Gender and Private Security in Global Politics

Oxford Studies in Gender and International Relations

Series editors: J. Ann Tickner, University of Southern California, and
Laura Sjoberg, University of Florida

GENDER AND PRIVATE SECURITY IN GLOBAL POLITICS

Edited by Maya Eichler

OXFORD
UNIVERSITY PRESS

OXFORD
UNIVERSITY PRESS

Oxford University Press is a department of the University of
Oxford. It furthers the University's objective of excellence in research,
scholarship, and education by publishing worldwide.

Oxford   New York
Auckland   Cape Town   Dar es Salaam   Hong Kong   Karachi
Kuala Lumpur   Madrid   Melbourne   Mexico City   Nairobi
New Delhi   Shanghai   Taipei   Toronto

With offices in
Argentina   Austria   Brazil   Chile   Czech Republic   France   Greece
Guatemala   Hungary   Italy   Japan   Poland   Portugal   Singapore
South Korea   Switzerland   Thailand   Turkey   Ukraine   Vietnam

Oxford is a registered trademark of Oxford University Press
in the UK and certain other countries.

Published in the United States of America by
Oxford University Press
198 Madison Avenue, New York, NY 10016

Library of Congress Cataloging-in-Publication Data
Gender and private security in global politics/edited by Maya Eichler.
pages cm. — (Oxford studies in gender and international relations)
ISBN 978-0-19-936437-4 (hardback : alk. paper) — ISBN 978-0-19-936438-1
(paperback: alk. paper)   1. Private security services.   2. Women soldiers.   3. Military
policy—Moral and ethical aspects.   4. International relations.   I. Eichler, Maya, 1974– editor.
HV8290.G46 2015
355.3'5—dc23
2014028998

9 8 7 6 5 4 3 2 1
Printed in the United States of America
on acid-free paper

To Ann and Cynthia, for paving the way

CONTENTS

ACKNOWLEDGMENTS

I thank Cambridge University Press for permission to reprint slightly edited versions of the following two pieces: chapter 4 (pp. 198–215) in *Altered States: The Globalization of Accountability* by Valerie Sperling, originally published by Cambridge University Press in 2009; and the article "(Re)Producing American Soldiers in an Age of Empire" by Isabelle V. Barker that originally appeared in *Politics & Gender*, volume 5, issue 2 in June 2009 (pp. 211–235).

I dedicate this book to two leading figures of feminist international relations—J. Ann Tickner and Cynthia Enloe—who paved the way for so many of us. Without their scholarship and example, I doubt that asking feminist questions about private security in global politics would have been possible in the first place. They have taught us to speak truth to power, question what is taken for granted, and listen carefully to those on the margins of international relations. Without asking feminist questions, they have insisted, we know less and are collectively worse off. This book is motivated by the kind of feminist questioning and scholarship that Ann and Cynthia have pioneered.

Over the past few years, a small but dedicated group of scholars has worked to develop feminist and feminist-informed analyses of security privatization and private military and security companies (PMSCs). In assembling this volume it was my goal to bring these scholars together and both showcase and advance this emerging research. The chapters make it evident that there are *multiple* ways of studying private security through gendered lenses. In this volume we have not exhausted feminist analyses of private security but instead aimed to inspire others to ask feminist questions and further develop the emerging field of "critical gender studies in private security." It has been my utmost privilege to work with the contributors to this volume. I am grateful to each one of them for agreeing to be part of this project. Without their commitment the volume would not have materialized. I thank Anna Leander for her enthusiasm for this project and for supplying such an insightful afterword.

Several of the contributors to this volume participated in ISA panels on gender and private security. In 2012 I organized the panel "Gender and the Privatization of Military Security," and in 2013 Amanda Chisholm and I co-organized the panel "Silences and Margins: Interrogating the Intersections of Gender, Race, Class, and Citizenship in Private Security." I thank the panel discussants—Anna Leander and Cynthia Enloe respectively—and the audience members for their engagement and comments. The Feminist Theory and Gender Studies Section of the ISA has offered important institutional space that encourages and enables the kind of research presented in this book.

I am especially grateful for the support that my book proposal received from the editors of the Oxford Series in Gender and International Relations, J. Ann Tickner and Laura Sjoberg, and my editor at Oxford University Press, Angela Chnapko, who expertly guided me through the publication process. My thanks also go to editorial assistants Peter Worger and Princess Ikatekit, project manager Peter Mavrikis, production editor Leslie Johnson, and copyeditor India Gray for their part in bringing this book project to completion. I am indebted to Soumita Basu, Amanda Chisholm, Deborah Cowen, Cynthia Enloe, Jane Parpart, Kim Rygiel, Valerie Sperling, Saskia Stachowitsch, and Sandra Whitworth who all at different times discussed the ideas for this volume with me and encouraged me to pursue it. I deeply appreciate the two anonymous reviewers who took the time to carefully read the manuscript and provided excellent and thoughtful feedback that has made this a stronger piece of collective scholarship.

The idea for this volume was born during a Gender and International Security Fellowship at the Harvard Kennedy School in 2010–2011 that offered support to me at a critical phase in my academic career. I also acknowledge the financial support I received from the Social Sciences and Humanities Research Council of Canada Postdoctoral Fellowship and the Lilian Robinson Visiting Scholars Program at the Simone De Beauvoir Institute at Concordia University while working on this edited volume. The Department of Geography at the University of Toronto, my institutional home for the past few years, was a most welcoming and intellectually stimulating place, in particular with Deborah Cowen as my postdoctoral supervisor. The final stages of work on this volume were completed at Mount Saint Vincent University in Halifax, my new home. As I embark on this new phase in my academic career, I am once again reminded of the importance of collaboration and mentoring as key values of feminist scholarship (and activism). I look forward to new opportunities to learn from my colleagues and students in order to advance together our understanding of the world and make it a truly more secure and just place for all to live.

Maya Eichler
Halifax

LIST OF CONTRIBUTORS

BIANCA BAGGIARINI is a PhD candidate in sociology at York University, Toronto. Her research interests lie in feminist critical security studies, citizenship studies, and international political sociology. Her PhD dissertation examines how states respond to the "crisis of military sacrifice" in late modern, biopolitical societies. She has published on the gendered and sociopolitical effects of military privatization in *Gendered Perspectives on Conflict and Violence* (2013) and *St. Anthony's International Review* (2014) and has as a forthcoming (2015) article on military drones and sacrifice, which will appear as part of a special issue on Mimetic Theory and International Studies in the *Journal of International Political Theory*.

ISABELLE V. BARKER is an assistant dean at Bryn Mawr College. She has a PhD in political science and has research interests in immigration, feminist political economy, and political theory. She has published on topics ranging from geopolitics and women's human rights to the rise of global Pentecostalism as a response to dilemmas of social reproduction produced by neoliberal economic restructuring.

AMANDA CHISHOLM recently completed her PhD in international relations at the University of Bristol. Her dissertation focuses on Gurkhas in PMSCs and examines how reproductions of colonial histories and raced and gendered practices underpin representations of Gurkhas' labor. She has published articles on this topic in the *International Feminist Journal of Politics* and in *Security Dialogue*. Since completing her PhD, Amanda has taken a position as lecturer in international relations at Newcastle University. Her research continues to be motivated by how colonial histories, race, and gender condition and discipline military and security labor globally.

MAYA EICHLER is Canada Research Chair in Social Innovation and Community Engagement and assistant professor in the Department of Political and Canadian Studies and the Department of Women's Studies at Mount Saint Vincent University (Halifax). Her research focuses on feminist international relations theory, gender and the armed forces, the privatization of military security, and post-Soviet politics. She has published the book *Militarizing Men: Gender, Conscription, and War in Post-Soviet Russia* with Stanford University Press (2012) and recent articles in *Critical Studies on Security, Citizenship Studies, Brown Journal of World Affairs,* and *International Journal.* She currently serves as an Associate Editor for the *International Feminist Journal of Politics.*

CHRIS HENDERSHOT is a PhD candidate in the Department of Political Science at York University. His dissertation is titled "Corpses, Guns, Penises, and Private Military and Security Corporations." This project undertakes a posthuman, queer, and feminist analysis of the work that PMSCs do for and through privatizing, militarizing, securing, and commercializing processes.

PAUL HIGATE is reader in Gender & Security at the School for Sociology, Politics and International Studies at the University of Bristol. He has researched the gendered culture of the military, the transition from military to civilian life, and gendered relations in peace support operations. He is a former Fellow of the Economic and Social Research Council (ESRC) Global Uncertainties Programme with a project entitled: "Mercenary Masculinities Imagine Security: The Case of the Private Military Security Contractor."

JUTTA JOACHIM is associate professor of political science at Leibniz University Hannover, Germany. She received her PhD from the University of Wisconsin-Madison and her MA from the University of South Carolina. She is the author of *Agenda Setting, the UN, and NGOs: Gender Violence and Reproductive Rights* (Georgetown University Press 2007) and co-author of *International Organizations and Implementation: Enforcers, Managers, Authorities* and *Transnational Activism in the UN and the EU: A Comparative Study* (both Routledge 2008). Her current project concerns the role of private actors in security governance. Her articles have appeared in, among others, *International Studies Quarterly, Millennium: Journal of International Studies,* and the *Journal of European Public Policy.*

ANNA LEANDER is a professor (MSO) in the Department of Management, Politics, and Philosophy at the Copenhagen Business School and professor of international relations at PUC Rio de Janeiro. Her research focuses on commercial security and on the development of sociological approaches to international relations. She has recently published the edited volumes *Business in Global Governance* and *Commercializing Security* and articles in *Global Constitutionalism, Leiden Journal of International Law,* and *Review of International Studies.*

ANDREA SCHNEIKER studied political science and sociology in Lille, France, and Münster, Germany, from 2000 to 2004. She received a PhD in political science from the University in Münster in 2008 for her research on the self- and co-regulation of PMSCs. From 2008 to 2013 she was assistant professor at Leibniz University Hannover. She is currently a junior professor in political science at the University of Siegen, Germany. She has published in, among others, the peer-reviewed journals *Millennium: Journal of International Studies, Comparative European Politics, Security Dialogue* (all co-authored with Jutta Joachim), *Disasters,* and *VOLUNTAS: International Journal of Voluntary and Nonprofit Organizations.*

VALERIE SPERLING is a professor of political science at Clark University in Worcester, Massachusetts. She received her PhD from the University of California, Berkeley. Her research interests include globalization and accountability, social movements, gender politics, patriotism and militarism, and state building in the postcommunist region. She is the author of *Organizing Women in Contemporary Russia: Engendering Transition* (Cambridge University Press 1999), which is about the emergence and development of the Russian women's movement, and *Altered States: The Globalization of Accountability* (Cambridge University Press 2009). Her latest book is *Sex, Politics, and Putin: Political Legitimacy in Russia* (Oxford University Press 2014).

SASKIA STACHOWITSCH is a postdoctoral research fellow and lecturer at the Department of Political Science at the University of Vienna. Her research areas are gender and the military, private security, feminist international relations, security studies, and global political economy. Recent publications include *Gender Ideologies and Military Labor Markets in the US* (Routledge 2012); "Military Privatization and the Remasculinization of the State: Making the Link between the Outsourcing of Military Security and Gendered State Transformations" in *International Relations* (2013); and "Military Gender Integration and Foreign Policy in the United States: A Feminist IR Perspective" in *Security Dialogue* (2012).

JILLIAN TERRY is completing a PhD in international relations at the London School of Economics and Political Science. Her doctoral thesis, supervised by Kimberly Hutchings, examines the contributions of feminist ethics to the burgeoning field of feminist security studies and the impact of feminist insights on the ethics of contemporary war practices including drone warfare, private military contracting, and counterinsurgency. Her recent publications include "The End of the Line: Feminist Understandings of Resistance to Full-Body Scanning Technology" with Stephanie Redden in the *International Feminist Journal of Politics* (2013).

ANA FILIPA VRDOLJAK is professor and associate dean (research) in the Faculty of Law at the University of Technology, Sydney. She was a contributor regarding women's issues to the European Commission funded research collaboration titled "Regulating the Privatisation of 'War': The Role of the

EU in Assuring Compliance with International Humanitarian Law and Human Rights (PRIV-WAR)." She has been Marie Curie Fellow and Jean Monnet Fellow in the Law Department of the European University Institute, Florence, and visiting scholar at the Lauterpacht Centre for International Law, University of Cambridge, and Global Law School, New York University. She holds a PhD (in Law) from the University of Sydney.

LIST OF ACRONYMS

CDU	Conduct and Discipline Unit
CE	Council of Europe
CEDAW	Convention on the Elimination of all Forms of Discrimination against Women
CIVPOL	Civilian Police
CP	Close Protection
ED	Erectile Dysfunction
EUPM	European Union Police Mission
GPE	Global Political Economy
HRC	Human Rights Council
ICJ	International Committee of Jurists
ICOC	International Code of Conduct for Private Security Service Providers
ICOCA	International Code of Conduct for Private Security Service Providers' Association
ICRC	International Committee of the Red Cross
ICTR	International Criminal Tribunal for Rwanda
ICTY	International Criminal Tribunal for the former Yugoslavia
IPOA	International Peace Operations Association
IPTF	International Police Task Force
IR	International Relations
ISOA	International Stability Operations Association
KBR	Kellogg Brown & Root
LNs	Local Nationals
LOGCAP	Logistics Civil Augmentation Program
MEJA	Military Extraterritorial Jurisdiction Act
MOU	Memorandum of Understanding
NGO	Non-Governmental Organization
OECD	Organisation for Economic Co-operation and Development
PMSCs	Private Military and Security Companies
POGO	Project on Government Oversight
PSD	Personal Security Detail

RMA	Revolution in Military Affairs
SEA	Sexual Exploitation and Abuse
SFOR	NATO-led Stabilization Force
SOFA	Status of Forces Agreement
SOMA	Status of Mission Agreement
SWAT	Special Weapons and Tactics
TCNs	Third-Country Nationals
TVPRA	Trafficking Victims Protection Reauthorization Act
UNDPKO	United Nations Department of Peacekeeping Operations
UNGC	United Nations Global Compact
UN-INSTRAW	United Nations International Research and Training Institute for the Advancement of Women
UNMIBH	United Nations Mission in Bosnia-Herzegovina
UNMIL	United Nations Mission in Liberia
UNOIGWG	United Nations Open-ended Intergovernmental Working Group
UNTAC	United Nations Transitional Authority in Cambodia
UNWGM	United Nations Working Group on the Use of Mercenaries as a Means of Violating Human Rights and Impeding the Exercise of the Rights of Peoples to Self-Determination
USDOD	United States Department of Defense
USDOS	United States Department of State
USGAO	United States Government Accountability Office
VAW	Violence Against Women

Gender and Private Security in Global Politics

Gender and the Privatization of Military Security

An Introduction

MAYA EICHLER

The past two to three decades have witnessed the increasing privatization of military security in Western states, with significant repercussions for global politics. Private military and security companies (PMSCs), especially those based in the United States and United Kingdom, have become central participants in contemporary warfare, selling services such as armed protection, training, intelligence, and logistical support to state and nonstate actors. It is estimated that the size of the global private security industry increased twofold between 1990 and 1999 (to USD 100 bln) and again doubled in size between 2000 and 2010 (Leander 2010, 209). The U.S.-led wars in Afghanistan and Iraq in particular led to burgeoning demand for private military and security services. In both wars, private contractors outnumbered or closely trailed U.S. troop numbers (see, for example, USDoD 2011).

It may be all too obvious to the casual observer (and therefore of little interest to the scholar) that the field of private military security is intensely gendered. The image of burly, masculine private contractors has become widespread over the past two decades, especially in media coverage of the wars in Afghanistan and Iraq. Private contractors have been cast, like mercenaries were previously, as the "whores of war" opposite the "just warriors" of state militaries. Reports which allege poor financial accountability, impunity for war crimes, and disregard for local populations but also sexual harassment and human trafficking have plagued the private military and security industry. In this context, the industry has begun to pay more attention to "women" and "gender" if only for the sake of reputation and revenue. Yet as gender is gaining in significance within the realm of private security, we continue to know relatively little about how and to what effect the privatization of military security is gendered.

This book brings together key scholars in the emerging research area of "critical gender studies in private security." The contributors to this volume contend that the privatization of military security is a deeply gendered process, with gendered underpinnings and effects. The contributors employ a variety of feminist perspectives, including critical, postcolonial, poststructuralist, liberal, and queer feminist perspectives, as well as a wide range of methodological approaches such as ethnography, participant-observation, genealogy, deconstruction, and discourse analysis. Located at the intersection of international relations (IR), security studies, and gender studies, this volume aims to push research in two key directions. First, it establishes gender as key analytical category for the study of private security in global politics, thus introducing new research questions and methods to private security scholarship. Second, the volume advances the field of feminist security studies by contributing new empirical and theoretical insights into the gendering of security today.

Gender is often misunderstood as being interchangeable with women, but a feminist-informed gender analysis goes beyond adding women and stirring. While this book does ask where the women are in the private military and security industry and how they have been affected by PMSCs in the field, the book as a whole offers an analysis of the varied ways in which masculinities and femininities constitute, and are constituted by, private security in global politics, with particular consequences for the global social order. The contributors interrogate security privatization as a gendered process, and the private military and security industry as a crucial site for the (re)production and contestation of gender norms in contemporary warfare and global politics.

The book not only contends that security privatization cannot be fully grasped without a consideration of gender but also presents a framework for studying security privatization from a critical gender perspective that emphasizes intersectionality, multiple scales, and the political nature of PMSCs. Collectively, the chapters in this book demonstrate that gender, in intersection with citizenship, national identity, race, class, and sexuality, is shaped by, at the same time as it helps constitute, the practices of PMSCs and their employees along with public perceptions of private contractors. The contributors to the volume recognize gender as a key structure in the multiscalar politics of security privatization, or, put differently, that security privatization is a gendered political process that takes place at and through multiple scales. Furthermore, we see PMSCs not simply as suppliers of security and security-related services but also as political actors who contribute to the production of gendered social hierarchies and the global social order. After locating this volume in the literatures on security privatization and feminist IR/security studies, I outline in more detail the framework of the book and describe how the individual chapters contribute to its development.

PRIVATE SECURITY IN GLOBAL POLITICS

Scholarship on the privatization of military security and PMSCs has proliferated in recent years across a number of disciplines, including political science, IR, international law, sociology, criminology, philosophy, geography, and business. Scholars in political science and IR have aimed to explain security privatization and assess its impact on the state's monopoly on legitimate force as well as to define, categorize, and regulate PMSCs (Singer 2003; Avant 2005; Kinsey 2006). In his seminal article and later book *Corporate Warriors*, Peter Singer (2001/02; 2003) identified a gap in the security market at the end of the Cold War, the changing nature of warfare, and neoliberalism as driving forces behind security privatization. Elke Krahmann (2010) more recently argued that the underlying ideology of civil-military relations (republican or neoliberal) plays a key part in explaining the willingness of state actors to privatize military security. Scholars have investigated how private force can enhance a state's military power but can also weaken transparency in states with high state capacity and increase vulnerability and conflict in states with weaker state capacity (Singer 2003; Avant 2005; Avant 2006). Much scholarly effort has gone into defining and delineating PMSCs in relation to mercenaries (Percy 2007), with most authors arguing that they represent a novel form of security actor despite their historical antecedents. Finally, much of the literature on security privatization has been driven by the practical challenge of how to regulate the industry and hold PMSCs politically, legally, and financially accountable. Here the existing institutional and legal frameworks have generally been deemed inadequate while industry initiatives toward self-regulation or voluntary regulation have been met with skepticism (Chesterman and Lehnardt 2007; De Nevers 2009; Carmola 2010; Dickinson 2011; Tonkin 2011). The research field of security privatization and PMSCs is highly dynamic, and contemporary scholarship goes well beyond these key themes. For example, lately more attention is being paid to the relationship between various security actors such as PMSCs, NGOs, and state forces in order to understand the complexities of today's military operations (Dunigan 2011; Berndtsson 2013; Birthe 2013), while questions of regulation, accountability, and ethics continue to be at the forefront of scholarly debates on private security (Tonkin 2011; Francioni and Ronzitti 2011; Huskey 2012).

Critical security studies scholars have made important contributions to research on private security. Importantly, they have questioned the public-private distinction that informs much scholarship on private security (Leander 2005; Krahmann 2008; Owens 2008; Abrahamsen and Williams 2011). As Patricia Owens (2008) argues, "there is no such thing as public or private violence. There is only violence that is *made* 'public' and violence that is *made* 'private'" (979). In analyzing the effects of security privatization on the state, critical scholars contend that security privatization should not be equated with the erosion of state power or its monopoly on legitimate force. Instead, security privatization is best conceived of in terms of a broader transformation in governance that involves public/private and local/global actors as part of global security assemblages (Abrahamsen and Williams 2011) and the commercialization of security practices in both public and private spheres (Leander 2010). Critical scholars see security as essentially contested and political, and recognize that privatization involves not only a change in supplier but a reshaping of security itself (Krahmann 2008). Anna Leander (2005), for example, shows that security privatization reinforces militarized notions of security while depoliticizing security issues.

Feminist-informed gender scholarship has developed within, and draws on, this critical scholarship on security privatization but foregrounds gender, a hitherto neglected area of study within both mainstream and critical approaches. Feminist and critical gender scholars have investigated the significance of (hegemonic and subordinate) masculinities in the private security industry (Barker 2009; Chisholm 2010, 2014a, 2014b; Via 2010; Higate 2012a, 2012c, 2012d, 2012e) as well as examined security privatization as a process of remasculinization (Schneiker and Joachim 2012c; Stachowitsch 2013). Feminist scholars have also begun to address the lack of accountability of PMSCs toward female employees and local women in the field (Sperling 2009; Vrdoljak 2011). Taking a security studies perspective, Laura Sjoberg (2013) has conceptualized security privatization as a gendered state strategy in war that takes advantage of the gendered invisibility of the private sphere. This volume builds on and advances these existing feminist and critical gender studies contributions to scholarship on security privatization.

The book focuses on the recent outsourcing in Western states of military functions and military work to the private sector and the concomitant rise of PMSCs in global politics. The chapters in this volume primarily deal with the key players in the industry, that is, the U.S. and UK companies that operate globally. The book does not address the deeper historical phenomenon of mercenaries and mercenary armies or the broader phenomenon of private force in global politics, which includes pirates and non-state armed groups. The book deals with the market in security and security-related services in the context of warfare and to a lesser extent peacekeeping. While focusing on international war- and peacemaking, it is worth acknowledging that this global market for force cannot easily be separated from the market in domestic commercial security services that has sprung up globally (Abrahamsen and Williams 2011). Both international and domestic private security are manifestations of the larger neoliberalization of security and the increasing securitization of public and private life at the turn of the twenty-first century.

Various terms have been used to describe the private companies whose employees perform the work previously carried out by military personnel. Scholars refer to private military firms (Singer 2003), private security companies (Avant 2005), and private military companies (Leander 2005). The most common term used in the scholarly literature, however, is private military and security companies—PMSCs—and it is this term that is used throughout the book to refer to the globally operating companies that sell a combination of services ranging from logistical support for military operations, armed and unarmed security services, military training, intelligence, and more. While smaller companies might focus on one or two of these services, larger companies often sell an array of military support and security services. The term "contractor" or "defense contractor" also appears in the book to refer to the employees of PMSCs, and the term "third-country national" (TCN) is used when speaking of employees who are citizens of neither the company's host country nor the country of operation. Overall, the book deals with three distinct aspects of private security in global politics: the processes of military security privatization, the companies themselves (the PMSCs), and the employees of PMSCs (contractors). It is, then, a book about both the structural changes *and* the agents shaping and shaped by the privatization of military security.

GENDER AND SECURITY

What distinguishes the contributors to this book is that they analyze private security through a primary (though not exclusive) focus on gender. Feminist scholars in IR (and other disciplines) distinguish between gender and biological sex to underscore that the meanings associated with masculinity and femininity are socially constructed rather than biologically given, and therefore vary across place and time.[1] Gender refers to the expectations, behaviors, and norms associated with being a man or woman in particular historical, cultural, social, and economic contexts. Feminist scholarship is interested in understanding how gender has been used to justify hierarchies and unequal power relations between people designated as "women" and "men." Thus gender is more than a variable—it is intrinsically linked to gendered relations of power that are reflected in processes of masculinization and feminization. Crucially, gender is "a primary way of signifying relationships of power" (Scott 1986, 1067). Gender structures social life as it assigns power to those institutions, practices, and activities associated with masculinities. For example, what has traditionally counted as political and thus relevant has gained its predominance by association with men and masculinity and in opposition to femininity and subordinate masculinities. The political leader, citizen, or warrior has long been imagined as a man and as displaying masculine characteristics (Tickner 2001). Significantly, gender also informs interstate relations whereby states try to project images of strength stereotypically associated with masculinity and aim to avoid their feminization within international structures (Sjoberg 2013). Gender is therefore a key social structure of domestic and international orders (Connell 1987, 2005).

The contributors to this book, while coming from a range of disciplines and employing diverse theoretical perspectives, all substantially draw on feminist IR theory to develop their analyses of the privatization of military security. Feminist IR scholarship has made important contributions to research on war and militarization. Over the past decade, the subfield of feminist security studies has emerged within feminist IR (Blanchard 2003; Sjoberg 2010; Wibben 2011). This new area of study is primarily focused on the public security sector even as it has paved the way for the kinds of analyses developed here. While there is significant diversity among feminist scholars of security, they share an interest in investigating how security practices are tied to norms of masculinity and femininity and tend to reproduce unequal gender relations. More specifically, feminist security studies makes four key contributions to the study of war and (public) security that inform the questions and analyses in this volume.

First, feminist scholarship has documented the important intersections between security, war, and national and global gender orders. Gender orders manifest themselves in gendered power relations, a gendered division of labor, and dominant sexual practices (Connell 1987). States' security and defense policies (including the waging of war) shape and are shaped by notions of masculinity and femininity that pervade domestic and global politics (Goldstein 2001; Tickner 2001; Eichler 2012a). For example, policies such as male conscription or female exclusion from combat draw on, at the same time as they reinforce, dominant notions of masculinity and femininity. The association of military strength with masculinity in global politics has dire consequences for international peace considering that states are "motivated in part by a desire to appear 'manly'" (Enloe 2000a). Therefore, we need to conceptualize security and war as gendered, and the organization of violence as intersecting with national and global gender orders.

Second, feminist scholars have shown that military organizations themselves are fundamentally gendered in that they represent a particular (micro) gender order within the broader societal (macro) gender order. Military labor and its management are deeply gendered. Militaries are male-dominated organizations that privilege masculinity and exclude or marginalize women and values associated with femininity or incorporate them in highly specific ways (Mathers 2013). The world's armed forces are overwhelmingly made up of men, and states choose to primarily rely on men to fight wars. Despite this, militaries in a variety of ways rely on women and notions of femininity such as loyal military wives or patriotic soldiers' mothers. Increasingly, armed forces across the globe are recruiting women into their ranks to compensate for the lack of military "manpower" (Enloe 2000b), and even opening direct combat roles to women, most recently in Australia and the U.S. Changing gendered recruitment and personnel policies both challenge and reproduce norms of militarized femininity and masculinity.

Third, feminist security studies scholars argue that key concepts of security, such as protection, are gendered, in that they are informed by particular understandings of masculinity and femininity (Stiehm 1982; Tickner 2001; Blanchard 2003; Young 2003; Sjoberg 2013). The gendered ideology of protection that defines men as the protectors and women as those in need of protection is informed by both masculinism and militarism. In this view, women's gender subordination is intrinsically tied to the organization of the means of violence in society. Feminists critique both the notion of the state as protector and of men as protectors, and document how policies of protection often increase women's insecurities.

Finally, this leads feminist scholars to critically interrogate the concept of security, both in terms of asking whose security counts and what makes up true security. Feminist scholars argue that we need to look at security from the perspective of ordinary women (and men) rather than the state. They also employ a multidimensional concept of security that goes beyond, or is even defined in opposition to, military security to include other dimensions of security such as personal, economic, environmental, or physical (Tickner 2001; Blanchard 2003). Therefore feminist scholars call on us to investigate the appeal that militarized security continues to have in domestic and global politics and to envision alternatives to current security narratives and policies (Wibben 2011).

These four insights into the gendered organization of violence and conceptualization of security lead to a set of feminist-informed questions about the privatization of military security and the private military and security industry. How is the privatization of military security connected to national and global gender orders and their current transformations? What type of gendered organizations are PMSCs and what notions of masculinity and femininity do they rely on and reinforce? What gendered conceptions of protection and security does the private security industry (re)produce? And, how does the private security industry affect women's and men's security, both as employees and locals in the field? What gender-specific problems of accountability does private security pose, and what is the potential for regulating and reforming private security from a feminist perspective? As the chapters in this volume answer these and other questions, they not only develop an in-depth analysis of gender and private security in global politics but also propose a unique approach to the study of gender and private security in global politics.

THIS VOLUME'S APPROACH: GENDER AND PRIVATE SECURITY IN GLOBAL POLITICS

This volume brings together the work of a multidisciplinary group of scholars—from political science, IR and GPE, sociology, and international law—working at the intersection of gender studies and private security. While there is considerable diversity in empirical focus and theoretical perspective among the chapters of this volume, they collectively put forward an innovative framework for how to study the privatization of military security through "gendered lenses" (Runyan and Peterson 2013). This framework consists of the following four pillars:

1. A feminist-informed critical gender approach: This volume employs an explicitly critical rather than problem-solving approach to the study of gender and private security.[2] A problem-solving approach tends to instrumentalize gender in the interests of business, public image, accountability, or operational effectiveness while taking for granted the activities of PMSCs. In contrast to problem-solving approaches that treat gender/women as a variable to be added without changing how we study security privatization, this volume asks feminist-informed critical questions about gender and the privatization of security: How is security privatization a gendered process? How does it rely on, reinforce, and reproduce gender difference and inequalities? The feminist-informed critical gender approach employed here has both analytical and normative goals: an interest in improved analysis and better understanding of gendered power relations in the private security sphere as well as an interest in transforming security practices that reinforce gender (and other) hierarchies in global politics. Importantly, such an approach is interested as much in men and masculinities as it is in women and femininities.

2. Intersectional analysis: The contributions of this volume go beyond an analysis of masculinities and femininities in private security. Various strands of feminist scholarship, such as socialist (Hansen and Philipson 1990), critical race (Wing 1997), queer (Butler 1990), and postcolonial feminist (Mohanty 2003), emphasize that gender intersects with other categories of social difference and that an exclusive focus on gender misses the complex intersecting hierarchies of oppression and subordination

that shape women's lives. Many of the individual chapters in this volume emphasize the intersecting inequalities of gender with class, race, nation, citizenship, and sexuality and their significance for a better understanding of the practices of PMSCs. Thus the volume asks not only how is security privatization a gendered process, but how does its gendering intersect with other social hierarchies?

3. Multiple scales of analysis: Feminist scholars and activists have argued that the personal is political and international (Enloe 1989). Feminists are keenly attuned to how various scales[3]—such as that of the body, the household/family, the nation/state, the region, and the global—are intimately connected rather than distinct. The contributors to this volume, while each focusing on a particular scale or scalar process (such as globalization), shed light on how security privatization is made possible and experienced differently at various scales. Many of the chapters speak to the recent interest in feminist IR to place the body at the center of the study of war, focusing on how war is experienced by ordinary people and differently gendered, raced, classed, or sexed bodies (Sylvester 2013a). In this volume private security is seen not only as a local, regional, national or global practice (as it might in conventional studies on private security) but also as an embodied practice. Security privatization becomes materialized through particular gendered, raced, classed, and sexed bodies and has different effects on these bodies. The volume examines security privatization both "from above" and "from below": How is security privatization connected to gendered state transformations and shifts in global markets? *And* how is private security a gendered experience for those individuals providing, buying, receiving, or exposed to privatized security, that is, how is private security embodied in particular contexts?

4. PMSCs as political: Animated by feminist concerns about gendered power relations and inequalities, the contributors bring a unique political view to the study of PMSCs. They do not treat PMSCs as neutral market actors filling a void in security provision but as political actors shaping not only security environments but also the global social order and its gender, racial, and economic foundations. Following from this, the volume asks the important question: How does gender help us see the ways in which PMSCs are implicated in reproducing and securing an unequal global order?

Structure of the Book

The book is organized into four parts, with the chapters in part I focusing on feminist theorizing on military privatization; parts II and III on empirical explorations of masculinities; and part IV on political issues regarding accountability, regulation, and ethics. That being said, a clear distinction among the theoretical, empirical, and political is not given as several of the empirically oriented chapters make strong and innovative theoretical contributions, and all chapters underline the gendered political nature of security privatization.

The first set of chapters by Saskia Stachowitsch, Bianca Baggiarini, and Maya Eichler (part I) advances feminist theorizing on military security privatization by focusing on neoliberal transformations of state structures and discourses. For political reasons the state has long been a key concern for feminist theorists (see e.g., MacKinnon 1989; Brown 1992). Feminists have scrutinized the state's role in upholding unequal gender relations through economic, social, and military policies, making it a crucial site for feminist activism. But feminists have so far not paid much attention to security privatization as an aspect of neoliberal state transformation. Stachowitsch in "Military Privatization as a Gendered Process: A Case for Integrating Feminist International Relations and Feminist State Theories" argues that military privatization is a gendered process that is best understood as a result of interactions between gendered states and the gendered international order. Military security privatization is not an effect of state erosion to the advantage of the global market for force but rather defined by the dynamics between neoliberal restructuring at the national and global level. These dynamics include the transformation of military labor markets, de-democratization, and discursive remasculinization. Stachowitsch develops a theoretical framework that integrates feminist IR/GPE and feminist state theories and allows us to capture the "hybrid character" of privatization as an aspect of both changing gender orders within the state and the gendered dynamics of the global economy. The military sector, public and private, she argues, is a state *and* international space, and thus an approach that is sensitive to changing gendered power relations at multiple scales— within and beyond the state—is needed for a deeper understanding of military privatization and its gendered implications.

Increasingly, governments have had to contend with their citizens' unwillingness to sacrifice soldiers in military operations in distant locations. The move from conscription to all-volunteer forces as well as the privatization of military security can be understood as mechanisms to deal with aversion to casualties. In "Military Privatization and the Gendered Politics of Sacrifice" Baggiarini considers how states and militaries are responding to the contemporary problem of sacrifice and how their responses are gendered in the context of military privatization. As the author argues, states have conceived of PMSCs as one solution to the problem of sacrificing soldiers, and military privatization is thus integral to the broader shift toward "bodyless warfare." By tracing the genealogical trajectories of privatized violence, she establishes PMSCs as a biopolitical component of the so-called revolution in military affairs (RMA). Baggiarini concludes that the incorporation of private contractors into the theater of war is an important but insufficient move toward overcoming the limits of the body. States' increasing reliance on PMSCs highlights the paradox between bodyless war and sacrificial violence in contemporary warfare.

Another central issue at the nexus of state, military service, and citizenship has been that of gendered protection. My chapter "Gender, PMSCs, and the Global Rescaling of the Politics of Protection: Implications for Feminist Security Studies" begins from the feminist insight that states have historically entrenched unequal gender relations through an ideology of protection. While recent feminist work has moved beyond a focus on the geographic space of the nation-state, it has only begun to consider the implications of the privatization of military security for the gendered politics of protection. As I show in chapter 3, PMSCs have an active interest in extending the politics of protection to the global scale in order to extend the market for security. I argue that today feminists must question protection anew, by examining how protection is being marketized and rescaled, and racialized, gendered, and classed in new ways. The logic of global masculinist protection is increasing our dependency on the market while reducing our political autonomy.

Part II moves to a more empirically driven but nonetheless theoretically rich collection of chapters. The three chapters in part II investigate the widespread use of racialized "foreign" labor in the global private security industry by analyzing the varied masculinities that security privatization entails and relies on, and their intersections with race, class, nationality, and citizenship. The vast majority of employees who have been hired to work in Iraq and Afghanistan under U.S. defense contracts are in fact not U.S. citizens but citizens of states on the periphery and semiperiphery of the global economy. They have included so-called TCNs from countries such as India and the Philippines as well as "local nationals" (LNs) from Iraq and Afghanistan. TCNs and LNs have performed much of the logistical work in support of U.S. military operations in Iraq and Afghanistan, but they have also worked in the provision of armed and unarmed security services.

Isabelle Barker's chapter "(Re)producing American Soldiers in an Age of Empire" examines the use of TCN labor for reproductive work—such as cleaning, food preparation, and laundering—on U.S. military bases in Iraq. As a result of military privatization, vital support services have been increasingly outsourced to migrant men from India, Bangladesh, Sri Lanka, the Philippines, Nepal, and Pakistan. Barker argues that this globalized division of reproductive labor is a site of symbolic politics that reinforces the gendered dimensions of U.S. soldiers' national identity and is rooted in a long history of gendered military service. The use of migrant labor to perform feminized reproductive labor previously performed by military personnel helps construct a more unified image of the U.S. soldier as warrior. Barker argues that this division of labor also reproduces neocolonial global relations and is thus integral to an aggressive U.S. foreign policy and the making of the U.S. empire.

Amanda Chisholm in her chapter "From Warriors of Empire to Martial Contractors: Reimagining Gurkhas in Private Security" brings to our attention the experiences of one particular subset of security contractors, namely Gurkhas. Gurkhas hail from Nepal and have fought in the British, Indian, and Nepalese armies. Long imagined as a "martial race" they have become sought-after workers in the global private security industry. Employing a feminist postcolonial approach that is sensitive to the intersections of gender with race and class and based on fieldwork conducted in Nepal and Afghanistan, Chisholm shows how Gurkhas and Gurkha agents view the industry and their own (martial and masculine) role within it. She examines historic constructions of Gurkhas and how Gurkhas and others reproduce or refashion these in the context of the contemporary market for force. Linking individual experiences to larger processes of colonialism and global migration (as does Barker), Chisholm's analysis highlights the centrality of individual agency even for those on the margins of the globally operating private security industry.

The final chapter of part II, "The License to Exploit: PMSCs, Masculinities and Third-Country Nationals," written by Jutta Joachim and Andrea Schneiker examines the labor of TCNs in the global private security industry from another angle. Drawing on an analysis of company websites, the chapter explores how the construction of Western contractors as the world's "best security experts" intersects with culture, race, and class to reinforce social inequalities and keeps from view the subordinate masculinities it relies on. The authors argue that the power of PMSCs rests not only on efficiency and cost-effectiveness but also on a hierarchy of masculinities. PMSCs allow state militaries to associate with accepted notions of militarized masculinity, such as the peacekeeper, and outsource less accepted ones. But, as the authors argue, the private provision of security services relies on hegemonic and subordinate masculinities that are constructed through "othering" and reproduce (post)colonial dichotomies. Significantly, their analysis highlights the political nature of PMSCs and the ways in which they contribute to the construction of masculinity norms in global politics.

Part III explores the masculinities of white Western contractors in relation to excesses and restraints of violence, and how these are perceived and interpreted. The chapters in this section also highlight the intersections of gender, masculinities more specifically, with nationality and sexuality in private security settings. Paul Higate's chapter "Aversions to Masculine Excess in the Private Military and Security Company and Their Effects: Don't Be a 'Billy Big Bollocks' and Beware the 'Ninja!'" develops a microanalysis of protection and masculinity in the private military and security industry. He argues that recent feminist analyses of security privatization that focus on the state and global levels need to be supplemented with an examination of the everyday experiences of security contractors. Based on participant-observation, where the author trained as a close protection officer in preparation for working in the industry, and equipped with a gender-sensitive lens, Higate interrogates the conditions that help constitute particular gendered and national contractor identities. UK and U.S. contractors are framed by training instructors through the binaries of the professional versus the hypermasculine "other." His analysis challenges simplistic assumptions about the use of violence by private contractors and shows that contractors' masculinized identities are shaped by a complex interplay of continuity and discontinuity with military identities.

Chris Hendershot in his chapter "Heternormative and Penile Frustrations: The Uneasy Discourse of the ArmorGroup Hazing Scandal" brings a queer perspective to the study of PMSCs, focusing on the intersections of gender and sexuality in privatized and militarized security contexts. The chapter focuses empirically on the Kabul hazing incident involving ArmorGroup contractors that came to light in 2009 as a result of an investigation by the Project on Government Oversight. The chapter examines overt and implied expressions of phallic unease and anxiety in public reactions to this incident. Hendershot concludes that the Kabul hazing incident illustrates the complex ways in which heteronormativity and phallo-centrism are (re)produced in global politics (including in global private security), and the difficulties states and PMSCs encounter when male bodies do not perform as expected in privatized-militarized (post)conflict zones.

Part IV moves from the study of masculinities in private security to the gendered problems of accountability in relation to PMSCs. The privatization of military security raises issues of accountability and ethics that are of particular concern to feminists. It not only enables states to circumvent citizens' democratic control over questions of war and peace, but it also undermines the claims for greater consideration of feminist concerns in the military sphere made by women's rights activists over the past decades. Valerie Sperling's chapter "Engendering Accountability in Private Security and Public Peacekeeping" shows that peacekeeping missions not only often take place in states with weak capacity but also often rely on private contractors. Together these two factors can have negative consequences for women's security in those particular postconflict settings, leading to gender-based exploitation and violence. The chapter reviews examples of UN peacekeeping missions in Bosnia, Congo, and Cambodia to illustrate how the UN has failed to adequately respond to allegations of sexual exploitation and abuse of women by peacekeepers, how contractors have been permitted to violate human rights with impunity, but also how U.S. legislation and UN policy has developed in an effort to strengthen accountability vis-à-vis local citizens.

The author concludes that the use of transnational military force (including private contractors) in postconflict settings has contradictory effects in terms of increasing stability while at the same time undermining political accountability between citizens and their governments as well as accountability of global actors to local populations.

The next chapter offers an in-depth analysis of international law to investigate gender-specific problems of accountability and regulation in relation to PMSCs. Ana Vrdoljak in her chapter "Women, PMSCs, and International Law" shows that shortcomings of existing regulatory regimes covering PMSCs reinforce concerns about transparency and accountability in respect to gender-related violence, harassment, and discrimination. The chapter considers the key recommendations of recent national and international initiatives covering PMSCs and women, including the Montreux Document, the International Code of Conduct, and European Union efforts. Vrdoljak also summaries existing international humanitarian law and human rights provisions relating to women and examines developments within the United Nations, the International Committee of the Red Cross and international criminal law jurisprudence shaping these legal norms. The author argues that the existing regulatory framework regarding PMSCs poses serious challenges for the security of women and other vulnerable groups. While gender considerations are being incorporated into nonbinding good practices guidelines, what is needed is an international legal instrument regulating PMSCs that can hold perpetrators accountable and secure reparations for victims.

Part IV of the volume closes with a theoretically driven chapter that explores the significance of feminist ethics for the realm of private security. While feminist engagement with PMSCs and their impact on global politics is growing, feminists have barely begun to examine the complex moral and ethical question of employing private force. "Empathy, Responsibility, and the Morality of Mercenaries: A Feminist Ethical Appraisal of PMSCs" written by Jillian Terry shows the utility of a feminist ethical framework for uncovering the ethical complexities involved in the use of private force. Mainstream scholarship stresses the individualistic and self-motivated ethical dilemmas of private contractors in the context of the market. In contrast, a feminist ethical framework premised on empathy and responsibility can help us recognize the relational and contextual nature of PMSC employees' lived experiences, bringing to light a more complex and varied set of moral quandaries than captured by the existing literature. Terry does not take a stance in support or opposition to PMSCs but rather suggests that a feminist ethical framework can enhance and broaden our understanding of the ethical and moral dilemmas inherent in the use of private force as well as point the way toward stronger, more effective regulation.

The conclusion, written by me, highlights the unique and innovative contributions of the volume in theoretical, empirical, and methodological terms.

It summarizes the most important insights into private security that the volume offers and recaps the framework presented in this book for "critical gender studies in private security." Furthermore, the conclusion draws out how the volume can advance the field of feminist security studies, in particular by establishing private security as a key area of feminist research, by furthering the study of masculinities and intersectionality in feminist security studies, and by contributing to the development of a feminist political economy of security. The conclusion also speaks to feminism's political project and what the analyses presented in this volume might imply for feminist politics, activism, and critique of (private/public) security as well as for a feminist rethinking of security more broadly. The afterword written by Anna Leander frames the volume's contributions in terms of four central themes of feminist research—(in)visibility, materiality, affect, and expertise—and considers how the analyses presented in this volume shift and unsettle the disciplinary boundaries of gender studies, global politics/IR, and private security studies.

NOTES

1. For introductions to feminist IR see, for example, Runyan and Peterson (2013) and Shepherd (2010a).
2. I draw on Robert Cox's (1981) distinction between problem-solving and critical theory approaches to the study of IR. As he argues, problem-solving approaches study the world as it is and aim to improve its management, while critical theory approaches ask how the current order came about and consider the potential for its transformation.
3. The concept of scale is informed by scholarship in geography; see, for example, Sheppard and McMaster (2004). For the utility of scale-sensitive scholarship in IR, see Sjoberg 2008.

PART I

Beyond the Public/Private Divide

Feminist Analyses of Military Privatization and the Gendered State

CHAPTER 1

Military Privatization as a Gendered Process

A Case for Integrating Feminist International Relations and Feminist State Theories

SASKIA STACHOWITSCH

In her introduction, Maya Eichler situates this volume within feminist security studies. She emphasizes the contributions that scholars in the field can make to strengthen analyses of the privatization of military security, PMSCs, and their clients and employees.[1] This chapter aims to advance feminist theorizing of military privatization by integrating a state-theoretical perspective with a feminist IR, including feminist GPE, approach. Such an integrated theoretical perspective, I argue, allows us to grasp the hybrid character of military privatization as both an aspect of gendered state transformations and of the gendered dynamics of global markets. Crucially, this approach requires us first, to widen the focus beyond the private military and security industry, its gendered practices, discourses, and effects and link scholarship on private security to transformations in global and local gender relations under neoliberalism. Second, we need to abandon the "decline of the state hypothesis" that dominates mainstream discourses on security privatization and has also found its way into some of the gender literature on the subject. This hypothesis suggests that the allegedly more women-friendly state is eroding at the expense of a masculinized global market for force. Such reasoning is built on the notion of a clear-cut distinction between state and market, public and private, and national and international—dualisms that feminist theorists have identified as central to upholding gendered hierarchies (Boyd 1997; Youngs 2000; Blanchard 2003, 1296; Löffler 2011, 194). This chapter moves away from these dualisms to conceptualize the gendering of private security as an interaction between gendered states and global markets in the course of which the boundaries between these entities shift. I do not view gender as a phenomenon or variable, but rather as a relational approach that transcends the conventional theoretical boundaries between the above-mentioned categories and makes evident their mutual constitutiveness. Indeed, the drawing of these boundaries itself becomes the focus of analysis.

The wider literature on new global security regimes acknowledges the relevance of state transformations for understanding the phenomenon of privatized security, but these transformations have mostly been understood in terms of state erosion or state weakness (Strange 1996; Zarate 1998; Singer 2001/02; Sperling 2009; Feil et al. 2008; Carmola 2010; Krahmann 2010; Musah 2010; Avant 2011; Dickinson 2011). In contrast, Anna Leander analyzes security privatization as an aspect of neoliberalization that is "not only allowed but designed and encouraged by states" (Leander 2007a, 50).[2] Instead of being a sign of state erosion, the neoliberal order works through state actors and leads to mutual empowerment of political and economic elites (Leander and Van Munster 2007, 213). Neoliberal restructuring initiates changes in power relations, which benefit geopolitically powerful groups and states, and exacerbate inequalities within and between societies (Peterson 2005, 506). This restructuring does not simply take place on both national and international levels but is also characterized by a changing relationship between them (Brand 2010). In this process, the lines between public and private, state and market, and national and international are not only being blurred or made irrelevant—they are being redefined, shifted, and reconstructed, and this process is fundamentally gendered.

The state, its transformation, and shifting boundaries with global markets and the international arena have so far not been adequately theorized in the gender literature on military privatization. This chapter aims to show that the privatization of military security represents an ideal starting point for reconsidering the interconnections between gendered states and global markets. For this purpose, the analysis links feminist state theories with feminist IR and GPE. These theoretical traditions share a commitment to disrupting taken-for-granted theoretical boundaries and unmasking the universalized masculine bias of dichotomous concepts, such as the public-private divide, which have defined much of conventional state, IR, and economic theorizing. Nonetheless, feminist IR and state theorists have seldom directly engaged with each other. In this chapter, I propose that a more integrated approach is helpful in order to identify the interactions between gendered states and gendered international relations as they pertain to private security.

My approach is not meant to reaffirm state-centrism but aims to fine-tune feminist IR's analyses of the gendered state in the international system. Instead of abandoning state-level analysis, I examine the state and the international system in their relationship with one another. Such an approach opens up the field of feminist security studies to feminist discourses outside of IR that bring new insights into the relationship between individual lives, state structures, and the international system. At the same time, this approach advances feminist state theorizing by incorporating an analysis of the internationalization and globalization of the state as gendered processes.

The chapter first reviews conceptualizations of the state-international relationship in feminist IR and identifies relevant aspects for the study of military privatization as a process transcending the boundaries between the "levels of analysis." It then goes on to evaluate feminist state theories for their possible contribution to a critical gender analysis of military privatization. In the final section, an integrated perspective bringing feminist IR/GPE and state theories together is employed in the analysis of (military) privatization processes. To illustrate the benefits of such an integrated theoretical perspective, I discuss the transformation of military labor markets, the loss of transparency and democratic control, and discursive remasculinization as gendered outcomes of the shifting boundaries between states and (global) markets.

GENDERING THE INTERNATIONAL AND THE STATE: TOWARD AN INTEGRATED PERSPECTIVE

Feminist IR (Enloe 1989, 2000b; Tickner 1992a; Sylvester 1994, 2002; Shepherd 2010a) provides rich theoretical and methodological resources for a critical gender analysis of military privatization. Feminist IR scholars have made a strong case for overcoming the constructed separation between individual, local, and global "levels of analysis" that characterize mainstream IR approaches. They criticize such a separation as arbitrary, gender-biased, ahistorical, and blind to social power relations and struggles (Sjoberg 2011). The aim of feminist interventions has been to challenge "strict state–inter-state distinctions" (Hutchings 2008a, 100) and to reconsider the allegedly gender-neutral state. By showing that the state is gendered and that we need to understand its gendered nature to make sense of international affairs (Sjoberg 2011, 116), feminist IR has challenged the (neo)realist conceptualization of the state as a unitary and monolithic actor in the international system (Sjoberg 2006, 65–66) and of "states as 'individuals' separated from history" (Sylvester 1994, 90). The (neo)realist focus on state behavior diverts attention from "race, class, national, and gender differences" within the state (115). Feminist scholars have established gender inequality at the state level as the root cause of women's exclusion from the international arena (8). It follows that international relations can only be fully understood when "we ask how states have been constituted historically and how they are currently being sustained or transcended" (Tickner 1992b, ix). These theoretical insights of feminist IR highlight the importance of integrating the analysis of current state transformations with investigations of global developments (such as military privatization).

The concept of the gendered state (Peterson 1992a) has been developed by feminist IR to understand the state as a process rather than a set of institutions (Kantola 2007, 271). In feminist IR scholarship, gender is used not as a variable but as an analytical category. This shifts the focus "from women's exclusion from state institutions to understanding the gendered structures of these institutions" (271). Feminist IR thus proposes an alternative, gender-sensitive, and relational approach to the state, "an ontology of social relations in which individuals are embedded" (Tickner 2006, 24). However, in practice the primary focus of feminist IR research has been on the power relations within the state that neorealist theory underestimates or even ignores rather than on an explicit theorizing of the state and its role in the constitution of these power relations. While feminist IR scholars have argued for addressing gendered state structures and their outcomes at the international level, state-theoretical considerations have remained scattered and relatively vague as Johanna Kantola (2007, 270) argues: "The state, thus, is 'everywhere' and, yet, definitions, theories and discussions of it are increasingly rare. One could argue that the state remains under-theorised in feminist IR. Since V. Spike Peterson's (1992) explicit focus on the state, not much has been written about the concept." This is partly related to the fact that the critique of (neo)realism's state-centeredness has been such an important tool in feminist deconstructions of mainstream IR theory (Kantola 2007, 272). This critique has inspired feminist IR to start analysis from "below the state level—with the lives of connected individuals" (Tickner 2006, 25). As a consequence, emphasis on the state has frequently been associated with positivist and masculinist approaches. This relative disinterest in the state also reflects a broader "cultural turn" in feminist theory as well as the advancement of (inter)dependence and critical IR approaches that also problematize the discipline's sole focus on the state (Kantola 2007, 272–273).

Feminist Global Political Economy (Marchand and Runyan 2000; Peterson 2003; Bezanson and Luxton 2006)—"a blend of feminist work primarily but not exclusively in economics, development studies, political economy, international relations and international political economy" (Peterson 2005, 518)—has been less reluctant to address the state. The transition from the welfare to the neoliberal state has been studied as a complex interplay between social reproduction, state regulation, and the globalized political economy (Cossman and Fudge 2002; Bakker 2003; Bezanson and Luxton

2006). The emphasis in feminist GPE on households, social welfare, and social reproduction highlights the link between neoliberal state transformations, the evolution of global markets, and women's lives. Feminist GPE approaches contribute to our understanding of the broader socioeconomic contexts in which military privatization is taking place by analyzing globalization as a gendered process of "global neoliberal restructuring" (Marchand and Runyan 2000, 3). They help us contextualize private security within the neoliberal transformation of capitalism, processes of marketization and commodification of public goods, shifting power relations between markets and states, and their combined effects on gender relations.

The prevalent focus on social reproduction, however, has so far limited feminist GPE analysis of privatization to functions associated with reproductive capacities—that is, to domestic policy areas rather than the military and security sector. As a consequence, current transformations in warfare have rarely been systematically related to broader processes of neoliberalization, such as growth of financial markets, flexibilization and informalization of labor markets, *and* increases in gender inequality (Peterson 2008, 8–9).[3] Furthermore, compared to the concepts of "market" and "economy," the state has generally been under-theorized in feminist GPE (Brand 2013, 301). However, as the state is a driving force in privatization processes, a comprehensive gender analysis of military privatization requires consideration of the state's gendered foundations. I argue that feminist IR/GPE should be complemented by feminist state theories for a deeper theorization of the gendered state.

FEMINIST APPROACHES TO THE STATE

Feminist state theorists have not developed a unitary, coherent account of the state (Jessop 2001, 152) but utilize "insights from different state theories relevant to the different faces that the state presents to women" (158). Early contributions to feminist state theories originated from feminist engagement with, and critiques of, Marxism and focused on the relationship between capitalism, patriarchy, and the state (Eisenstein 1978; McIntosh 1978; Mies 1986; MacKinnon 1989). Until the 1980s, feminist state theorists were preoccupied with social institutions regulated by the state such as welfare systems or marriage laws (Löffler 2011, 190). In the 1990s, the focus shifted toward a more process-oriented understanding of the state (Franzway, Court, and Connell 1989) and toward poststructuralist and discursive approaches (Pringle and Watson 1992).[4] Recent feminist work on the state (Ludwig, Sauer, and Wöhl 2009) has built upon neo-Marxian and poststructuralist theory traditions, innovating the ways in which these can be connected to each other (Sauer 2001). Nicos Poulantzas' (1978) view of the state as a material condensation of social power relations has been influential in the feminist study of state transformations and their relationship to changing gender orders. Feminist state theorists have also employed Michel Foucault's concept of governmentality to examine the state's role in constructing gendered subjectivities under neoliberalism (Ludwig 2011).

Despite different emphases, feminist state theories share key theoretical cornerstones such as a critical stance toward political/state power, an open, process-oriented, and broad definition of the state, a focus on social power relations and struggles within and beyond the state, and an interest in the interrelations between structural and discursive phenomena. Feminist state theorists view the state as changing and contested. The state is seen to have a certain degree of autonomy, observable in state policies, but it is not an independent subject (Löffler 2011, 102). As a social process and manifestation of political power relations, the state is structured by gendered practices and discourses. Vice versa, gender as a structural and ideological category is constructed and organized through state institutions, policies, and discourses. Unlike static concepts of the eternally patriarchal state, such a conceptualization allows us to grasp the interconnections between transformations of the state and changes in gender relations, in the course of which masculinities and femininities are redefined and gender-specific patterns of labor division are reconstructed (Sauer 2008, 35). These dynamics of gendered state transformations can potentially undermine traditional gender relations and stereotypes but also introduce new inequalities (Bakker 2003, 66).

Feminist State Theory and Military Privatization

A state-theoretical perspective is useful for examining global security markets and military privatization for, at least, three reasons. First, it enables us to address the interrelatedness between state (trans)formation, warfare, and gender relations (Hagemann and Pröve 1998). Feminist research has shown that the coevolution of the Western nation-state, modern military institutions, and hierarchical gender orders led to a privileging of militarized masculinity in the political sphere and institutionalized gendered dichotomies of "just warriors" and "beautiful souls" within the state (Elshtain 1995). In the nineteenth-century, the military was the central state institution establishing and sustaining the special relationship between the state and men, and the strong association of citizenship and masculinity organized through compulsory military service provided the basis for women's political exclusion (Frevert 1996). The military thus represents a main site where hegemonic masculinity and masculinism as a political ideology are generated and where hierarchical gender relations are institutionalized in and by the state (Kreisky 1994).

In many Western countries, this historical connection between state, military, and masculinity has been transformed with the abolishment of the draft—an important precondition for increased female representation in the military (Segal 1995). Since then, women's (limited and selective) integration has challenged but not fundamentally changed the role of the military as a male resource of power establishing a direct link between masculinity, citizenship, and the state. Military privatization—as an aspect of neoliberal state restructuring—once again transforms the relationship between state, military, citizenship, and gender (Eichler 2014).

Due to the historical interconnections between state formation, military institutionalization, and hierarchical gender relations, the military sector is not merely another policy area affected by neoliberal reforms; it is a central sphere in which the gendered war-state-citizenship nexus is reconstructed in the neoliberal era. The literature on private (military) security has so far not adequately accounted for this (Stachowitsch 2013). A gender-sensitive approach to the state and the gendered dimensions of its transformation is therefore needed to better understand the dynamics that neoliberal restructuring initiates in the relations between gender, war, and state.

The second rationale for including feminist state theories is the different perspective they enable on gender and privatization through a more sophisticated conceptualization of the state. Feminist state theory does not focus on state institutions and governmental processes in a narrow sense but on the hybrid and changing boundaries between the state and other spheres, for example, the market or the international system. This allows us to address the global market for force and the transnationally operating military and security industry in their interrelatedness with the gendered state. Furthermore, taking into account the structural and institutional as well as the discursive aspects of the state enables a view of military privatization not only as a policy or an institutional process but also as a discursive process in which state and nonstate actors interact to support their shared or conflicting interests in the neoliberal project. We can thus, for example, examine how neoliberal arguments regarding the superiority of the private market over the state are gendered and how gender ideologies are used to promote or criticize neoliberal policies of military outsourcing.

This theoretical move also speaks to Kantola's (2007) critique of feminist IR in which she suggests that instead of abandoning the state as a relevant analytical category, we are to focus on the "gendered reproduction of the state" and discuss the state "as an effect of discursive and structural processes" (270). She highlights the importance of studying "the various ways that boundaries of the state are redrawn, since they are likely to have significant impacts on the state's policies that influence gender relations" (280). An approach starting from the gendered reproduction of the state offers a different perspective on military privatization—one that enables an understanding of how privatization as a discourse and practice reconstructs the state and its boundaries as gendered entities.

A third asset of feminist state theories is their sensitivity to state *transformations* (Löffler 2012) that first, counters simplifying notions of state decline (Youngs 2000; Rai 2004; Kantola 2007) and second, enables contextualization of military privatization within neoliberal state restructuring and associated changes in gender orders. Although the relationship between the national and international has so far not been a major focus in feminist state theories, recent feminist work has shown that global governance constitutes a "new form of statehood based on unequal gender relations" (Sauer and Wöhl 2011, 119), rather than a "counter model" to the eroding nation-state (114). The restructuring of gender relations in a globalized world leads "to new forms of gendered exploitation" (114). The ongoing transition from the welfare to the neoliberal state (Cossman and Fudge 2002; Sauer 2008) is based on specific gender arrangements, which it reproduces and thereby modifies locally and globally (Marchand 1996, 602). In this process, neoliberalization reconstructs rather than dissolves hierarchical gender regimes. Neoliberal policies of privatization and outsourcing have deteriorating effects on women's status in different economic, social, and political contexts and contribute to the hierarchization of gender relations (Marchand 1996). They create new forms of inclusions and exclusions, often exacerbating existing inequalities (Marchand and Runyan 2000, 2) and in particular "harm women as a structurally vulnerable population and as the main care-takers of society's dependent members" (Peterson 2007, 15).

Relating military privatization to these analyses of neoliberal restructuring highlights how the gendered state is involved in shaping the gendered structures of private security through its outsourcing policies, the promotion of neoliberal ideology, and gender-based inclusions and exclusions in state (military) institutions. Rather than being the gender-egalitarian counterpart to the security industry, the gendered state and its military provide the background for the gendered dynamics of privatization (Stachowitsch 2013). State and nonstate actors interact to uphold state interests and marginalize women's rights (Johnstone 2009, 1).

By employing a state-theoretical perspective in the research on gender and private security, the process of military privatization can be theorized as an aspect of both gendered state transformations and global neoliberal restructuring, in the course of which the boundaries between state and market, public and private, and national and international are shifting. Following the concept of the internationalization of the state (Brand 2013), the emergence of global security markets is dependent on internal state transformations which in turn enable international deregulation and the emergence of a global neoliberal consensus in favor of outsourcing. This highlights the privatization of the military security sector as a gendered process related to the transition of the neoliberal, internationalized state. The following section illustrates this reconfiguration of state-international, public-private, and state-market relationships by integrating feminist state theories with feminist IR/GPE.

GENDERING MILITARY PRIVATIZATION AT THE STATE AND THE GLOBAL LEVEL

Military privatization is shaped by the changing relationship between the gendered state and global markets that increase gender inequality locally and globally. I next discuss central processes associated with neoliberal restructuring in the context of military privatization: the transformation of (military) labor markets, the loss of transparency and democratic control, and discursive remasculinization. These processes have been identified in the gender literature on the subject as centrally problematic aspects of security privatization. Scholars have emphasized gendered and racialized inequalities in private military labor markets (Eichler 2013; Chisholm 2014a), highlighted how a lack of accountability and democratic control leads to violence against women (Schulz and Yeung 2008; Vrdoljak 2011), and scrutinized the masculinist discursive practices of PMSCs (Joachim and Schneiker 2012c) and embodied practices of contractors (Higate 2012a, 2012b, 2012c).

In these analyses, negative consequences of privatization have so far mostly been studied in terms of the industry's structures and practices. Some—particularly those taking the accountability and violence angle— implicitly or explicitly argue that more egalitarian national or international institutions are eroding at the expense of the private market and need to regain their former regulatory capacity and/or monopoly on violence. This follows the mainstream consensus that the state is being undermined through privatization (Strange 1996; Zarate 1998; Singer 2002; Sperling 2009; Feil et al. 2008; Carmola 2010; Krahmann 2010; Musah 2010; Avant 2011; Dickinson 2011), rather than transformed or even strengthened. While critically investigating the industry is an important step, I argue that to grasp the gender-specific implications of privatization, we need to foreground the interactions and shifting boundaries between private and public sectors. This is because first, the state cannot be assumed a gender-egalitarian counterpart to the private military and security industry, and second, privatization is a state-induced process and an expression of the state's internal transformation as well as its internationalization. To investigate the dynamics between public and private structures of inequality, I integrate feminist approaches to global economic and political phenomena with feminist theories on the state. From this theoretical perspective, I examine the gendered dynamics that result from redrawing boundaries between state and market, public and private, as well as national and international levels.

Transformation of Labor Markets

The internationalization of capital and the explosive growth in financial markets that have "disembedded" capital and financial flows from national contexts (Altvater and Mahnkopf 1996, 107) have also led to the transfer of public responsibilities to the market by way of direct privatization, outsourcing, or public–private partnerships (Leander and Van Munster 2007, 204). This marketization is not just a reaction of the state to the internationalization of capital but is also dependent on national policies of deregulation. It is in this context that labor markets have been globalized and deregulated, which increases informalization and flexibilization of labor, and leads to "growing inequalities of ethnicity/race, gender, class and nation" (Peterson 2008, 9). Feminist GPE has identified the feminization of employment as one central aspect of these developments, indicating both an increase in the proportion of women on labor markets and the deterioration and devalorization of working conditions: "In short, as more jobs become casual, irregular, flexible and precarious, more women—and feminised men—are doing them" (Peterson 2005, 509). This reinforces an unequal global labor division between powerful and peripheral states as well as hierarchical gender orders within the state. "Low quality jobs" are increasingly outsourced to the exploited workforce at the global margins. Meanwhile, the (re)privatization of public responsibilities shifts social welfare onto households and particularly onto women (Marchand and Runyan 2000, 17) and decreases public sector employment, which also disproportionally and negatively affects women (Peterson 2005, 506).

In military labor markets, this neoliberal restructuring has led to the increasing integration of private actors and has also rearranged gender orders. Both forms of feminization of labor can be observed here: First, privatization excludes women from an increasing number of military jobs and limits them to unskilled and stereotyped positions in the private military and security industry (Eichler 2013). This is a result of the dynamics between gendered state structures, expressed in unequal access to the armed forces, and the gendered and racialized recruitment conditions on the global market for force. PMSCs largely draw from personnel pools consisting of ex-military personnel trained in (ground) combat-intensive occupations in national militaries (Schulz and Yeung 2008, 4)—occupations from which women are legally excluded or in which they are strongly underrepresented. The male workforce trained in these capacities has become increasingly available to the industry as a result of military downsizing after the end of the Cold War

(Singer 2001/02). At the same time, national militaries have become more dependent on female recruits, particularly in noncombat support jobs at the lower and middle ranks (Stachowitsch 2012a, 2012b). Neoliberal state transformations thus lead to both the establishment of a masculinized, lucrative private military job market and the feminization of lower quality jobs in the state forces. Women's discrimination in the private sector is rooted in unequal gender relations in the state military. At the same time, inequality in the military sphere as a whole reaches new dimensions with privatization because a hierarchical gendered labor division between public and private is established.

Second, the labor of marginalized men is feminized and exploited on private military labor markets. (The chapters by Isabelle Barker and Amanda Chisholm in this volume discuss this in more detail.) Deregulation and the internationalization of recruitment have made contractor firms less dependent on the national workforce, because they can recruit globally in search of the most cost-effective ways to provide their services. As a result, menial, unskilled, and reproductive labor is assigned to men from the global periphery, that is, from poorer countries providing cheaper labor (see Barker's chapter), and dangerous work is outsourced to "martial races" with which the companies' home countries share a colonial history (see Chisholm's chapter). The global private security industry has become an important source of revenue for states that export this type of migrant labor (Avant and Sigelman 2009, 13–15). The most prestigious and best paying jobs are reserved for those who conform to hegemonic Western masculinity ideals (Chisholm 2014a). Women are excluded from even the least lucrative jobs in favor of "feminized" men from the global margins. Gender provides a framework through which the relations between the global center and the periphery are being defined and military labor is distributed, not only between men and women but also between different national, social, and "ethnic" groups.

These interactions between national and global military labor markets reinforce hierarchical patterns of gendered and racialized labor divisions. This does not solely reflect the practices and discourses of the male-dominated contractor industry but is also an outcome of state transformations and their effects on global markets. Taken together, state and global transformations create a two-tiered feminization of military labor. Neoliberal state reforms and changing geopolitical conditions after the end of the Cold War led to the downsizing of Western state forces and put pressure on them to function according to market laws of cost-effectiveness and economic rationality. Outsourcing capacities to the market was one way for state militaries to concede to this pressure. The state has enabled the flexibilization and internationalization of military labor markets and in turn has benefited from exploitative global work relations that facilitate otherwise too costly foreign interventions. At the same time, many regular militaries could not be upheld without the increased integration of women into lower and medium-quality jobs (Segal 1995). State policies have codified women as an unequal military workforce, which now limits their ability to transition into private military labor markets. These dynamics between the gendered state and gendered global markets reconstruct gender hierarchies and inequalities and reproduce both spheres as structured by racialized and gendered hierarchies.

Loss of Transparency and Democratic Control

The boundaries between the state and the market, public and private, and national and international are also reconstructed with gendered effects in the realm of policy. In the neoliberal era, the state's "centralized power, regulatory capacity and public accountability . . . is [sic] eroded in favor of unaccountable decentralized markets, international agencies and private interest networks" (Peterson 2008, 14). This also affects the state's ability to regulate the conduct of war (8–9). Outsourcing of some state functions to global markets limits the state's ability to influence related policy matters through legislation and public action. Gender equality in the military and security realm is a case in point. While gender mainstreaming and equality measures are increasingly implemented and more women are integrated into the structures and practices of state forces, gender equality plays virtually no role in the military and security industry—aside from a few rhetorical references to "gender issues," for example, in the International Code of Conduct for Private Security Providers (Swiss Confederation 2010). Elected representatives have less access to international private security markets compared to the state military and no direct instruments to implement and monitor gender equality in the industry. This negatively affects the legal status of women in the private military workforce and decreases the protection of local women from gender-based human rights abuses (Harrington 2005; Gumedze 2007; Schulz and Yeung 2008). In their chapters in this volume, Ana Vrdoljak and Valerie Sperling explain what implications this loss of accountability and transparency has for gender-related violence and women's security in post-conflict peacekeeping. Jillian Terry's chapter links accountability issues to violence and the moral and ethical implications of military privatization.

This decrease in political control over a key policy area does not indicate a general weakening of the state. Rather, the neoliberal state accepts and at times actively initiates a certain degree of de-democratization of decision-making processes, while flexibility and independence of the executive branch from the legislative are strengthened and the "coercive and surveillance capacities [of the state] are . . . enhanced" (Kantola 2007, 271). The state loses influence in some areas of military policy, for example, recruitment requirements for private contractors, in exchange for more flexibility in others, for example, the ability to extend troop sizes through private forces without requiring approval from elected representatives (Avant and Sigelman 2009, 2) or being held less accountable for human rights abuses committed by private forces. Thus the state is not losing power to global markets but functionally redrawing the boundaries of its legal authority; and this reconstruction of the state's reach is gendered.

Areas formerly covered by equality laws guaranteed by the state are not just being outsourced to the unaccountable global market; rather, masculinist state structures are being internationalized—exported to the global arena where they have new effects. In the state context, the privileging of male citizenship via military service historically justified discrimination against women, the militarization of everyday life continues to marginalize women and their interests, and exclusionary state policies define military women as less-than-equal service members which causes elevated levels of gender-specific violence against female soldiers (Segal 1999; Enloe 2000b). This state-made masculinist military culture and structure are being outsourced to global markets, while public oversight and accountability are eliminated in favor of cost-effectiveness, efficiency, and economic rationality—values that are also being privileged through neoliberal state reforms.

At the same time, gender discrimination in the state forces is upheld and women's rights and status are attacked in other policy fields by neoliberal reform, for example through cuts in state support for social reproduction and the privatization of public services (Marchand 1996).[5] In the U.S. case, neoliberalism's alliance with neoconservatism (Virchow 2008, 238) devalues gender equality as a political goal in those areas that the state still effectively controls. Neoconservative forces which typically blame the welfare state and feminism simultaneously for social and political problems (Marchand and Runyan 2000, 18) have worked hard to curtail women's roles in the armed forces, albeit with limited success. State transformations have not only led to the (intended) loss of accountability and regulatory capacity over selected policy issues but also to power gains for political forces attacking women's rights.

The image of the eroding state unable to intervene in gender policy matters cannot be upheld when looking beyond the industry and its practices. What we see is not the loss of state authority but a process of de-democratization of key policy areas in the course of the state's internationalization and associated outsourcing to global markets. While accountability of public actors is lacking on the global security market with gender-specific effects, gender-based discrimination and violence in private security result just as much from the state's "absence" as from its globalized presence. The state's gender-discriminatory policy and culture, particularly within the military, are outsourced to deregulated global markets, while neoliberal restructuring threatens women's status in civilian policy areas. The boundaries between state (national policy-regulated fields) and nonstate (international unregulated markets) are redrawn in a way that exacerbates inequalities and reaffirms both as gendered spheres. It follows that the problems that private military security can create for states in the form of public scandals are not an issue of regulation alone. Attempts to further regulate the industry, for example by introducing codes of conduct or gender-mainstreaming mechanisms, will not automatically make private security a more gender-equal sphere.

Discursive Remasculinization

In addition to structural transformations in labor markets and in the realm of policy, new arrangements between the state and private actors also affect the discursive level. Here, military privatization is accompanied by a process of remasculinization (Jeffords 1989), which reconstructs masculinities and adapts them to the current challenges raised by social change in a way that reaffirms the political sphere as masculine. In discourses on private security, masculinity is emphasized as a core competence in national security and foreign policy as well as a privileged category in international business (Stachowitsch 2014). This is most evident in the marketing strategies of PMSCs identified by Jutta Joachim and Andrea Schneiker (2012a), which rely on (hyper)masculinization and feminization to promote their services. PMSCs draw on notions of ideal versus deviant masculinity to position themselves as the efficient, assertive alternative to state forces and "mercenaries." Neoliberal discourses, in which "the state is typically 'feminised' in relation to the more robust market" (Kantola 2007, 271), provide the argumentative backdrop for these strategies in which the state and its military are typically portrayed as inefficient, weak, and incapable (Joachim and Schneiker 2012a).

Though different in content, critical accounts of the contractor business, particularly in the media, take part in this gendered framing of the new state-market relationship and rely on the ideal of soldier masculinity associated with state forces. The stereotype of the hypermasculine, aggressive, greedy, and unpatriotic contractor is contrasted with the image of the disciplined, restrained, patriotic, and self-sacrificing state soldier. Articles in the *New York Times*, for example, portrayed contractors as "amateurish, overpaid and, often, trigger-happy," as "beefy men with beards and flak jackets" (Glanz and Lehren 2010), who did not show "the same commitment and willingness to take risks as the men and women of the military" (Glanz 2009). The state soldier, in contrast, was depicted as "motivated by, and schooled in, the common good and simple patriotism—not profits or private ambitions" (Friedman 2009). This essentially masculine figure of the ideal warrior draws on the citizen-soldier model that historically linked political participation to (male) military service and militarized the gender order of the nation-state (Snyder 1999). To utilize this image is a gendering strategy, in which the state is constructed as the true bearer of appropriate and legitimate masculinity, while the market appears as a symbol of uncontrollable, profit-seeking, and ruthless hypermasculinity (Stachowitsch 2014).

Overall, the shifting boundaries between the nation-state and the (global) market lead to discursive remasculinization through which state and market are both confirmed as masculine resources of power. Masculinity is adapted to the challenges raised by new security regimes that question the traditional bases of male power, such as state warfare, military institutions, conscription, and the masculine protector status historically derived from them. In discourses that affirm privatization, the public-private divide is redefined and its gendered meaning reconstructed. The main demarcation line no longer lies between the masculinized public sphere, which includes the state and the market, and the feminized private household but between the market as the masculine (efficient, cost-effective, technologically advanced, managerial) sphere and the state as the feminine (weak, democratic, inefficient, and bureaucratic) sphere. Resistance to neoliberal ideology does not aim to disrupt its gendered narrative, but simply genders it differently. The state is associated with "appropriate" masculinity and the market with hypermasculinity. Public and private are defined and valued differently, but a clear gendered hierarchy is retained. Discursive remasculinization is thus not only an effect of the private military and security industry but also a result of power struggles between state and market actors. Both instrumentalize gender ideologies as power tools that ultimately reproduce both the state and the market as separate, distinguishable entities that are hierarchically gendered.

Discursive redefinitions of security, which Leander (2007a, 2009a) has identified as a central aspect of the privatization process, are also affected by remasculinization. Leander's research suggests that privatization shifts our notion of security and that PMSCs and their "security experts" have gained a monopoly on defining (in)security, threats, risks, and solutions—with real effects. This redefinition is gendered; it is deeply associated with state-defined notions of militarized masculinity as well as market-oriented ideals of neoliberal business masculinity. On the one hand, private security is associated with militarized masculinity, casting PMSCs as willing, risk-taking, and affirming military values and culture in opposition to naive, gender-integrated, and thus feminized state forces, NGOs, and the UN.

With this militarization of discourses, private security draws on masculinist protectionism (Young 2003), a gendered definition of security that developed in the process of state formation (Peterson 1992b, 49–51) and conceptualized protection as based on "the exchange of obedience/subordination for (promises of) security" (Blanchard 2003, 1297). Historically, this notion of protection was state-centric. Representations of the state as the legitimate protector of not only women but also of a feminized public became the basis for the justification of state power (1297). Such an understanding of protection was also exclusionary because it created systematic insecurities for women (Peterson 1992b, 49–51) and other marginalized groups. In her chapter, Maya Eichler discusses how the gendered politics of protection is now extended to the global scale through military privatization.

On the other hand, security is redefined in market-related terms. From a public good provided by the state for communities or populations, security turns into an excludable and marketable good, restricted to clients who can afford to pay for it. In this process of security commodification (Abrahamsen and Williams 2008), understandings of security are depoliticized through a narrow focus on technicalities and cost-effectiveness (Leander and Van Munster 2007, 201). A managerial, technocratic approach enables private companies to market their expertise as the logical solution to all kinds of social problems and political conflicts, which are redefined as "security threats." These discourses draw on professionalized, managerial masculinity ideals whereby the private sector is portrayed as rational and guided by calculable market laws, as opposed to state forces that are dependent on the irrationalities inherent in a democracy.

Taken together, militarization and commodification restrict the concept of security to exclude notions of human security with their focus on social or environmental aspects. They also exclude marginalized groups, that is, those who cannot afford to pay for their own security or are themselves considered "security threats" by security elites (such as immigrants, protesters, refugees, and others). And they exclude civilians, non-Westerners, and women from participating in the process of defining security. They devalue alternative, nonsecurity framings and solutions, such as local knowledge and diplomatic options (Leander and Van Munster 2007, 201); militarize foreign policy (201); and normalize violence in security provision (Higate and Stachowitsch 2013a). These developments result in lower levels of security for civilian actors (Fitzsimmons 2012) and particularly marginalize the security concerns of women and other vulnerable groups in (post)conflict settings.

This discursive remasculinization of security does not result from security functions being "taken away" from the state, but from a new and complex interplay between state- and market-related discourses. Private security providers draw on market-defined ideals of professionalized business masculinity in rhetorical opposition to the state just as much as they draw on state-defined notions of militarized masculinity and state traditions of masculinist protectionism. The state provides the basis for masculinist protectionism as a narrative for private security, and neoliberal state ideology allows private actors to capitalize on the positive bias that exists toward business solutions as more effective than public sector solutions (Leander

2007a, 14). State transformations thus enable the globalization of a commodified form of masculinist protectionism (also see Eichler's chapter in this volume). This leads to a mutual empowerment of security elites within and beyond the state "that share a 'techno-managerial understanding of security'" (Leander 2007a, 15). As the executive branch is strengthened in matters of security policy, masculinist protectionism is invigorated because an even greater degree of unquestioning obedience is demanded from a feminized global public.

CONCLUSIONS

In the course of national and global neoliberal restructuring, the boundaries between the state and the market are being redrawn discursively and structurally. Feminist state theories provide a strong critique of the gendered state, feminist IR highlights the genderedness of global politics, and feminist GPE points to the gendered (and racialized) character of global markets. Taken together, an integrated perspective enables an in-depth analysis of the relationship between state transformations, global market relations, and global and national gender orders. Systematically embedding military privatization within neoliberal state *and* global transformations offers new insights into the gendered aspects of the privatization phenomenon and the changing state-war-gender nexus in the contemporary period. The contextualization within broader processes of social change enriches research on gender and the global market for force by going beyond a focus on the industry and linking the emerging field of "critical gender studies in private security" (see the introduction to this volume) to debates on gender relations in the neoliberal era. As the analysis has shown, gendered state structures and their transformation are central to understanding the gendered effects of private security.

Gender relations are transformed in the process of military privatization, reinforcing and even exacerbating inequalities. Gender discrimination at the national and international level marginalize women and sustain hegemonic concepts of masculinity. This defies idealizations of the state as the guarantor of gender equality as well as myths of the market as the "great equalizer." The above analysis shows that exclusions at the state level attain new qualities in the course of the state's internationalization. State policies have gendered effects in the private sector and structure global markets, for example by inhibiting women's equal participation in global labor markets. At the same time, global restructuring transforms gender orders within the state, for example by eroding women's public support structures.

The advancement of private security is not a sign of state erosion but an outcome of gendered state transformations and the changing relationship between the state and the international sphere as well as the state and the market. Identifying the gendered effects of these shifting boundaries and the dynamics they introduce between gendered state and global orders enables a more radical critique of private security, a critique that goes beyond attempts to solve the industry's problems of gender-based violence and inequality. It also moves debates away from "industry-bashing" or nostalgia for an imagined past in which the egalitarian state allegedly ruled over gender relations to the benefit of women. The study of military privatization thus provides an ideal starting point for revisiting the relationship between the gendered state and the gendered dynamics of global politics.

NOTES

1. The research presented in this chapter was funded by the Austrian Science Fund (FWF): Project V 291-G22. The author would like to thank Rahel Kunz, Maya Eichler, Kathrin Glösel, and the "Habil Kolloquium" at the Department of Political Science, University of Vienna, for their feedback on and contributions to this chapter.
2. Consequently, some scholars have abandoned the concept of "privatization" and reformulated research agendas in terms of commercialization, commodification, governance or governmentality (Leander 2009a, 2) to highlight that this phenomenon is implicated with state policies in many ways. In this chapter, privatization is retained as a concept to emphasize state transformations and associated shifts in the private-public relationship, while questioning these very categories.
3. The chapters by Chisholm as well as Joachim and Schneiker in this volume indicate that this might be changing in the future.
4. For a detailed discussion of additional influences on feminist state theory see Löffler (2011, 192).
5. Legal gender discrimination in Western armed forces is gradually being removed. For example, the United States has recently announced that women's last remaining exclusions from ground combat positions will be lifted. However, women are extremely underrepresented in key areas of the military despite decades of integration. High levels of sexual abuse of female recruits also indicate that women are still not considered equal service members.

CHAPTER 2

Military Privatization and the Gendered Politics of Sacrifice

BIANCA BAGGIARINI

In the right of sovereignty, death was the moment of the most obvious and most spectacular manifestation of the absolute power of the sovereign; death now becomes, in contrast, the moment when the individual escapes all power, falls back on himself and retreats, so to speak, into his own privacy. Power no longer recognizes death. Power literally ignores death.

Michel Foucault, *Society Must Be Defended*

Every act of identifying an enemy is fraught with risk, for if the populace fails to see that person or group as the enemy, it will see only murder, not sacrifice.

Paul Kahn, *Sacred Violence*

This chapter explores how military privatization challenges the relationship between gendered, sacrificial violence and soldier-citizenship. Private means of governing redraw the parameters between the public and private spheres (Hibou 2004), which is underscored by a shift "beyond the social contract on which modern citizenship was configured" (Rygiel 2008, 231). I argue that privatization, a chief technique for governing at a distance (Brown 1995), depoliticizes war by rendering violence beyond the scope of the social contract and norms of reciprocity, which have governed war since the early twentieth century. These interrelated processes—governing at a distance and the departure from the norms of the social contract—compel feminists to investigate the productive potential of gender in international relations writ large, as well as the meanings of gender in privatized military settings. As the boundaries between the public and the private spheres are reconstituted through the neoliberal restructuring of capitalism, feminist theorists are concerned with foregrounding the body within mainstream security studies (Sylvester 2012), a subdiscipline of IR, which is still chiefly defined by realist theory and problem-solving approaches to social issues (Eichler 2012b). I extend a shared (although heterogeneous) feminist approach to security studies: because war and gendered discourses are mutually reinforcing, the study of state and nonstate violence requires a concurrent analysis of securitization as it pertains to power and the gendered body.[1]

Postmodern wars contain perplexing visions of the body, particularly in relation to combat unmanning—the replacement (or supplementation) of bodies with technology.[2] Mainstream security discourses regard bodies, which are vulnerable and require ongoing care, as an obstacle to network-centric warfare (Masters 2008). Although conceptualizations of the body are integral to theorizing and strategizing war, alluring promises about the benefits of so-called bloodless war argue that it is possible (and in fact desirable) to move beyond the body, eclipsing all its vulnerabilities—including gendered politics. Christine Sylvester states, "Wars are not indicative of a breakdown of inter-state balances of power, norms or structures of conflict resolution as much as they are an intensification of social relations" (2012, 489). Yet military privatization is neither just an effect nor an intensification of relations contained by the neoliberal restructuring of capitalism. It is also a response to the problem of how to sacrifice soldiers in late modern, casualty-averse, liberal-democratic societies. As such, the body is of central concern in the negotiation of who ought to sacrifice and who will be sacrificed. Since "the boundaries of the self only become clear through the imagination of sacrifice" (Kahn 2008, 109), citizens' subjectivity is predicated upon an understanding of the micro and macro effects of state power in the organization of the meanings of violence—meanings that gain content in relation to sacrifice. Postmodern war does not erase sacrifice but instead redistributes the material burden of it, revealing how sacrificial narratives are informed by whether war is thought to be public or private. Given that PMSCs avoid the discourse of sacrifice (see Taussig-Rubbo 2009a), I ask: What is the meaning of bodies, soldiering, and citizenship in postmodern, privatized wars?

Sacrifice offers a clue as to how to begin to address this question. I explore how sacrificial discourses informed the disciplining of citizenship within the Western nuclear family during the first half of the twentieth century. Historically, women's sacrifice has been defined relationally and negatively, while men's sacrifice has been regarded as transcendent and self-sufficient by way of the symbolic capital that citizen-warriors' sacrifice generates for the nation. The various potential constructions of women, as passive victims ("sacrificial objects"); as "unsacrificeable"; and now as active and, presumably equal to men, as "sacrificing subjects," in military settings suggests an unraveling of the traditional relation between masculine (universal) citizenship and sacrifice, as anchored in a relation of mutual reciprocity between citizen and state. Women's bodies, their mere presence in militarized settings and in combat roles, therefore trouble the normative gender order that has historically informed masculine sacrifice.

Further, I show how PMSCs emerged as a seemingly permanent feature in thinking about security. Privatization is not solely a matter of economic maneuvering; it reveals historically specific ideas of how war should be governed in relation to soldier-citizens. I use a genealogical method in this regard, since it takes illegitimate knowledge and contradictions as rich sites of truth-making processes and critiques the effects of linearity in traditional historical projects (Foucault 2010). Society cannot function without the idea of the sacred (Girard 1979), thus genealogy reveals the paradox of bloodless war and sacrifice's reliance on bloodshed. Sacrifice is a material phenomenon, albeit now an increasingly uneven one. PMSCs are an effect of the neoliberal construction of capitalism, the revolution in military affairs (RMA), and a response to how, and under what conditions, casualty-averse liberal societies sacrifice soldier-citizens. I argue that the tension between sovereign and biopolitical power (Mutimer 2007) is partly resolved by PMSCs (Baggiarini 2013), enabling the functioning of liberal warfare. Since contractor deaths do not correspond to a single national public, PMSCs, which are notoriously impenetrable (Avant and Sigelman 2010), save North American audiences from confronting the realities of war.

I conclude by exploring the sociopolitical implications inherent in fantasies of disembodied combat. One implication is that sacrifice appears anachronistic. Casualty-aversion provokes policies that replace bodies with technological rationality and solutions, bloodless war. In closing the gap between sovereignty's right to kill and biopolitical power's life-enhancing aspirations, PMSCs free states from the democratic impulses that have traditionally defined territorial warfare: accountability, collectivism, and transparency. The corporatization of war, which results from a political ethos of wide-scale privatization, seems to do away with the need for a nationalized narrative of sacrifice as integral to imagining war. However, I argue that this bracketing of sacrifice reveals less about whether sacrifice is happening from a material standpoint and more about how states manage the contradictions of liberal warfare.

GENDERED SACRIFICE AND THE DISCIPLINING OF CITIZENSHIP

In this section, I trace the historical development of sacrifice with reference to the expansion of the nation-state system, and the gendered expectations and qualities of the nuclear family. I illustrate how sacrifice, as a discourse and practice, became integral to the formation of the soldier-citizen as an archetype of heroic masculinity in North American social consciousness. Militarized notions of sacrifice, rooted in nationalized origin stories, were instrumental in the realization of state sovereignty and, in turn, in defining gendered norms. Military sacrifice, first and foremost, has historically worked to politicize and to publicize the suffering, injury, or deaths of soldiers. The individual's self-sacrifice, or death, is thought to serve a purpose beyond the scope of the individual: sacrifice is for the greater good of the national community and subsequently the life of the body politic. As a result, it has a communicative effect (Taussig-Rubbo 2009a). Sacrificial actions must be recognized and represented as sacrificial by a validating authority, and, as such, it is an essentially contested concept. Rather than existing as a universal given, sacrifice is discursively constructed. It draws upon foundational narratives, protection myths, and symbols of masculinized courage—an entrenched lexicon of heroism—to militarize collective consciousness and reify the social contract between the citizen and the state.

In foundational narratives, women are constructed as the symbolic, cultural, and biological reproducers of the nation. Women occupy the home front as the Good Mother or Beautiful Soul, while "the male heterosexual human or citizen is firmly located in the public sphere, disassociated from the female private sphere, or the realm of necessity of the body" (Lister 2002, 194). Woman's sacrifice is defined relationally or by lack. Her body is in and of itself insufficient, so sacrifice is experienced through men, embodying "men's honor [and] their accomplishments, and [woman] is the repository of all that should be protected and conserved" (Pin Fat and Stern 2005, 44). Jean Bethke Elshtain (1993) comments: "[T]he state's proclamation of its own sovereignty is not enough: that sovereignty must be recognized. War is the means to attain recognition, to pass, in a sense, the definitive test of political manhood" (162). Sacrifice and sovereignty are realized together, by being tested in the theater of war, where men occupy natural positions as embodied combatants. Soldier-citizens, through death or injury, have come to represent the highest expression of sacrifice. Through the interpellation of soldier-citizens, state and military power maintains and perpetuates affective economies that constitute war as the "soul" of the nation. In this vein "[f]allen soldiers remain the property of the state," Jenny Edkins (2003, 95) points out. In death, the nation reclaims the loss of soldiers as a remainder or surplus that arises in the remaking of the state (95). Only male individuals are capable of transcending the body; women, as sexual beings and bearers of children, are not (Lister 2002). Yet, private contractor deaths are not claimed on behalf of the nation. American PMSCs are not required to publicize the deaths of their employees. Their deaths therefore offer no meaningful surplus for the state in the construction of foundational narratives. This, at the very least, seems to trouble the straightforwardness of sacrificial myths insofar as killing and being killed for the nation are concerned.

Sacrificial discourses are written upon disciplined, sexed bodies and therefore contain a deeply gendered logic of transcendence over the impure feminine: that is, over the female/feminized body (Jay 1992). Composed of two mutually constitutive processes, sacrifice is first a microembodied practice in which the sovereign right to kill intersects, in contradictory and historically uneven ways, with life-enhancing biopolitical powers. The effects and narrative frames invoked by sacrifice are often governed according to gendered norms, protection myths (Young 2003), and sex-role stereotypes, which then serve in the construction of sociopolitical relations more generally within nation states. In this way, sacrifice has a macrohistorical dimension, which sustains the state's supposed monopoly on the means of war, its status as the sole legitimate wielder of violence. Sacrificial violence reproduces "schemes of significance and insignificance" (Taussig-Rubbo 2009a, 87), which signify whose bodies are capable of transcendence and who—and what—is to be transcended.

Traditional theories of sacrifice (Hubert and Mauss 1964; Girard 1979; Nancy 1991; Agamben 1998) do not offer much detail about the gendered effects of sacrificial transcendence. These theories, while certainly valuable, often ignore the misogynistic and racialized assumptions that underpin sacrifice, such as the unequal social and political conditions that fix meaning to who is capable of sacrifice and who must be sacrificed. Instead of inquiring about the role of women in these sacrificial narratives, curiously such specificities are omitted. Henri Hubert and Marcel Mauss (1964) argue that "sacrifice is a religious act which, through the consecration of a victim, modifies the condition of a moral person who accomplishes it or that of certain objects with which he is concerned" (13). This definition can refer to personal and/or objective sacrifices, depending on the context and goals of a given ritual. Further, Hubert and Mauss do not claim that there is an origin of sacrifice, yet they state that all sacrificial acts establish "a means of communication between the sacred and the profane worlds through the mediation of a victim, that is, of a thing that in the course of the ceremony is destroyed" (97). Secularization offers new opportunities for self-sacrifice. In an ostensibly post-Christian era, everyone can sacrifice him- or herself; it is about the genuine, mimetic giving of the self (Nancy 1991). Here the connotations of sacrifice are positive. René Girard (1979), however, argues that sacrifice is meant to create the necessary conditions for the socially acceptable use of violence. For him, sacrifice and violence are inextricably linked. Sacrifice allows for the circulatory movement or displacement of vengeance onto a scapegoat. Unchecked violence is only tamed through sacrifice or through the implementation of a judicial system. Sacrifice is an act of violence without the risk of vengeance. Girard, like Hubert and Mauss, seems to suggest that a clear, identifiable essence links and homogenizes all sacrifices. Yet, like all social concepts, sacrifice is susceptible to contestation.

The opposition between the sacred and the profane is cited as key to sacrificial rituals: it is often women's bodies that represent the impure. Sacrificial rituals unite community members by disavowing outsiders, such as women, foreigners, or "undesirables." Naturalizing men's transcendence over the constraints of womanhood, particularly in the area of reproduction, sacrifice is the site in which men's historical need to establish and maintain the integrity of kinship relations is contingent on controlling "reproductive resources"—childbearing women. Sacrifice is performative because it causes what it signifies (Jay 1992, 37); as such, it cannot be understood outside of the historical conditions in which its discourse takes shape. Robin Schott (2010) argues that sacrifice reveals the potential of violence that is imminent in society. She claims that sacrifice can be used as a diagnostic tool to ascertain how violence informs the political. There is no universal theory of sacrifice worth pursuing that would also satisfy the sociological need for an emphasis on the importance of particularity. Sacrifice implies the power to name and legitimize certain deaths as having public significance, to recognize certain deaths as legitimately lost, and to rank those deaths according to a schematic of who is worthy of recognition.

Further, sacrifice confirms the state as the sole legitimate wielder of violence. In this vein, sacrificial rhetoric proliferates when states authorize or remember violence through an invocation of collective memory, ethnicity, or nationhood. The expansion of the nation-state system required not only the individual disciplining of men and women but also the nationalization of the population. Soldiers were to be drawn from the population, and it was argued through a biological account of the natural—differentiated roles of men and women—that the vitality of the soldier, and as such the virility of the nation, began in the home. These beliefs mobilized hegemonic narratives of soldiering, warfare, and the normalization of the "warrior" construct of masculinity and soldiering. Nation building contributes to the broader moral and disciplinary project of making "good" citizens. As a result of the state's desire to monopolize the communicative potentiality of sacrifice, disciplinary power and its effects are integrated into the broader biopolitical concerns over the nation-state: the practice of exteriorizing and militarizing violence, as well as efforts to nationalize the economy and territorialize sovereignty. While having myriad trajectories, disciplining occurs in the solidification of the nuclear family. The family is one space in which conceptions of intimate, private power and public, legal power intersect in ways that legitimate the economic and political subordination of women.

In the twentieth century, the family provided a space for the soldier to be nurtured, solidifying his symbolic place in national politics. The soldier-citizen was unquestionably a body of sacrifice—but his sacrifice would not be possible without the unevenly shared sacrifice that permeated the home. In this regard, women made up a reserve or surplus army of labor and were folded in and out of the military as workers, nurses, wives, mothers, and as (unequal) sacrificing bodies. Thus the nation-state system was born in tandem with the soldier-citizen archetype and its associated expressions of symbolic nationalized performance, which hinged on a complex imaginary of sacrificial discourse. In this vein, Anne McClintock (1993) argues that nationalism is transmitted primarily through fetishistic spectacle: nationalism's translation takes place because of the ceaseless circulation of fetish objects, such as: "flags, uniforms, airplane logos, maps, anthems, national flowers, national cuisines and architectures, as well as through the organization of collective fetish spectacle—in team sports, military displays, mass rallies, [and] the myriad forms of popular culture" (71). The military and its soldier-citizens are actively involved in the reification of fetish objects. Likewise, the soldier-citizen as a model is deeply rooted in a political imaginary that renders nation-states as discrete, territorially contained entities—opposed to other states. National armies facilitated the symbolic and material development of the nation-state and were the product of a newfound securitized, technocratic reason. This rationality required soldier-citizens to undergo systematic physical and moral disciplining so that, ideally, their own vitality would contribute to the overall strength of the military and the population.

In the aftermath of World War II, the sacrifices of soldier-citizens were met with social entitlements for the soldiers and their dependents—health care, social and job security, retirement—benefits that are typically encountered in a robust welfare state with enshrined rights. Much of this was the result of feminist praxis that unfolded as both an intervention into the military as servicewomen but also a theoretical critique of the universal/particular dichotomy that had marginalized women and naturalized their subordination. An analysis of the soldier-citizen as a working and laboring body, a body that required care and maintenance, was made possible in this context. Subsequently, the soldier-citizen was the first body to receive these benefits. While the soldier-citizen might be the embodiment of the highest expression of sacrifice, and thus of citizenship, the soldier-citizen nonetheless served to signify the mode of proper conduct for civilians—the citizen who sacrifices the self for a particular body or association, and is thus regarded as a "true" citizen (Burchell 2002). In the 1960s, benefits were extended to civilians. Yet national duty continued to inform the discourse on rights. This rights-based discourse framed the parameters of the social contract as an exchange between state and citizen—a reciprocal give-and-take in which national duty was exchanged for social entitlements. In other words, the state had special claims on its citizens (claims to loyalty and potentially military service), while the citizenry had special claims on the state (rights of entry and residence, rights to political participation, or claims to diplomatic protection abroad) (Brubaker 1992, 63). This exchange of claims also institutionalized and normalized the male-breadwinner family model through the notion of a family wage; this model features the real citizen as an autonomous masculine subject. The organization of the nuclear family had material implications for class, gender, and race relations and facilitated new gender-specific expectations of citizenship (Lister 2002, 195); specifically, women's political relation to the nation was submerged as a social relation to men through marriage (McClintock 1993). Beyond the confines of the home, however, women's incorporation into the military, both as crucial characters in the narrative of national sacrifice and as actual employees was in part productive: it was predicated on a simultaneous celebration of "modern women." At the same time, it was also negative and repressive, which created new mechanisms by which to discriminate against women (Cowen 2008, 95).

Feminists have been concerned with how the politics of representation relates to publicity and how women have been able to overcome their status, drawing on Immanuel Kant's language, as mere "auxiliaries to the commonwealth" (Benhabib 2004, 46). The public sphere indicates a struggle in making a particular topic worthy of publicity, since "the struggle to make something public is a struggle for justice" (Benhabib 1992, 79). Cindy Sheehan famously became a focal point for discussion of the sacrifice made by mothers of fallen soldiers, when speaking of her own sacrifice as a mother, as well as the sacrifice made by her son, she critiqued then President Bush's attempt to minimize her loss. Accordingly, she was able to "mobilize her private suffering in the public domain" (Taussig-Rubbo 2009a, 108), destabilizing the hegemonic interpretation of the public and private spheres, and to unsettle the gendered expectations of citizenship (Lister 2002)—namely, that she would, as a mother, reserve her grief for the private sphere only and accept her son's fate as being in the service of a greater national good. Sheehan's claim was grounded in the fact that her son was a state-soldier and not a private contractor. Her claim gained momentum due to her assessment that her son's sacrifice was meaningless and not a real sacrifice. Sacrificial narratives must be represented by a notion of legitimacy that goes beyond individual action.

To comprehend the relationship between the disciplining of citizenship in North America during the twentieth century and the military and security privatization of the current moment, one must investigate the historical ebbs and flows of the role that bodies have played in giving meaning to nation-state power in the private and public spheres. Privatized violence has existed for centuries: "Our general assumption of warfare is that it is engaged by public militaries, fighting for the common cause. This is an idealization. Throughout history the participants in war were often for-profit private entities loyal to no one government" (Singer 2005, 19). The discontinuities of the commercialization and bureaucratization of violence are traceable to the emergence of European states: having once been a tool of monarchs attempting to secure territory and private property, the use of privateers diminished after the French Revolution when "wars became wars between nations, fought by citizens of those nations, as opposed to between monarchs with private armies" (Kinsey 2006, 23). At this time, the state placed the populace at the center of its story. "The people" were thus ideologically suited to administer warfare. Today, wars are no longer anchored by the concept of "the people," as flexibility and globalization erode the synthesis of citizenship and sacrifice.

Like international relations, sacrifice is deeply gendered. I have so far argued that sacrificial discourses gained momentum in relation to total war, crystallizing in the resultant social contract in the second half of the twentieth century, which offered a normative framework to organize relations of mutual reciprocity between citizens and states. Yet, such mutual reciprocity no longer characterizes citizenship. As professional armies replaced citizen armies, sacrifice was severed from its historical connection to citizenship. Although by itself it is insufficient to explain the entirety of the social changes that took place in the twentieth century, the question of sacrifice is fecund given the problem of how military privatization comes to bear on the historical synthesis of soldiering and citizenship. The soldier-citizen, an archetypical figure that dominates social consciousness in commonwealth countries, has long legitimized nation-states' right to violence. The nation-state's legitimizing power is dependent on the maintenance of hierarchical race, class, and gender relations, in which (middle-class white) male subjectivity is understood to be universal. "True" citizens or "citizen-warriors" are marked by their willingness to sacrifice in order to protect defenseless women (Yuval-Davis 1997; Young 2003).

There has been an increase in the number of women in public and private military settings as a result of the professionalization and modernization of militaries (see Stachowitsch 2012a); this reality confronts deeply gendered ideas about whose bodies are capable of real violence, of real sacrifice. The incorporation of women's bodies as active and self-sacrificing in war zones troubles the masculine logic of sacrifice. Historically, discourses of sacrifice have been instrumental in legitimizing militaries' use of violence. Given that sacrificial rhetoric gains meaning through protection myths, which view women as passive bodies requiring protection (see Eichler's chapter in this volume), the inclusion of women in militarized spaces corrupts, at a very basic level, the logic of sacrificial narratives. If sacrifice is partly about transcendence over the profane, represented by the impurity of foreign "others," and signified by the female/feminized body, then the physical presence of women as equal combatants in militarized settings disrupts the workability of sacrifice. Subsequently, a descent into the ordinary emerges (Das

2007)—the revelation that ordinary and exceptional manifestations of violence are intertwined.

This revelation renders the violence of war outside of its supposed exceptional space, exposing a central contradiction of war: rather than being external phenomena, violence and war are in fact integral to the founding of political communities; they are absolutely crucial to the ways in which we historicize, regenerate, and memorialize the nation-state. However, the incorporation of PMSCs into the war theater disrupts this idealization. States, I argue, use PMSCs in part to establish monopoly over the terms and conditions of sacrificial violence. PMSCs refuse the language of sacrifice (Taussig-Rubbo 2009a), instead self-representing as "true professionals" and "ethical hero-warriors" (Joachim and Schneiker 2012a). While heterogeneous, PMSCs are nonetheless symptomatic of the shift beyond the social contract. When war is no longer a collective social practice but an individualized corporate one, politics—including gender politics—are eclipsed. A tension is produced, though, when this corporatization of war rubs up against sacrificial narratives. State use of PMSCs legitimizes violence while simultaneously stripping citizenship of its sacrificial dimension. As Mark Duffield (2001, 52-61) argues, despite issues surrounding regulation and legitimacy, PMSCs will continue to influence military and security practices, especially in light of the crisis of sacrifice and the conflicting needs of maintaining a conventional military and responding flexibly to new wars.

A GENEALOGY OF PRIVATIZED VIOLENCE

In this section, I explore how PMSCs reconcile the tension between the liberal humanitarian impulses to preserve life, or "make live," and the need of sovereign power to effect legitimate violence against politically disqualified others—to "let die" (Foucault 2003). Military and security privatization are effects of the neoliberal restructuring of capitalism that began after the Cold War. Military privatization is also a response to the ways in which states, particularly the United States, govern the sacrifice of soldiers by reconciling the incongruent trajectories of sovereign and biopolitical power, which have become exacerbated under globalization: PMSCs let states use violence without drawing in a national population, undermining the hierarchical and centralized structure of military forces that defined traditional interstate wars and instead relying on privatization and marketization—the introduction of "private sector accounting and management techniques" (Duffield 2001, 48–60). Thus states (can claim to) protect their citizens, while easing the burden of killing noncitizens. I argue that capital-intensive weapon systems, or the revolution in military affairs (RMA), are intimately connected to military privatization: privatization grants the economic and sociopolitical preconditions that render PMSCs as the bearers of expertise and the arbiters of how to apply network-centric military technology and technological solutions to conflict; conflict that states are no longer regarded as capable of managing unilaterally. The U.S. military famously showcased its capacity to "make live" during the first Gulf War in 1991. Here, about 240 coalition lives were lost. This success has been largely attributed to the unprecedented application of military technology (Shimko 2010). Yet, as will be explained in more detail below, the RMA does not just refer to technological advancements in "smart" weapons (precision-guided munitions). As Eric Blanchard claims (2011, 153) drawing on John Arquilla, the RMA was activated by the perceived need to "stabilize defense spending" in an era of financial austerity and "to demonstrate the continuing usefulness of various military tools in an environment seemingly devoid of serious threat." PMSCs satisfy both of these perceived needs.

Privatization implies a shift in citizenship away from collective or public ideals (or to use Rose's [1999] phrasing, governing from the social point of view) toward consumer-based, individualistic, securitized, and militarized modes of subjectivity. In the 1990s, or "Washington Consensus" era, the military was a primary target of privatization schemes. The privatization of security from above, as exemplified by the outsourcing of military operations, reflects a broader ideological push toward privatization, where many of the state's institutions, such as schools, prisons, and policing, are turned over to the marketplace (Singer 2004). Initially, these ideas came from conservative coalitions in the United States and Britain in the 1980s; however, the collapse of the Soviet bloc, the privatization of state-owned industries across Europe, and the International Monetary Fund's and World Bank's endorsements of these principles made privatization seem inevitable (Avant 2007, 183). In line with neoliberalism's privileging of the unfettered market, security has been transformed from a public good into a commodity, packaged as a private service, delivered by private enterprises, and consumed by individuals as well as state and nonstate actors (Avant 2005). Following the end of the Cold War, warfare has increasingly involved the use of PMSCs, as evidenced by the U.S. war in Iraq (Wedel 2008). This war required greater expertise and resources than the Pentagon had anticipated or could supply (Dodge 2005, 710). For military planners, PMSCs are "necessary" in light of ongoing recruitment struggles: the military now spends considerable money (in the form of signing bonuses and incentives) to attract and retain soldiers (Stiglitz and Blimes 2008, 55).

PMSCs are therefore an integral feature in how states conceptualize conflict and in how they imagine and respond to new, and indeed proliferating, security threats such as the illegal drug trade; uncontrolled immigration; and, particularly after September 11, 2001, global terrorism. The widening of the meaning of security has meant that the traditional boundaries of the nation-state are no longer regarded as capable of managing conflict, as expressed by asymmetrical wars (Duffield 2001). As a result, PMSCs close the gap between what is required and the inadequate capability of national militaries. After 9/11, in the quest for full-spectrum dominance over the "arc of instability," strategies have come to enfold "all elements of national power: economic, diplomatic, financial, law enforcement, intelligence, and both overt and covert military operations" (Gill 2005, 35). Instead of boots on the ground—which signify the presence of a body politic or community, which has a collectivizing and nationalizing effect—governing at a distance through privatization and marketization renders violence a commodity to be managed within the neoliberal marketplace.

In contrast, in the eighteenth century the sovereign exercised his right of life only by exercising his right to kill, or by refraining from killing. He demonstrated his power over life only through the deaths he was capable of causing. This right, which was formulated as "the power of life and death," was in reality the right to take life or let live. Its symbol, after all, was the sword (Foucault 1978, 136). Sovereign power is invested in the spectacle of death. Territorial wars were waged on behalf of the sovereign and in the name of the sovereign. Biopolitics, however, transforms war as a vehicle for attaining collective interests—"we the people"—in the realm of the production, regulation, and maintenance of life. Wars are not about defending the sovereign but are waged on the behalf of populations who are "mobilized for the purpose of wholesale slaughter in the name of life necessity: massacres have become vital" (137). Biopolitics marks the transformation of war in defense of the sovereign to securing populations. The war on terror has been routinely justified as a war for the protection of ("civilized" or Western) life, both "at home" and "abroad."

Illiberal techniques of rule are exposed when liberalism is analyzed in relation to both biopolitical and sovereign power: "liberal societies find themselves entering a new stage of development requiring their permanent mobilization against an enemy said to move in unforeseeable ways, which strikes at unforeseeable times, festering in the hidden recesses of their own defense infrastructures" (Reid 2006, 3). Drawing on Giorgio Agamben, Cristina Masters (2005) explains that the preoccupation with security as a central task of the state, and its source of legitimacy, runs the risk of turning the state itself into a terrorist. Notably, there is a contradiction at the intersection between sovereign power and biopolitical power (Mutimer 2007), namely, how liberal states are able to pursue both sovereign and biopolitical power at once. Still, this does not resolve the question of how populations, which are presumably national, can be "permanently mobilized" in relation to war, while privatizing the tasks so that permanent mobilization is ensured.

Championed by the architects of the U.S.-led war in Iraq, especially Donald Rumsfeld, the RMA extends an explicit desire to replace military labor with technology, capital, or "dead labor" (Parenti 2007, 88), producing a base of technologically savvy, highly educated and trained personnel, invoking an elite transnational business masculinity (Connell 2000b) that, although lacking in state militaries, is available for hire via private firms. However, significant force reduction is required to finance technology (Moskos, Williams, and Segal 2000, 5). The military was not exempt from broader institutional transformations in industrial societies during the 1990s: it too shifted from a labor to capital-intensive organization (Manigart 2003). As Catherine Lutz (2002, 727) argues, nineteenth-century industrial warfare not only required the raising of mass armies but also centered on manufacturing labor; it thus required a sizeable number of workers to produce relatively simple guns, tanks, ships, and eventually airplanes. The inaccuracy of the newly acquired firepower of World War I resolved itself during the nuclear revolution of World War II, which revealed the "speed with which total annihilation [could be] carried out, and the ability to do so without first achieving success on the battlefield" (Lieber 2005, 126). The decline of this mass army was a consequence of restructuring toward professionalization. Now, managers and technicians increasingly conduct war, as opposed to combat leaders (Moskos 2000, 15). The professionalization of the military was essential for the realization of the goals of the RMA: "a policy agenda emphasizing the exploitation of technological advances to preserve and even improve the United States' long-term strategic position" (Shimko 2010, 2). Without professionalization, the ideals of the RMA, particularly the incorporation of precision-guided weapons as a means to give qualitative advantage to the United States over the quantitative advantage of the Soviet forces, would not have been realized (Adamsky 2010, 59–61).

Notably, these business elites are not necessarily trained to execute physical force: "neoliberalism in the metropole does not indulge in the warrior cults, the enthusiasm for blood and iron that earlier masculinities did" (Connell 2000b, 221). Raewyn Connell argues that neoliberal leadership values a mediated, technological violence (221). High-tech weapon systems are often operated by private employees, since training public soldiers is too time-consuming and costly, given that solutions are required instantly, and yet are always changing. "The result is a steep rise in the number of private sector employees—technicians, programmers, systems analysts, and simulation specialists—on the virtual 'battlefield'" (Uesseler 2008, 123). The transition from military masculinity to transnational-business masculinity emerged alongside the normative rise of privatization. Through technological advancements and political restructuring, the marketization of violence allows liberal states to effect violence while creating distance from their populations and the everyday practices and realities of war.

PMSCs perpetuate this distancing by turning violence into an economic or development problem instead of a sociopolitical problem. While there is a marked moral and physical distancing in remote fighting, which is exacerbated by military technology, such as drones and unmanned systems, there is also a political distancing that misidentifies the subject and the object of violence. When contractors suffer death or injury, states are not responsible for confronting the consequences, or for providing care or benefits, since the relationship between the two is a corporate rather than a social contract. Hence private contractors are unsacrificeable subjects, since no single national public can validate their actions as such (Taussig-Rubbo 2011). Instead of being worthy of sacrifice, their presence in the war theater protects American life and saves American audiences from confronting a national past that, following defeat in Vietnam, includes collective mourning, "body-bag syndrome," and emasculation of the body politic (Masters 2008). It is no surprise then that privatized war is, quite literally at times, private.

The idea of casualty aversion necessitates that the success of war is reduced to the number of casualties on "our side." With modernizing and downsizing of militaries, efficiency and the success of war have been linked with casualty minimization (Shimko 2010). The question of counting the dead and/or injured implies a disturbing hierarchy of "who counts." Geopolitically, the question of who is counted is related to the question of "who counts?" and "who cares?" The "fatality metrics" of body counts is clearly lopsided in the context of Iraq: victimhood is commodified and patriotism publicized for soldiers making the ultimate "sacrifice," while Iraqi deaths are framed as "the price that must be paid" for introducing "freedom and justice" (Hyndman 2008, 199). This privileges American life over politically marginalized others, resulting in a highly racialized hierarchy of suffering in which some lives are worth mourning and others are not (Butler 2006). As Masters (2007) argues, "Dead US soldiers, for instance, get counted. They tell a story about which bodies count as politically qualified life" (47). The RMA, which is defined by "technological mastery, omnipotent surveillance, real-time 'situational awareness,' and speed-of-light digital interactions" (Graham 2008, 37) claims that

> remote sensors and computer tracking of numerous targets supposedly allow sophisticated combat operations to out maneuver foes and destroy opposition targets relatively easily with few casualties. This requires a reorganization of armed forces with large tank and infantry divisions broken into smaller units to be more flexible and capable of moving much faster over long distances. (Dalby 2008, 3)

"Casualties" in this context are American soldiers. When officials do acknowledge "collateral damage" there is an implied assumption that, because the technology is "smart" and kills relatively fewer people, it is more humane. This rhetoric further dehumanizes victims and survivors of state violence, reentrenching a racialized hierarchy of suffering.

CONCLUSION: THE PARADOX OF MILITARY PRIVATIZATION

In this chapter, I examined military privatization through a theoretical tradition of feminist critiques of violence to ask what is gained in the affirmation or negation of sacrificial rhetoric. A paradox remains. It is unclear what happens to sacrifice when it is supposed to be absent, as military privatization—illustrated by postmodern depoliticization and combat unmanning—would seem to imply. I argued that sacrifice is most fruitfully understood not in a quantitative manner—sacrifice as an individual act is not empirically disappearing; yet PMSCs' avoidance of sacrificial rhetoric suggests a disruption of the sacrificial system insofar as the meaning of war is concerned. It seems that contemporary war-making negates sacrifice, *except* in moments when states want to authorize or remember the collectivism of an original founding moment of sovereign power. The RMA, which includes technological advancements, as well as a fundamental rescaling and reorganization of violence, reveals concerns about the liabilities and limitations of human bodies in terms of their inherent and growing financially costly vulnerability, but also their politics. It is worth considering the ongoing sexual assault crisis in the U.S. military (see e.g., McVeigh 2013; Steinhauer 2013) and the fact that there is no trace of a sexual assault crisis within PMSCs. It is not the case that there is no gendered violence of note *within* PMSCs, but instead, since military privatization *makes violence private*, questions of sexual violence can be perceived as problems to be solved by the market or through private legal means, such as arbitration. The privatization of violence depoliticizes suffering, rendering it invisible and inaudible (Baggiarini 2013). Since state military and private militaries are mutually constitutive, however, it is imperative to avoid analyzing them as discreetly bounded entities, each in its own social vacuum. The key point is that PMSCs allow states the flexibility to override parts of the gendered politics that characterize contemporary Western militaries.

Society must have an idea of the sacred, even if it is contested. The paradox gains complexity through imaginings of the body: sacrifice, in its highest militarized expression, requires the potential for the *publicization* of death or injury. Yet, public and private militaries no doubt collaborate on some level; state violence is never entirely public or entirely private. Instead of attempting to objectively define public and private, the goal should be to capture the effects wrought from each term, in relation to how war is exercised. As Dominique Memmi (2002) argues, the use of "public" and "private" simplifies complex realities that are value laden. She claims that these terms are in fact relational and the emotional, cognitive separation of them serves a political purpose. The effect of the turn toward and indeed the reification of the private military contractor as necessary in contemporary conflict resolution, combined with the myth of bloodless war, implies that sacrifice will become more unevenly distributed amongst "us," and the decision to sacrifice (racial) "others" will likely be made in terms of dehumanized corporatist techno-rationality rather than in consideration of social objectives. I have argued that liberal wars capture an historically unprecedented slippage between citizenship and sacrifice (Baggiarini, 2014), an unresolved anxiety about what the meaning of bodies is in techno-centric, privatized wars, and a fracturing of the symbolic content of the social contract of the golden age. Indeed, war and corporatism do not mix well (Duffield 2001).

Further, configurations of biopolitical and sovereign power reveal how killing and being killed are shored up by imperialist justifications for violence, despite legal and liberal democratic developments aimed at minimizing war. Illiberal war, particularly exposed after 9/11, renders bodies in pain invisible. In U.S. detention centers, the boardrooms of PMSCs, and in military "black sites," the effects of violence are subsumed by economic and technocratic rationalities. In this context, the precariousness of those understood as enemy bodies has come to affect the legitimacy and therefore the transparency of war. The "absence of an enemy means that there is no legitimate claim on Americans to sacrifice their lives. Nor is there ground for Americans to be killing Iraqis" (Kahn 2008, 156). PMSCs, and private means of governing, suggest a scaling back of the conditions that gave rise to the imaginary, yet productive, category of the "the people." Even so, enemies must be knowable if permanent war, and the technologies that sustain and justify it, which are honed by PMSCs and their personnel, will be realized.

Soldiering is shifting away from service to the nation-state, in the confines of a rights-based discourse, toward an increasingly individualized, antisocial, and risk-averse practice. This transformation is the antithesis of the idealism and philosophical etiquette of mutual reciprocity, which came to constitute social consciousness in the post–World War II period. State militaries underwent professionalization and modernization in the 1990s so that they could appear "family friendly" and therefore women friendly. While women are now officially being folded into combat roles in the United States and thus apparently achieving equality of opportunity, private military settings show no interest in gender equality. However, "even when women are fighters, they are treated as exceptions that prove the rule that war is for men" (Gray 2003, 215). A tension remains in how states include women in national militaries and employ PMSCs, which offer the possibility of bypassing gendered, sexual, and racial politics.

Inclusion through exclusion is accomplished via a bricolage in the organization of military masculinities (Gray 2003). PMSCs, like all corporations bent toward growth, profit-generation, renewal, and serving a host of varied and expanding clients, offer a range of services. Thus it is not surprising that these different services would require a range of masculinities that might contradict or complement those masculinities that are championed in national militaries. As Paul Higate (2012b, 359) explains, bodies trained in violence are inseparable from the macrohistorical conditions that facilitate the coming into being of these bodies. The preservation of warrior masculinities requires the physical denial of women's bodies but also the ideology of a feminine presence as contamination and coterminous with weakness and suffering. But at the same time, states require multiple constructions of masculinity depending on the nature of the conflict and the proposed solution. The presence of women as active in combat, as bodies in scenes of death and killing who are ostensibly those who transcend, rather than transcended over, disrupts the reified masculine privilege of negotiating and controlling the terms of sacrificial violence—of killing and being killed. The presence of women in militarized space therefore troubles the masculine grammar of sacrifice, compelling a descent into the ordinary (Das 2007). This is problematic for the stability of the military's organization, because military settings, and indeed war, are thought to be exceptional in liberal democracies, not ordinary. Hesitation about women in combat shows that gender is unstable and requires ongoing maintenance, particularly in military settings, where its finality is essential. However, the point that militarized violence requires a stable masculine/feminine dichotomy does not imply that the dichotomy cannot shift over time.

Sacrifice is a deeply political system that invokes ideas about what constitutes the social realm. To overcome the contradictions of liberal warfare, sacrifice, as a concept and practice, must be carefully managed. If not, the gap between "the people" and "the state" will widen and become potentially unbridgeable. In the period of nation-state formation, sacrifice had a collectivizing effect. It was anchored in ideas about nationhood, citizenship, and democracy (Brubaker 1992). The willing giving of the self, and the public acceptance of mass casualties in defense of the homeland, helped construct the fabric of national identity. Modern citizenship was informed by the legacy of the French Revolution and has long been characterized by a formal institutionalized, nationalist willingness to sacrifice oneself. The existence and maintenance of the first regularly trained and highly skilled standing armies in the eighteenth century expressed this willingness. Here, the mobilization and deployment of a mass armed force was contingent on conscription. Within an expanding military apparatus, soldiers' roles were defined and experienced through the body: the spilling of blood, origin stories, primordial ties, and the potential for death—and as a result, sacrifice.

Giving the self through the negation of the body had productive purposes in territorializing sovereign power and securing the nation, in an era when war was conceived of as necessarily between states and in which defending the state from foreign invasion was a chief concern. The turn away from sacrifice through the incorporation of private contractors, and the substitution of advanced technology for the use of bodies, invites the question of why states, and the mechanisms of warfare therein, might desire the end of sacrifice.

NOTES

1. This chapter is the product of spirited conversations, careful editorial guidance, and invaluable insight offered by Maya Eichler, Sean Rupka, Fenn Stewart, and Lorna Weir.
2. Postmodern approaches to IR build on the discursive turn in critical security studies. Emphasizing deconstructive methods, these approaches often apply Michel Foucault's concepts of power and governmentality—control techniques and practices that are not reducible to state politics—to securitization (Edkins, Pin Fat, and Shapiro 2004; Dauphinée and Masters 2007). Postmodern wars reveal a crisis insofar as they increasingly rely on technology for "full-spectrum dominance," and yet in reality the most powerful military technologies cannot be used (Gray 2003, 215). Speed has replaced geopolitics as the basis of military logistics (Hooper 2001, 111, drawing on the work of Der Derian) extending (simulated) battlefields beyond national borders (Uesseler 2008). This illuminates the amalgamation of public (state) and private (nonstate) powers to realize the goals of liberal "wars of choice"; wars that are conceived of in humanitarian terms, yet perpetuate modes of violence.

    American military strategy is concerned with supplementing missions with modern weapons/robotics systems and technocratic rationality in order to lift "the fog of war" and minimize (U.S.) casualties with "smart," precision-guided weapons. Although the state still suffers casualties, casualty aversion, as a hegemonic ideology that became entrenched following the first Gulf War, is the primary mechanism by which to measure the "success" of war (Mandel 2004). The central aim of advanced military technology, and the data wrought by it, is to protect the soldiers who use it by enhancing their situational awareness.

CHAPTER 3

Gender, PMSCs, and the Global Rescaling of Protection

Implications for Feminist Security Studies

MAYA EICHLER

One of the foundational assumptions of security studies—informed by the dominant research tradition of Realism—is that military protection is the sine qua non of statehood.[1] Central to war discourses is states' claim to protect their citizens, in particular their "womenandchildren" (Enloe 1989), from external military threats. While protection is a central theme in the study and practice of international relations, it is rarely problematized. Critical and feminist scholars call on us to consider the "politics of protection," drawing attention to the ways in which protection is implicated in relations of power and the construction of identities (Runyan 1990; Huysmans 2006). Notions of protection shape and are shaped by economic, social, political, and cultural factors as well as understandings of gender and race. To conceptualize protection in terms of its politics allows us to interrogate rather than take for granted dominant meanings and practices of protection. The politics of protection centers on the following questions: Who provides protection? Who is defined as needing protection? And what relations of power exist or are created between protectors and protected? By posing these questions scholars have demonstrated that far from being a straightforward process, the answers remain contested and part of ongoing struggles in national and global politics.

Despite the tight association of protection with the state and its military, there has recently been a proliferation of new actors claiming protector status and hoping to gain the legitimacy it confers. Anne Orford (2011) comments on the increasing currency of protection in global politics today: "A range of actors, from US counter-insurgency specialists, through UN officials to human rights activists and Christian aid workers, have enthusiastically begun to redescribe and reconceptualize their missions in terms of protection" (9). One important group missing from her list is the globally operating private military and security companies (PMSCs) that have gained prominence over the past three decades. They have not only become central actors in support of military and peace operations, but also contenders in the contemporary politics of protection. PMSCs define threats (Leander 2005), sell a range of armed and unarmed protection services (in addition to logistical support services, training, intelligence, etc.), and compete with the state (and increasingly, other actors) by claiming the role of protectors in global politics. As security comes to be provided and defined by private actors, the private sector becomes a crucial site to consider in investigations of the politics of protection (Leander 2005, 2006).

One line of inquiry into security privatization and the politics of protection that has so far been neglected is how security privatization challenges, shapes, or redefines the specifically gendered aspects of the politics of protection (with the exception of Higate 2011). Feminist scholars show that "protection" is not only a response to violence but is also productive of violence. Historically, the protector has been constructed as masculine, and women have been cast as needing protection. The gendered ideology of protection that normalizes such gender roles helps justify women's gender subordination as well as the waging of war (Stiehm 1982; Runyan 1990; Sjoberg 2013). While earlier feminist accounts of the gendered politics of protection largely remained limited to public militaries and the geographic space of the nation-state, more recent feminist work has considered how unequal gendered (and racialized) relations of protection are being reproduced at the global scale through peacekeeping and peacebuilding (Agathangelou and Ling 2003; Whitworth 2004; O'Reilly 2012), humanitarian interventions (Doty 1996; Orford 1999), the responsibility to protect (Hall and Shepherd 2013), and the "war on terror" (Hunt and Rygiel 2006; Riley, Mohanty, and Pratt 2008). Furthermore, earlier feminist work emphasized a gendered story of male protectors/female protected and of the gendered political and physical violence that is made possible as a result of protection, while more recent feminist interventions have shed light on women's role in violence and militarized protection (Sjoberg and Gentry 2007; McEvoy 2010; MacKenzie 2012). Thus, feminist scholars are painting an increasingly complex picture of the gendered politics of protection. I argue that attention to how security privatization affects the gendered politics of protection is crucial to this endeavor.

While Paul Higate (2011) has focused on the everyday interactions between security guards and clients in one particular setting to show the complexity and fluidity of gendered protection relations at the micro level, my focus in this chapter is on the interactions between the gendered national and global politics of protection. I sketch the recent and ongoing shifts in the national gendered politics of protection, that is, in the particular nexus of citizenship, nationalism, and military security that characterized nineteenth- and twentieth-century statehood in the West. These shifts include women's deepening integration into public militaries which unsettles the automatic association of protection with masculinity and men; Western states' increased use of new forms of military intervention (humanitarian intervention, peacekeeping, peace and stability operations, etc.) that point to a global rescaling of the politics of protection; and finally, the privatization of security which calls into question the state's dominant role as protector in global politics. I furthermore investigate how PMSCs shape notions of protection by examining how the market produces relations of protection and through these also contributes to particular notions of gender, class, race, and scale in global politics.

Drawing on critical feminist IR, feminist political economy, and feminist political geography, my argument is twofold: (1) Security privatization needs to be understood in the context of broader contemporary shifts in the national gendered politics of protection that have challenged men's *and* the state's status as sole protectors. (2) The market shapes relations of protection in (at least) three key ways: it regenders the relationship between protector and protected beyond the male-female dichotomy of protector/protected (e.g., by creating masculinized protected and feminized unprotected); it contributes to a global rescaling of the politics of protection (both symbolically and materially); and it enables the globalizing of classed, racialized, and gendered protection work. PMSCs challenge the national gendered politics of protection and take an active interest in extending the market (in services and labor) for protection globally. As the chapter demonstrates, they thereby rely on and reinforce global relations of protection that rest on hierarchies of class, race, and gender. PMSCs are not so much actors who step in to fill a void in protection but actively shape the emerging global politics of protection.

Focusing on transformations at the national level as well as the emerging global politics of protection, this chapter complements the microanalysis that Higate develops of close protection training in his chapter in this volume (also see Higate 2011). Together, Higate's and my chapters illustrate the different ways in which protection plays out at the national, global, and the local/personal scale. This chapter also closely speaks to Bianca Baggiarini's historic analysis of the shifting politics of sacrifice within the nation-state, which illuminates a particular aspect of the gendered politics of protection that I examine here more broadly, as well as to the discussion by Saskia

Stachowitsch (in this volume) on the discursive remasculinization of security, including of protection, as a result of privatization. Finally, the chapter addresses the globalization of racialized security work, which the following three chapters (part II of the volume) examine in more detail.

The primary focus of this chapter is theoretical, but it draws empirically on the experiences of the United States, and to a lesser extent other Western states, and on the Western-based globally operating private security industry. I begin with a discussion of the central place of protection in IR, focusing on the feminist contribution to understanding protection as a gendered relationship. Second, I examine recent and ongoing challenges to the national gendered politics of protection, with a focus on the privatization of security. Third, I examine how the market for force is shaping and reshaping relations of protection in terms of class, gender, race, and scale. In conclusion, I consider the implications of security privatization for feminist interventions into the study and politics of protection.

INTERROGATING PROTECTION FROM A FEMINIST PERSPECTIVE

According to mainstream IR theory, states' essential role is to defend their territory and protect their population from internal and external threats. This understanding of the state's role as protector draws on the social contract theory put forth by Thomas Hobbes. In this view, state authority depends on the state's "capacity to guarantee protection," but the guarantee of protection comes in exchange for citizens' consent to the authority of the state (Orford 2011, 15–16). James Pattison (2010) explains that "the state's right to rule over us, and our obligation to obey its rule, depend on the provision of national defence and the maintenance of internal security" (436). The state's role as militarized protector and the legitimacy that the state derives from its protector role are intrinsically tied to the state's "monopoly over the legitimate use of violence within a given territory" (Weber 1994, 38). Protection in IR is therefore traditionally understood as protection by the state and by military means, and is seen as essential to the social contract between state and citizens.

Feminist IR scholars have critiqued this conceptualization of militarized state protection and domestic social order for overlooking the ways in which it normalizes gender inequalities and gendered violence. Feminists offer four connected insights into the politics of protection. First of all, feminist scholars "problematize the state and raise questions as to its status as protector of women" (Blanchard 2003, 1297). They are skeptical of the state's (and men's) role as protector and document how policies of protection tend to increase women's insecurities. While wars are often justified as being fought to protect women, military violence results in increased insecurities for women (UN Secretary-General 2002; Sjoberg and Peet 2011). In fact, women are intentionally targeted in war as a result of gendered protection relations: "belligerents victimize (women) civilians seen as the property of the enemy under the same logic that motivates them to provide protection to the (women) civilians that they see as their own property" (Sjoberg 2013, 201). The gendered ideology of protection is thus inherently violent, with negative effects for women's security.

Second, at a conceptual level, feminist scholars show that notions of protection are informed by, and help shape, dominant notions of masculinity and femininity (Elshtain 1995). The protector is associated with stereotypically masculine characteristics such as rationality, agency, autonomy, strength, while the protected is associated with feminized dependency, passivity, weakness, irrationality, and vulnerability (Peterson 1992b, 54; Wadley 2010, 49). The protector, "a pervasive model of masculinity" (Wadley 2010, 51), offers an "apparently more benign image of masculinity, one more associated with ideas of chivalry" than with masculine domination (Young 2003, 4) or warrior masculinity (Sjoberg 2013, 149). While the warrior may be linked to hypermasculine traits of aggressiveness and excessive violence, the male protector is seen as "courageous, responsible, and virtuous" (Young 2003, 4). Gender thus is constitutive of dominant understandings of protection at the same time as ideas about protection shape gender norms and help legitimize patriarchy through a seemingly benign form of militarized masculinity.

Third, the labor of militarized protection—soldiering—has historically been and remains to this day deeply gendered. The soldier has almost exclusively been conceived of as masculine, and the military created as a masculinized space that excludes or marginalizes women and privileges traits associated with masculinity (Mathers 2013). The military institutionalizes gendered protection roles that inform the societal gender order more broadly. In her seminal article on gendered protection, Judith Hicks Stiehm (1982) comments on the making of gendered protection roles: "For the most part, then, men have forbidden women to act either as defenders or as protectors. At the same time a government's very existence affirms the need for defenders or protectors. In this situation all women become 'the protected.' Some men become actual protectors; the rest remain potential protectors" (367). State and military policies such as conscription and the waging of war help establish and reproduce the link between masculinity, protection, and soldiering and thereby construct the norms of masculinized protectors and feminized protected (Tickner 1992a, 58; Mathers 2013).

And finally, related to the above points, feminist scholars show that protection is intimately tied to women's gender subordination. The gendered division into protectors and protected legitimizes unequal relations of power because the relationship between protector and protected is one of dependency and asymmetry (Stiehm 1982, 374). Feminist scholars see the state as upholding a male protection racket, whereby women pay for their protection with their political and personal autonomy (Runyan 1990; Peterson 1992b). Women are deemed as needing protection but have "little control over the conditions of their protection" (Tickner 1992a, 28).

Feminist critiques of protection have made a key contribution to problematizing "protection" in IR and security studies, showing that the dominant notion of protection centrally informing IR is not gender neutral, but rather assumes and legitimates unequal gender relations, which in turn enable military violence. The male protector represents a hegemonic form of militarized masculinity that is central to the legitimation of patriarchy and the (inter)national organization of violence. More recent feminist IR work has begun to question the automatic association of militarized protection with masculinity, showing the various ways in which women have participated and increasingly participate as combatants in militaries and paramilitaries (Alison 2009; MacKenzie 2010; Parashar 2010; McEvoy 2010; MacKenzie 2012). Furthermore, recent feminist IR scholarship has begun to interrogate gendered protection relations at the global, not just national, scale. This work has shown how, for example, peacekeeping (Agathangelou and Ling 2003; Whitworth 2004) and humanitarian interventions (Orford 1999) are implicated in reproducing unequal gendered and racialized relations of protection in global politics. Other feminist IR work has critically investigated the discourse of protecting women's rights in Afghanistan that has helped legitimate the global war on terror (Hunt and Rygiel 2006; Väyrynen and von der Lippe 2011). This recent feminist work points to the need for a more systematic consideration of how the national gendered politics of protection is being transformed and rescaled, which requires us to rethink existing conceptualizations of gendered protection. Security privatization, as I show next, is intimately connected to these changes.

CHALLENGES TO THE NATIONAL POLITICS OF PROTECTION

This chapter locates the privatization of security within the context of recent and ongoing shifts in the national gendered politics of protection. The national gendered politics of protection refers to the nexus of citizenship, nationalism, and military security that characterized nineteenth- and twentieth-century statehood in the West. This national gendered politics of protection relied on male citizen-soldiers, protection of the nation, and the public provision of security. The transformation of this national gendered politics of protection—largely, but not exclusively, a result of neoliberal globalization—has entailed shifts in (1) militarized, gendered citizenship; (2) the state's role as sole provider of security and protection; and (3) in the scalar politics of protection as I outline here. As such, the social contract based on state protection is giving way to new conceptions of citizenship, community, rights, and responsibilities.

Militarized citizenship has historically been a key component of the national politics of protection. Not only the state's claims to sovereign power and legitimacy, but also the very conditions of citizenship are tied to the politics of protection. In explaining the citizenship-protection nexus, Anna Leander (2009a) describes "protection as a (or *the*) fundamental citizenship right" (4). The right to claim protection in turn requires citizens' participation in their protection through military service (4). While the model of the male citizen-soldier as protector goes back to the Greek polis, the relationship between citizenship, soldiering, protection, and masculinity became solidified with the rise of nationalism and the spread of conscription across European nation-states starting in the late eighteenth century (Frevert 1996; Blom 2000, 15; Kronsell 2012, ch. 1; Feinman 2000; Snyder 2003; Yuval-Davis 1997, ch. 5). For much of the nineteenth and twentieth centuries obligatory military service for men elevated their citizenship status over that of women in Western nation-states. In this way states and militaries institutionalized the norm of masculinized protection that defined women as the objects of protection (at the same time as women were called upon to support military efforts in other roles, see Enloe 2000b). In the national gendered politics of protection, women stand in for the nation that requires protection (Yuval-Davis 1997). Laura Sjoberg (2013) explains: "Masculinity becomes that which defends the nation, while femininity holds it together, and women's need for protection *and* men's obligation to protect combine to justify *both* wars and individuals fighting in them" (199). The "imagined community" (Anderson 1991) of the nation is based on the fraternal community of masculine citizen-soldiers.

The increasing abandonment of the male citizen-soldier model in the West over the past few decades has challenged the national politics of protection. Countries such as the United States, Germany, Italy, Sweden, among others, have terminated conscription for a variety of reasons (Leander 2004), but at least partly as a result of broader neoliberal transformations in citizenship (Cowen 2006). The trend away from male conscription has shifted military service from a citizenship duty to a market relation. While this does not imply that recruits sign up only for economic reasons (though these are often front and center), it does underline that the military now competes for recruits with other employers.

The shift from the logic of citizenship to that of the market has also entailed changes in the military gender order. The all-volunteer forces that have been introduced to replace conscription armies are still overwhelmingly male, but women's increased entry into Western militaries has led to a potential reconsideration of gendered protector roles. In the United

States, for example, the proportion of active-duty female military personnel increased from 1.6 percent in 1973 (when the draft was terminated) to 14.5 percent at the beginning of 2012 (The Women's Research and Education Institute 2013), and the restrictions excluding women from direct ground combat roles were lifted in 2013. These developments in the military's gender order challenge, even if they do not break, the link between masculinity and protection.

At the same time, we have seen the rise of new market-based protector masculinity as a result of security privatization, further complicating earlier feminist analyses of the gendered politics of protection based on male protectors and female protected in the context of state militaries (Eichler 2013). The public provision of security has had a central place in the national politics of protection. While historically the use of private force was widespread, the rise of the modern Westphalian state system went hand in hand with the growing exclusion of private military force, the state's consolidation of its monopoly over the legitimate means of violence, the rise of nationalism, and the establishment of conscription (Abrahamsen and Williams 2008, 134). The rise of neoliberalism across the United Kingdom, United States, and other Western nation-states since the 1980s has made the historical linkage of the nation-state with military (and socioeconomic) protection increasingly tenuous (Cowen and Smith 2009, 43). The neoliberal state has transferred many functions and capacities to the private sector in an attempt to support profit-making opportunities for business. Privatization is a key neoliberal state policy, as David Harvey (2006) explains: "The neo-liberal state is particularly assiduous in seeking the privatization of assets as a means to open up fresh fields for capital accumulation" (25). Neoliberalism in the United States, for example, has led to the outsourcing of state functions across a variety of sectors such as public utilities, transportation, and health services. Neoliberalism erodes some forms of protection (such as social and economic) while creating new forms of market-based protection (e.g., private security services).

While the neoliberal state has actively created the market in private protection services, PMSCs challenge the state's status as sole protector (at the same time as they support state military operations). PMSCs offer a range of specialized protection services such as risk mitigation, commercial and residential security, executive protection, mobile and static security, private security details, or asset protection. Companies such as Academi, Triple Canopy, Unity Resources Group, and many others offer these protection services in support of global military operations. PMSCs provide protection services for state representatives and personnel, nongovernmental and international organizations, international businesses, infrastructure, military convoys, military bases, embassies, oilfields, mines, and more. Protection is sold to whoever can pay for it, thus delinking protection from citizenship and tying it to the ability to pay. Leander (2009) argues: "The consequence [of privatization] is a profound reshuffling of the politics in the citizenship-protection nexus. New market based hierarchies of rights are created and at the same time the politics of protection is increasingly negotiated in markets and based on market practices" (7). Privatization opens up new areas of profit making for capital and redefines protection from a citizenship right to a market relation.

In addition to new market-based protection, the past two decades have witnessed the rise of protection narratives that are rooted not in the nation, but rather assert a global responsibility toward other peoples on the basis of humanitarianism (Doty 1996; Orford 1999 and 2011; Hall and Shepherd 2013). In the post–Cold War period, we have seen the making of a "new humanitarian order" (Mamdani 2009), based on the proliferation of new forms of military intervention (humanitarian interventions, stability and peace operations, etc.) and a redefinition of the acceptable use of force in the name of protecting human rights. Critical voices have emphasized the neocolonial mold of the new interventionism and the way in which it reproduces notions of "first-world" saviors and "third-world" victims that require protection (see Darby 2009 on liberal peacekeeping; for feminist critiques, see Agathangelou and Ling 2003; Whitworth 2004; O'Reilly 2012). Mahmood Mamdani (2009) explains: The new humanitarian order "draws on the history of modern Western colonialism. At the outset of colonial expansion in the eighteenth and nineteenth centuries, leading Western powers—Britain, France, Russia—claimed to protect 'vulnerable groups'" (274) and described "colonial intervention as a rescue mission" (277).

Importantly, the contemporary global rescaling of protection reinforces unequal relations between the West and the global periphery, in ways that are profoundly racialized but also gendered. The national protection story of men defending and protecting "their" women in and through the space of the nation-state is reinvented as a global protection story of heroic, masculine Westerners who save and protect vulnerable, racialized, feminized, passive third-world populations (Wilcox 2010, 76). This global protection story has helped legitimize the "humanitarian" wars of the 1990s and 2000s, including the international U.S.-led wars in Afghanistan and Iraq that were in part justified in the name of protecting local women's rights (Young 2003; Hunt and Rygiel 2006).

These recent and ongoing shifts in the national gendered politics of protection are redrawing the interconnected lines between domestic/external, state/market, feminine/masculine, us/them, national/international, and public/private. Next I focus on security privatization to explore in more detail how the politics of protection today is being remade in terms of its marketization, scale, gendering, and racialization.

PMSCs AND THE GLOBAL POLITICS OF PROTECTION

Elke Krahmann (2008) argues that privatization indicates more than a change in the supplier of security (from states to PMSCs), because it also reshapes the meaning of security (also see Leander 2005). Building on this insight, I argue that the privatization of security is not simply a redrawing of the line between public and private but rather a struggle over the scale of the politics, and political economy, of protection. Security privatization challenges the national politics of protection and is a driving force behind the global rescaling of the politics of protection. The global politics of protection is characterized by liberal, neocolonial narratives and practices of global protection; a perceived proliferation of threats (military and nonmilitary) and a spatial and temporal unboundedness of war;[2] and new assemblages (Abrahamsen and Williams 2011) of global protection actors (states, international organizations, NGOs, private companies, individual activists, etc.). The emerging global politics of protection is to a large extent a product of neoliberal globalization (though with historical antecedents in colonialism), and at the same time it further pushes a global neoliberal agenda. It contributes to global relations of protection that rest on hierarchies of class, race, and gender, and are deeply implicated in the reproduction of the current global social order.

Just as states do, PMSCs cast themselves as masculine protectors. While states, even in an era of the global rescaling of protection must remain wedded to protecting the nation, PMSCs claim a global protector role. As companies themselves put it, they can "deliver the impossible 'anytime, anywhere'" (quoted in Joachim and Schneiker 2012a, 497), offer "the best possible security on any scale, anywhere in the world," in "any place on earth," and "even in the most hazardous situations' (501–502). These examples illustrate the ways in which PMSCs actively contribute to extending narratives and claims of protection to the global scale in order to expand the market for protection. The politics of protection entails both a symbolic struggle over narratives that define who is a legitimate and effective protector and who and what needs protecting *and* a material struggle over the opening up of new global markets and sources of profit making to the private security sector.

Gendering Global Privatized Protection

Privatization challenges the state's dominant role as protector, but, importantly, it does not challenge men's protector role (or a militarized version of protection). Global market-based protection is heavily masculinized, as I have argued elsewhere (Eichler 2013). The privatized protector is most likely to be a man, as it is first and foremost men in PMSCs who work in security and risk management, security services, and on field deployments—all areas associated with global protection work. There are extremely few women who work in private security details providing protection to a client. Instead, female employees in the private military and security industry are concentrated in feminized tasks associated with support functions and least likely to be hired for masculinized tasks associated with security and protection services. Gendered recruitment practices pose one of the main barriers for women's employment in the more "hard-core" armed security and protection area of the private military and security industry. Employees who are hired to perform security services are mostly recruited from public security and military forces, particularly the army and special forces. Privatization thus reinforces and even intensifies the gendered division of protection that has historically characterized the public sphere (Eichler 2013, 318–319).

Privatization reinforces masculinized notions of the protector but also shifts the gendered politics of protection to one equally informed by class. PMSCs mainly provide protection to masculinized clients privileged enough to afford private protection services: state representatives and international business people, that is, the transnational political and economic elite. PMSCs also provide protection for the assets of this global ruling class; assets such as military bases and military convoys, oilfields, and other valuable resources and infrastructure. Thus, while services are offered globally, they are accessible only to a small fraction of the global population—the small, masculinized, mostly Western (or Westernized) elite, and its property and military-economic resources. The relationship between protector and protected here is an intramasculine one rather than the masculinized-feminized protection relationship described by feminist scholars in regards to the national gendered politics of protection.

The privatization of security produces new inequalities and hierarchies in protection, on the basis of existing socioeconomic inequalities. Pattison (2010) explains: "[R]elying on the market to provide military services creates massive inequalities in access to security. It is not simply a question of benefiting one set of individuals: *insecurity is deflected onto those who cannot afford private protection. . . . those who can afford it employ the best protection, whilst those who cannot have to depend on weak or nonexistent forces which have been deprived of many of their best personnel" (445). Thus privatization of security leads to a (global) polarization between the masculinized protected and the feminized unprotected, between those who have the privilege to be subjects of protection and those who the market for protection renders abject, which reinforces global class inequalities that cut across gendered and racialized hierarchies. For example, while reinforcing masculinized protection, the market reduces the significance of gender by creating new inequalities *among* women. The market in protection enables women with access to economic resources to buy protection services and, in effect, to temporarily escape the gendered protection racket (cf. Higate 2011). But for women on the lower rungs of the socioeconomic ladder, the increasing privatization of protection that turns protection from a right into a service to be bought makes protection less accessible. Privatization thus partially erodes and partially intensifies the specifically gendered aspects of protection and challenges a simplistic male-female dichotomy of gendered protection characterized by male protectors and female protected.

Global Protection Narratives: Expanding the Market for Protection

While democratic access to protection shrinks as a result of privatization, PMSCs aim to expand the market for protection services. As part of this attempt, PMSCs and industry representatives portray private contractors as global protectors of vulnerable third-world populations and thus contribute to and help construct the "new humanitarian order" (Mamdani 2009) that has arisen over the past two decades. "PMCs can go where Western militaries fear to tread and protect or even rescue those the World abandons," wrote Doug Brooks in 2002, then president of the International Peace Operations Association (renamed the International Stability Operations Association in 2010), which is the Washington-based trade association representing PMSCs operating globally (Brooks 2002). This quotation highlights one of the main claims of the private security industry, that private companies can be more effective and reliable global protectors than states or the international community if only they were allowed to play a more active role in the global politics of protection. One way the industry has tried to legitimate itself and establish its global protector role is by "employ[ing] the rhetoric of humanitarianism, selling itself as a 'peace and stability industry' vital for the protection of human rights worldwide" (Pattison 2010, 444). Jutta Joachim and Andrea Schneiker (2012b) convincingly argue that the adoption of a "humanitarian frame" by PMSCs has been instrumental in their struggle for greater legitimacy.

Similar to the depiction of vulnerable, passive women in need of protection in state-protection narratives, PMSCs and the private military and security industry depict third-world populations as vulnerable, passive, and in need of protection. They thereby reinforce relations of unequal power between the West and the "developing" world, making sense of their relations in protector-protected terms. PMSCs reproduce the scripts of "muscular interventionism" that Orford (1999) describes in her analysis of humanitarian interventionism: they construct a particular view of the world as chaotic, fragmented, where "knights in white armour" protect helpless victims (692). As Lauren Wilcox (2010) notes in relation to the new humanitarianism: "While seemingly benign, such chivalric discourses require helpless, feminized victims: not full and equal citizens capable of defending themselves. . . . The protector and the protected cannot be equal to one other" (75). In claiming global protector status, PMSCs render populations in Africa and Asia passive, feminized, racialized, and as sources of instability in the world that they offer to stabilize. Here, those "deserving" of masculinized protection are feminized but valued by the market.

Unlike the national politics of protection defined by states and citizens, the global politics of protection is defined by the ever-growing need to extend the market in security. The U.S.-led wars in Afghanistan and Iraq led to burgeoning demand for private military and security contractors. But the private military and security industry and its members have been concerned with what they refer to as the "Iraq bubble" (and the now looming "Afghanistan bubble") associated with a decrease in business as a result of the pull-out of United States and other troops from Iraq in 2011 and the planned withdrawal from Afghanistan by 2016. Malcom Hugh Patterson (2009) explains, "[T]hese companies face pressures—notably in the form of gradually declining opportunities in Iraq and the deepening global recession. This ebb in Iraq in particular has spurred corporate expansion elsewhere" (4). Christopher Spearin similarly (2008) argues that PMSCs "increasingly look to humanitarianism as a future market opportunity" (364). As this example shows, privatization creates a continuous push to expand the market for security provision and protection services in ways that "broaden and deepen" the ambit of security and lead to the deeper securitization of more and more aspects of global politics, including peace operations and development work.

The Global Labor Market in Protection Services: Subordinate Protector Masculinities

PMSCs rely on a global labor market in protection services that "both reflects and reproduces global class difference" (Cowen and Smith 2009, 37) in addition to racialized and gendered hierarchies. The Western-based, globally operating private security industry heavily relies on the labor of non-Western citizens, which includes locals in the country of operation as well as what the industry refers to as "third-country nationals" (TCNs): men (and some women) from countries in the global South such as the Philippines, Bangladesh, Nepal, El Salvador, Chile, India, Pakistan, and Uganda. The global labor market in protection services fundamentally challenges the national framework of protection: instead of citizens protecting citizens, migrant and local workers from the periphery and semiperiphery of the global economy disproportionally provide the labor of global privatized protection, even if their role is rarely acknowledged (Chisholm 2013; Eichler 2014).

The global labor market in protection services rests on a hierarchy that constitutes racialized men from the global South as subordinate masculinities vis-à-vis the hegemonic masculinities of white, Western contractors, as Isabelle V. Barker, Amanda Chisholm, and Jutta Joachim and Andrea Schneiker discuss in more detail in their chapters in this volume. These differences are evident not only in pay and working conditions but also in the kind of work performed. The more dangerous the work, the higher the proportion of local and migrant workers among private security employees. For example, out of 102,000 private contractors performing unarmed security and logistical work for the U.S. Department of Defense in Afghanistan in 2011, 78 percent were non-U.S. citizens; and out of 53,000 private contractors in Iraq, 70 percent were non-U.S. citizens. But when we look at armed security work, out of 22,000 armed security contractors working for the U.S. Department of Defense in Afghanistan in 2011, 93 percent were locals and 4 percent were TCNs. Out of 100,000 armed security contractors in Iraq, 87 percent were TCNs and 4 percent locals. Only a small minority of private contractors working in armed security in Iraq and Afghanistan for the Department of Defense were in fact U.S. citizens (USDoD 2011).

Thus PMSCs reinforce a global division of labor that is racialized, and this is particularly pronounced when it comes to protection work. Ironically, these workers are often unprotected themselves, toiling under poor working conditions and recruited specifically because of their spatial and social precariousness. While the use of foreign nationals in the provision of security and protection challenges the national politics of protection, there are important continuities between national public and global privatized military and security work. The classed and racialized hierarchies of the global labor market in privatized protection reflect but also globalize and deepen the class and racialized make-up of today's Western militaries. This is the case, in particular, in the United States where since the termination of the draft and the introduction of an all-volunteer force, the burden of military service has fallen disproportionally on the working class and working poor, especially on the racialized and rural lower-middle class (Cowen 2006, 176). Thus, we can conceptualize the privatization of military protection work as enabling a global rescaling of recruitment that geographically extends the class and racialized determinants of military labor increasingly found within the nation-state (see Eichler 2014 where this argument is more fully developed). Both at the national and global level, some of the least protected in society are performing the work of militarized protectors.

PMSCs as Global Protectors?

I have argued that the market for force shapes relations of protection in (at least) three key ways: by regendering the relationship between protector and protected, by contributing to a global rescaling of the politics of protection, and by enabling the globalization of classed and racialized gendered protection work. PMSCs challenge the national gendered politics of protection and take an active interest in extending the market (in services and labor) for protection globally. They thereby rely on and reinforce global relations of protection that rest on hierarchies of class, race, and gender. PMSCs actively shape, and benefit from, the emerging global politics of protection.

However, PMSCs' claims to protector status have not gone unchallenged. Common media (and scholarly) images of PMSCs emphasize the hypermasculine, aggressive aspects of PMSCs associated with mercenarism (Via 2010; Kruck and Spencer 2013). Much of the debate on PMSCs has focused on how to protect civilians *from* private contractors who violate human rights and what forms of regulation are necessary to avoid impunity (see chapters by Sperling and Vrdoljak in this volume). PMSCs increasingly contest their association with excessive violence and strive to depict themselves as benign protectors of both clients and vulnerable populations (cf. Higate's chapter in this volume). As Joachim and Schneiker (2012a) write, PMSCs "seek to rid themselves of the mercenary image by replacing the negative, subordinate forms of masculinity associated with that image with more accepted forms" such as those of humanitarians, security experts, and protectors (500). Thus, the status of PMSCs as protectors remains contested even as the market for protection is expanding globally. While a focus on the state is no longer sufficient to understand the politics of protection, we must also be attentive to how a critique of PMSCs tends to reify and romanticize the state's role as protector. Instead, contestations of PMSCs as protectors could serve to open up space for a reconsideration of protector masculinities—public and private—more broadly. However, as I show in the conclusion, privatization produces new challenges for feminist reconceptualizations of protection, which may limit the potential for a reconsideration of protector masculinities.

CONCLUSION: IMPLICATIONS OF PRIVATIZATION FOR FEMINIST CRITIQUES OF PROTECTION

The dominant norm of state protection in international relations is based on a militarized and masculinized notion of protection that helps legitimate not only the modern state, but also its waging of wars and subordination of women. While feminist IR scholars offer an important critique of the politics of protection, they do not pay enough attention to the market as a new site for the making of unequal protection relations. I have argued that we need to consider how the privatization of security is shifting gendered relations of protection to produce and reinforce global hierarchies and inequalities along classed, gendered, and racialized lines. While state militarism has historically relied on a division into masculine protectors and feminized protected (Runyan 1990), recent feminist scholarship has shown that this masculine/feminine dichotomy is less than clear-cut and that gendered relations of protection shape politics beyond the nation-state. Privatization further complicates the gendering and scale of protection. In addition to the masculinized protector, privatization creates three new gendered classes of people: those who can afford protection (masculinized), those who find themselves outside the market for protection (devalued feminized), and those populations who are poor but are considered deserving of protection (valued feminized) in the context of global-protection narratives. Gender remains constitutive of protection in the private realm of the global market but intersects with class and race to create a complex set of relations between protected, protector, and unprotected, highlighting new divisions and inequalities among protectors and protected. While Western-based PMSCs seek legitimacy as new global protectors, racialized men from the global South disproportionately carry out protection work in today's conflict zones. Western elites who buy protection exist alongside those vulnerable populations defined as needing and deserving protection, while those outside the market of protection are rendered unworthy and unprotected.

Beyond the focus on security privatization, the analysis underscores three important lessons for feminist security studies. First, it highlights the need for more accurate and nuanced analyses of the shifting national politics of protection that increasingly defies a clear division into masculine protectors and feminine protected as both more women join the ranks of today's public militaries and the market regenders protection relations. Second, the analysis in this chapter points to the need for feminist scholars to reconceptualize the gendered politics of protection along a public-private continuum (cf. Eichler 2013; also cf. Baggiarini in this volume), at different scales (cf. Sjoberg 2008), and in intersections with class and race (cf. Chisholm 2013; Barker 2009). And finally, security privatization underscores that the politics of protection is both an ideological struggle over protection narratives and a material struggle over global markets in protection services and labor, highlighting the importance for feminists to consider both material and ideological factors in the study of protection more generally.

Privatization challenges not only feminist approaches to the study of protection but also one of the central tasks of feminist security scholarship which is to envision alternative forms of security and protection (Blanchard 2003; Wibben 2011). As discussed earlier, feminists are critical of how protection has historically been conceptualized (as militarized, state-centric) and organized (around male citizen-soldiers), and how it has legitimated unequal gender relations and the waging of wars. Stiehm (1982) argues that allowing both women and men to act as "defenders" (rather than "protectors") offers a way out of the unequal gendered politics of protection. Others have sought to redefine security in nonmilitary, nonstate, and multidimensional ways that recognize the interdependence of human, social, and environmental security (Tickner 1992a), and to reconceive of protection in terms of a nondependent relationship (Peterson 1992b; also see Bigo 2006). Young (2003) asserts, "Democratic citizenship thus means ultimately rejecting the hierarchy of protector and protected" (22). Anne Sisson Runyan (1990) elaborates on this point: "Just as we must resist the dichotomous constructions of masculine and feminine, ally and enemy, and protector and protected, we must seek . . . [alternatives] in which there would be no necessity for protection of one given order, and particularly one based on the dynamics of the militarily strong protecting and, thus, dominating the weak, at all costs" (31). Thus, rethinking protection requires a wholesale rethinking of gender and social orders.

The privatization of protection—allowing protection to become a commodity provided by the private sector—creates new challenges for feminist reconceptualizations of protection. Privatization entrenches the masculinization and militarization of protection and leads to a depoliticization of protection (as much as this depoliticization itself is political), which hinder the development of alternatives to the norm of the masculinized protector. Privatization makes it more difficult to envision protection in nonmilitarized, non-gender-hierarchical terms and allows for a "displacement of political process" (Leander 2009a, 11), making it harder for all citizens, including women and women's rights activists, to intervene in the politics of protection. The shift from the logic of citizenship to the logic of the market dislodges citizen "defenders" (Stiehm 1982) and democratic citizenship (Young 2003) from the politics of protection (see Stachowitsch 2013).

While neoliberalism promises greater freedom, privatization, in fact, creates new dependencies on and exclusions from the market for those seeking protection in the context of a neoliberal state that is shedding some of its protection functions. Under neoliberalism, we need to attend not only to the violence of national and global masculinist protection across public and private spheres but also to the political violence inherent in being deemed undeserving of protection (because one is unable to pay for protection or nobody is willing to pay for one's protection). Equally problematic, the logic of market expansion has led to a "broadening and deepening" of security and protection services offered by private companies that constitute an ever-expanding market for war, peace, stability, development, and humanitarian operations. Thus, we need to be attentive to how the revisioning of protection in nonmilitary, nonstate ways in the context of privatization may be quite profitable and desirable to PMSCs. Today feminists must question protection anew, by examining how protection is being marketized and rescaled, and racialized, gendered, and classed in new ways and how the logic of global masculinist protection is increasing our dependency on the market while reducing our political autonomy.

NOTES

1. I am grateful to Soumita Basu, Amanda Chisholm, Sandra McEvoy, Saskia Stachowitsch, and one anonymous reviewer for providing helpful feedback and comments on this chapter.
2. See Gregory (2011) on the "everywhere war" and Bacevich (2010) on the U.S. "permanent war."

PART II

Rethinking the Private Military Contractor I

Third-Country Nationals and the Making of Empire

CHAPTER 4

(Re)Producing American Soldiers in an Age of Empire

ISABELLE V. BARKER

I spent my entire career watching soldiers pulling KP [kitchen police] in the kitchen. Why do we have to do that with soldiers? Why can't we outsource that mission? . . . [W]hat we're trying to do is assist the war fighter and get him prepared to go do the mission with a proper attitude in a proper environment.

> Paul Cerjan, retired Army lieutenant general, at the time vice president of Kellogg Brown & Root Worldwide Military Affairs, April 13, 2005

The reason we have contractors is that they take the place of soldiers. And it doesn't matter whether they're guarding a facility or a convoy or cooking meals.

> Secretary of Defense Robert Gates, October 3, 2007

This chapter was written in 2008 in an effort to track the effects of military privatization within the geopolitical context of an aggressive neoconservative U.S. foreign policy.[1] The chapter focuses on how the intersecting dimensions of gender/race/class/nationality shaped the reproductive labor at the heart of U.S. military operations at the time, in particular the war in Iraq. While U.S. foreign policy has since shifted, as has the U.S. position in geopolitics, this chapter provides an analysis of the effects of military privatization on the division of labor that may be used as a lens to explore other moments of U.S. foreign policy and global engagement.

In the 2005 *Frontline* film, *Private Warriors*—a documentary about outsourcing military services in Iraq—nonmilitary men from South and Southeast

Asian countries are an undeniably ubiquitous presence (Gaviria and Smith 2005). In one scene, a South Asian man donning a "Pizza Hut Iraq" baseball cap serves pizza to soldiers in the food court of Camp Victory in Baghdad. Another scene takes place 40 miles north of Baghdad in Camp Anaconda, a vast base housing 28,000 soldiers and 8,000 contractors. Here, we see a Southeast Asian man pushing a laundry cart past countless aisles of washing machines and dryers. In several other scenes shot in Camp Anaconda, a South Asian man serves a cheeseburger to an African American male soldier, and another South Asian man scoops ice cream for a young white male soldier. And finally, in another scene, yet another South Asian man is filmed moving in and out of individual portable latrines, cleaning each, while two white soldiers sit by. The filmmakers never explicitly discuss these South Asian men and the work that they do, but the film visually illustrates the significance of their presence in the kitchens, laundry rooms, and barracks of the military bases across Iraq.

The presence of migrant workers in service occupations suggests that the division of labor on twenty-first century U.S. military bases has taken on a set of characteristics representing an underexplored axis in the global division of reproductive labor.[2] As with other instances of this division of labor, we see the convergence of migrant labor serving as a structural stopgap *and* as a site for symbolic politics in the arena of social reproduction. In this case, the gendered symbolic politics of what is essentially a reliance on low-wage migrant labor serves to reinforce both the neoliberal privatization of the U.S. armed forces as well as neoconservative American foreign policy ambitions.

Dating back to the Revolutionary War, the U.S. military has always outsourced some degree of military services (Woods 2004, 3). Since the early 1990s, however, this outsourcing has intensified. The U.S. involvement in Iraq under Operation Iraqi Freedom brought attention to the existence of the privatized military, the "corporate warriors" hired by contracting companies who work alongside military personnel (Singer 2003). Since the September 2007 allegations of Blackwater personnel's disproportionate use of force, this privatized dimension of current U.S. military engagement has been the subject of intensified public scrutiny. But this chapter turns attention to another aspect of outsourcing in the U.S. military, one which has gone relatively unnoticed by scholars and by mainstream media.[3] In addition to the privatization of security services, the Department of Defense has also restructured the provision of so-called vital support services to the armed forces.[4]

Reflecting more general economic trends toward restructuring and flexible production (Peterson 2003), in 1985, the army formally created the Logistics Civil Augmentation Program, or LOGCAP. This program institutionalized practices of outsourcing already increasingly in place following the Vietnam War. LOGCAP originally served as means to plan in peacetime for "the use of civilian contractors to perform selected services in wartime and other contingencies to augment U.S. forces in support of Department of Defense missions" (Woods 2004, 3). With civilian contracting far more centralized than ever before, LOGCAP served as a mechanism to establish an umbrella contract for delivery of a vast range of support services. The first five-year LOGCAP contract was awarded in 1992 to Brown & Root Services Corporation (Singer 2003, ch. 9; Briody 2004, 185). In 2001 the Department of Defense awarded Brown & Root another LOGCAP contract, this time extended for 10 years. In Iraq, the renamed Kellogg Brown & Root (KBR) supported all the U.S. and remaining coalition forces, relying primarily on hundreds of tiered subcontractors to perform a host of vital support services. These services covered the whole range of operations involved in the life-cycle of a military base and of the individual soldiers on that base. Services included base construction and maintenance, delivery of fuel, transporting cargo and personnel, generating power, food service, laundry and field show-ers, latrines, and sewage and solid waste removal (Woods 2004, 6).

The focus of this chapter is a particular aspect of the outsourcing of sup-port services—namely the staffing involved in the organization of social reproductive labor in the theater of war. I ask the following questions: Who does the laundry, who prepares the food, and who cleans the facilities on military bases? As illustrated in the aforementioned vignettes, evidence suggests that the vast majority of the outsourced vital support service labor is performed by men migrating from India, Bangladesh, Sri Lanka, the Philippines, Nepal, and Pakistan (Simpson 2005, 2006a, 2006b; Raz 2007). The majority of KBR staff in Iraq were noncitizens—out of 48,000 employ-ees, 35,000 were neither Americans nor Iraqis. Beyond KBR, other estimates suggest that contractors in Iraq numbered 180,000 with only a small frac-tion of these working as security contractors. Here, again, most were not U.S. citizens (Broder and Risen 2007; Raz 2007).

The use of those the military refers to as third-country nationals, or TCNs, in Iraq represents a massive enhancing of decades-old migration pathways in place between Asian countries and the Middle East (Seccombe 1985; Castles and Miller [1993] 2003, 159–160). For example, the Jordanian migrant recruitment agency, Morning Star for Recruitment and Manpower Supply, has for years brokered the placement of South and Southeast Asian migrants as low-skilled assembly workers and as maids for wealthy Jordanians. Since the U.S. involvement in Iraq began, the business of recruiting migrant labor-ers to work on American bases has been booming (Simpson 2005).

The vast supply of low-wage migrant labor is structurally absolutely cen-tral to the calculations involved in the military outsourcing support services in the first place. In an interview with the producers of *Private Warriors*, Paul Cerjan, at the time vice president of Kellogg Brown & Root Worldwide Military Affairs, defends the controversial high wages earned by KBR's truck drivers (who generally are U.S. citizens) by pointing out that the privatization of services actually saves taxpayer dollars precisely because of low-wage migrant labor. He baldly puts the matter as follows:

> Wait a minute now. You're paying some people more money. . . . There's an American truck driver who gets more money, but you don't take into account the third-country nationals we hired at less wage, because they can come over here and do it cheaper. They don't have deployment issues that they have to contend with. They don't have mobilization issues—that's on their nickel. We use subcontractors from around the area so you don't have to mobilize them. They take care of their own living conditions and what have you. (Cerjan 2005)

It is of course unusual to hear such an honest appraisal from official channels regarding the United States' structural dependence on low-wage migrant labor. Cerjan freely and unapologetically admits that migrants working in reproductive arenas of food preparation, laundry, and cleaning services make a very low wage and so end up costing KBR, and U.S. taxpayers, far less.

Reflecting larger patterns of post-Fordist cost-containment through flexible labor arrangements and outsourcing (Peterson 2003), exploitation of foreign labor is crucial to keeping reproductive labor costs low. Whereas the military estimates that a soldier costs about 100,000 USD a year in pay, benefits, and training, migrant workers earn only about 20 USD a day (Brodie 2007; Raz 2007). Labor practices that are commonly enforced in the United States do not apply, since migrant workers are the employees of any one of the hundreds of regional subcontractors. Therefore far more labor can be extracted from each migrant worker. For example, the Saudi-based food services firm Tamimi contracted migrant workers to work in U.S. bases for two years at 1.25 USD an hour and, on average, migrant service workers work 12-hour shifts, seven days a week (Raz 2007). The outsourcing of reproductive services represents a remarkable and, in light of these labor conditions, unsettling reorganization of the division of labor within the military. In this chapter, I also suggest that this reorganized division of labor reinforces the devaluation and disavowal of social reproduction and in the process serves as a site of symbolic politics underwriting the gendered dimensions of the national identity of the American soldier. This symbolic politics appears to serve multiple ends. First, it helps to rationalize the privatization and outsourcing of reproductive labor. Secondly, it underwrites the imperial posture assumed by the United States in the context of neoconservative foreign policy. Consider again the words of Paul Cerjan in the *Frontline* documentary. In defending the outsourcing of vital support services, Cerjan points out that this outsourcing serves in part as a means to reduce costs *and* in part as a way to enable the soldier to maintain a "proper attitude" as a "war fighter." Cerjan laments that he "spent his entire career watching soldiers pull KP [kitchen police] in the kitchen."[5] He goes on to ask rhetorically, "Why do we have to do that with soldiers?" A soldier pulling KP—performing the feminized repro- ductive labor of preparing and cooking food and cleaning a kitchen—is for Cerjan unnecessary work that has the added disadvantage of detracting the soldier from his/her proper masculinized role as a war fighter.

This essay explores the underlying gendered dimensions of this division of labor on U.S. military bases, where as we have seen, most reproductive labor is performed by men from poor Asian countries. Lying at the intersec- tion of gender, race, class, and nationality, the structure of this organization of social reproductive labor builds on a long tradition of gendered dynamics framing military service. I open the discussion with a survey of the evolution of this tradition in the organization of modern soldiering. Taking gender as a lens by which to unpack the naturalization of multiple intersecting hier- archies (Peterson 2003, 36), the discussion then explores how the outsourc- ing of social reproduction on military bases updates the tradition of armed masculinity. This is done by reinforcing the aggressive masculine production of the American soldier as a "war fighter"—regardless of the race, economic class, or even gender of that soldier. The remainder of the discussion is dedi- cated to revealing the multiple ways that the displacement of reproductive labor, which remains coded as effeminate, onto poor, nonwhite, migrant men from South and Southeast Asian countries may reinforce the aggressive mas- culine version of American soldiering. One key effect of the symbolic politics of off-loading this feminized work is that the resulting masculinist image of the military serves to rationalize the privatization of the armed forces. That is, the symbolic politics of this outsourcing is such that emphasizing the feminization of this labor serves to reinforce the neoliberal model of a leaner and more effective and efficient armed forces. Outsourcing this labor enables a division of labor that symbolically reinforces the soldier's role as a masculinized war fighter with a second level of implications, supporting the corresponding and increasingly imperial posture that the United States has assumed in the world in this first decade of the twenty-first century. The division of labor on the military base has become a site for positioning mem- bers of the U.S. military first as bearers of a superior masculinity vis-à-vis feminized migrant workers who are, significantly, *non-Americans* performing devalued feminine reproductive labor. In addition, it serves to mute signifi- cant race, class, gender, and regional differences between service members. Finally, this gendered symbolic politics appears to play a role in obscuring the disconnect soldiers experience between their training for combat and the actual daily "nation-building" operations of occupying Iraq. As we will see, the link between the symbolic politics of the division of social reproductive labor with the ambitious and aggressive aspects of U.S. foreign policy echoes earlier colonizer-colonized relations in that domestic life and reproductive labor continue to be critical sites for demarcating lopsided positions of power in international relations.

THE GENDERED DIMENSIONS OF REPRODUCING SOLDIERS

There is, of course, nothing new about the fact that military service is a gendered arena. Feminists have noted that over the course of the Western tradition gendered practices have always underwritten the theory and practice of military service. There is a long tradition of associating soldiering with masculinity, both in Western political thought as well as in the practice of armed forces (Snyder 1999; Enloe 2000b). The tradition of modern "armed masculinity" (Snyder 1999) can be traced back to Niccolò Machiavelli's celebration of the manly citizen-soldier as the key figure in a republican polity. Reading *The Prince* alongside *The Discourses of Livy*, R. Claire Snyder (1999, 25) explains that "the civic virtue of the citizen and the combatively masculine action of the soldier come together in a figure that exhibits both characteristics at once." Embodying republican civic virtue, citizen-soldiers are motivated to act for the good of their community. They are characterized by their courage, patriotism, and selflessness along with their willingness to take action (23–24). For Machiavelli, these traits of civic virtue are interchangeable with masculinity. As Hannah Pitkin points out, Machiavelli repeatedly defines *virtù* against all that is "*effeminato*" (quoted in Synder 1999, 24)—all that is either passive and meek on the one hand (25), or wily, cunning, and unpredictable on the other (Brown 1995, 89). This array of feminine traits stands in stark opposition to the qualities of the citizen-soldier. Courage, patriotism, and so forth are realized through action that defies the passivity of Christian effeminacy and that subdues the fickle ways of feminine *Fortuna*. And, as Snyder (1999, 25) highlights, by way of this opposition to all that is associated with femininity, the figure of the citizen-soldier brings together "soldiering, masculinity, and citizenship."

The armed masculinity of Machiavelli's citizen-soldier reverberated centuries later in the organization of the Revolutionary-era U.S. military, as did its symbolic feminine counterpart. But in this instance, femininity was linked less with passivity or cunning seductiveness than with domesticity and reproductive labor. Indeed, the attributes associated with soldiering alongside those associated with "republican motherhood" put the gendered dynamics of the division of labor into stark relief. The masculine citizen-soldier was counterpoised against the middle-class ideal of the republican mother—the embodiment of feminine citizen virtue realized through performing reproductive labor. The concept of republican motherhood has become ubiquitous in feminist scholarship, but its origin lies in Linda Kerber's (1980) analysis of women's roles in the American Revolution. Republican motherhood derived in part from the role assigned to women to perform the social reproductive labor to support members of the army. While often used to define the tasks of middle-class mothering of future citizen-soldier sons, for Kerber, the concept of republican motherhood also serves to highlight the gendered division of labor in relation to the armed forces. She explains that

> the American army offered political uses for traditional domestic skills. . . . Wives and children who had no means of support when their husbands and fathers were pressed into service followed after and cared for their own men, earning their subsistence by cooking and washing for troops in an era when the offices of the quartermaster and commissary were inadequately run. (Kerber 1980, 55)

A sense of women's distinctive civic duty came to be associated with this social reproductive labor, as captured in the words of James Fenimore Cooper's character Elizabeth Flanagan, a "female sutler, washerwoman, and . . . petticoat doctor to the troops" in his novel *The Spy*. Emphasizing the civic significance of her work, she asks, "What would become of the States and liberty if the boys had never a [clean] shirt, or drop to comfort them?" (quoted in Kerber 1980, 56). Based on the reproductive work performed by women, alongside the cultural narratives that emerged on the subject, the Revolutionary War occasioned the attachment of civic importance to women's work in the gendered division of labor, all the while clearly demarcating soldiering as masculine.

Women have always had a place in supporting members of the army, though they have not always been celebrated as the republican ideal. Cynthia Enloe (1988) notes that, historically, female "camp followers" were often associated with promiscuity and disorderliness; however, their labor was absolutely essential with women playing key roles as "soldiers' wives, cooks, provisioners, laundresses, and nurses" (3). In the twentieth century, as the armed forces modernized, reproductive work on the battlefield was undertaken less frequently by women than by soldiers themselves. In spite of this, however, Enloe is certainly right to point out that the paradoxical dynamic of misogyny toward and simultaneous dependence on "camp followers" has permeated the military's unspoken reliance on military wives to sustain soldiers (4–6).

Profound historical shifts in the allocation of reproductive work occurred in the early twentieth-century military. Reproductive tasks came to be folded into the armed forces as part of an overall reorganization of the logistical support needed to maintain a modernized and highly bureaucratic military (Keene 2001, 39). During World War I, due to civilian labor shortages alongside relatively high civilian wages, the armed forces could no longer rely on civilians to perform these noncombatant tasks. Moreover, fighting overseas precluded significant reliance on unpaid nonmilitary resources—that is, wives and mothers—to support soldiers as they had when soldiers remained on American soil (51). As a result, and enabled by the 1917 establishment of the national draft, the armed forces—the army in particular—significantly expanded its population of noncombatant troops.[6] This had implications not only for logistical support, but for the organization of reproductive work as well.

Beginning with World War I, units of the armed forces increasingly became "self-sufficient societ[ies]" (Brotz and Wilson 1946, 374). In the early twentieth century military, soldiers' duties in these self-contained societies were numerous, extending to social reproductive labor, or "housekeeping functions" (374). This reorganization of the division of labor ultimately reinforced gendered orderings, with male soldiers uneasily assuming "feminine" reproductive tasks which continued to be devalued. As described by sociologists in the 1940s, "to a former professional who is an enlisted man, policing the area, cleaning latrines, kitchen police, and care of the barracks is at first an imposition" (374). As evidence of its undesirability, KP, or kitchen police has historically been assigned either by rotation or as punishment for minor infractions.

It is not hard to imagine that in a military system that promulgated the image of the soldier as warrior, this extensive reliance on soldiers to perform, among other tasks, those associated with women in the gendered division of labor sat uneasily alongside soldiers' sense of their masculinity. The gendered politics of dependence and disavowal of social reproduction have, after all, historically proven tenacious. Writing of the huge pool of noncombatant soldiers in World War I, historian Jennifer Keene (2001) suggests that these soldiers struggled with the disconnect between the aggressive ideal of soldiering fostered by the armed forces culture and the actual work they did. She writes, "the contradiction between the belligerent posture the army enticed all recruits to embrace and what military service actually entailed for noncombatants precipitated an unforeseen crisis of identity for noncombatants in the wartime army" (36). For example, according to a War Department investigator at the time, soldiers complained that "their manpower was wanted but not their manhood" (40). What is key here is that this perceived disconnect on the part of conscripted soldiers existed because military service was associated with masculinity—and vice versa.

Due to the history of armed masculinity in the Western tradition, it is not surprising that this link has been longstanding. In spite of women's integration into the modern military, the association of soldiering with masculinity continues to prevail (Faludi 1994; Herbert 1998; Snyder 2003).[7] In fact, the combination of the privatization of the military over the last two decades alongside the posture assumed by the United States in foreign policy under the George W. Bush administration appears to have had the effect of invigorating the tradition of armed masculinity. To make sense of this aspect of the military requires unpacking the symbolic politics that produce and reinforce the narratives of hypermasculinity surrounding American soldiering today.

The twenty-first century U.S. military looks quite different from its early twentieth-century progenitor. For one thing, it is a vastly smaller military made up of an all-volunteer force. Since the end of universal conscription in 1973, the U.S. armed forces have diminished from over 3 million in 1970 to 1.4 million in 2002. A second and related difference is the increased flexi- bilization of the military and the attendant reliance on private channels to perform necessary services. Former Secretary of Defense Donald Rumsfeld summed up the contemporary amalgam of public and private entities that comprise the armed forces as follows: "The U.S. military is more than its fighting forces. It is a broad complex of military, civilian, and contract per- sonnel who equip, support, and sustain—in hundreds of thousands of ways every day—the men and women who put their lives on the line" (quoted in Woods 2004, 1). A final difference is the role of the U.S. armed forces in the world today—a world in which the United States is increasingly viewed as, and increasingly considers itself to be, an imperial power. These conditions combined have profoundly altered the organization of social reproductive labor within the armed forces so that today, this organization is quite dis- tinct from the model that prevailed for much of the twentieth century. At the same time this organization has taken on new symbolic roles.

The United States as empire is a condition alternately hailed and con- demned by commentators, but this disagreement should not detract from the remarkable consensus that empire has become an accurate way to describe the United States today.[8] The events of September 11, 2001, ush- ered in an era of emboldened and militarized U.S. presence in global affairs. Having espoused a mostly isolationist approach to international relations in his first presidential bid, following 9/11 George W. Bush and his admin- istration undertook a far more aggressive and ambitious approach to world affairs. While the United States has been the dominant world power since the collapse of the Soviet Union, recent events have laid bare the lopsided relationship of American power with regard to the rest of the world. In the 1990s, the United States maintained the Department of Defense's Unified Command Plan, a Cold War–era military organization of bases around the world. It did so without meaningful opposition from Russia, much less any other state. This residual Cold War–era global military structure combined with post–Cold War military and economic preeminence and the United States' activities undertaken under the aegis of the "global war on terror" together today position the United States as an imperial power.

This structural position of primacy is further bolstered by the foreign policy approach adopted by the Bush administration. The 2002 National Security Strategy explains this posture in no uncertain terms: "the U.S. will use this moment of opportunity to extend the benefits of freedom across the globe. We will actively work to bring the hope of democracy, development, free markets and free trade to every corner of the world" (U.S. White House 2002). Ann Norton (2004) has provided an astute excavation of the intellectual roots of the neoconservativism that has shaped recent U.S. foreign policy, noting the gendered dimensions of its "expansive internationalism" (187). She sums up the argument as follows: "America can not only be great among nations, with a power 'unmatched since Rome,' it can impose upon the world a *Pax Americana. . . .* The nation [can] shake off the effeminacy and apathy of containment and extend itself" (190–191). In *Present Dangers: Crisis and Opportunity in American Foreign and Defense Policy,* William Kristol and Robert Kagan (2000) give voice to the neoconservative drive to establish American greatness in the world, advocating a return to "a robust brand of internationalism" built upon "honor and greatness" (23). What we see in U.S. foreign policy under the Bush administration is putting into practice this intellectual call for aggressively maintaining the United States as a preeminent global power. Underlying current ambitions lies the neoconservative thrust to purportedly spread the practices and values of American liberalism far and wide—even if this must be done at gunpoint.

The military plays a significant and unique role in this foreign policy vision. The expansion of military presence is specifically mandated by the 2002 National Security Strategy which holds:

> The presence of American forces overseas is one of the most profound symbols of the U.S. commitments to allies and friends. Through our willingness to use force in our own defense and in defense of others, the United States demonstrates its resolve to maintain a balance of power that favors freedom. To contend with uncertainty and to meet the many security challenges we face, *the United States will require bases and stations well beyond Western Europe and Northeast Asia, as well as temporary access arrangements for the long-distance deployment of U.S. forces.* (U.S. White House 2002, 29; emphasis added)

Based on this directive and on the estimation that the United States has over 700 military installations in nearly 40 countries around the world, Chalmers Johnson (2004) argues that in the place of achieving political power through direct administration of foreign governments, the United States has instead established an "empire of military bases" (6). Driven by a quest for national security in an era of nonstate threats, the United States as empire rests heavily on the capacities of the military to undertake this emboldened foreign policy strategy.

In advocating for a liberal American empire, historian Niall Ferguson (2004) worries that the American public is not up to the task—the American electorate would be unlikely to support an imperial undertaking. He is correct to note that the political impossibility of universal conscription certainly calls into question the viability of an empire modeled on earlier versions of colonialism that deployed colonial administrators across the globe. There are simply not enough American citizens willing to work as administrators of an American system of colonization.[9] Moreover, the relatively small numbers of the all-volunteer armed forces limits the possibility of a colonizing empire administered by the military. Reinstituting universal conscription remains utterly unrealistic in today's political climate. So it would seem that, desirable or not, a colonial-style empire, one organized along the lines of creating settlements in foreign countries to reinforce a dominant country running the domestic and foreign policies of weaker countries, is not a viable option. This is why Jan Pieterse (2004, 49) writes of what he calls "imperial understretch."[10] And yet, while nonmilitary colonial-style settlement is not an option, and even military settlement is apparently questionable due to the relatively small size of the U.S. armed forces, the alarming expansion of U.S. military presence in countries around the world seems to, for the moment, have prevented a self-defeating "understretch" with regard to manpower.

This points to a central strategic paradox at the heart of today's *Pax Americana,* but one that has been managed to date.[11] The only way that the United States can support an empire of military bases with a trimmed-down force comprised of all volunteers is through outsourcing services. The privatization of key components of the military in an era of neoliberal ideological dominance has turned out to be absolutely crucial to enable a militarized imperial turn on the part of the United States. Thus it is more accurate to term this a *neoliberal* empire of bases—one that relies heavily on nonstate, private entities to support all the activities of the military—from security services to logistics and vital support services (Singer 2003). In this neoliberal era, due in part to the all-volunteer army as well as to the availability of a low-cost and mobile global labor force of migrants, the U.S. armed forces have reverted back to a pre–World War I organization of both logistical support *and* the division of labor, outsourcing reproductive activities, among others, to nonsoldiers through privatized channels.

In the case of outsourcing reproductive labor, which is the focus of this discussion, it is of note that we are not witnessing a simultaneous reverting back to relying on the unpaid labor of female "camp followers." And so neither are we simply reverting back to the dual cultural politics of republican motherhood and misogyny to prop up armed masculinity. But this is *not* to suggest that narratives of armed masculinity and the politics of dependence on and disavowal of social reproduction are waning. Quite the opposite. For example, even in an era of gender integration, when women make up 16 percent of (active-duty and reserve) personnel in the U.S. armed forces (USGAO 2005), armed masculinity is alive and well. As scholars have noted, the presence of women in the military has instead led to a militarization of femininity and a corresponding masculinization of female service members (Herbert 1998).[12] The tenacity and capacity of armed masculinity to thrive in spite of the presence of women raises the question of how armed masculinity is being produced today.

What is the corresponding symbolic politics underwriting the "expansive internationalism" of neoconservative foreign policy administered by neoliberal armed forces? In what ways does the division of labor reinforce a demarcation between soldiers and those who labor to reproduce them? How in turn does this divide, which perpetuates the politics of dependence and disavowal of social reproduction, shape what it means to be a soldier in the neoliberal militarized American empire? In order to explore this aspect of the post-9/11 *Pax Americana*, I return to investigations of gender and the military. However, as we will see, gender as a category on its own is insufficient for unpacking the cultural work being done by the division of labor on military bases. Even when adjusted to incorporate dimensions of race and class, the division of labor in the neoliberal empire presents yet another factor, that of national citizenship status. When the vast majority of the people performing social reproductive labor on military bases are men emigrating from poor South Asian countries, what we have is an instance of what V. Spike Peterson (2003, 36) terms the "corollary exploitation of all who are denigrated by association with the feminine."[13] This globalized organization of reproductive labor thus raises the question of what symbolic work is being done. That is, we must consider how the "armed masculinity" of American soldiers—men *and* women—is being recoded and, in turn, precisely what kind of narrative of soldiering may be emerging.

THE REPRODUCTION OF THE AMERICAN SOLDIER IN AN AGE OF EMPIRE

With assertions linking aggressive and ambitious foreign policy with "manliness," the symbolic politics of the division of labor within the military arm of the current *Pax Americana* take on a gendered valence similar to that of earlier European empires. As many scholars of European empires have noted, the organization of domestic colonial life was a key locus for the organization of the politics of inclusion and exclusion and the distribution and demarcation of power. For instance, Cynthia Enloe (2004) has pointed out that "empires are built in allegedly 'private' places" (270). Historian Ann Stoler (2002) further explains that management of the intimate spheres of life was crucial to the symbolic politics of modern European empires; she writes, "the very categories of 'colonizer' and 'colonized' were secured through forms of sexual control that defined the domestic arrangements of Europeans and the cultural investments by which they identified themselves" (42). So, while there are great differences between the imperial adventure on the part of the United States and earlier empires, it should come as no surprise that with regard to the location of symbolic politics in the domestic sphere, there are striking parallels. The organization of the "domestic" arena of social reproduction in today's U.S. empire and the corresponding symbolic and political meanings echo the operations of the symbolic politics of demarcation in earlier European empires. In the case of American "empire," the symbolic politics emanating from the reliance on low-wage migrant labor to perform reproductive tasks is constitutive of multiple narratives: on one hand, it serves to underwrite the neoliberal privatization of today's all-volunteer military, and, on another, it serves to reinforce a neoconservative foreign policy.

With regard to legitimating a trimmed-down, privatized military, as Cerjan (2005) suggests, why not outsource social reproductive tasks that have nothing to do with the masculine role of the combat soldier? To continue to have these tasks performed "in-house" is not only inefficient as understood in economic terms but also would effeminize members of the military, thus weakening their effectiveness on the battlefield. Moreover, the outsourcing of staffing of reproductive labor to poor men from South and Southeast Asia makes a smaller force possible, which in turn makes certain kinds of U.S. involvement overseas politically viable (outsourcing security has a similar effect of keeping the number of deployed active duty personnel relatively low [Singer 2003]). Finally, in the case of an all-volunteer army, this outsourcing and the corresponding symbolic politics of disavowal facilitate recruitment in an increasingly challenging climate. Military recruitment experts suspect that recruitment would be that much more difficult if the military were still associated with the labor of "pulling KP." Michael P. Peters, executive vice-president of the Council on Foreign Relations, explains that "in order to make service more attractive, the military had to eliminate a lot of the less-glamorous aspects" of military service, including the "less-glamorous"—read feminized—tasks of cooking and cleaning (quoted in Pan 2004).

But it is also of significance that this symbolic politics reinforces the United States' aggressive foreign policy posture toward the world by way of underscoring the role of armed masculinity through the global division of reproductive labor. With regard to reinforcing neoconservative foreign policy, outsourcing plays multiple symbolic roles. It enables the U.S. armed forces to be figured first, as made up of soldiers endowed with attributes of aggressive masculinity, and second, as an apparently homogenous middle-class entity. Third, it also serves to obfuscate the realities of daily operations undertaken on the part of soldiers on behalf of an occupying power. It is of note that the severely lopsided structural conditions shaping the experience of migrant workers reinforce all of these symbolic narratives regarding members of the American armed forces.

That service members are not performing reproductive labor can function on the symbolic level to underscore a figuration of American soldiers as endowed with armed masculinity. These are precisely the kind of soldiers that KBR Vice President Paul Cerjan advocates as necessary—necessary, that is, for the task of enforcing neoconservative imperial ambitions that reverberate around the globe. This gendered dimension is of course nothing new in the cultural politics of empire. In his trenchant work on the subject, Ashis Nandy ([1983] 1988) explains that colonialism "produced a cultural consensus in which political and socio-economic dominance symbolized the dominance of men and masculinity over women and femininity" (4). Edward Said (1978) echoes this in his analysis of the gendered dimensions of orientalism as an epistemological project. As illustrated in Gustav Flaubert's nineteenth-century writings about Kuchuk Hanem, an Egyptian dancer with whom he had an affair, orientalism was undergirded by a particular form of sexual politics. Said explains:

> Flaubert's encounter with an Egyptian courtesan produced a widely influential model of the Oriental woman; she never spoke of herself, she never represented her emotions, presence, or history. *He* spoke for and represented her. He was foreign, comparatively wealthy, male, and these were historical facts of domination that allowed him not only to possess Kuchuk Hanem physically but to speak for her and tell his readers in what way she was 'typically Oriental.' . . . Flaubert's situation of strength in relation to Kuchuk Hanem was not an isolated instance. It fairly stands for *the pattern of relative strength between East and West, and the discourse about the Orient that it enabled.* (Said 1978, 6; emphasis added)

The gendered symbolic politics of U.S. empire takes multiple forms. For example, the prisoner abuse in Abu Ghraib that was brought to light certainly was produced by and in turn constituted a complex terrain of symbolic sexual politics (Kaufman-Osborn 2005; Tétreault 2006). Building on contemporary feminist applications of postcolonial scholarship to the analysis of American involvement in Iraq, I suggest that the organization of social reproductive labor on military bases may well present an additional dimension of gendered symbolic politics.

As suggested by Paul Cerjan, to have service members "pulling KP," doing laundry, cleaning the latrines, and so forth, is to disarm them—they are directed away from the attitude that would be proper for an aggressive enforcer of expansive internationalism. Deploying the politics of disavowal and displacing effeminate reproductive labor onto others reinforces the aggressive nature of armed masculinity required of such a bold and ambitious undertaking as securing America's position of preeminent global power and legitimates the privatization of the armed forces. This is not a task for the unmanly. Soldiers are reminded of this on a regular basis, several times a day in fact. The people who serve them pizza, ice cream, and hamburgers, the people who do their laundry, and the people who clean the latrines they use are *not* soldiers. For the most part, they are not women either. Here we see the symbolic politics of gender overlaid with an imperial posture toward the world. In this case, the aggressive undertaking on the part of the United States is emboldened by its masculine qualities—which in turn are emboldened by the *emasculation* of the rest of the world. This emasculation is reinforced in the staffing of devalued and disavowed reproductive labor activities on the American military base with poor men of color migrating from South and Southeast Asia making up the vast majority of these workers. The division of labor on the base also serves as a daily invocation of the orientalism of colonial projects, and the corresponding pattern of relative strength on the part of the United States in relation to the rest of the world. It is this kind of gendered symbolic politics that serves to reinforce the neoconservative foreign policy message that the United States is in a unique, but tenuous, position of preeminence. As such it is endowed with a set of global responsibilities and so must not shirk "the cause of American leadership" (Project for the New American Century 1997). This is a manly undertaking if there ever was one—in fact it reverberates with Machiavellian civic virtue in the sense that the rest of the world is figured as feminine, unequal, and in need of being directed.

In addition to demarcating gendered boundaries of who is American and who is not, this symbolic politics generates a homogenizing effect by underscoring the commonality of American nationality amongst an otherwise disparate and potentially conflict-laden group of service members. These sets of symbolic politics have a particular significance due to the nature of U.S. military service today. Endowing an all-volunteer force with the task of reinforcing America's preeminent power in global affairs entails a significant degree of symbolic politics—particularly since the actual daily tasks involved in occupation detract from the combative behavior associated with armed masculinity. The symbolic politics of social reproductive labor downplays this disconnect to avoid a crisis of identity by redirecting soldiers toward their role as masculine enforcers of *Pax Americana*.

Consider the demographics of the enlisted population that comprise the armed forces today. With regard to geography, most active duty service members are from the southern and western parts of the United States. More specifically, most are from rural communities (USGAO 2005).[14] Most service members hail from the lower-middle class, with median household incomes ranging from 30,000 to 59,999 USD. As the bipartisan National Priorities Project (2006) explains, "neighborhoods with low- to middle-median household incomes are over-represented." Most have completed high school, but far fewer have attended college (USGAO 2005). The make-up of the armed forces is racially and ethnically diverse, though only 16 percent of the forces—including active-duty and reserve forces—is made up of women service members.[15] Significantly, the members of the armed forces—the face of the U.S. empire—are not members of the elite. They are just barely, if even, members of the middle class. Instead, they are oftentimes individuals who find themselves on the downside of the globalized labor market of the United States. With the reorganization of global production and the attendant demise of urban and rural manufacturing, jobs for those without college degrees are fewer, are less secure, and are generally poorly remunerated. In a postindustrial economy, joining the military is one of the few available means of economic mobility left.

In spite of various identifications amongst service members along the lines of race, class, and gender, the contrast with TCNs on the base serves to smooth over the edges of these differences along with their potential for political disunity. This social operation of homogenizing a "we" by way of contrast with "them" permeates all imperial projects. Writing of the function of racism in nineteenth- and twentieth-century empires, historian Stoler (2002) explains, "colonial racism was more than an aspect of how people classified each other, how they fixed and naturalized the differences between We and They. It was also how people identified the affinities they shared, how they defined themselves in contexts in which discrepant interests, ethnic and class differences, might otherwise weaken consensus" (24–25). In the U.S. involvement in Iraq, the contrast with the "enemy" can perform similar work. However, in light of the elusive and ever-changing nature of this enemy, the existence on military bases of a class of non-American low-wage laborers performing devalued feminized reproductive labor serves as a meaningful site for the daily reproduction of military service members as having in common their status as *American* citizens. This is particularly important symbolic work due to the disparate racial and ethnic makeup of the armed forces, as well as the differences between rural and urban recruits. Potential contestations between service members, as well as between enlisted service members and officers, are attenuated by way of a symbolic politics that serves to reinforce what all members of the military have in common—they are Americans enjoying the semblance of a middle-class lifestyle, food courts and all.[16] This lifestyle is made possible due to the low-wage labor of non-American migrant men of color. Again, it is of note that the military services are for the most part comprised of nonelite enforcers of empire. But, on the imperial bases in theaters of war, with a low-wage class of migrant laborers performing the vast majority of the reproductive labor previously performed in their families (most likely by women—wives, mothers) these nonelite so-called "imperial grunts" (Kaplan 2005) are positioned as elites vis-à-vis service workers. Moreover, due to structural shifts in the U.S. labor market, ironically, the migrant food service workers in particular—the burger flippers at Burger King, the cashiers at "Pizza Hut Iraq," and even the barristas at Green Beans Coffee—are performing the kind of low-skilled service jobs that their enlisted customers would most likely have back in the United States were they not serving in the armed forces.

The symbolic politics of low-wage migrants performing feminized labor has served yet another purpose. In the daily operations of the U.S. involvement in Iraq, there existed the potential for a similar kind of crisis of identity found by historian Keene (2001) to have existed in World War I. In that case, noncombat soldiers socialized to be aggressive warriors struggled with the mundane and decidedly nonaggressive nature of their daily tasks. Similarly, in Iraq, as the initial war dragged into a far longer and far more complex operation of nation building, soldiers came up against the disconnect between their training as combat soldiers and their daily reality. In a documentary film on the daily life of a battalion in Iraq, Sergeant Toby Nunn expresses this frustration in an interview. Commenting on his actions vis-à-vis Iraqi police officers he believes to be working with insurgent forces, he explains that "[t]he warrior in you is telling you to go over there and whack every single one of them, engage them, let them know that you know that they're the enemy. But then, you know, the leader and politician in you is saying this is not gonna help the cause, this is not gonna win their hearts and minds" (Scranton 2008). The theater of war of the U.S. occupation of Iraq has been marked by a divided and contradictory set of tasks, with moments of combat required in the midst of what is by and large an operation of nation building. This requires soldiers to tack between the masculinized role of combat soldiers and more often something else, something akin to what is often viewed as a feminized role of nation building. It would seem likely that the symbolic politics of disavowal of feminized reproductive labor on bases across Iraq would help to smooth over the potentially jagged edges of this gendered identity crisis.

This othering operation vis-à-vis TCNs along the lines of gendered politics and of the politics of national citizenship is further reinforced by the dreadful conditions shaping the lives, choices, and work of migrant workers (also see the chapters by Chisholm, and Joachim and Schneiker in this volume). As a structural stopgap, TCNs are hired because they are willing to work for comparatively far lower wages than American citizens. Salaries range from 65–112 USD a week (Simpson and Madhani 2005). Anecdotal evidence suggests that their working conditions fall far below U.S. labor standards—and these appalling working conditions further reinforce the devaluation of the reproductive labor that these workers perform. Working long days throughout the week, TCNs are housed in comparatively poor conditions and are given inadequate food (Simpson 2006b). Moreover, these employees lose their freedom of movement, with recruitment agencies and local employers often confiscating their passports upon arrival. Identification practices on military bases include badges for all workers with their names, the names of their employers, their designated jobs, and their nationalities, one more means of marking them as distinct from U.S. service members (Simpson and Madhani 2005).[17] Along with the structural positioning of migrant workers performing devalued reproductive labor, these poor labor conditions serve to further reinforce the powerless position that migrant workers find themselves in, in contrast to the relatively powerful position of the service members of the U.S. armed forces.

This chapter aims to illustrate how the posture of U.S. foreign policy under the Bush administration has a long tradition of symbolic politics to invoke in producing a culture that reinforces the lopsided vision of the world at the core of *Pax Americana*. Gendered symbolic narratives surrounding the military have been particularly salient due to the central role the military plays in U.S. foreign policy at the outset of the twenty-first century. The modern military has always been formed by way of gendered politics, and so it should come as no surprise that a version of this symbolic politics has surfaced in the contemporary empire of bases. In addition, in today's stripped-down, neoliberal military, outsourcing is a central factor. The corresponding reliance on low-wage migrant workers to perform reproductive labor serves a structural purpose as well as a symbolic purpose. The multiple effects of this symbolic politics of disavowal ultimately support a key narrative. That is to say, the globalized division of labor on military bases helps to figure soldiers of a neoliberal, all-volunteer force as enforcers of the muscular ambitions of a foreign policy that asserts that the United States is endowed with the global responsibilities of greatness.

NOTES

1. This chapter is a slightly edited version of the article "(Re)Producing American Soldiers in an Age of Empire" by Isabelle V. Barker which originally appeared in *Politics & Gender*, volume 5, issue 2 in June 2009 (pp. 211–235). The title references the feminist political economy concept of social reproduction. Social reproduction encompasses the physical and emotional care of dependents, but it also has generally been held to include subsistence and educational activities involved in reproducing the labor force. For a thorough overview of the concept see Isabella Bakker (2007). Many thanks to Kathy Ferguson and to audience members at the panel "Families Under Fire" at the Western Political Science Association Conference 2008 for their helpful suggestions regarding an earlier version of this paper. Thanks also to the editors of *Politics & Gender* and four anonymous reviewers for their insightful comments.
2. On the global division of reproductive labor, see Ehrenreich and Hochschild (2002).

3. Exceptions include Raz (2007) on National Public Radio and Simpson's (2005, 2006a, 2006b) investigative work for the *Chicago Tribune*, both of which I rely on heavily in this chapter.
4. The military's use of the word vital to describe the work migrant laborers are performing is revealing. Vital comes from the Latin root *vitālis* meaning "functions indispensable to the maintenance of life" (*Oxford English Dictionary*)—precisely the kind of functions that fall under the feminist political economy category of social reproductive labor.
5. According to the *Dictionary of United States Army Terms* (U.S. Army 1983, 104), kitchen police refers to "military or civilian personnel detailed or hired to perform noncook duties pertaining to preliminary preparation of fruits and vegetables, sanitation and cleaning of dining facility building and equipment."
6. In the Civil War 90 percent of troops were combat troops. By World War I, this had dropped to 40 percent (Keene 2001, 39).
7. It is due to this prevailing masculinity that women in the armed forces must navigate a climate that can be hostile if not outright abusive.
8. For some, however, "empire" is a misleading term which obfuscates the unprecedented nature of the contemporary unipolar power of the United States, a power that is in fact constrained by having to operate within a world of other powerful polities, including Europe, Russia, Japan, and China. The imperial behavior of the United States toward weaker states cannot be deployed in relations with these states, thus significantly narrowing when and where the United States can act as an empire (Ikenberry 2004). This qualification on the designation of "empire" does not change the fact that regardless of the actual viability of the United States as an empire, current U.S. foreign policy has assumed an "attitude" of empire. This in turn points to the significance of symbolic narratives in underwriting this attitude.
9. Consider the difficulty the State Department has had in recruiting foreign-service officers to work in Iraq (Cooper 2007).
10. This contrasts with Paul Kennedy's (1988) notion of "imperial overstretch" to explain the demise of the British Empire.
11. This is one of many paradoxes. For example, Chalmers Johnson (2004) points to the problem of financing the U.S. empire of bases. Previous empires extracted revenue from their colonies to the point that they were self-financed. This is not the case with the U.S. empire (24–25).
12. This leads to a host of contradictions for individual women soldiers and officers navigating the gendered minefield of being viewed as too masculine and dismissed as either lesbians and/or as bitches.
13. Along these same lines, consider the wide range of gendering operations reinforcing geopolitical inequalities and conflicts. See for example, Tickner (1996), Mohanty (2003), Narayan (1997), and Goldstein (2001) among many others.
14. The 10 states with the highest rate of recruits in 2005–2006 were: Arkansas, Oklahoma, Montana, Texas, Maine, Alabama, South Caroline, North Carolina, Alaska, and Kansas. The bottom 10 (note the high representation of states in the Northeast) were Connecticut, New Jersey, DC, Delaware, Utah, Massachusetts, Vermont, Rhode Island, Minnesota, and Pennsylvania (National Priorities Project 2006).
15. According to a 2005 publication by the U.S. Government Accountability Office, the ethnic and racial makeup of the armed forces is as follows. The military has proportionately fewer whites (67%) than the civilian workforce (71%), but,

at 17%, it has more African Americans than the civilian workforce (11%). The representation of Latino/Hispanics in the armed forces has grown (9%) but remains about on par with the civilian workforce (11%). Similarly, Asian and Pacific Islanders are about equally represented in the military (3%) and in the civilian workforce (5%). The U.S. military has a policy of recruiting noncitizens and offers favorable naturalization procedures in return. Noncitizens make up 2% of the armed forces and hail primarily from the Philippines, Mexico, and Jamaica (USGAO 2005).

16. This is the case in spite of the fact that noncitizens have been recruited into the American military. While this is a notable phenomenon, noncitizens only make up 2 percent of the armed forces (USGAO 2005).

17. In addition to the troubling labor practices mentioned, the recruitment of migrant workers into Iraq is a process rife with examples of bribery, fraud, and coercion (Simpson and Madhani 2005; see also Associated Press 2007 on interventions undertaken by the International Organization for Migration).

CHAPTER 5

From Warriors of Empire to Martial Contractors

Reimagining Gurkhas in Private Security

AMANDA CHISHOLM

We are known [as] the Gurkhas all over the world . . . People understand [the Gurkha] as loyal, honest, honorable, and disciplined. The Gurkhas are very well mannered, very good person[s], very energetic. Whatever instructions come down from higher we will obey.

Kivendra, May 2009

It all comes down to the training. The raw material is key. The trick is the training that turns that raw material into someone who is incredibly disciplined and proud.

Tristan Forster, FSI Worldwide, September 2012

T he above quotations, one from an interview with a Nepalese man working as a Gurkha security contractor in private security in Kabul, the other with the director of a security company specializing in providing Gurkha security, speak to the notoriety Gurkhas have within international security and military realms.[1] They also speak to Gurkhas' ascribed racialized attributes rooted in the British Empire's colonial enterprise. Gurkhas, a group of men originating from the hills of Nepal and sharing over 200 years of military history with the British, have, like other militarized men from the global South, made their way into private security as racialized security laborers. Kivendra and other men I interviewed in

Afghanistan and Nepal are identified as Gurkhas because they are Nepalese nationals who have served within the British or Indian militaries or the Singaporean Police. The security industry seeks out Gurkha men because of their long-standing ties with western militaries; their racialized representations of being hard workers who follow orders; and their bravery, which, so the story goes, makes them more amenable to dangerous work. Labeled third-country nationals (TCNs) by security practitioners and academics, these men represent a growing labor force from the global South whose labor experiences are marked by increasingly fragile, dangerous, and flexible work. While some of these men are fortunate enough to garner management positions, most of them take up positions in static guarding and convoy protection. These positions are poorly paid, considered of lesser importance, and are often more dangerous. Importantly, a homogenous TCN security experience does not exist. More accurately, it is defined by experiences that vary depending upon how the individual men associate with and measure up to the ideal (white) security contractor. While these men and their stories remain largely absent within the mainstream literature on private military and security companies (PMSCs), their representations and participation demonstrate how the industry rests upon and reproduces racial and gender hierarchies.

This chapter examines Gurkhas who participate as TCNs in private security. Gurkhas are an interesting group of men to study. They are largely understood as martial men, deep-seated in colonial histories with the British Empire. Their notoriety has a global reach, and mention of them often brings up conflicting images of fierce little men who employ brutal tactics, yet are disciplined and loyal to their western superiors. It is these colonial attributes that make them an "easy sell" in the security industry, as well as set the terms under which they participate. Relying on colonial imaginings of martial race, security companies, agents, and Gurkhas themselves are all reconstituting the Gurkha in the realm of private security. Pictured as little men with kukris who adhere to their motto "Better to die than to be a coward," exhibiting stealth in their movements and natural fierceness in battle, these men are revered for their loyalty, determination, and courage (Bullock 2009). For the security world, the martial Gurkhas are an ideal substitute for the expensive western contractor. Westerners love these men, enemies fear them, security companies make money off them, and their participation continues, at least in part, to be constituted through colonial martial histories.

Focusing on gender and racial mechanisms within private security, this chapter is theoretically positioned within emerging scholarship in "critical gender studies in private military security" (see the introduction to this volume). Western PMSCs, western states, western security contractors, and western clients have been the main points of inquiry in critical gender studies in private military security. The experiences of men and women from the global South, and by extension, the intersectionalities of race and gender, have largely remained absent in this scholarship (with the exceptions of Barker 2009; Higate 2012e; Chisholm 2014a, 2014b; Eichler 2014; and Schneiker and Joachim as well as Barker in this volume). As a result, much of the emerging critical gender research inadvertently reinforces the discrete categories of global southern versus global northern men because it does not interrogate the practices that sustain this division. By bringing to the fore the particular techniques and histories that give rise and make intelligible particular security subjectivities, this chapter moves beyond reinforcing and naturalizing racial hierarchies.

The chapter focuses on how Gurkhas understand and negotiate their positions as TCN security laborers. I use Gurkha experiences and histories to illustrate how Gurkhas' lives were and continue to be intimately connected to the British military and are also intimately connected to western PMSCs. Drawing on interviews from my fieldwork in Afghanistan and Nepal, I argue that instead of looking at private security as a world constituted as white and western, or even as constituted by the dichotomy of global South/global North, private security industries should be understood as economies/worlds (Agathangelou and Ling 2009) where men and women from a variety of histories and situational knowledge come together to produce and reproduce fragmented and hybrid subject positions. I ask how Gurkhas and Gurkha agents understand their subject positions and make sense of their relationships with each other and with the western men who they work alongside. This analysis reveals fragmented, interconnected, and hybrid martial security contractor subjects; each interviewee seeks different ways of understanding himself and others and attempts to find personal agency in an industry that works to marginalize Gurkhas.

The remainder of this chapter is divided into five sections. The first briefly details the challenges and opportunities my ethnographic fieldwork presented and offers an introduction to the men I interviewed. Second, I describe the theoretical gender concepts I employ to help me understand and analyze in what ways gender hierarchies are produced and how Gurkhas are complicit in these productions. Section three demonstrates the importance of Gurkhas' colonial history not only in making these men intelligible to larger (mostly western) audiences but also in terms of how these men invest particular meanings into this history. The next section explores, through interview transcripts with Gurkhas, how racial logics underpinning Gurkhas' colonial histories are reproduced in contemporary private security operations. The final section examines how the Gurkhas I interviewed make sense of and find meaning in their relationships with the British and their marginalized positions within private security markets.

Security markets, observed through recruitment and marketing, highlight the different value that is placed upon Gurkhas and their skill sets. Yet, while these men are complicit in market practices, they also actively resist and adapt them, using them for their own ends. This chapter draws upon the personal stories of Gurkhas who have worked or currently work as armed private security contractors. These accounts were gathered from in-depth interviews in both one-on-one and focus group formats, with 14 Gurkhas of British, Indian, or Singaporean military/police training. The interviews took place in Kabul, Afghanistan, and Kathmandu and Pokhara, Nepal, from January to July 2008 and September 2009 through May 2010.

The interviews in Afghanistan were with Roshan, a young Indian military Gurkha who left military service to work with a security company in Afghanistan; Jitendra, a retired Singaporean police Gurkha who took up work in private security in Iraq and Afghanistan; a focus group with Fabien, Tek, and Tikaraj, three Indian Gurkhas who left service with the Indian military to work in private security; Rabindra, a retired Indian army Gurkha who currently works in Afghanistan; and Pun, a young Gurkha who left the Indian military to work in Kabul. Further interviews conducted in Nepal included a focus group with four former British military Gurkhas: Kivendra, Kitendra, Jitendra, and Randhoj. These men have worked in private security in Angola, Iraq, and Afghanistan but currently live in Nepal. The interviews were complemented by 10 months of participatory observations of security contractors in Afghanistan. Combining observations with interviews allowed me to gain a deeper insight into how Gurkhas understand contending masculinities and representations of themselves and others within PMSCs. The research revealed complexities of identity formation, acts of resistance, and ways of seeking agency.

Ethnography is a method that is used by many feminist scholars (Skeggs 2009). While a particular feminist ethnographic method does not exist, what makes ethnographies feminist is a focus on the ethical and political aspirations of specific research projects, borne out of feminism and feminist debates over epistemology, constructions of knowledge from multiple locations, and research ethics (Skeggs 2009, 429; Hemmings 2012; J. Tickner 2013). As such, feminists have sought to situate themselves in their research (through participation and nonparticipant observations) and to write themselves into their research through reflexivity.[2] These strategies are applied with the political aspirations of disrupting power practices embedded in the research process and to draw upon the importance of the researcher's positionality in understanding the meanings behind social concepts and the ways in which the research community has a stake in the research being produced (Skeggs 2009, 426; Hemmings 2012).

Conversely, even with the best feminist intentions to pay attention to gendered power relations, ethnography is not a perfect methodology and can reproduce the silences and inequalities the researcher seeks to expose (Vrasti 2008). Ethnography has a past deeply embedded in colonial knowledge production, which reinforced and perpetuated historical power imbalances. It was a central method used to understand and know the Gurkha at the time the British military sought to employ Gurkhas in its colonial army throughout Asia (Caplan 1995; Streets 2004). The irony of using a method that was integral to the initial shaping and knowing of Gurkhas and to positioning them as subordinate to the British in the very Gurkha communities I sought to understand, was not lost on me.

We can stand to learn much about power by not only understanding the colonial history of ethnography but also by reflecting on how research is produced through intersubjectivities and practices of power in the interactions between the researcher and the researched (Ramazanoglu and Holland 2002, 118; Pintchman 2009). Such a reflexive strategy requires one to pay attention to "how the researcher is socially situated, and how the research agenda/process has been constituted" (Ramazanoglu and Holland 2002, 118). Reflexivity also offers a trustworthy and dependable account of how research was produced. By placing oneself in one's research, the reader is able to understand the particular set of social conditions and contexts that have led the researcher to her particular conclusions and analysis (Higate and Cameron 2006, 223). Through this, we "become answerable for what we learn and how we see" (Haraway 1988, 583, quoted in Gunaratnam 2003, 33). Not only does reflexivity offer a transparent account of our research, it also disrupts power practices and the privilege of the researcher that is embedded in all research projects (Skeggs 2009).

To this end, it is worth noting that I am a white, English-speaking, middle-class Canadian woman. I have military experience—I served for five years in the Canadian Armed Forces (CAF) as a medical assistant. My background afforded me as many opportunities as it presented challenges. From the onset of my research I was an outsider to the Gurkha military family, a military family deep-seated in colonial history. With only four years to *know* the men constituted as Gurkhas, I could only begin to forge a relationship with and understanding of them and their histories. Yet my accounts and understandings of these men are mediated through my background as a white middle-class Canadian woman with some military experience, and through my identification as an academic researcher with the men I interviewed.

During my fieldwork, I was situated in a highly masculinized space (cf. Cohn 2007, 97), predominantly containing men with former military experience working in private security. The insider community I was researching distinguished civilians from security contractors with military backgrounds, although this distinction became more dynamic and multilayered the more I became immersed in the community. My gendered subjectivity as a young civilian woman, seen as nonthreatening, allowed me certain access to security contractors and made me privy to conversations that others may have been excluded from. Specifically, many of the men I interviewed (either formally or informally) were very forthcoming with their personal experiences, insights about the security industry, their positions, and their understandings of Gurkhas in the industry. My status as a white, middle-class, and young female academic who was "out there" in Afghanistan garnered a lot of credibility, resulting in fairly substantial, generous, and forthcoming responses.

STRIKING A BALANCE: NEGOTIATIONS OF HEGEMONIC MASCULINITIES AND SUBALTERN MASCULINITIES

Private security contractors are predominantly men and the industry is highly masculinized. Yet, as others in this volume also show, this does not mean that the security industry produces a monolithic understanding of masculinities or that all men in the industry have equal amounts of power. Marysia Zalewski (2010) argues that a feminist engagement with masculinities reveals "the varying and contradictory ways that masculinities are weaved through the theories and practices of international politics" (37). V. Spike Peterson (2007) explores masculinities in international relations by emphasizing "affective investments and the mutual constitution of subject formation" (10). Subject formation determines who we are, how we think, and what we do as men and women. Thinking through the intersections of gender, class, and race highlights how gender coding not only privileges some men but also how some masculinities are understood to be more appropriate than others (Peterson 2007).

Masculinities within private security are constituted through colonial histories. These histories produce a hierarchy of men and masculinities demarcated largely along lines of the global North versus the global South. Raewyn Connell (2005) is one of the pioneering scholars in masculinities studies who explores colonial gendered relations among men. Connell provides a historical gender analysis as she traces the violent practices that were carried out by westernized men (such as soldiers, sailors, traders, administrators, and missionaries) from the metropolis. The frontier masculinities embodied by these men often resulted in sexual exploitation of local women and in the establishment of new economic and administrative systems, significantly changing local men and masculinities through these processes (Connell 2005, 75; also see Fanon 1967; Streets 2004; Morrell and Swart 2005; Ouzgane and Morrell 2005).

These colonial processes do not simply work top down, as local men negotiate their subject positions. The postcolonial masculinities literature tends to argue that the west (the white man) continues to exercise power over developing countries (nonwhite man) as a result of colonial legacies. Postcolonial masculinities and discourses surrounding them produce and sustain representations of gender and actual men "that serve to create, perpetuate and reinforce First World norms of masculinities and heterosexuality" as an ideal (Stanovsky 2007, 495). As indicated by Andrea Schneiker and Jutta Joachim in this volume, the archetypal security contractor continues in the image of the white, specially trained, western man. Yet, like the Gurkha, this image does not come into play without a history or an immediate relation to national and global politics in which the western security contractor finds himself. The dominant white, western contractor masculinities rely on colonial logics that constitute and, at the same time, silence racialized others. White men garner employment with PMSCs largely as a result of their experience with western militaries. Their years of service, military skills, and time spent in hostile environments determine whether they can move into commercial security in places like Afghanistan and Iraq. A part of the postcolonial commitment, as depicted by Anna Agathangelou and Heather Turcotte (2010), a commitment this chapter shares, is to demystify and denaturalize these seemingly geographically positioned global North (white) and global South (nonwhite) subjectivities and histories.

Gurkhas, like the TCNs described by Joachim and Schneiker in this volume, are represented by the security industry as lacking the necessary (white) security skill sets to garner the higher paid and higher status security positions. Not only are their experiences considered nonstandard or out-of-date, the security managers and directors I interviewed maintained that the inability of Gurkhas to fluently converse in English impeded their ability to effectively communicate with clients. Similarly, many security company country managers in Kabul expressed a need for security contractors to maintain a competency in English business culture, which meant a security contractor could easily converse with a client, exude confidence in their ability to protect (even if they were not overly confident), understand sarcasm and humor, and socially relate to westerners (author's communications with representatives from IDG Security, CRG, AEGIS, ASI Security, and FSI Worldwide Jan.–Jul. 2009). This desired skill set reinforces the white security contractor as the ideal and positions the TCN as forever lacking.

Where western security contractors are valued as a result of their military training and acquired professional skills, Gurkhas are valued on the basis of their raw/natural talents, which have been further refined through their military experience. The distinction is important as Gurkhas continue to be seen as raw security contractor talent, not highly skilled professionals. In interviews and conversations, when I asked why martial men are more suitable

TCN security labor, industry practitioners and managers in Afghanistan and Nepal pointed to these men's military training and biological martial attributes, which are seen to provide them with discipline and the ability to handle (without complaint) the monotony of long hours standing in front of buildings or driving vehicles in remote (and often hostile) settings.

Such representations of Gurkhas can also be found on Gurkha security company websites. The rebranded representations of Gurkhas, drawing upon a shared military history with the British and reinforcing their raw and natural martial talents and physical robustness, appear on a variety of PMSC websites such as Gurkha Security Services, G4S Gurkha Services, and Everest Security. These companies' websites, like popular books about Gurkhas, illustrate to the public audience who Gurkhas are and how they are to be understood.[3] They also underscore the historical martial roots of Gurkhas either through direct quotations from former British officers or through colonial images of these men. The consistent message is that Gurkha men carry timeless virtues of bravery, heartiness, and loyalty. The repeated references to the long martial history and association of Gurkhas with the British contribute to a commodification of Gurkhas as unique martial TCNs, made intelligible through their shared colonial history with the British.

COLONIAL IMAGININGS: THE BEGINNINGS OF THE GURKHA

The British began to know and define Gurkhas as martial during their military and colonial operations along the Nepalese border in the early nineteenth century. British officers at the time wrote about these "mysterious hill men" with admiration for their military skill and ridicule for their lack of military equipment. As British colonial expansion came in direct conflict with Nepalese expansionist policies, the British finally went to war against Nepal in 1814. It was during this two-year war that the Gurkha martial race was constructed and documented by the British. Most documented was how these "fierce men" could hold up against such a formidable British force for so long with very little military equipment. British military writers claimed their natural fierceness, commitment, and fortitude accounted for their bravery in battle (Pemble 1971; Caplan 1995; Coleman 1999; Bullock 2009).

After the war, the British identified biological fierceness in certain communities of Nepalese men and actively recruited them under the Nepalese government's radar. A Nepalese man who sought employment with the British Indian army would travel across the Nepalese border into India (Des Chene 1991). Here he would be measured, weighed, and assessed based on notions of sexual prowess, martial performance, and cultural heritage (Tucker 1957; Coleman 1999). Despite the belief of British officers in Gurkhas' martial abilities and their loyalty to the British, Gurkhas were only used in small numbers and regiments within the British Indian army. During the Great Sepoy Mutiny in May of 1857,[4] the Gurkhas proved their loyalty to the British by refusing to side with the Bengal army mutineers and Indian national deserters. It was after this mutiny, and in subsequent battles, that the Gurkha reputation for being martial, disciplined, loyal, fierce, and subservient to the British was solidified (Coleman 1999; Roy 2001). For British officers fighting alongside Gurkhas, Gurkhas "would in every way be [a] more efficient, courageous and trustworthy body of men than any to be had in the plains" (E. Drummend, magistrate of Dinajpur, quoted in Smanta 1996, 25). Both military writings of Gurkha valor and the scientific classification of Gurkhas were coupled with specific institutional practices involving detailed dress, histories of recruitment, and military ceremonies (Caplan 1995; Streets 2004; Kochhar-George, 2010). Military writings of their valor during war throughout Europe, Asia, and Southeast Asia further entrenched the popular representation of the Gurkha as the gentleman soldier who was steadfast, fierce, and feared by the enemy but kind, loyal, and hospitable to his British leaders. In fact this representation of the Gurkha remains so strong today that, as J. P. Cross and Buddhiman Gurung (2007, 27) succinctly capture, Gurkhas are not inherently fearless but are afraid to show fear. These writings, ideologies, and institutional practices turned racialized men into a race of men.

The construction of martial men was not simply a process whereby the colonizer bestowed practices and images upon the colonized men. Gurkhas were complicit in the construction of their reputations and identities. These men were able to economically provide for their families and their communities through employment with the British and Indian armies (Enloe 1981; Des Chene 1991). Lionel Caplan (1995) argues that the employment of Gurkhas with the British Indian army resulted in substantial social changes in the villages to which they returned. These men were able to challenge the social hierarchy founded in class/caste structures in Nepal—often to the frustration of Nepalese elites (Caplan 1995; Des Chene 1991). They did this by returning from a career with the British military with a pension that allowed them to economically move up the class hierarchy, which was very difficult to achieve in Nepal (Caplan 1995). Many Gurkhas built expensive homes and financially supported their communities. Their ability to provide financially increased their status, and this status continues today, as a sense of exceptionalism amongst Gurkhas was repeatedly highlighted in my interviews.

While the number of Gurkhas in the British military service is decreasing, their popularity in the Indian army remains unquestionable (Khalidi 2001/02). Gurkhas' martial notoriety also provides them an easy entry into private security. Interestingly, with their entry into private security, newly emerging representations of the Gurkha are coming to the fore. The colonial and seemingly static understanding of these men is, in fact, unstable. The new privatized Gurkha identities are constructed through a dynamic and relational process involving Gurkhas, their agents, security companies, and clients who consume their racial representations. All these actors work to produce hybrid forms of collective and individual Gurkha identities.

FROM MARTIAL MEN TO RACIAL CONTRACTORS

Often Gurkhas are recruited for armed security work through word of mouth. Recruitment is established in regions of the country that are known to have large Gurkha settlements, and very few recruitment agents publicly advertise. The Nepalese Gurkha agents are in positions of power, acting as gatekeepers for Nepalese men seeking economic opportunities with western security companies. Many Gurkhas working with PMSCs have served in the Indian military and have had to seek out Gurkha security agents in Nepal to assist them in gaining employment in private security. For these men, finding reputable agents can be difficult and can have drastic implications for their work experiences abroad. Some more fortunate Gurkhas access the security industry through immediate connections with British national white men, formerly Gurkha officers in British military Gurkha regiments, who are in management positions with security companies.

Sante, an Indian Gurkha with 22 years of military experience, was new to the private security industry. In our interview he talked about the circumstances of his recruitment: "I placed my document in Kathmandu, and then the man there told me that this man from [the] UK was coming, and I should come for [an] interview." Sante's wife agreed to let him work abroad for a limited time, although he wanted to stay in Afghanistan as long as his contract would allow. Sante was recruited through a company that solely works with Gurkhas. The owner, a former British Gurkha officer working with the Singaporean police Gurkhas, started his business with the aspiration to create job opportunities for Gurkhas in the private security sector. Sante managed to find employment via an agent working directly for this security company, and Sante remained quite positive about his working conditions and experiences.

Other Nepalese men were not as fortunate as Sante and had to go through third-party agents to get contracts in Afghanistan. These Gurkhas experience a higher risk of exploitation from the agents. Sante explained that "agents are getting a bunch of money from these men and these men's families to get over here and [these men] then have [few] opportunities." He further commented that "the Nepali Gurkha is so happy that someone will get him a job and will immediately trust . . . him." As Sante surmised, it is important to be vigilant. Another interviewee, Fabien, further described how finding the right agent has immediate implications on one's living and working conditions while in Afghanistan. He stated that "sometimes work opportunities promised are OK, and sometimes they are not. Sometimes a Gurkha is staying at a local camp and we need money and we call our family [to] please send us 1,000 dollars [because] we are hungry. Sometimes there are visa problems, and the Gurkha is sent to jail." For many Gurkhas, the agent remains the vital link for contract opportunities.

This vital link opens up space for the Gurkha contractor to be exploited. Both security managers in Afghanistan and Gurkhas themselves told me in great detail of Nepalese men who pay considerable amounts of money to come to Afghanistan for work. Once they arrive in the country, they are often without the proper work visa and have no support in finding employment (Gurkha focus group in Kabul, Feb. 2010). Interviewees also told stories of Nepalese farmers who came to Afghanistan and had been promised jobs as Gurkha security contractors, but found themselves without work, work permits, or cash, yet owed an agent back in Nepal a lot of money. Bishal, a Gurkha agent working in Afghanistan, had met many men in this precarious situation and commented on the overall economic and political concerns these men face:

You know [that it is difficult to work] in this market nowadays. Everywhere guys are cheating each other. Gurkhas [trust too easily and invest] a lot of money to come [to Afghanistan]. When they get here they find themselves without the proper documentation to work. So many guys come to me because they have lost a lot of money, [owe their respective agents, and have no means to pay their debts]. They meet me because I have a registered company, and I try to get them a job. Unscrupulous agents are easily cheating Gurkhas over here, and we [don't have] any embassy or consultancy [to aid these Gurkhas]. Our embassy is in Islamabad in Pakistan, and sometimes we deal with them [but it remains difficult]. If we run into a problem, we have no one to take care of ourselves.

Conversely, not everyone obtained work through agents. In a focus group with Jitendra and Randhoj, they detailed that the men who had served as British Gurkhas or in the Singaporean police relied on their relationships with their former British commanders who were employed in private security (referred to in interviews as their second career in security). Jitendra explained:

I did not have such a problem. First my second career was [in] Angola . . . there was a British major, a retired major that served in our own regiment, and we went through him. We had no problem and no payment . . . not even a single payment . . . and [a] second [position] in Yugoslavia, no problem. The same major came here as well . . . I went to Afghanistan by the time a British guy came and I interviewed and they said: "We like you and we will take you there but you have to pass your medical. It will cost you 3,000 rupees, and once you [have] passed you will be reimbursed." But I have no knowledge of [contractors who pay agents and experience labor exploitation]. So I went through the British people. I didn't pay any money. This is my story.

While some men can secure a contract without paying, they continue to rely on colonial relations. As Jitendra commented, "my old commander request[ed] me . . . [to] come here. [I responded:] OK, I will go sir, I will obey your orders.'" Order, loyalty, and discipline for the British officer were important factors that secured Jitendra work in the security industry.

It is not only the relationships with British and western company managers that are important in determining the type of contract and conditions of possibility that Gurkhas have access to within the industry. Gurkhas are also assessed on the basis of their military skills, an assessment that relies on the ideal western military contractor. Bharat, a former British Gurkha who owns a Gurkha manpower agency that provides Gurkhas for larger security companies, discussed in detail how Gurkhas are assessed for private security. Bharat classified Gurkhas into three categories: A, B, and C. Category A refers to Gurkhas from the Nepalese military or with Indian army experience. These Gurkhas are seen to have limited ability to converse in English and are primarily hired for security work in Nepal or India but may also go to Afghanistan. Category B refers to Gurkhas who speak English well and who work primarily for western clients. They earn a salary of 750 USD to 1,000 USD a month and are often contracted to places in Africa. Category C was reserved for Gurkhas who excelled in their professional background as well as in their ability to converse in English. These men would go to the highest-paid positions with clients in Bahrain and Afghanistan. These men could command anywhere from 900 USD to 2,000 USD a month.

In contrast, when it comes to unarmed security, the image of Gurkhas is more fluid and the guidelines for recruitment are much less strict. In the unarmed security market, women can also be contracted as Gurkhas. Quatta, a former Gurkha stationed in Hong Kong and now an owner of a security company in Nepal, marketed both men and women in unarmed security. Quatta went into business with a former British Gurkha officer who also worked with Gurkhas in Hong Kong. These men specialize in providing unarmed Gurkhas to cruise lines. Quatta claimed that Gurkha, as a historical colonial image of a fierce soldier coming from a landlocked country, was not a difficult sell to the cruise lines. For his company, he and his British officer counterpart stressed the trustworthiness, heartiness, and loyalty attributes of the Gurkha. These attributes could transcend gendered bodies, and therefore both women and men were actively recruited.

NEGOTIATING "ALMOST BUT NOT WHITE": GURKHAS' UNDERSTANDINGS OF SELF AND OTHER

Gurkhas' experiences of being recruited and vetted validate and reproduce a white privilege within the industry. Consequently, much of Homi Bhabha's (2004) analysis of the colonial relationship and mimicry whereby the colonial subject is constituted "as a subject of difference that is almost the same but not quite" resonates here (122). Gurkhas like other TCNs continue to be "almost but not white" (as also discussed by Joachim and Schneiker in this volume). They are positioned in relation to their white security contractor counterparts. The white contractors assume the benchmark against which Gurkhas are measured and their value as security laborers is determined. The men who have a closer personal relationship with their white managers or who closely mimic the archetypal white security contractor in skill sets and behaviors enjoy more opportunities and material benefits. However, as a result of Gurkhas' colonial reputations and exotic subject positions, no Gurkha could ever be constituted as the same as their white counterparts. Gurkhas' positions within PMSCs are reminiscent of Bhabha's (1994) concept of "almost the same but not quite" (122). This concept is used to describe the ambivalent position of the colonized vis-à-vis his white colonizer other, where ambivalence both ruptures and creates alternative spaces in the colonial discourse. Gurkhas' ambivalent relations to their western others illuminate the colonial tension upon which colonial enterprise rests—tension that attempts both to fix Gurkhas as natural martial and to transform (modernize) them into exceptional (almost white) security contractors.

Each Gurkha I interviewed dealt differently with his almost-but-not-white position in the security industry. They were all proud of their Gurkha history, and, at the same time, they recognized their subordinate status vis-à-vis their white counterparts. Overall, interviewees reinforced the ideal of the white western security contractor, yet there was not much support for the vast material differences between Gurkhas and westerners. In many of my interviews, Gurkhas expressed a general frustration with how security companies were using the Gurkhas' global reputation and selling them as ideal while paying them very little in comparison to westerners. Murat explained: "I don't know why there is such a big difference in pay and living . . . I know the British are [better] educated than us and are more professional than us and in that case the salary could be different. But in some cases, Nepalese are talented and educated but even they are not getting that salary." The pay was not the only source of frustration, interviewees also felt that they were not treated as well once they were working in Afghanistan and had little negotiating power to improve their conditions. Here Fabien commented:

> It is fine, not bad, but there is also huge discrimination between expats [westerners] and third-country nationals in the salary and also the living and clothing is different. Like the expats used to stay in [single] room[s], and we are staying in one room for five to six people. There is different dining and different food and different drinks. Whatever food is in the kitchen they [the westerners] can take whenever they want but we cannot. We have specific times. Always one food, same meal every day.

The Gurkhas who did not completely accept the colonial logics of difference in living and working conditions were additionally frustrated over their inability to change their immediate situation. For example, Rabindra rhetorically asked: "I feel bad, but what to do?" He claimed he could not raise concerns because "if you do you will be kicked out." Many Gurkhas appeared to have an overall frustration with the global private security industry and their lack of agency within its structure. Rabindra commented on this situation: "The security companies are getting the contracts because of the Gurkha. They convince their clients that we are good, but these same companies have cheated us. This is because they are using your name and yet you are treated completely different."

How Gurkhas understand their representations and experiences within private security is far from simple. Many move into private security work because it offers them not only financial incentives, regardless of the significant pay gap between them and their western counterparts, but also a space to claim and live their martial masculinities. For Gurkhas like Tek and Fabien, working in private security reinforced their martial attributes as being somehow biological. Being a Gurkha, they felt, was in their blood, and it was a calling. These men believed and stated that there was something exceptional about their martial status. For them, white men had to be trained, whereas the Gurkha had natural attributes that only needed to be harnessed. Gurkhas could learn certain skills from their white mentors, but those white men could never have the natural warrior spirit that was in the Gurkha bloodline. Their masculinities were wrapped up in a warrior understanding of self and a sense of natural physical strength and mental courage in battle, things extensively written about in many Gurkha officer memoirs.[5]

These Gurkhas drew upon their reputations for uncompromising bravery to redefine their subordination as TCN security contractors. It allowed them to construct an identity as strong martial men; men who were stronger and braver than a lot of white westerners who worked from fortified places, whereas the Gurkhas sought work in dangerous parts of Afghanistan and Iraq. Cross and Gurung (2007), in a detailed discussion of interviews with retired Gurkhas, provide a thought-provoking analysis of how, while Gurkhas are not fearless, their fear of showing fear is strong (27). The authors cite one Gurkha claiming: "[I]f you think you'll get back home, you'll be no use in war. You're only any use if you think you won't get back" (26). This quotation and others like it place a great deal of emphasis on the resolve to face death. The men I interviewed shared similar stories, passed down by their fathers, uncles, and grandfathers. Their understanding of their masculinity and of what it means to be a Gurkha is wrapped up in histories and long-held views of how to behave in the face of violence and possible death. Showing fear was simply not an option.

The brave and fierce imagery of the Gurkha embodied in this particular masculinity helps Gurkhas cope with dangerous incidents they encountered in their private security work. When I asked Kavijdra how he felt about performing dangerous tasks in Afghanistan, he stated that "we are already Gurkhas, and this is how they [our forefathers] got their name." Recounting the Gurkha motto, Kavijdra continued: "[I]t is better to die than to be a coward. We are also afraid of dangerous things, but we have to still put the name Gurkha forward and do these dangerous jobs. Because my grandfather and father [have] done this, so we have to." Not wanting to tarnish the Gurkha reputation, this man accepted most tasks his employer assigned him. Rather than not being afraid, he was determined not to show fear (cf. Cross and Gurung 2007; also Des Chene 1991). For most of the men I interviewed, fear was something to suppress in order to perform their jobs. Exposure to violence and danger were articulated as part of the job—a job they freely signed onto and that their fathers and grandfathers had performed. Fear was also not to be shown in private spaces with family. In many interviews, Gurkhas working in Afghanistan claimed to downplay the level of potential violence to their family in order to ease family concerns. One interviewee claimed that there was no need to feel fear since Gurkha bravery kept them safe. He then explained that, to the date of the interview, there had not yet been a Gurkha fatality. Any feelings of fear were reassured and silenced by affirming the formidable martial attributes of the Gurkha, which provided them with bravery and kept them alive.

Some Gurkhas I interviewed expressed a commitment to taking more dangerous work in Afghanistan and Iraq in order to protect their white managers. They felt they were in a better position to protect white contractors because of their better cultural understanding of Afghans (being Asian and nonwestern) as well as their martial roots. The gendered divide between the male protector and female protected discussed by Judith Hicks Stiehm (1982) is being challenged in private security practices (Higate 2011; also see Eichler's and Higate's chapters in this volume). My research suggests that the protector/protected relationship is more dynamic than the male/female dichotomy indicates. Specifically, the protector subjectivity is used by

Gurkhas to reclaim their martial masculinities, which have been devalued by their subaltern status in private security markets. Cynthia Enloe (2007, 93–115) pays particular attention to the ways feminization is used to devalue and humiliate particular men (as in the case of the Abu Ghraib torture and abuse scandal) but does not focus on how feminization is also used by the devalued and racialized man to reclaim his own authority, self-respect, and dignity. Interviews with white British national, former Gurkha officers within British military Gurkha regiments, who are now security company owners, and with Gurkhas themselves, indicate that both groups of men use the protector/protected discourse to assert their own masculinities. British Gurkha officers feminize Gurkhas by retelling colonial histories, marking Gurkhas as underdeveloped and in need of mentoring. They further feminize them in the security industry by stating that these men need Gurkha officers to provide them with economic opportunities and manage them properly— reducing the potential for them to be exploited by unscrupulous Nepalese agents. In response, Gurkhas feminize their western managers by assuming the protector role in operations on the ground in hostile environments. These men reclaim their masculinities (and their self-respect) by appropriating the devalued roles of static guard and convoy protection, arguing that it is their instincts and knowledge of local culture, not their feminized, devalued skill sets, that position them in these peripheral and dangerous places. They are in these places to protect their western managers. The potential for violence and exposure to danger reinforced for many of the men interviewed their martial masculinities. It offered them a space to regain authority and practice power in the protection of their western managers and clients.

Conversely, other Gurkhas recognized the paradoxical and unstable nature of their representation and participation in the industry. Men like Jitendra and Randhoj saw working in the security industry as something short term and as a sacrifice in order to provide an education for their children. Jitendra spoke highly of his four daughters and one son, three of them at universities in the United States and Australia. He was very impressed that I was doing a PhD. For him, education meant a better material life because it enabled more opportunities in the global market. Education was the tool required to financially take better care of your family and community. He stated that he had become a Gurkha because he had failed in school. When I asked him if he encourages his son to become a Gurkha, he said that he did not talk to his son much about his work because he would prefer him not to become a Gurkha. Jitendra continued: "Without education you cannot get anything. If you can't study, you don't have a future. So what I did for my children [is] I did a time set. You come from school you have to eat then you have to study, and I always check their homework and their bags to make sure they are good. I always go to see their teachers and the principal to see how they are doing." Jitendra expressed a sincere desire to have the Gurkha martial identity end with him.

Others interviewed such as Bharat and Randhoj agreed with his point of view. Yet for others, Gurkha identity lay somewhere in-between a realized commodified construction necessary to meet family educational needs and something biological or a calling within them. A few men I interviewed over a period of several months told me that they were proud of their Gurkha service and bragged about being part of a particular regiment. They did not necessarily see being a Gurkha as something in their blood but as something deeply rooted in their family or community history. Whilst Gurkhas have been constructed through colonial practices and imagery, they believe that they continue the Gurkha reputation through their conduct during military service and through their work in private security.

GURKHAS CONSTITUTING PRIVATE SECURITY
WORLDS: CONCLUDING THOUGHTS

Exploring Gurkhas through a postcolonial frame allows us to see the myriad subject positions of private security contractors. The preceding analysis highlights the pervasive nature of colonial logics that continue to operate in the background of the industry by framing the conditions of possibility for men working in private security. While the example of Gurkhas shows that the security industry benefits from and works to sustain a heavily racialized form of governance, it also shows that there is room for resistance and appropriation. Interrogating not only why these men participate but also how they, while at the margins, use their ingenuity to achieve "the good life" is an important line of inquiry if we want to see alternative ways of being.

The interviews show that being a Gurkha is associated with the ability to provide financially for one's family. It also affirms masculinity and access to authority. It provides a valuable sense of history and pride, an identity that offers comfort and strength in the physically dangerous situations in which Gurkhas find themselves through their private security work. While their martial history and identity as a Gurkha provides these men with esteem and a sense of belonging, they nonetheless have to negotiate the pecking order in the international security market. While some men successfully claim their self-worth by assuming the role of protector and by enduring the violence that many expats do not expose themselves to, their vulnerability and the hierarchy of labor are revealed when they become physically injured and are unable to continue to work. The lack of social networks and programs, found in most western countries but unavailable to them as Nepalese nationals, makes their ability to work even more paramount and means any loss of work through injury is to be feared.

Like other martial men, such as Fijians and Chileans, Gurkhas continue to access private security markets as a result of their martial race (in contrast to other men from the global South who might be denied access and perform reproductive labor instead, see the chapter by Barker in this volume). Their marketability is attributed to their long history of military service involving exemplary courage and commitment to the British military as well as the discourse centering on Gurkhas as cheaper and therefore desirable alternatives to white westerners. Their employment in private security is being disrupted in Afghanistan through the employment of other racialized contractors such as Ugandans and Fijians. Fijians in particular are increasingly garnering contracts in private security in Iraq and Afghanistan largely because of the same discursive basis that brands the Gurkhas (MacLellan 2007).

The rise of alternative martial men comes at a time when Gurkhas are becoming more politically mobilized and are fighting for equal treatment in Nepal and in the UK. Certainly their understanding of inequalities, their research, and their mobilization afford them the chance to settle in the UK, to advance educational and employment opportunities for their children, and to allow them better life choices within Nepal. Unfortunately, their individual and group mobilizations do not appear to be dismantling the oppressive system that provides marginal opportunities to subaltern men. As Gurkhas seek greater political and economic opportunities for themselves and their families, another racialized group—one that is willing to work under worse conditions than the Gurkha—will likely come to fill their role in the neoliberal private security market.

NOTES

1. Both quotations are from author interviews.
2. Feminist ethnography has been informed by debates within feminism more generally that are historically situated. Skeggs (2009, 429) for example details how during the 1980s radical feminism informed feminist ethnography and the point of ethnography was to research and write women into male-stream knowledge and knowledge production. Today, a poststructural understanding of gender and the importance of seeing how social categories of women and men relate to ideologies of masculinities and femininities inform much feminist research.
3. The Gurkha Security Services' website (http://gurkhasecurityservices.co.uk) details the services they offer within the UK. It also makes reference to Gurkha martial attributes and their origins in the Anglo-Nepalese war. The Everest Security's website (http://www.everestsecurity.co.uk) also points the viewer to the Gurkhas' martial attributes and makes reference to the "colonial" Gurkha through black-and-white photos of Gurkhas serving in the British colonial army. Like Gurkha Security Services, the services that Everest Security offers involve not only security but also cleaning services, largely geared to the UK client. The Global Gurkha Security Services' website (http://globalgurkhasecurity.com) draws attention, through images, not to colonial histories but to more recent Gurkha military experience in contemporary British military operations. They,

like the two aforementioned companies, employ British Gurkhas and appear largely for the UK audience. Finally, the G4S Gurkha Services website (http://www.g4s.uk.com/gurkhaservices/) draws attention to Gurkhas' management style and notes that all managers are former British army officers. The images associated are more modern and do not make reference to colonial Gurkha histories yet cite their martial attributes of discipline and honor.

4. The Great Sepoy Mutiny refers to an internal Bengal army revolt as a result of growing religious and labor grievances the Indian nationals had against their British officers. It resulted in a mass desertion of Indian nationals from the Bengal army and an armed revolt. The British revere Gurkhas for their loyalty to the British during this mutiny and their taking up of arms against the Indian mutineers. Military historians and British Gurkha officers alike refer to this mutiny as the defining moment where Gurkhas' martial attributes and their loyalty to the British were cemented in history. For further details of the mutiny and changing British attitudes toward mass recruitment of Gurkhas into the British Indian army, please refer to Bullock (2009, 28–41) and Coleman (1999, 197).

5. See, for example, Parker (1999), Cross and Gurung (2007), and Bullock (2009).

CHAPTER 6

The License to Exploit

PMSCs, Masculinities, and Third-Country Nationals

JUTTA JOACHIM AND ANDREA SCHNEIKER

Military and war are sites were gendering takes place through the construction of masculinities. Because the multiple forms of masculinity that exist in these militarized spaces " . . . depend . . . on the clear dichotomy of *us* versus *them*" (Sharoni 2008, 152), they can be conceived of "as a discourse of power" (151) and "discourses of domination" (152). Common dichotomies constitutive of dominant masculinities in the context of war and the military have historically been that of "peaceful women/bellicose men," "protector/protected," or "colonizer/colonized" (152). However, complex demands posed upon states by the changed nature of warfare and the multidimensional character of peacekeeping missions increasingly require "hybrid" forms of masculinity (Mannitz 2011, 690). Today, soldiers have to be warrior, peacekeeper, humanitarian aid worker, and manager all at the same time. As we have illustrated elsewhere (Joachim and Schneiker 2012a) PMSCs can be regarded as "masculinity multipliers" in this respect. They help states and their militaries negotiate the various, and sometimes contradictory, roles they have to perform in the course of international interventions, allowing them to claim accepted forms of masculinity and ones that help boost their image, such as the peacekeeper and the manager, and outsource the less accepted ones, like the warrior, to the private sector (Joachim and Schneiker 2012a; also see Barker's chapter in this volume on the outsourcing of social reproductive work). However, rather than simply absorbing lesser valued masculinities, PMSCs also compete and therefore take part with state militaries in what Steve Niva (1998) refers to as "complex struggles to define and control individual and collective identities as well as domestic and international political orders" (111).

Like states and their militaries, PMSCs strive for hegemonic masculinity and they construct, or rather, assert it by setting themselves apart, claiming their superiority in opposition to a different "other" or by appropriating desired masculinity attributes from a different "other." State militaries and mercenaries play an important role in this respect. "Compared to the latter, PMSCs claim to provide security in a professional, ethical manner and to care about the world rather than profits. Unlike states, PMSCs pride themselves on being able to offer all-encompassing protection and of having the resolve to go anywhere, at anytime, whatever the risks entailed" (Joachim and Schneiker 2012a, 507). In this chapter we illustrate that "othering," in the sense of asserting one's own masculinity while questioning and/or devaluing that of other actors, takes place not only with respect to security actors outside the PMSC industry but also within and among companies that belong to it. As such, PMSCs together with other multinational corporations constitute new "transnational arenas . . . where hegemonic and subordinate masculinities are constructed" (Connell 2005, 849) and in which the global gender order is currently reconfigured. They are characterized, according to Raewyn Connell (2012), by a "strong gender division of labor and a strongly masculinised management culture" (4). The recruitment of third-country nationals (TCNs) from the global South is exemplary of this gender order. Several companies, especially those that carry out logistics and other support activities, mainly recruit men from the global South because of their cheap labor.

While the hiring of TCNs is often silenced, PMSCs assert that their Western employees are the world's best security forces recruited from elite units of state militaries. Discourses and practices related to the employment of TCNs not only reflect structural discrimination within the private security industry more generally but are also constitutive of subordinate masculinities. As in the military they are, on the one hand, linked to ethnicity and race, and on the other hand, based on dichotomies such as the colonizer/colonized and center/periphery. The invisibility of TCNs in and of itself may not be too surprising, especially from a gender perspective which draws attention to the opaqueness of the private. However, as we suggest, the case sheds new light on this *problematique*. It shows that there exists a dividing line between what is a public and what is a private issue and, hence, what is made visible and what stays invisible, not only in regards to public and private actors or sectors, but instead, that the public-visible/private-invisible divide runs squarely through the private security sector, and runs predominantly along the global North–South fault line. The subordinate masculinities that are constructed, but silenced, help and are critical, as we will show, to "sustain global corporate capital, First World identities, and masculine hegemony" (Kempadoo 1999, 18). Hence, what we can observe with respect to the private security industry is not limited to this specific industry but reflective of general trends within the globalized economy.

Because hegemonic and other forms of masculinity are constructed discursively, including through speech, images, and practices, we undertake a discourse analysis of the web pages of PMSCs and articles by representatives of the PMSC industry that have been published in the *Journal of International Peace Operations* (JIPO), which is the journal of the U.S.-based industry association International Stability Operations Association (ISOA).[1] The materials we analyze cover the following nine PMSCs: AKE, Assured Risks, Atlantean, Blackwater, Blue Hackle, DynCorp, FSI Worldwide, SCG International, and Specops.[2] When analyzing these companies' web pages, we paid attention both to written text and to images, including photos and symbols, indicative of hegemonic masculinity as well as subordinate forms of masculinity. The sample is representative of PMSCs based in the United States and the United Kingdom, which are currently the biggest markets for transnational PMSCs in the OECD (Organisation for Economic Co-operation and Development) world. The sample represents the wide spectrum of companies that offer diverse services, work for a variety of clients, and adopt a range of practices and policies. We focused on U.S. and UK companies in order to demonstrate how they contribute to the construction of hegemonic and subordinate masculinities through strategies of "othering."

The chapter is structured as follows. We first discuss the concept of masculinity more generally, which we assume to be plural, contingent, and intersecting with other identity-forming categories, before we turn to the results of our analysis of how subordinate masculinities are constructed within and between PMSCs specifically. We illustrate how the provision of security services rests on a gender hierarchy whereby the masculinities of employees from the global South are regarded as essential for but of lesser value to the presumed hegemonic masculinity of Western employees. We conclude with a discussion of the implications of our findings, suggesting that unveiling how PMSCs are implicated in the construction of masculinities is important since it helps dispel the myth that they are neutral, apolitical actors and draws attention to their political face and their role in the constitution of gender norms.

GENDER, THE CONSTRUCTION OF MASCULINITIES, AND THE MILITARY

Militaries have been identified by scholars interested in gender hierarchies as a central site where masculinities are constructed. As Marcia Kovitz (2003) points out, "The military is an organization that values, promotes, and engages in practices that are the inverse of those valued, promoted, and practiced in the civilian sphere" (9). Mandated to "perfect the techniques of lethal violence, of killing . . . they must construct different kinds of lives and deaths, and they must assign them meaning" (9). Drawing on the works of Kimberly Hutchings (2008b), we conceive of military and masculinity as being "mutually constitutive and mutually reinforcing" of each other (391),[3] and therefore militarized masculinity is far from static or universal. "[D]iscursively, rather than materially, produced or caused" (391), it is both plural and fluid (Cornwall and Lindisfarne 1994, 12; Petersen 2003, 57–58; Higate and Henry 2004, 483). It encompasses a range of possible positions, identities, or performances (see, for example, Connell 2000a, 21–33; Blanchard 2003) that are shaped by and intersect with other identity-forming categories, such as ethnicity, race, disability, religion, age, or class (Higate and Henry 2004, 481–498).

Thinking of masculinity and particularly militarized masculinity in the plural has ontological consequences. It moves our focus from men to patterns of gender relations and hierarchies that exist between different masculinities (Kaufman 1994, 144; Kimmel 1994; Hooper 1998, 35; Wadley 2010, 49). Hence we are able to, for example, identify hegemonic masculinity, which Jennifer Heeg Maruska (2010) defines as "one type of identity construct, at the top of a hierarchy that includes subordinate masculinities and femininities" (238) and which according to Charlotte Hooper (1999) relies on other masculinities and sometimes on an eclectic mix of competing and partially overlapping and historical archetypes.

Gender and feminist scholars have, for example, argued that since 9/11, the U.S. military and its allies have "re-creat[ed] the old colonialist narrative of Western/'enlightened' men waging war against 'other'/often dark-skinned men" (Sharoni 2008, 152). In this respect, "the white, wealthy, western, heterosexual hegemonic male identity is constituted, in part, by constructing other groups of men as threatening, including men of Muslim and Arab background and those identified as 'non-western,' as well as people of color, immigrants, refugees, non-status people and women" (Rygiel 2006, 147). Furthermore, feminist critiques of the international political economy literature have made apparent how the construction of the worker in the transnational context rests on a colonialist logic with supposedly irreconcilable differences (Agathangelou 2002, 143; Peterson 2003; see also, for example, Gibson-Graham 2006) between, for example, "history-making capitalist economies vs. history-lagging non-capitalist ones; wealthy centers vs. exploited peripheries; transnational firms vs. territorially bound states; globe-straddling cosmopolitans vs. locally bound parochials" (Chang and Ling 2000, 32). Others have illustrated how feminization can be used to upgrade some masculinities or devalue others. Several studies show how hegemonic masculinities are constructed in the military through the degrading treatment of new recruits. By assigning them tasks traditionally associated with women, such as cleaning (Apelt and Dittmer 2007, 71) or clerical work (Higate 2003b, 31) or by calling them "pussies" or "ninnies" when failing to perform a task assigned to them (Barrett 2001, 77; Hockey 2003, 17), they are treated like "female objects" (Apelt and Dittmer 2007, 71). Regardless of the kind of strategies through which gendered identities are constructed, they all have in common that they involve "othering," that is, an identity that is distinct from and perceived as being subordinate to one's own. As Nicola Pratt (2013) observes in her postcolonial feminist critique of Security Council Resolution 1325 on "Women, Peace and Security": "Practices and understandings of security and insecurity depend upon the identification of boundaries between 'us' and 'them' and particular constructions of Self/Other which are gendered, racialized, sexualized, and class-ed" (772).

Colonization, femininization, and masculinization are also helpful to understanding the ongoing privatization of security. Isabelle Barker (2009), for example, suggests that in the case of the U.S. Army outsourcing "social reproductive tasks that have nothing to do with the masculine role of the combat soldier" (226) to poor men from the South allows "the U.S. armed forces to be figured, first, as made up of soldiers endowed with attributes of aggressive masculinity, and second, as an apparently homogenous middle-class entity" (227). This division of labor, she argues "symbolically reinforces the soldier's role as a masculinized 'war fighter' with a second level of implications: supporting the corresponding and increasingly imperial posture that the United States has assumed in the world in this first decade of the twenty-first century" (217). Furthermore, it "echoes earlier colonizer-colonized relations in that domestic life and reproductive labor continue to be critical sites for demarcating lopsided positions of power in international relations" (217; also see the chapters by Barker and Chisholm in this volume). As much as traditional militaries are trying to boost their masculinity (Joachim and Schneiker 2012a) by relying on the private sector, so too do PMSCs use strategies of masculinization to distance themselves from subordinate masculinities such as "mercenaries," "war profiteers," or "guns for hire," which are often used in the media to discredit PMSCs (see, for example, Fainaru 2008; Jackson and Grotto 2008; Westcott 2010).

PMSCs are also responding to the challenges confronted by contemporary state militaries as a result of the shift away from the traditional "warrior" type masculinity. As Claire Duncanson (2009) points out, the growing involvement in complex peacekeeping missions since the end of the Cold War and state building more recently have imposed new demands on soldiers and their masculinity, asking them to show understanding for locals and build connections. And again others note that technological developments in the military increasingly require both managerial and professional skills (Woodward and Jenkings 2011). The emerging hegemonic military masculinity is not only demanding but is also characterized by tensions between its constituent elements, especially between the traditional "'warrior' combat leader," on the one hand, and the "rational manager" (Nuciari 2006, 68) and the "peacekeeper" on the other hand, as complex operations such as those in Iraq or Afghanistan illustrate: "[S]oldiers are expected to win hearts and minds, create peace and security, yet [are] also [required to] use their combat skills" (Duncanson 2009, 76).

PMSCs allow state militaries to live up to and reduce the tensions between the conflicting demands of multiple masculinities. For example, when state militaries have to be peacekeepers and hence become feminized, PMSCs can perform the warrior masculinity role that does not necessarily involve fighting per se but, as Paul Higate (2003b) notes in his reflections about military masculinity, involves "traits—both performance and ideology—[that] cluster around violence, aggression, rationality, and a sense of invulnerability" (29). PMSCs, in other words, represent the different "other" against which state militaries can construct what in the postheroic age appear to be more accepted masculinities, such as the rational manager and the tender peacekeeper. Hence, PMSCs perform a similar role vis-à-vis the feminine other, that is, the "beautiful soul" (Elshtain 1995) that has to be protected and against which the tough warrior has traditionally been constructed, or the prostitute, which allows men "to 'other' women and understand themselves as masculine" (Jeffreys 2007, 18). Seen this way, PMSCs function as "masculinity multipliers" for state militaries which are under pressure due to complex demands of contemporary civil-military operations (Joachim and Schneiker 2012a). Producing these masculinities is, as we illustrate in the following section, accomplished in part through the subordination of others.

PMSCs AND THE CONSTRUCTION OF (SUBORDINATE) MASCULINITIES

PMSCs often claim that their employees are the world's best security experts recruited from the elite units of Western militaries. The company Specops, for example, asserts to "distinguish . . . itself by recruiting only highly motivated and professional personnel drawn from various elite governments [sic] units and Special Forces personnel" (Specops Company 2012). Such special units are generally those of Western militaries. The company Assured Risks, which recruits "only former members of the UK Special Forces, Royal Marine Commando's and the UK security services" (Assured Risks 2011), refers to itself as a security specialist whose "security consultants are the very best in the market having gained extensive experience from careers in the British Military" (Assured Risks 2010b), while the staff of Blue Hackle "are of the highest caliber and include experienced former Special Air Service (SAS) personnel" (Blue Hackle 2011), a special forces regiment of the British army. Statements such as these are reflective of what some masculinity scholars refer to as "trans-national business masculinity" (Connell 1998). They are reflective of, on the one hand, the (re)construction of masculinities that PMSCs take part in, and on the other hand, how in this process subordinate masculinities are upgraded, sanitized, or rendered invisible.

Although employees are hired from Western militaries where they have undergone training for combat, in the web pages of the respective companies, both a distancing from and an upgrading of warrior masculinity related to violence occurs through an exclusive emphasis on the rational expert with superior skills (e.g., Hearn and Parkin 2002; see also Connell 2000b; Connell 1998, 16). Blue Hackle, for example, considers itself "to be an innovative, minimally intrusive, low-profile security solution designed for challenging and complex environments" committed "to safely and discreetly execut[ing] security activities while providing the flexibility to deliver rapid turnkey protection and risk mitigation services" (Blue Hackle 2013a). Moreover, company web pages are also indicative of a postcolonial narrative in which Western forces are identified with the protectors and securitizers, while the South, though in theses quotes not explicitly mentioned, operates in the background as the site of insecurity inhabited by men who are either portrayed as a threat to security or as being unable to provide security for their families or their countries. At the same time as Blue Hackle declares to "value the caliber of our people, and we continuously employ the most highly trained employees, inclusive of former U.S. and UK Special Operations Forces" it explains that the company "strive[s] to **work by, with and through the local communities** where our customers operate. Our approach means that we give back to the local economies by using local vendors and partners to the maximum extent possible" (Blue Hackle 2013a; bold/italics in the original). Finally, statements of PMSCs hide the other side of the gender hierarchy associated with employment and, more precisely, that of third-country nationals who are often less qualified or even unqualified staff from so-called third-world countries. Consequently, they have to be trained in order to become qualified. This training is provided by white Westerners. A photograph on the web page of Blue Hackle entitled "Our People" shows three white males, two of them in combat fatigues, who look directly into the camera, next to nine men of color, most of them with black beards, who hold a certificate in their hands and who mostly have their faces lowered or have their eyes covered by a cap (Blue Hackle 2013b).

Several companies, especially those that engage in logistics and other support activities, recruit TCNs from the South because they constitute a cheap labor source. TCNs earn between 100 and 1,000 USD a month, which is significantly less than what well-trained employees from industrial countries would earn doing the same job but still more than what they would earn in their home countries (Chatterjee 2006; Chatterjee 2009, 19–20). TCNs come neither from the country where PMSCs operate nor from the country of the company for whom they work. A lot of them stem from Bangladesh, India, Pakistan, the Philippines, the Fiji Islands, or Sri Lanka (Chatterjee 2006; Chatterjee 2009, 19). In Iraq, approximately over 40,000 TCNs worked for companies that had contracts with the U.S. Army or government (CorpWatch 2004, 4; Elsea and Serafino 2007, 4). When taking a closer look at how industry officials justify their employment and payment, the literature on gender and globalization as well as postcolonial feminism is instructive. The term TCNs itself is reflective of differences in power between the economically dominant and affluent North and the politically weak and economically poor South. Moreover, TCNs illustrate that "masculinities are involved in the cultural remaking of gender meanings under globalization" (Connell 2000b, 44), or as Pratt (2013) puts it, "hierarchies of race, gender, and sexuality . . . are central to the political economy of imperialism" (774). A photo on the web pages of DynCorp, for example, shows a Western man in military gear searching an Arab man (DynCorp International 2013). While the focus of (postcolonial) feminist critiques has primarily been on the gendered script involved, which Gayatri Spivak (1988) described as "white men saving brown women from brown men" (92), studying PMSCs also sheds light on the varied relationships between "white" and "brown" men that are a central part of the security industry.

According to the (then) president of the International Stability Operations Association (ISOA) Doug Brooks there is an absolute need for PMSCs to employ third-country nationals: "TCNs come from all over the world and they add enormous capability and value to contingency operations. No international stability policy could succeed without the cost-effective labor, expertise and off-the-shelf experience TCNs bring to the field" (Brooks 2011, 6; also see Brooks 2012, 5). TCNs, according to Brooks, fill a void. Yet, contrary to the specialized and highly professional training that their Western employees enjoy and that companies pride themselves in, TCNs are a cheaper resource. Similar to what Anna M. Agathangelou (2002) found in the case of domestic and sex workers, these men are portrayed as "natural resources or objects for the use of the new emerging professional class of men and women . . . in multinational corporations" (155). The treatment of TCNs is reminiscent of colonial days when raw materials were of interest to imperial nations or when locals where employed as servants in the colonizers' households. Now, as in the past, the relationship is hierarchical and not questioned.

Industry representatives like Brooks (2012), who conceive of the hiring of TCNs as not only "mak[ing] sense" but also as "a practice that is standard procedure" in the industry, regard the qualifications of TCNs as being of a lesser kind than those of the "extremely skilled experts" from the North (5). TCNs bring with them "non-standardized experiences," such as docility, while at the same time they are readily available, hence "off-the-shelf." Similar to women employed in third-world manufacturing, who are assumed to have "naturally nimble fingers" and are "naturally more docile and willing to accept tough work discipline and less inclined to join trade unions (Elson and Pearson 1981, 93), TCNs are hired because they are assumed to be naturally suited for the job. Not only are they "non-skilled" or "semi-skilled," but they also essentially complement the masculinity of the highly trained professional security expert, who produces analyses and forecasts but does not fight. Binaries such as these are also telling of a hegemonic masculinity that is presumed Western in origin yet is universal, and with which other subordinate masculinities are compared, as the following statement in an article authored by Whitney Grespin (2012), an operations associate at Atlantean, LLC, a PMSC, in the *Journal of International Peace Operations* illustrates: "The teams with rescue missions vary in quality from those with world class training from Western countries to ad hoc teams with little to no training in third world countries" (18). The difference in training and expertise is also what—in the eyes of Western employers—justifies lower wages, as the former director of the ISOA (then still IPOA) stated: "Few would argue against the notion that soldiers from western countries are some of the best trained in the world. So, based on experience, should someone who has worked 20 years for the U.S. military be paid the same as someone who was part of an under-resourced developing country's military?" (Messner 2007, 32)

The way in which representatives of the IPOA/ISOA describe the work performed by TCNs affirms what Ayesha Imam (1997) refers to as the "sexual narrative of consumption" in which those "providing services are never positioned as agents" (295). Instead Northern employees define the norm, possess superior skills and resources, and therefore manliness while those in the South are the "different other," subordinates who are controlled by the norm, have lesser abilities, and are less masculine. The "sexual narrative of consumption" (295) "exhibits a clear connection between low wages and the definition of the job as supplementary . . . and the fact that the lifestyles of people of color are defined as different and cheaper" (Mohanty 1997, 6). Lower living costs of TCNs in their home countries, in addition to the lack of training, serves as a reason for the wage difference between Northern and Southern employees: "From a fairness perspective, even though TCNs and LNs [local nationals] often earn substantially less than their Western counterparts, they also enjoy an even lower cost of living back home" (Messner 2007, 32). The relations depicted here are reflective of a gendered division of labor and similar to one that Cynthia Enloe (1989) described and criticized when discussing sex tourism:

> To succeed, sex tourism requires Third World women to be economically desperate enough to enter prostitution; having done so it is made difficult to leave. The other side of the equation requires men from affluent societies to imagine certain women, usually women of colour, to be more available and submissive than the women in their own countries. Finally, the industry depends on an alliance between local governments in search of foreign currency and local and foreign business men willing to invest in sexualized travel. (36–37)

Similarly, the provision of security through private companies requires men who are desperate enough to sell their bodies or labor and, as we will show, even their identity.

The PMSC industry conceives itself as helping people in need and rescuing them from their misery. Similar to women in developing countries, they are "naturalized as the poor and despondent who are to be provided a job, room, and board by the emerging upper- and middle-class" (Agathangelou 2002, 156). In the words of Doug Brooks (2011): "For many, these jobs are a path out of abject poverty and misery. . . . TCNs are able to contribute substantially more support to their families than had they stayed at home" (6). Exploitation is justified with what used to be former feminine attributes but which by now form part of modern masculinity, that is, kindness and concern for those who are less than masculine because they are unemployed and poor, and therefore cannot provide for their families.

Although representatives of the ISOA/IPOA claim that "TCNs work in stability operations because they want to be there" (Brooks 2011, 6), the argument that TCNs are "freely choosing to go to Iraq for the very reason that the money on offer is not only good, but even irresistible" (Messner 2007, 32) already suggests that there might not be a real choice to begin with in light of the miserable living conditions in most of the TCNs' home countries. Moreover, claims such as these hide the fact that for some the promised Garden of Eden turns out to be "hell" (Indian employee of a Halliburton subcontractor, quoted in CorpWatch 2005, 10). In recent years a number of reports have pointed to the miserable working conditions of TCNs (CorpWatch 2004, 2005, 2006; Chatterjee 2006). One report by CorpWatch (2006) states: "Many are said to lack adequate medical care and put in hard labor seven days a week, 10 hours or more a day, for little or no overtime pay. Few receive proper workplace safety equipment or adequate protection from incoming mortars and rockets" (10). This is why some countries, such as Nepal and the Philippines, prohibit their nationals from working in Iraq

(Chatterjee 2006; CorpWatch 2006, 10). Nevertheless, many are forced to work there because "unscrupulous employment agencies" (Chatterjee 2006) promise them jobs in Kuwait but fly them to Iraq instead. On arrival they are robbed of their identities. Their passports are confiscated, and they are threatened with torture if they protest (Chatterjee 2006; CorpWatch 2005, 10). In April 2006, the U.S. military issued an order in Iraq that passports confiscated by PMSCs from their employees should be returned, but it did not stop the illegal practices (Chatterjee 2006).

"White"/Hegemonic and "White"/Subordinate Men/Masculinities

While the employees of PMSCs who come from Northern countries and are mostly male are often presented as being exceptional and well-trained experts, they, like TCNs, are subject to subordination. For example, they do not enjoy the same labor rights and social security coverage as the personnel of regular Western armed forces. Instead of being given long-term contracts, they are often hired as contractors for single missions that frequently last only a few months. For example, a former Blackwater spokesperson declared, "The people who provide security services abroad are independent contractors," and "[w]hen their 60- to 90-day contracts with us expire, they can seek employment with whomever they choose" (Anne Tyrell, quoted in Nordland 2009). According to a report by CorpWatch, employees of Halliburton, the former mother company of Kellogg Brown & Root (KBR), were "contracted to a Cayman Islands subsidiary of Halliburton named Service Employees International" (CorpWatch 2005, 9) and once their contract ends, they "are not entitled to unemployment benefits" (9–10). Labor practices such as these clash with the corporate responsibility norm to which many PMSCs officially claim to adhere. AKE (2010b), for example, promotes a "highly developed sense of corporate social responsibility or duty of care" and "believe[s] in teamwork rather than hierarchy" (AKE 2010a), while DynCorp (2012) asserts on its web page to "[c]are—for the safety, security, development, and well-being of our employees," and Assured Risks prides itself on an equal opportunity and diversity policy and is "keen to develop good relationships to everyone within our organization with the purpose of increasing quality of work, skills, effectiveness and commitment to the company" (Assured Risks 2010a). Apart from calling into question the self-professed company norms, the different conditions of PMSCs' employees draw attention to the gender structure and the role of power in PMSCs. While this up- and down-grading of masculinities is not exceptional to PMSCs but also pertains to the military and to conventional companies (see, for example, Hooper 1998), it is reflective of the way in which PMSCs are implicated in the (re)construction of masculinities.

The exploitation narrative is not quite as seamless as one might expect. The following statement by Brooks (2012) from an article on labor trafficking published in the *Journal of International Peace Operations* illustrates an additional dimension of the (re)construction of masculinities by PMSCs:

> Local nationals and third country nationals (TCNs) bring enormous efficiencies and value to international missions. Their costs can be as much as 50 times less than imported Western talent with similar skills. They often bring experiences and backgrounds from unstable areas that make them more hardy, savvy and resilient than skittish Western employees. (20)

At the same time as Western employees are portrayed as representative of hegemonic masculinity with superior skills and training, their masculinity is also called into question while that of TCNs appears to be upgraded. However, this too is indicative of devaluation. The ascription of hypermasculine qualities such as "hardy" or "resilient" represents what Hooper (2001) refers to as "pathologization"—the "branding of subordinate masculinities as pathological, aberrant" (74)—and highlights the ways in which the provision of security services rests on, and requires, not only different but also flexible masculinities.

As much as employees at the top of the masculinity ladder are subject to subordination, they are at the same time implicated in the construction of subordinate masculinities. Representatives of Western PMSCs conceive of themselves as superior to the staff that Western companies employ in the countries in which they operate. According to Brooks (2010), then president of the IPOA, "it is . . . quite normal to see local nationals being trained by international companies on the skills necessary to operate and manage contracts to Western standards" (4). And the PMSC SCG International distinguishes four tiers of personnel. While tier one staff requires a minimum of eight years of experience in, for example, the U.S. Special Operations Command, which oversees the various special forces units of the U.S. Army (SCG International 2013a), the company declares that "[w]e recruit, screen, train, and manage what we categorize as our Tier 4 Personnel"—"vetted, trained foreign nationals with area familiarity and local area language skills" (SCG International 2013b). Statements such as these as well as others are reflective of the colonizer/colonized dichotomy where "brown" men living on the periphery of the global economy are conceived of by "white" men as savages that have to be civilized and taught what is regarded as "normal" in the metropole. An article published in the IPOA/ISOA journal concerned with the medical treatment of PMSC staff, for example, identifies TCNs as one of the "major roadblocks to primary care" (Dahmer et al. 2009, 25) because they may have, for example, "pre-existing, chronic conditions that are difficult to

manage in theater, [when] not appropriately screened out prior to hiring"
(25). Furthermore the authors of the article argue:

> With many companies employing TCNs, companies must understand the spe-
> cific challenges that pertain to medical care with this population. The initial
> prescreening process is a vital step, as certain diseases are endemic and com-
> mon to that part of the world. These screening exams should be conducted
> by skilled providers committed to enforcing the same standard of health
> and fitness that is mandated in the contract. In situations where a physical
> is done sloppily, with the boxes checked unscrupulously, that individual will
> ultimately become a liability to the site manager and the company as a whole.
> (Dahmer et al. 2009, 26)

Similar to colonized men who were regarded as "dirty, sexualized and
effeminate or childlike" (Connell 2000b, 49), so too TCNs are portrayed as
different and abnormal. In the case at hand, they do not meet Western standards with regards to their health: "Without proper medical pre-screening,
preventive care, education, and access to competent primary health care, the
TCN work force will be unduly limited" (Dahmer et al. 2009, 34) in what
is regarded as a cornerstone of Western-type masculinity, its "productivity"
(34). Yet, subordinate masculinities are not only constructed by holding men
in the South to different standards. Instead, hierarchization and competition occur also among men and masculinities that are considered of lower
value, as, for example, a statement from a former Colombian PMSC employee
in Iraq illustrates: "Colombians are not as cheap as the nationals of other
developing nations, but if one needs a more sophisticated level of security,
Colombians are a good option" (Guerrero 2008, 22). This statement highlights and lends force to what masculinity scholars, such as Hooper (1998)
have claimed, namely, that men, consciously or not, collaborate or identify
with hegemonic masculinities "to boost their own position" (34). In the case
at hand, Colombians upgrade their own masculinity by "othering" and setting themselves apart from lesser masculinities (nationals from other developing countries) while at the same time appropriating aspects of a higher
form of masculinity (the security expert). Through these processes masculinities are reconfigured.

The concern that Northern-based PMSCs and, more precisely, their execu-
tives express about TCNs supports what Connell claims to be characteristic
of transnational business masculinity today. It is marked by "increased ego-
centrism, very conditional loyalties (even to the corporation), and a declining sense of responsibility for others (except for purposes of image-making)"
(Connell 2000b, 52). According to two representatives of the company FSI
Worldwide, appeals to treat TCNs with "respect and dignity" (Forster and
Sinclair 2009, 15) are not justified with basic norms, such as human rights,

but are regarded as a matter of reputation: "In order to ensure that your company is not the focus of unwelcome media or legal investigation, it is important that all companies are fully aware of where their personnel come from and the way in which they are recruited" (15). Transnational business masculinity is also reflected in the ways in which PMSCs dissociate themselves from "[p]roblems [that] arise when rules are ignored, or brokers . . . demand money from the desperate TCNs willing to pay exorbitant amounts to get the relatively high-paying jobs, which is illegal" and those that may result when "potential employees" are not informed "about the risks, the potential salaries," and that "confiscating their passports so they cannot travel" might happen (Brooks 2011, 6). As two representatives of the PMSC FSI Worldwide wrote: "Many will claim to be former soldiers who are trained in the use of weapons and who will be resolute in the face of attacks. Sadly, these claims are often untrue and the results in terms of serious security breaches, examples of which we are all aware, can be disastrous" (Forster and Sinclair 2009, 15). Hence, rather than taking responsibility for their staff and employees, PMSCs blame the individual, insufficient regulation, or subcontractors for the infractions that might occur as a result of employing unqualified staff.

CONCLUSION

In this chapter we have shown that while PMSCs claim to recruit the world's best security forces from the elite units of Western militaries and to care for them, the provision of security services relies on the employment of less qualified or unqualified staff. This staff from so-called third-world countries is often expected to work and live under very bad conditions. Like many multinational corporations, PMSCs exhibit a gendered division of labor, one which is intimately linked to and intersects with race, ethnicity, culture, and class. In this context, the power of these companies rests not on efficiency and cost-effectiveness, as is often claimed by policymakers, but in part on constructed hegemonic masculinity, subordinated masculinities, and the competition between them. The highly trained and skilled white security expert requires a different other—the unskilled, economically desperate, brown male—in order for PMSCs to be able to provide security on any scale, anywhere, and any place. These dichotomies are, however, far from fixed and static. Just as Western employees are often portrayed as representative of hegemonic masculinity, their masculinity is also at the same time subject to devaluation. The same applies to TCNs or local nationals whose masculinity is either viewed as being of a lesser or a more valued kind, depending on the security requirements or the competitors from which individual contractors try to set themselves apart by claiming aspects of hegemonic masculinities.

The case of PMSCs illustrates and provides empirical evidence for what has thus far been a theoretical claim that transnational businesses are arenas where masculinities are (re)constructed. In that sense it lends itself to comparisons with studies concerned with women employed by transnational businesses to tease out more precisely how the gendering that goes on is different or similar for different groups and in different spaces. However, uncovering the masculinization script of the security industry is important for another reason. PMSCs are often depicted by policymakers and scholars alike as neutral and apolitical entities solely providing needed services. If their political role is acknowledged at all, it is with respect to companies participating in multistakeholder dialogues concerning their national and international regulation or their lobbying activities. Therefore, detailing how PMSCs are implicated in the construction of hegemonic and subordinate masculinities highlights how their political role is also inherently gendered and influences societal gender norms.

NOTES

1. Before the fall of 2010, the association was called International Peace Operations Association (IPOA). In July 2012, the ISOA replaced *JIPO* with a magazine called *Stability Operations*. According to ISOA, "The rebranding follows the name change of ISOA from the International Peace Operations Association in late 2010" (ISOA 2012).
2. Blackwater is now called Academi.
3. See also Kovitz (2003) for a historicized perspective.

PART III

Rethinking the Private Military Contractor II

Masculinities and Violence

CHAPTER 7

Aversions to Masculine Excess in the Private Military and Security Company and Their Effects

Don't Be a "Billy Big Bollocks" and Beware the "Ninja!"

PAUL HIGATE

Growing interest in private military and security companies (PMSCs) from critical scholars of gender has seen a number of these commentators engage the concept of remasculinization in their analyses. The concept of remasculinization has been considered discursively in relation to company websites (Joachim and Schneiker 2012c) as well as at the level of state policy and ideology (Stachowitsch 2013). Taken together, these contributions illuminate private security's reinvigoration of masculinity in ways that reposition it as the prime guarantor of security in relation to the alleged feminization of the armed forces over the last two or so decades. Through a foregrounding of the close links between power and masculinity as they are inflected by market dynamics in a sphere of growing importance to conflict and its aftermath, this literature throws light on particular aspects of the industry's gendered terrain by raising the question to what extent it can be conceived of as a site/sight of remasculinization.

Set against this backdrop, I also use a gender-sensitive approach in the current chapter but apply it to contractors' practices on the ground—more specifically, the classroom. More broadly I consider the concept of remasculinization through the manifestation of the so-called cowboy contractor versus his professional foil envisioned as a discrete and restrained contractor equipped with the capacity for violence. Here, my aim is to deepen and

broaden understandings of remasculinization in the private security industry through an ethnographic and empirical approach focused on the training
of student contractors as armed close protection (CP) officers. This hitherto
unconsidered learning environment represents an analytically significant
gendered aspect of security privatization, providing insights into a social
environment within which individuals are prepared for employment in the
industry. Perhaps more importantly, it also demonstrates that remasculinization can be a process of both conscious strategy *and* a partly unintended
outcome of gendered and national identities, where the mercenary figure
is found to be distasteful at the level of men's self-identification. Taking a
step back, internal struggles around masculine identity—including aversion to masculine excess in the case of armed contractors—help legitimize
an industry based ultimately on the potential and actual use of violence.
Complementing Maya Eichler's chapter in this volume, where the global scale
of the politics of protection is foregrounded, I develop a microfocused analysis of protector masculinity.

This chapter is structured around three main sections. The first provides
a brief overview of the remasculinization thesis, where state-level and discursive perspectives reveal the importance of remasculinization for the
legitimacy of the industry, as it reconstitutes and recuperates masculinity's
authority in both ideological and policy terms. Discussion then shifts to
the methodological approach used in the chapter where background details
of field research are provided. Third, this leads to the empirical material,
where the metaphors of "Billy Big Bollocks" and "Ninjas" are used to capture training instructors' binary framing of the professional and the oppo-
sitional hypermasculine other—distinctions configured to large degree
through the American versus British masculine archetype. Consideration of
this empirical material follows where I focus on convergence and divergence
with the remasculinization thesis, as well as argue that in the final analysis,
self-referential intramasculine rivalries play their own role in the militarization of security since they proceed from the unquestioned, intuitively held
belief that violence is inevitable. A brief conclusion follows.

PMSCs AND REMASCULINIZATION

Drawing on Susan Jefford's (1989) use of the concept in her groundbreak-
ing book *The Remasculinization of America*, Saskia Stachowitsch (2013) highlights the term's sensitivity to the means by which the project of patriarchy
is revived through signs, symbols, and popular culture. These combine in
specific ways to help reestablish the dominance of men and masculinity in
American culture. Stachowitsch then turns to feminist theories of the state
to make sense of the gendered aspects of neoliberal restructuring and the

strategic importance of private military labor. Here, the concept of remasculinization is used to underscore women's relative exclusion from PMSCs, a sector that "impedes gender equality policies and reconstructs masculinist ideologies" (Stachowitsch 2013, 75). In this way, women's overall status and rights are eroded as a consequence of military privatization where masculinity is reanimated as "the efficient guarantor of national security" (Stachowitsch, 2013, 87; also see Leander 2006). This observation is reminiscent of Judith Hicks Stiehm's (1982) and Iris Marion Young's (2003) work on masculinity and protection that has enduring relevance in the contemporary sphere of the PMSC in regard to research conducted on G4S in Kabul (Higate 2011). There, armed contractors were noted to explicitly identify with their role as protectors of female clients who, while framed as the protected, eschewed such labels.

While the revival of masculinity's authority at the level of the state and military privatization is significant, Jutta Joachim and Andrea Schneiker complement state-level analysis through a gendered decoding of PMSC websites, which they argue propagate a pluralized hybridization of privatized masculinities. Given that these websites may function as the primary interface with customers and company market shareholders, their gendered framing is of considerable analytical significance. In this way, dominant constructions of acceptable and normalizing "benchmark" masculinities in the form of the professional, ethical warrior hero are considered (Joachim and Schneiker 2012a, 2012c). Explanations for the particular framings these gendered constructions take lie in all three categories of institutional isomorphism identified by Paul J. DiMaggio and Walter W. Powell (1983), demonstrated empirically in the case of white, Western former special forces veterans as well as those who trade on the Ghurka label in order to generate an income within the industry (Chisholm 2014a). More broadly, these commodified representations are characterized by a widely held aversion to the mercenary archetype since he is ultimately bad for business (Via 2010; Higate 2012a; Joachim and Schneiker 2012a, 2012c; Leander 2012; Stachowitsch 2013, 84). Rather, market-driven processes commodify competing forms of masculinity in-line with companies' presumptions around clients' preference for expertise and professionalism in their risk managers (Leander 2006, 2012). This is more than a matter of pluralizing masculinities in occupational terms as noted in national state militaries (Morgan, 1994; Barrett, 1996; Higate 2003), but rather within the context of the market place, can be seen as key to the survival of companies offering niche, securitizing masculinities. Here, the gendered contours of PMSCs follow a pattern established since the end of the Cold War and the relative crisis in legitimacy experienced by Western militaries. These historical shifts stimulated the emergence of softer, more sophisticated and palatable masculinities often dovetailing with national, state military identity (Whitworth 2004;

Duncanson 2009). Set against the backdrop of the increasing securitization of aid (Duffield 2001), these modes of masculinity can be seen as hybridized forms of the warrior archetype, fusing the ability to conduct peacekeeping operations with compassion whilst simultaneously embodying the capacity to respond with force when necessary. In turn, these shifts in military and militarized masculinities have helped create the gendered and humanitarian logics within which PMSCs have evolved (Joachim and Schneiker 2012b). Scholarly contributions examining the PMSC industry through state and labor market policies and company websites thereby underscore the regenerative mutability of masculinity in this sphere as, phoenix-like, it seeks (and largely attains) authority in private security such that PMSCs "derive their growing importance not solely from being effective force multipliers [an industry justification for privatization], but also because they are effective masculinity multipliers" (Joachim and Schneiker 2012a, 507).

Guided by these critical gender scholars' insights, the following discussion based on ethnographic observations of an armed CP officers training course provides an original contribution to a literature that has yet to engage directly with contractors' social practices on the ground, and in turn with how these might speak to the wider legitimacy of the industry.

METHODOLOGY: FIELD RESEARCH

The field research on which this chapter is based was carried out in the United States in the summer of 2011. I attended a training course for potential contractors seeking employment in hostile regions in the role of an armed CP officer working in a personal security detail (PSD). Put in lay terms, the most significant aspect of this body-guarding course turned on the attainment of safety, proficiency, and accuracy in the use of a number of weapons systems (the AK 47, Uzi, various pistols, sniper rifles, and so forth), which were used extensively during training with live ammunition. It also taught a wide range of skills argued to be vital for the security of clients. These included specialized walking formations designed to protect clients, response drills when under attack, the identification of improvised explosive devices (IEDs), security surveys of hotels and other buildings, drills for extricating clients from vehicles when threatened, and the compilation and use of route cards integral to the secure movement of clients by road. Crucially, the course also provided the opportunity to develop a close rapport with fellow students who were seeking employment in the industry; although, this chapter deals specifically with the two instructors of the program.

As a student enrolled in all aspects of the course, I was required to reach the same standards as my peers. Since I was integrated fully into the program, and partly because of my background in the military, I quickly built a comfortable relationship with the student group, further strengthened through time spent eating, socializing, and swimming together in the hotel facilities, and when shopping for food at the local supermarket. The all-male group of 13 students were drawn from the European and American continents, ranged in age from mid-20s to early 50s, had attained different education levels (one held a PhD), and had a mix of military/law enforcement and civilian backgrounds. Many of the former had seen combat in Iraq and Afghanistan, while the latter had neither knowledge nor the prerequisite weapons skills considered relevant for work as an armed contractor. I kept a detailed fieldwork diary, recorded in note form in the classroom—where it was legitimate to write in one's course book—and then in more detail on return to the hotel at the end of the sometimes lengthy training day. Once back in my room, and after completing written work set by the instructors, I turned my attention to the field notes. Applying gender sensitivity to the data, and drawing on a mix of deductive and inductive approaches characteristic of the grounded theoretical method of data generation and analysis, it became clear that the instructors (two British, former military men in their early 50s who I shall call Rich and Ken), relied heavily on narratives of masculinity in their discussions about security—specifically the binary of professional versus cowboy in relation to contractor competence. As the course progressed and the volume and depth of data focused on instructor narratives increased, further analysis began to reveal patterns of gender talk invoking remasculinization.

(Man)aging the Fine Line between Arrogance and Confidence

Unlike the professional activities of an academic for example, the work of security professionals is often perceived both implicitly (Pelton 2006) and explicitly (Higate 2012b) through its embodied dimensions. From door bouncers tasked to control entry to, and maintain order in, nighttime venues (Monaghan 2004), through to the stereotypical, pumped-up Blackwater guard, security contractors have become synonymous with hypermasculine presentations of self, as a form of security through intimidation (Schumacher 2006). In stark contrast to these explicit modes of embodied masculinity where brain might be seen as subordinate to brawn, we were told repeatedly on the course that security was "a thinking man's game," where "unlike the U.S. approach," according to Rich, "everyone can do everyone else's jobs. We want to see flexibility . . . you need to adapt . . . think on your feet." This way, it was possible to keep the job "varied" and ultimately be an "ambassador for the profession . . . since you won't get bored." Important as it was to be "switched on, think ahead and . . . strive for the highest standards," we were also reminded in the very strongest of terms that use of weapons "was *not* glamorous in the slightest." To further reinforce this point, it was stated with considerable solemnity by Rich that "the best weapon we have … [points to his head] is this," and that we should exercise "humility" in our security work through using *both* our "heads and our hearts." At this juncture we were asked to raise our hands if we had children and/or partners (the majority did) and to reflect on how we would feel if they were killed by a "trigger-happy" contractor. Framed in this way, the ethos of security work demanded, on the one hand, utter proficiency in the use of weapons, while on the other, frowned on the actual use of these weapons since armed contractors had in their hands the power of life and death. This power, it was argued, could feed the arrogance of some operatives who made life difficult for local people "because they can … and they fucking-well do," as Rich put it. He then invited us to contemplate the fine line between "arrogance and confidence," where exercise of the former was harmful to the mission, and the latter, something to which we should aspire "every single working day" as the hallmark of a "true professional." While the student group was encouraged to be confident, considerate, and set about their work with humility and modesty, these narratives were invariably conveyed with a tangible sense of frustration in relation to particular others working in security devoid of such attributes. These demeaned individuals "gave the industry a bad name" because of their "sheer incompetence" revealed to the instructors when attending training courses at the school. Not only did they serve as the primary foil against which professionalism was constructed, but, most strikingly as I show next, both instructors invoked these men in terms of an aberrant hypermasculinity as well.

Ninjas and Roly Polies: The Irony of Hypermasculinity

While "the Americans" were seen as the most likely to demonstrate forms of deviant hypermasculinity in tension with professional approaches to security work (perhaps aware of the need to strike some balance in the classroom for the benefit of the American student cohort), Rich also made references to "the SAS" [Britain's Special Air Service], stating that "some of them are idiots … and can be just as bad!" However, though elite soldiers and law enforcement officers from both the U.S. and UK came within his critical orbit, Rich tended to concentrate on the former, using such derogatory words as "retards" and "sheep" to describe what he saw as their inability to "think on their feet … it's beyond them," he told us. He also argued that they followed each other "blindly … using methods that are counterproductive … and just plain stupid," going on to say "it's like they've had their fucking brains removed!" Rich was passionate during these moments and would often apologize for outbursts that flowed from his belief that security was a "craft," where one is always learning, refining, and honing skills to the highest possible standards. "If anyone comes through that door and . . . can show me how to do it better, I'll do it . . . I am willing to learn, I want to learn" ("I am still waiting," Rich told us). Commenting further on incompetence, deep unease was expressed at those who presented themselves in light of "what they *had* done or who they *had* been . . . they are all has-beens" he stated with contempt. Grounding his by now visceral sense of chagrin of those who traded on their previous status but had "nothing to offer the industry," he drew attention to the wider culture in the United States "where everyone's a has-been . . . look at their bumper stickers . . . 'Nam Veteran, Gulf Veteran, US Marine Corps Veteran . . . I don't give a fuck what you've done, show me what you can do *now*," he told us.

During these sometimes protracted monologues—most evident in the classroom prior to departing for the firing range—the American students in the group were somewhat muted and on no occasion did they question Rich's strongly held opinion on these matters. Consequently, this appeared to reinforce the instructor's belief that those with service in the American military (numerous veterans were present in the class) had been indoctrinated into an enduring and strictly hierarchical system that crushed any sense of agency. For Rich, this meant they were unable to challenge or even contribute constructively to decisions made further up the chain of command, but in reality these individuals were almost certainly intimidated by the instructor standing before them, alongside the extent to which questioning might jeopardize their chances of success on the course. Yet, one domain within which the much-demonized American contractor was seen to excel, albeit in ways that stood as a salutary lesson of how not to approach security work, was captured in the explicitly gendered metaphors used by Ken and Rich referring to an unknown, though illustrative number of American contractors, law enforcement officers, and military veterans. With some irony, these men were labeled "Ninjas" and "Billy Big Bollocks," and it is to these instructor narratives that the discussion now turns.

Beware the Ninja . . .

Framed in sardonic terms, Rich made repeated references to the Ninjas that had completed earlier courses, and in so doing invoked a cultural trope familiar to many in the class. The Ninja figure was popularized in 1984 through a comic book entitled *Teenage Mutant Ninja Turtles*, leading to an animated TV series and associated merchandise that has gained widespread appeal. Ninja Turtles (or Ninjas for shorthand) are known for battling good with evil through martial arts techniques learned from an anthropomorphic rat, their *sensei* (master). Ninjas are superhumanly athletic, made possible by their animated status, and the early comics depicted a good deal of violence, which many considered unsuitable for children. Whether the instructors were aware of the deeper roots of the word Ninja is unclear, but by some coincidence, the Ninja was a mercenary or covert agent in feudal Japan who specialized in unorthodox warfare and open combat (Ratti and Westbrook 1991). Either way, the Ninja label derived its particular trivializing status from the cartoon-like and infantilizing sense in which those deemed as such were constructed. Substantive examples were given over the duration of the course including most notably, the operational procedures of particular American Special Weapons and Tactics (SWAT) teams.

One morning while receiving instruction in the course gymnasium on basic self-defense, including how to resist an individual with a pistol trained at the back of one's head in a hostage situation, Rich described particular "moves" made by members of a SWAT team who had attended the school for a week's training a few months prior. Barely concealing his mocking disdain, he painted a somewhat humorous, yet ironic picture of the ways in which prior to contact (the moments leading up to shots being fired), SWAT team members would perform a highly choreographed series of forward rolls, or "roly polies," across the floor. After these elaborate roly polies, they would pop up and assume a crouching position with pistol drawn, ready to engage the enemy. Another similarly "ridiculous" ritual he discussed concerned the Secret Service PSD teams who jog alongside the U.S. president's vehicle as it proceeds through crowds. One lunchtime, Ken played a training video of a well-known U.S. private security training company showing an operative rolling on his back and firing his weapon under a vehicle. Finally, one of the instructors mentioned the American and Israeli Secret Services who confront threats to their (highly distressed) clients by wrestling them to the ground while, with weapon drawn, they respond to enemy contact. Each of these examples was systematically critiqued by both Rich and Ken. For example, questions were raised over the operational rationale for jogging alongside a limousine that has five-inch thick military-grade armor, doors that weigh as much as Boeing 757 cabin doors, its own oxygen system, tear gas, and smoke grenades. What value is added to the security of the president by these sunglass-wearing individuals? The most obvious limitation of firing a weapon under a vehicle underscored a point made earlier about "collateral damage" since, as Rich put it, "you can't see who the fuck you are shooting at . . . and run the risk of rounds ricocheting off the underside of the car!" Similarly, why roll across the floor prior to using one's weapon when such a procedure provides the enemy with (albeit a moving) target and at the same time impedes contractors' response time? The instructors argued instead for the clients' *removal* from the threat as paramount, in contrast to exposing oneself to further risk during the moments in which less-than competent CP officers may fumble for their weapon while their client is restrained underneath them.

Though there are complexities here regarding an infinite number of potential scenarios and the most appropriate tactical response, the instructors noted how threats to clients were *not* "military situations" that required an unthinking return of fire but, rather, demanded a qualitatively *different* and "smarter" reaction. Here, staying and fighting should be seen as the last course of action rather than the first. Taken together, these "lessons in incompetence" served to graphically illustrate the triumph of security's performative dimensions (exemplified in the Ninja metaphor), over those of operational effectiveness and "common bloody sense." How then did the instructors explain the tensions between performance and this questionable practice? Why were these (according to Rich and Ken, mainly American) men apparently devoid of common sense? It was at this point that gendered understandings augmenting the frivolous, masculinized Ninjas gave rise to the metaphorical figure of Billy Big Bollocks. That he relied on hypermasculine security practice revealed his status as a "weak man . . . who had something to prove," in the words of Ken and, in turn, suggested a form of compensatory masculinity desperate to reaffirm its manly self (Kimmel 1997).

Don't Be a Billy Big Bollocks!

Second only to the penis, the bollocks (a euphemism for testicles) are an irrefutable masculine cue. The oft-heard jibe that "your balls are not big enough" is addressed to those men perceived to fall short of an acceptable masculinity, or in the case of women, masculinity will always remain out of their reach since they are not in possession of the male reproductive organs. Interestingly then, the derogatory narrative used by the instructors subverts this dominant trope by supplanting it with reference to an *excess* of masculinity—balls that are "too big," and as such, a further instance of the condemnatory mercenary narrative. Thus, closely bound up with the Ninja metaphor, the student group was frequently reminded of the characteristics of Billy Big Bollocks—aspects of embodied identity and social practice that should be avoided at all costs or at least downplayed if at all possible. Here, the operational rationale for effecting a security persona that deflected rather than drew attention to itself, turned on the enemy's identification of the "real" (i.e., operational) reason for one's presence in a hostile region. It was also linked in the mind of Rich to the intramasculine dynamic of competition between differing modes of manhood where "pumped-up bodies" might be interpreted as a provocative "come on" in those stereotypically macho contexts characteristic of "seriously dangerous [South American] countries." Frequented by Rich and Ken for the purposes of CP work for a client located in a particular South American city, this region was often invoked in regard to its exemplary levels of violence (noted further below). In an allied sense we were told that "tattoos are stupid . . . they don't frighten the enemy one bit [since] these guys have been fighting wars for thousands of years . . . what is needed is confidence." Rich then rolled up his sleeve to expose a number of tattoos that he "got done when he was a young lad" that he now "regretted." Further examples used to underscore the operational futility of excessive iterations of masculinity included the "big muscle-bound idiots coming on the course," many of whom were believed to have achieved their extreme size through the use of steroids, and/or long periods working out in the gym. These hypermasculine symbols undermined the low-key professional approach and could threaten operations and ultimately the safety of the client. "From the moment you land [at the airport]," Ken informed us "the bad guys are clocking [watching] you . . . this is even more likely if you turn up in a tight fitting t-shirt with bulging muscles and tattoos up yer' arms . . . for fuck's sake don't advertise yourself."

Students who had attended earlier courses were also mentioned. Rich described one of them as "so large that he could barely lift himself from the ground" after firing from a prone position on the range. With his disproportionately large biceps limiting movement, another student struggled to hold a pistol straight out in front of him—"he was a monster of man," we were told. "When you're that size, you can't run, you can't be agile . . . and you make a great target," Rich noted; and to illustrate the increased vulnerability characteristic of this muscle-bound physique, he stated with a wry smile that "bullets travel far quicker through muscle than fat!" Developing the theme of how Billy Big Bollocks' use of weapons demonstrated weakness was the tendency for some contractors to "flag [point at] people with their weapons . . . they are fucking idiots . . . they are aggressive, don't care, and are just motivated by money," argued Rich. With this in mind, he relayed the story of an American military officer who had told the instructors that his rules of engagement provided for the shooting of *anyone* carrying a weapon, no matter what the circumstances (even if the weapon did not have a "mag" [magazine] on and was being carried in a nonthreatening manner). "This" stated Rich was "totally crazy . . . a weapon is a reminder *not* to use it . . . just as much as body armor creates a false sense of security." What was needed was "respect for the locals . . . not aggression and intimidation."

On the wall of the course coffee area were 15 or so black-and-white and color photographs depicting grisly images from the South American country where the instructors regularly worked. These showed decapitated bodies, dismembered heads, and other scenes of death and mutilation. One showed five bodies hanging from the steel frame of a child's swing in a nondescript, inner-city play area. We were asked to gather around these images. Rich and Ken were present and, pointing to the photographs, the former stated, "if you think you're a tough guy then we'll get you to [names the country] . . . you couldn't make the brutality up . . . kids and all . . . these people are barbarians." The aim of this moment was to reinforce the by-now, well-rehearsed observation that security was not the place for bravado and big men, but rather was a highly skilled occupation to be treated with great respect. Put succinctly, those who thought CP work or body guarding glamorous and the ideal site to deploy an (arrogant) hypermasculinity were, as Rich put it to the amusement of the student group, "well 'ard . . . not!"

The Billy Big Bollocks metaphor contained a final, explicitly gendered component. This concerned Rich's respectfully framed reference to his "old mum" who, he stated repeatedly on the firing range, "can shoot better than the lot of 'yer'"! He made much of this retort—usually accompanied with a joke or two—and sought to publicly criticize those who failed to hit the target through the twin tropes of femininity and old age. Given the prevalent status of those with this doubly-disadvantaged identity, by invoking his old mum, Rich positioned (incompetent) men as submasculine in relation to an elderly woman, who by implication should barely be able to hold, let alone use, a weapon proficiently. In sum, unlike the well-documented observations drawn from military and militarized settings where women and gay people exist as the ubiquitous subordinate foil, in the current field research, evidence of this narrative was limited and replaced with running commentary on the perils of excess masculinity as a prime indicator of cowboy or rogue contractor status.

DISCUSSION

In general terms, these findings resonate with Joachim's and Schneiker's (2012a) contribution in their analysis of PMSC websites where they developed three gendered strategies of legitimation: pathologization, masculinization, and feminization. Most striking in the current data was the extent to which Rich and Ken pathologized the aberrant other through narratives of the hypermasculine Ninja or Billy Big Bollocks. Through criticizing those perceived to be less than professional, the instructors replicated wider traits in the industry noted on company websites and beyond that "devalue the masculinity of other security actors, such as conventional military forces, mercenaries and even other PMSCs, by depicting them as weak, incapable, ineffective and immoral" (Joachim and Schneiker 2012a, 507). In contrast, and central to the industry's remasculinizing narratives that potential clients may find appealing, is Rich's and Ken's implicit construction of the exemplary protector figure. This resonates with a bourgeois, rationalist masculinity equipped with "superior intellect and personal integrity [which is] valued over physical strength or bravery" (Hooper 2001, 98, quoted in Joachim and

Schneiker 2012c). The invitation to reflect on our connection with loved ones who might be killed through the incompetence of trigger-happy contractors can be read as an instance where compassion and empathy—more typically understood as feminized traits—were invoked as key facets of professional practice "upgraded" to further legitimize contractor masculinity (Joachim and Schneiker 2012c, 78).

While the field research elicited findings that broadly mirror the industry's wider attempts to constitute professionals of certain kinds by differentiating themselves from the archetypal cowboy, in certain respects, the current findings also depart from this general theme. For example, unlike company websites that framed the expertise of their operatives alongside superior technology (Joachim and Schneiker 2012c, 71), Ken and Rich stressed the importance of operating effectively even when drastically *underresourced*, hence the need to develop skills in a wide range of weapons "'coz you never know what [weapon] you're gonna' get given in these places." Findings from unpublished field research by the author echo the importance of adaptability, where it is imperative that contractors make the best of what limited means they have at hand. In the words of a former New Zealand special forces manager in a private company: "We want guys who can go anywhere in the world with only a passport and 5,000 dollars . . . and just get on with it." And, in contrast to companies that are pitching to a global market through narratives of omnipotence and unlimited capacity (Joachim and Schneiker 2012c, 86), the instructors were very clear about what could and could not be realistically achieved with modest resources. They were cautious about overselling themselves and selected only those jobs deemed manageable; the notion that they cared "for the whole world" was anathema, unlike the message conveyed through a number of PMSC websites (Joachim and Schneiker 2012c, 81). It is through these observations that we note the *differences* between the presentation of masculinities in the market for force through the websites (Joachim and Schneiker 2012a) and their empirical manifestation on the ground in this particular (nongeneralizable) instance. However, what are the implications of the instructors' narratives for wider questions of the legitimacy of PMSCs?

Remasculinization and the Effects of the Professionalism Narrative

The findings included above provide for numerous lines of original inquiry. Among others, these include an interrogation of the historical and cultural conditions that make possible the degrading of U.S. military and militarized masculinity by the British in the context of PMSCs and national militaries. While this topic is dealt with elsewhere (Higate 2012a), the current chapter takes its analytical cue from Anna Leander's (2012) work on the jurisgenerativity of Codes of Conduct in the industry since her observations have analytical utility for instructor narratives in regard to their constitutive dimensions (92).

Though their otherwise sophisticated lexicon on all matters relating to violence was indisputable, Rich's and Ken's use of the word "violence" was notable in its absence and mirrors wider trends that reach into the realm of international relations scholarship (Thomas 2010). Indeed, the bedrock of the instructors' respective identities and material existence turned on their ability to deploy violence when required (in their case to protect a South American client), as well as to instruct others in a craft requiring humility, dedication, and integrity nested within a modest masculine self. In this way, we might read their practices as tantamount to an informal process of (industry) regulation, to argue for the appropriate bodies and minds through which particular gendered beings can legitimately exercise violence in order to, as they put it, "lift the industry up." Framed in these terms, the authority of the remasculinization narrative was derived from the implicit assumption that the existence of violence—used by perpetrators and countered by CP officers in line with their bourgeois, rational masculine ethic—was a given. Violence is the norm rather than the exception. As an unavoidable tenet of everyday social relations, what really matters is *who* (or what form of masculinity) has the right to deploy practices intended to kill and injure others for reasons of client protection. Seen against the backcloth of the wider industry then, invocations of Ninjas and Billy Big Bollocks serve to normalize the privatization of security by self-referential distraction and a gendered-doctrinal binary; violence's illegitimate (hypermasculine) proponents versus those superior others who respond with due professionalism (Leander 2012, 100). That these narratives were infused with humor, self-deprecation, and irony may well have helped reinforce their impact on a subordinate student group keen to learn from expert instructors imbued with the kudos of military masculinity (Belkin 2012). In microcosm, and in parallel to Codes of Conduct in the industry, these classroom narratives mimic wider trends that "produce distinctions among respectable and non-respectable firms . . . [in turn, these] generate a misrecognition of the overall increase in the weight of military professionals; respectable or not" (Leander 2012, 105).

Yet, unlike the case of ArmorGroup employees, remasculinization in the current example turned on highlighting rather than obscuring "disorder and uncertainty" in the conflict context (Leander 2012, 103; also see Hendershot's chapter in this volume)—underscored by the violent images we were encouraged to view and reflect upon. To put this differently, a key incentive for the student group to develop a professional approach to security work was to acknowledge the potential chaos of the operational context through developing a contingent masculinity imbued with the capacity to adopt and adapt *in the right way*. This moment of quintessentially British remasculinization called forth a subtle, understated, restrained, tempered, and contemplative masculinity (Paris 2000; Plain 2006) noted in other militarized contexts (Nagl 2002; Aylwin-Foster 2005) and invoked those attributes that point to "gender and nation as unchanging essence" (Dawson 1994, 11). That these masculine traits were conveyed persuasively through the instructors' charisma (especially Rich) also helped distract from the legitimacy or overall inevitability of the industry as an instrument of militarization (Leander 2012, 92). In this way, Rich intuitively maneuvered students within a social universe of his own making by engaging the affective and embodied dimensions of identity, the (appropriate) use of violence, and two imagined communities of contractors comprised of either big men or modest men. To which should we subscribe? How far could we reject his seductive promise to attain an ontologically secure identity in respect of the latter?

Seen in this way, instructor narratives turned on a politics of gender inhering within the charismatic dimension of leadership defined by Max Weber and conveyed through a blend of passion, authority, and due responsibility (Adair-Toteff 2005, 197). Conceived of in positivist terms, the influence of charisma as an integral element of (informal) industry regulation is "irrational" yet remains key to processes of remasculinization in the current example. Charisma is the imperceptible social quality of interaction that, while existing beyond quantification, nonetheless carries with it powerful transformative effects (Adair-Toteff 2005). And it is the ethnographic rather than discursive or state-level data approach to knowledge generation derived from face-to-face interaction that leads me to argue that these narratives were *not* derived from a rational, instrumental, business strategy driven by profit margin as in the case of company website construction of masculinities (Joachim and Schneiker 2012c, 81), but rather from a strongly held sense of professionalism, largely without market logic, manifest through deeply embodied identity. Thus, it is not only that military professional and national identity get commodified in the sphere of private security in ways that have utility for increasing market share, but also that this gendered practice is the partly *unintended* outcome of the ultimate desire to distance oneself from the persistent mercenary stereotype at the level of masculine self-identity. This is a question of how particular men position themselves in dense social relations that turn—as they see it—on matters of life and death.

CONCLUSION

This chapter has sought to develop the remasculinization thesis as it pertains to the PMSC industry through drawing on the contributions of Stachowitsch and, in particular, Joachim and Schneiker. Guided by original field research conducted with a training company run by two British, former military men in the United States, the analysis revealed the centrality of the national dimension. In its American guise, I argued that it provides for excesses of masculinity in ways that signaled contractor incompetence. These excesses, symbolized in the metaphorical figures of the Ninja and Billy Big Bollocks, were offset by the gendered architecture of professionalism residing in a quintessentially British militarized masculinity. In moving from the micro-interactional context, I also argued that these social processes contributed toward the affirmation of a consensual world view for those involved and, more widely, that violence is normal and natural, and it is the question of who has the authority to exercise it that occupied center stage. Given the recent proliferation of interest in PMSCs from critical scholars of gender, it might be worth asking how far and in what kinds of ways this scholarship may also, in some instances, help legitimate an industry through its problem-solving approach that leaves undisturbed the centrality of violence argued to frame the work of those in the armed CP role.

CHAPTER 8

Heteronormative and Penile Frustrations

The Uneasy Discourse of the ArmorGroup

Hazing Scandal

CHRIS HENDERSHOT

The U.S. Department of State's (USDoS) contract with ArmorGroup North America, a contract that had been signed in March 2007 to provide static security services for the U.S. embassy in Kabul, turned scandalous on September 1, 2009. Prior to this date, the USDoS had on at least three occasions expressed concern to ArmorGroup regarding deficiencies with their provision of security services (see U.S. Senate 2009). Primary among these concerns was ArmorGroup's continued failure to provide a properly prepared and staffed guard force, which "gravely [endangered] performance of guard services in a high-threat environment such as Afghanistan" (James 2008, quoted in U.S. Senate 2009, 3). On the first of September 2009, such staffing deficiencies became starkly apparent through a press conference conducted by Danielle Brian, executive director of the Project on Government Oversight (POGO), and a subsequent digital media story published by Gawker. In the POGO press conference, Brian presented a letter addressed to then Secretary of State Hillary Clinton detailing a litany of problems with the ArmorGroup contract. Beyond reiterating the USDoS' prior acknowledgement of staffing issues, this letter also detailed allegations, corroborated by eyewitness testimonials and visual documentation, of "Supervisors Engaging in Deviant Hazing and Humiliation" (Brian 2009, 6). As text from the letter to Secretary Clinton reads:

> Numerous emails, photographs, and videos portray a Lord of the Flies environment. One email from a current guard describes scenes in which guards

and supervisors are "peeing on people, eating potato chips out of [buttock] cracks, vodka shots out of [buttock] cracks (there is video of that one), broken doors after drnken [sic] brawls, threats and intimidation from those leaders participating in this activity. . . ." Photograph after photograph shows guards—including supervisors—at parties in various stages of nudity, sometimes fondling each other. These parties take place just a few yards from the housing of other supervisors. (Brian 2009, 6)

Although numerous issues with understaffing, overwork, language barriers, and unauthorized, armed excursions into Kabul are also detailed in the letter and press conference, the textual, photo, and audiovisual evidence of alcohol-fueled contractors in various stages of undress and cross-dress performing simulated sex acts proved too titillating for Gawker to pass up. At 4:18 p.m., over six hours after the POGO press conference (Cook 2009b), Gawker published a story with the title "Our Embassy in Afghanistan Is Guarded by Sexually Confused Frat Boys." The accompanying article contained eight photos of men, with all identifying markers blocked out, consuming alcohol (some of which is being poured across and down an orifice), standing around a fire naked, simulating anal penetration, and slapping and biting exposed nipples and buttocks (Cook 2009a).[1] With digital media breaking and making the story, mainstream print and television media coverage ensured that ArmorGroup's staffing issues transformed from a discourse of a problematic contract to one of scandal and embarrassment. Dubbed "Embassygate" by Daniel Schulman of *Mother Jones*, the media maelstrom prompted a USDoS and congressional investigation, the firing of 14 contractors, the replacement of the senior management staff, and the decision to not renew ArmorGroup's contract (CNN.com/asia 2009; Schulman 2011).[2]

As will be evidenced, journalists and editors, policy and regulatory officials, and netizens deploy heteronormative articulations in order to express unease with the sexualized activities of the ArmorGroup contractors. The articulation of these assumptions clearly signals unease that a presumed norm violation, transgression, or reevaluation has taken place, but it is not always clear what norms have been violated, transgressed, or reevaluated. In the majority of media and policy pronouncements, sexualized transgression, violation, and reevaluation are offered unreflexively. These discourses of unease construe the sexualized activities of ArmorGroup contractors as deviant, disgusting, depraved, and disturbing because they are apparently deviant, disgusting, depraved, and disturbing. It is tempting to critique this discourse as a tautology, thereby suggesting that unease is illogical or nonsensical, that is, the articulators cannot explain their disapproval, hence their disapproval is meaningless. I resist such a temptation because the disapproval and unease are not meaningless, but, as I argue, a sign that PMSCs and their male contractors are expected to uphold and further practices and institutions of heteronormativity—including the proper functioning of both symbolic and fleshy penises.

To demonstrate this assertion I analyze a series of forthright, intertextual, metaphorical, and euphemistic examples of heteronormal and penile unease with the intimacies enacted by the ArmorGroup contractors. To ensure a thorough analysis, I undertake a two-part investigation. In the first section, I engage with three groupings of heteronormal unease: (1) visceral, (2) staid, and (3) deflective. Subdividing this analysis into three groups is empirically necessary inasmuch as it is pertinent to individually address differing expressions of heteronormal unease. Such categorization is not intended to suggest that differing expressions are meaningful in isolation from one another. A key insight of this analysis is that we need to recognize the differing and sometimes contradictory or competitive articulations of heteronormative unease. In the second section, I undertake a more playful analysis that focuses on how unease with and between symbolic and fleshy penises can be read through the Kabul incident. Somewhat surprisingly, very few direct expressions of the problems of and with penises are found in the source material consulted for this analysis. Some comments jokingly riff on the name of ArmorGroup's parent company at the time: Wackenhut. Short of this word play, the vast majority of comments avoid referring to contractors as "dicks" or lamenting that the contractors need to start using what's between their ears rather than what's between their legs. Interpretation in this section must therefore be metaphorical, euphemistic, and intertextual. As discourses of penile unease are actualized figuratively, this section also delves into broader discussions of how penises matter to privatizing, militarizing, securing, and commercializing processes. Such a discussion contextualizes and historicizes penile unease by demonstrating how privatizing, militarizing, securing, and commercializing practices and institutions intra-act with erections, ejaculation, and phallo-centric carnalities and pleasure.[3] Reading penile metaphor and innuendo through the Kabul incident produces a not so subtle discourse of unease with the dysfunctions and deficiencies between and among symbolic and fleshy penises—and how men and their bodies are manifested to perform heteronormally in (post) conflict spaces.

UNEASY INTIMACY

The clearest way to establish the extent of the heteronormal unease with the Kabul incident is by slotting differing articulations into three categories of affective intent and inference. The first of these categories contains articulations and expressions that exude visceral disgust and revulsion.

Such expressions are often exceedingly direct: "the very disgusting photos" (quoted in Harper 2009), "[t]his is the sickest thing I have ever seen" (doge-ater99 2010), "[m]en's behavior in this country is really getting disgusting" (dsnj1-2009 2009), and "faggots" (TheFlex21 2010). My reasons for classify-ing these reactions as visceral rather than bigoted or hateful are that (1) vis-ceral properly conveys the psychosomatic intra-actions of senses, emotions, organs, and muscles that these commentators are experiencing through their encounter/witnessing of the sexualized pleasures enacted by the (male) ArmorGroup contractors; (2) embodying revulsion allows for understand-ings of personal unease that are not simply traceable to the mental faculties of commentators, that is, ignorance or stupidity; and (3) using visceral rather than bigoted or homophobic gestures toward conceptualizing this form of unease as only one method of the ways that sex, sexuality, intimacy and pleasure are regulated.[4] As Samuel A. Chambers (2007) notes: "Homophobia connotes both an individual act (something done by a person who is 'homo-phobic') and a psychological disturbance (a problem located in someone's head)" (664). Accordingly, not labeling strong, aggressive, or guttural inter-pretations as bigoted or homophobic avoids isolating this form of unease in the individual commentators, thereby opening the possibility to read vis-ceral unease through conceptions of heteronormativity. This is not to con-done visceral unease but rather to recognize that the heteronormalizing of sex, sexuality, pleasure, and intimacy is a multifaceted, contradictory, and hierarchical assemblage of sexualized, gendered, raced, and classed practices and phenomena (Seidman 2005; Jackson 2006; Hubbard 2008).

As Lauren Berlant and Michael Warner (1998) write, heteronormative arrangements are "more than ideology, or prejudice, or phobia against gays and lesbians" (554), they are "a constellation of practices that everywhere disperses heterosexual privilege as a tacit but central organizing index of social membership" (555). Heteronormalizing most readily flows through the structural and everyday actualizations of familial and kinship architectures, modes of consumption, popular culture, and geography (Berlant and Warner 1998; Hubbard 2000). In particular, sexualized or intimate practices and expressions are heteronormalized through the assignment of public, private, or marginal value. In Warner's (2005) words, "not all sexualities are public or private [or marginal] in the same way" (24). Intimate or sexual practices that have a public value are those which reaffirm, reify, or commodify the public space of the state, community, or street as a space of reproductive futurity (Edelman 2004), citizenship (Johnson 2002), and civility. Sexualized public intimacies can include practices like hand-holding, hugging, and nonerotic kissing (i.e., no tongue) among couples, friends, or family. Private value inti-macies need not bolster reproductive futurity, citizenship, and civility as private space better accommodates personal or self-expression and explora-tion,[5] so long as such expression and exploration are not deemed harmful to the self. This means that both vanilla and more adventurous intimate practices can be assigned private value. For intimacies such as viewing pornography, using sex toys and other apparatus, or role-playing to hold private value, their actualization must only occur in the privatized space of the bedroom, home, or in a legally regulated commercial site. Marginal value intimacies are not wholly harmful or threatening to heteronormativity but rather exceed or slip through the bounds of public and private space and therefore must exist on the peripheries. As such, marginal value intimacies can simultaneously be enacted or co-opted as threats and pillars of heteronormative ordering. Historically, marginal value intimacies have included promiscuity, prostitution, masturbation, homosexuality, and sadomasochism. Public, private, and marginal value intimacies are contextually actualized, meaning that heteronormative arrangements of intimacy are not the exclusive preserve of binary-sexed couplings that only enact procreative coitus. The slow, but advancing, acceptance of homosexual coupling is the most obvious sign of the contextual actualizing of heteronormative intimacies—which for some academics is translated into homonormative ordering (Puar 2006). Reactions of visceral unease must therefore be recognized as functioning through a complexity of potential transgressions of heteronormative ordering. Hence, it is not sufficient to contend that bigoted expressions or expressions of disgust are only manifestations of unease when encountering marginal value intimacies. The specific intimacies encountered through the Kabul incident are certainly marginalized, but the unease is more appropriately recognized as unease with encountering a spatial transgression rather than a specifically sexualized violation of the public and private value of heteronormative intimacies. The visceral reactions as represented above are expressions of unease with both a confusion of heteronormative and militarized spacing of intimacy. The overtly sexualized inflections demonstrate unease with confronting marginal value fraternal rituals (Higate 2012c) being performed in (proximity to) the public space of the U.S. embassy—which is located in a (post)conflict zone. Interestingly, (heteronormal) militarized spacing of intimacy leaves very little space for public value expressions of heteronormal intimacy save for nonsexualized fraternal intimacies of brotherhood such as hugging, high-fiving, fist-bumping, and hand-shaking. That the Kabul incident can be read as a performance of sexualized fraternal rituals that create bonds and cohesion among men living and working in male-only spaces (Higate 2012c, 455) seems not to apply to visceral reactions of unease and thus visceral reactions, even hateful and bigoted articulations, are better understood as expressions of unease with a violation of the heteronormal militarized spacing of (post)conflict zones.

The second category I discuss, staid expressions of unease, appear primarily in the headlines and titles of articles and videos. Like visceral reactions, staid expressions are forthright in their disapproval and unease with the (space of) intimacies enacted by the ArmorGroup contractors. Unlike visceral expressions, staid articulations are more measured in their affective intents and phrasing, thereby avoiding an obvious stigma as bigoted or hateful. The most common manifestations of staid references are to the offensive, deviant, lewd, vulgar, and/or obscene character of the sexualized activities of the ArmorGroup contractors. The POGO letter to Hilary Clinton is the original source of staid referencing by subtitling the section addressing the sexualized activities as "Supervisors Engaging in Deviant Hazing and Humiliation" (Brian 2009, 6). Similar examples of staid articulations include, "Embassy Guards Fired for Lewd Behavior" (CBS News 2009a), "Embassy Fires Security Guards Over Appearance in Vulgar Photos" (Brodsky 2009), "US Guards 'Drunk at Obscene Kabul Parties'" (Sky News 2009), "Kabul U.S. Embassy Guard: Sexual Deviancy Required for Promotion" (Ross, Schwartz, and Radia 2009), and "Embassy at Risk as 'Deviant' Guards Let Their Hair Down" (Whittell 2009). Reporting on the reactions of the USDoS, CBS News (2009) cites Hilary Clinton as being "genuinely offended" and quotes a USDoS spokesperson as saying "[t]his violated our values." Fox News (2009) also quotes Secretary of Defense Robert Gates as saying: "Those activities . . . [t]hey're offensive to us." The contentiousness of deeming sexual practices and intimacies as acceptable, legitimate, healthy, and moral or inappropriate, dangerous, and disorderly means that staid interpretations need to be read as unreflexively reconstituting historically pernicious hierarchies of appropriate sexualized behavior—hierarchies that have gravely disadvantaged and punished peoples deemed incapable or unworthy of reproductive futurity, citizenship, and civility. Moreover, because these staid expressions are articulated without subsequent explication of what actually makes the sexualized activities of the ArmorGroup contractors offensive and vulgar, it can only be presumed that, like visceral reactions, the behavior of the ArmorGroup contractors generates unease because it violates the heteronormal militarizing of space and the attendant values attributed to the intimacies permitted to be actualized in and through heteronormal militarized spaces. Framed as such, staid interpretations are more authoritative than visceral ones inasmuch as the determination of deviancy, lewdness, obscenity, and vulgarity has historically been the providence of reputable and indispensable practices and institutions such as law, medicine, education, and the military. As numerous (queer) social theorists have argued, the deployment of sexuality (Foucault 1978), invention of gender (Butler 1990), and normalizing of heterosexuality (Warner 1999) are intimately linked to Anglo-American "advances," "modernizing" and "institutionalizing" law, medicine, education, and the military. The social and historical links to reputable practices and institutions along with emotionally and politically tame(d) terms and phrasings have the effect of mainstreaming or, more appropriately, normalizing staid unease. That this form of unease is articulated predominantly by and through mainstream media sources and government officials only enhances its status as normal unease.

To be fair it is arguable that what is deviant, vulgar, obscene, offensive, lewd, and thus a transgression of values is more appropriately connected to the coercion and intimidation that is said to have occurred to get certain contractors to participate. In short, it is the accusations of hazing that make the Kabul incident deviant and offensive. There are some significant difficulties with maintaining this argument however. The first, and a most flimsy, counter is that the visual evidence does not depict any of the contractors in states of duress. To echo the sentiments of a variety of commentators, in the photos and videos the contractors appear to be enjoying themselves—many contractors are smiling and enacting celebratory body language. While there is an aesthetic of celebration to the photo and audiovisual documentation,[6] that no visual evidence of duress is seen in these documents does not rule out the possibility that coercion or intimidation were integral features of the sexualized activities of the contractors. A second and more nuanced point of contention was offered by Danielle Brian in response to the question, "And the lewd and deviant behavior, why does that matter?": "It is devastating to these people, many of whom have a law enforcement and military background . . . to show up in an environment that is so . . . debaucherous . . . and the fact that supervisors are using participation in these parties as kind of a weapon . . . so it's being used as weapon" (quoted in MoxNewsDotCom 2009).

Brian's response provides a key, yet troubling, qualification to the coercive character of the hazing. Brain's suggestion that the conservative, innocent, or reserved character of former police officers and soldiers needs to be considered when analyzing the effects of the coerced debauchery is a strange qualification if the coercion is what is actually deviant. Sexualized coercion and intimidation are certainly applied to make specific people as embodied entities do specific things, for example, satisfy interrogators in Abu Ghraib. The problem with labeling targeted coercion deviant, however, is that it opens the political possibility that not all coerced sexual encounters are problematic—or "deviant" for that matter. In short, it should matter little who experienced coercion or intimation and only that someone did. Likewise, the actualization of coercion or intimation through unsettling sexualized practices is certainly unsettling, but what should be primarily unsettling is that sex and intimacy are again deployed through expressions of (nonconsensual) domination and force. In a different interview, Brian does state that "this is not about guys in parties being naked, this is about a total breakdown of command structure" (quoted in baracine 2009). This phrase rings hollow however because it is the guys partying naked and the coercive participation of some of these guys that contributes to the breakdown of the command structure. Or as was put in an e-mail sent to POGO by one of the contractors, it is the "gay shit" that is the problem. Coercion needs to be taken seriously whatever the situation. Attaching lewdness or deviance to a coerced sexual situation signals more insidious forms of unease. In this case, it signals that unease is traceable to a failure of the ArmorGroup contractors to uphold the heteronormal militarized space of (post)conflict zones.

The third category of unease I identify is deflective. Deflective unease is articulated through irreverence, sophomoric humor, and pop-culture referencing. Deflective unease strips away the guttural righteousness of visceral readings and the intellectual disciplining of staid expressions by wrapping unease in playful wink-wink, nudge-nudge terms and phrasings. Notable examples include "Animal House in Afghanistan" (Schulman 2009), "U.S. Kabul Security Gone Wild" (CBS News 2009b), "Homoerotic 'Hazing' Turns U.S. Kabul Embassy into 'Animal House'" (Melloy 2009), and the headline that launched the scandal, "Our Embassy in Afghanistan Is Guarded by Sexually Confused Frat Boys" (Cook 2009b). The privatized and marginal heteronormative value accorded to frat-boy intimacies, including homoerotic ones, and the pop-cultural institutionalizing of these intimacies in the 1978 film *Animal House*, and the pornographic series of videos entitled *Girls Gone Wild* does not immediately signal unease with a deflective interpretation of the Kabul incident. The popular-culture references do, however, link the Kabul incident to a genre of films, which characterize male protagonist(s) as late 20 to early 30 somethings who are unable to grow up or mature. Embodied by the performances of Vince Vaughan, Will Farrell, Adam Sandler, and Seth Rogan, the boy-man character is a commercially very successful trope. The proliferation of the drunk, lazy, stupid, onanistic, still living with his parents male has, however, been cited, mainly by conservative critics, as the popular instantiation of a broader crisis of modern male immaturity (Crouse 2011). The core of this concern is encapsulated in the book *Men to Boys: The Making of Modern Immaturity* (Cross 2008), which makes the case that the rise of the boy-man (in pop culture) is causing a detrimental stunting of American masculinity.[7] This foregrounding of the immature, sophomoric, and childish antics of the Kabul incident links a deflective reaction to concerns with the general dumbing down of (Anglo-American) men and masculinity. The deflective unease cited above is not so much manifested through unease with transgression as it is with the unease that accompanies a reevaluation of masculine preferences and the subsequent effects on heteronormative ordering of space and intimacies. Frat-boy and spring-break antics and consumption of male-gaze pornography are not overly valued publically, but they are privately and marginally valued as rites of passage from boyhood to manhood. The operative word here is "passage," and the unease contained in the above cited deflective articulations is an expression of a sign that the ArmorGroup contractors are failing to complete this passage. In failing to pass from boyhood to manhood, the ArmorGroup contractors are also failing to manifest a heteronormal male body that is capable of disciplining urges for lesser pleasures derived from lesser intimacies, that is, nonreproductive intimacies.

With that said, Gawker and *Mother Jones* do use deflective articulations as a method of criticizing the intimacies enacted by the ArmorGroup guards. Jokingly, the concluding line from Gawker's initial post reads: "Are these guys asking, or telling?" (Cook 2009a). Along with playing off social and institutional unease with uncloseted gay, lesbian, bisexual, and transgendered people serving in the U.S. military, this "joke" invokes heteronormal-masculinist unease with penetration and reception, that is, "who's the pitcher and who's the catcher." The images of alcohol being consumed off an anus further unsettle penetrator-receiver intimacies as it is unclear who or what is performing penetration and who or what is the receiver. Another Gawker post that explains how Gawker came to obtain the "photos of [the contractors] acting out a gay porn version of Animal House" refers to the photos as "gross" (Cook 2009b). In a similar expression of ick, *Mother Jones* captions one of the more scrutinized photos with "And here's the infamous butt-shot shot—wrong on so many levels" (Schulman 2009). Ironically, compared to the off-handedness of writing "Are these guys asking, or telling?," these more direct expressions of distaste are not all that clear in explicating what it is that is distasteful about the images. Employing a deflective method of my own: Is it the aesthetics of the photos, for example, the lighting, angles, clarity, or fore- and background that makes the images and videos gross and wrong? Is it the varied aesthetics of male bodies, which cannot be said to conform to popular heteronormal and phallo-centric prescriptions for taught and hairless bodies? Is literal distaste generated by the thought of drinking alcohol that has sanitized the anus of a human? Before I get carried away, the wrongness and grossness of the images of the ArmorGroup contractors are traceable to numerous aspects and assumptions. Nevertheless, the meaningfulness of wrongness and grossness combined with the presumption that what is wrong and gross is obvious does rely upon a deeper presumption of the proper conduct and usage of male bodies to experience pleasure. Or, as I have reiterated throughout this section, the meaningfulness of wrongness and grossness rests upon presumptions and manifestations of male bodies as heteronormalizing entities or vessels.

Visceral, staid, and deflective methods of expressing unease do use differing terms, phrases, and inflections, and a potential for contention amongst what terms, phrases, and inflections are hateful, proper, or stupid must be acknowledged. Heteronormal unease need not be unilateral in scope, nor need it be discursively exclusive. As both queer and feminist scholars maintain, heterosexed and gendered expectations, performances, embodiments, and institutions are produced "as open-ended, multiple, and multidimensional processes" (Hooper 2001, 39). This means that the existence and actualization of multiple heterosexed performances and embodiments only become problematic or uneasy when such performances and embodiments are perceived to transgress, violate, or reevaluate heteronormativity—or more specifically heteronormal militarization. Construing visceral, staid, and deflective methods as differing methods of expressing heteronormal unease is not only an appropriate reading of the sources of sexualized unease with the Kabul incident, but it also creates the conceptual space to appreciate the intra-actions amongst privatizing, securing, militarizing, and commercializing processes and heteronormativity. I now turn to a discussion of penile unease in order to more concretely demonstrate that unease with the Kabul incident is assembled through unease with how men should live and work in (post)conflict spaces along with how privatizing, securing, militarizing, and commercializing processes fail to produce or govern men and male bodies capable of performing heteronormal-penile expectations.

OF PENISES AND PHALLUSES

It may seem strange to pursue an analysis of penises when the presence of this fleshy adornment is nowhere to be seen in the visual documentation of the intimacies enacted by the ArmorGroup contractors. Considering that (white, bourgeois, "civilized"[8]) penises have not until the 1990s been seen publically (Del Rosso 2011), it may actually be more shocking if the fleshy penises of the ArmorGroup contractors were visible—especially if those penises were also erect. Conversely, even if the contractors had not covered their penises with circular black material, censorship codes would have forced at least the mainstream media coverage to blur out any visible genitalia. The sociopolitical, cultural and economic ordering, and sorting of power manifested through fleshy penises and its metonym the phallus (Potts 2001) by privatizing, militarizing, securing, and commercializing processes ensures that invisibility should not be construed as absence or irrelevance.[9] Militarizing and securing processes, particularly the waging of war, are often justified by their need to protect and defend ways of life of which heteronormal spaces and intimacies must be considered a significant fixture. More specifically, as national militaries and security forces are tasked with protecting the nation, one feature that undoubtedly needs protecting is the need of a nation's citizens to reproduce. In this context, heteronormal intimacies, which require functional penises, are regularly upheld as practices and functions worth protecting. Specific to the military as an institution, the U.S. military's concern with providing genital protection to enlisted male personnel serving in Iraq and Afghanistan demonstrates a militarized structural need to keep soldiers' genitalia functional. Maintaining functional genitalia ensures that soldiers can fulfill their desires to reproduce. Keeping soldiers endowed with operative apparatuses also avoids the trauma of emasculation, which can be experienced through the loss of a functional penis as a result of a battle injury (Netter 2010; Sigal 2011).

Symbolically, militarized security discourses are laden with penile double entendres, euphemism, and innuendo. Carol Cohn (1987) sums this up nicely in her ethnography of American defense intellectuals:

> American military dependence on nuclear weapons was explained as "irre-sistible, because you get more bang for the buck." Another lecturer solemnly and scientifically announced "to disarm is to get rid of all your stuff." (This may, in turn, explain why they see serious talk of nuclear disarmament as perfectly resistible, not to mention foolish. If disarmament is emasculation, how could any real man even consider it?) A professor's explanation of why the MX missile is to be placed in the silos of the newest Minuteman missiles, instead of replacing the older, less accurate ones, was "because they're in the nicest hole—you're not going to take the nicest missile you have and put it in a crummy hole." Other lectures were filled with discussion of vertical erec-tor launchers, thrust-to-weight ratios, soft lay downs, deep penetration, and the comparative advantages of protracted versus spasm attacks—or what one military adviser to the National Security Council has called "releasing 70 to 80 percent of our megatonnage in one orgasmic whump." . . . There was serious concern about the need to harden our missiles and the need to "face it, the Russians are a little harder than we are." (693)

Whether "patting the missile" (693), assessing threats to soft targets, or "rolling hard" with other contractors, penises and their abilities to penetrate, engorge, and entice are even if not visible, ever present in militarizing and securing processes.

With regard to privatizing and commercializing processes, until the turn of the twenty-first century, consideration of the actual functionality of penises was a rather private affair. Masculinized anxiety about disrob-ing in the bedroom, locker room, or doctor's office signals that the failure to achieve and maintain an erection, premature ejaculation, and concerns about size are certainly not new issues (Del Rosso 2011). With the astro-nomical commercial success of erectile dysfunction (ED) medication and the sustainable profitability of pseudo-scientific measures to both get an erec-tion and keep it longer, the dysfunctional or faltering penis is no longer a private matter. In a study of erectile-enhancement discourse, Sarah Jane Brubaker and Jennifer A. Johnson (2008) demonstrate how (digital) adver-tising for erectile enhancements forthrightly, if not aggressively, articu-lates the (masculinized) problems of a smaller and weaker penis. By openly precipitating a "crisis" of poor or shameful penises, erectile-enhancement discourse not only publicizes penis issues but also commercializes them by offering a solution—through the consumption of pills (Brubaker and Johnson 2008). Similarly, and as mentioned above, until very recently penises adorning white, bourgeois, civilized, and/or heteronormal, that is, hegemonic, male bodies have only been publically visible through renaissance art and fascist sculpture (Bordo 1994). The marginal and sometimes private value of male-gaze pornography did mean fleshy penises adorning various male bodies could be glimpsed and enjoyed albeit in socioculturally scorned, politically monitored, and economically precarious establishments and neighborhoods. The proliferation of digital media, relaxing puritanical censorship standards, and the consistent profitability of disseminating male-gaze pornography have coalesced over the past 20 years to significantly lower the barriers to encountering visuals of fleshy penises. The rise of erotic, sensual, or artistic pornography also signals the movement and reevaluation of pornography from the margins to privatized spaces where heteronormal couples can "mutually" experience the pleasures of viewing penetrative sex. Unlike fleshy penises, phallic processes of marketing Anglo-American consumer goods have thoroughly produced the phallus as a desirable spectacle of the good life (Bordo 1994, 1999). Advertisements for automobiles, alcohol (especially beer), cigarettes, firearms, tools, fashion, sports and sporting events, film, and music are only the most egregiously clichéd propagators of phallo-centric consumption and commercialism. Continued cultural acceptance, as well as commercial deployment of phallo-centric marketing, is also metaphorically demonstrative of the pleasure and desire derived from spectacular visibility and penetration.

Selling cars, protecting genitals, and comprehending nuclear war are not the only ways that penises and the phallus matter. For example, Cynthia Weber (1999) makes a convincing case for a phallic reading of America's hegemonic relations with the Caribbean since 1959. Her rereading/rewriting of the dephallusization, rephallusization, and queering of the American Body Politic not only provides a cheeky analysis of American imperial relations but also demonstrates how international actors and nation-states in particular wield phallic power. Like phallo-centric advertising, wielding phallic power internationally need not require making fleshy penises visible. In Weber's estimation a nation-state need not actually possess the phallus in order to exercise phallic power and authority. A nation-state's efforts to demonstrate rigidity, potency, and virility are regularly and rightly interpreted as a sign that nation-state is not to be "fucked with." The size, strength, and global reach of a military are not only a practical demonstration of the ability to defend the heteronormal space of the nation-state but also a symbolic demonstration of phallic potential. Likewise, discourses of "unflinching," "unwavering," and "standing strong" ideologically array a nation-state's ability to withstand adversity and/or resist penetration. Phallic prowess, or lack thereof, can also be claimed, exhibited, or flaunted through economic and financial measures of the health, wealth, stability, independence, productivity, activity, and attractiveness of a nation-state. GDP, debt-to-GDP ratios, export-import gaps, and competitiveness are not readily apparent phallo-centric figures, measures, and statistics. Nor are they an obvious phallic/penile double entendre or innuendo. Nonetheless, as ostensive interpretations and demonstrations of a nation-state's health, wealth, and vitality, GDP and competitiveness are easily actualized as phallic performances.[10]

The invisibility of actual fleshy penises in the documentation of the intimacies enacted by the ArmorGroup contractors should not be read as a means to dismiss the import of penises to understanding unease with the Kabul incident or understanding the unease with PMSCs more generally. Be they symbolic, fleshy, ideational, and/or material, penises and phalluses are routinely assembled by and through (international) privatizing, militarizing, securing, and commercializing processes for purposes of claiming, exhibiting, and flaunting power, domination, and superiority. Penile performativity and phallic privilege are not unidirectional or everlasting. Privatizing, militarizing, securing, and commercializing processes also expose penises as vulnerable, faulty, and dysfunctional and to vulnerabilities, failings, and dysfunctions. The aforementioned concern of the U.S. military with genital protection for male personnel evidences the anxiety of upholding phallic standards while engaging in practices, for example, armed conflict, that can be literally castrating. Regardless of the apparent prowess, virility, or potency of phallic performances, be they interpersonal or international, there is a constant unease among these performances—an uneven, differed, and sometimes foregrounded unease.

PENILE UNEASE

Abstractly, penile unease is an unavoidable consequence of manifesting a metonymic relation among penises and the phallus. As Susan Bordo (1999) writes: "The phallus . . . haunts the penis [and] at the same time the penis . . . also haunts phallic authority, threatens its undoing" (95). To say that the phallus and penises haunt each other is to assert that while the phallus is certainly symbolic of penises, for fleshy penises to uphold phallic standards "the blood would have to be drained from it and replaced by an enduring artificial substance" (Bernheimer 1992, quoted in Weber 1999, 132). Furthermore, "Nature doesn't deal out the same pickle size to every man, and no exercise routine will enlarge or tone it if the owner feels he's been shortchanged. There is also the issue of shrinkage" (Wolcott 2012). As fleshy penises are "perhaps the most visibly mutable of bodily parts" (Bordo 1994, 206), the metonymic relation amongst penises and phallus is ontologically unsettled. Fleshy penises may "get hard," be able to penetrate, and expend for purposes of progeny; however, the majority of the time fleshy penises are flaccid appendages, hanging about requiring constant attentiveness in order to guard against injury. As a historically, materially, and morphologically contingent adornment, fleshy penises cannot be nor readily become the universal, ahistorical, and immaterial phallus. Phallic providence, power, and privilege are therefore unsettled insofar as providence, power, and privilege cannot be consistently derived from the thing that makes the idea of the phallus meaningful. Simultaneously, the unyielding straightness of the phallus creates an unrealistic standard for fleshy penises to embody (Bordo 1999, 95). Construing the penis as phallus produces an unrealistic set of performance measures that no fleshy penis can consistently attain. Phallusized bedrooms, locker rooms, boardrooms, and battlefields add the additional unease of performance anxiety, exposure, and/or castration, which only further dampens the phallic potentials of fleshy penises. Inability to uphold phallic standards and expectations are not just penile, personal, or personal penile failings but are also examples that masculinized male bodies are not the exclusive preserve of phallic authority. "Other" bodies whether adorned with a penis or not can, with exceeding difficulty, claim phallic authority.[11] Proximity to a fleshy penis strongly correlates to phallic privilege, but actually being adorned with a fleshy penis also means consistent unease with never actually being able to fulfill phallic demands. Construed as such, male phallic performativity is always also an uneasy performance. For masculinized bodies, institutions, and practices going harder, longer, and more vigorously is the primary method of claiming, exhibiting, flaunting, and maintaining penile power and privilege. Going harder, longer, and more vigorously also risks exposure that what is hard, long, and vigorous is likely less so and to risk exposure to the failings and dysfunctions caused by going harder, longer, and more vigorously.

In more practical and less euphemistic terms, penile unease is often made real and meaningful by the very practices and processes that desire and demand phallic prowess and privilege. As evidenced above, consumer goods, foreign policies, and security measures can all be assembled as phallic performances. However, alcohol and cigarette consumption, familial and social stress, battlefield injury, and full-body scanners are also meaningful causes of penile dysfunction, damage, exposure, and subsequently unease. It is at this juncture of penile prowess and unease where interrogating unease with the Kabul incident becomes most interesting. For the Kabul incident, penile unease takes on two forms: (1) as a sign of unreliable tumescence and (2) as a cipher for concerns that (post)conflict spaces arrange and assemble male bodies in emasculating ways.

Commenting on a MSNBC story, Robtice (2009) writes, "The use of mercenaries by a nation has always, 100 percent, been a sign that the nation is crashing socially, economically and psychologically. And, it's always ment [*sic*] the end of the nation as a power in the world." Although the historical inaccuracy of this comment is thoroughly rebuked by other commentators, the sentiment of declining American power is a common theme among pundits, politicians, and academics (Cox 2007). A conclusive determination of whether American power is or is not waning is not my concern here. Rather I suggest that PMSC usage as a sign of declining or waning American power offers an enticing phallic analogy of unease with the Kabul incident. Construed as phallic wielding exercises, the Anglo-American wars on al-Qaeda, the AfPak Taliban, and Ba'athists are better read as demonstrative of the quality of Anglo-American tumescence, that is, strength and hardness, rather than a reaffirmation of phallic possession. By this I mean that the "threat" posed by the aforementioned groups is not the threat of castration or phallic usurpation, but the threat of putting too much strain and pressure on the Anglo-American phallus thus resulting in a failure to rise to the occasion. The invasions of Afghanistan and Iraq are thus demonstrations that despite the discomfort or lack of confidence caused by the brashness of al-Qaeda, the United States and the United Kingdom, and to a lesser extent Canada and Australia, are willing and able to get hard and stay hard whenever and wherever. The reliance on PMSCs as force-multipliers to conduct these erectile-presenting endeavors belies some difficulty with the actualizing of Anglo-American tumescence.[12] While the Blackwater aesthetic of muscular aggressiveness lends credence to understanding PMSCs as phallic appendages or derogatorily as "dicks,"[13] the immense dependence of the Anglo-American defense, diplomatic, development, and intelligence apparatus in Iraq and Afghanistan on the logistical, training, and protection services performed by PMSCs suggests that PMSCs are more appropriately metaphorically prophylactics, "little blue pills" and "extenze." Although ArmorGroup was contracted to protect the U.S. embassy, the temporal coincidence of the Anglo-American turn to a commercialized solution for militarized phallic practices with the millions of Anglo-American men who turned to a commercialized solution for ED is a much more fruitful cipher. One source of general unease with PMSCs is thus traceable to the discomfort with the public exposure that the Anglo-American militarized phallic apparatus requires circulatory assistance to actualize and sustain its phallic capabilities. The public exposure of a need for an erectile enhancer, be it for individual men, the military or nation-states, is a direct confrontation with the inabilities of matter, male bodies or fleshy penises, to uphold symbolic pretenses of masculinity/phallo-centrism. The meaningfulness of this sort of penile unease is lessened when considering that both ED mediation and PMSCs were thoroughly instantiated in private and public phallic practices by the time the Kabul incident occurred in 2009. Accordingly, the Kabul incident signals a waning in Anglo-American tumescence because it demonstrates that the erectile aids used to achieve and sustain the necessary tumescence are at

best faulty and at worst inhibiting erection altogether. As such, concerns that "the management of the contract to protect the U.S. Embassy Kabul is grossly deficient" (Brian 2009, 2) cannot be simply read through gender- and sex-neutral managerial or oversight discourses. Breakdowns in command structure, lack of discipline, and poor morale (Brian 2009, 2) all signal uneasiness with the failure, if not denigration, of masculinized/phallusized processes in (post)conflict spaces. In phallo-centric penile parlance, breakdowns, lack, and poor are exceedingly troubling conditions and adjectives that require immediate redress or privatization in order to prevent (further) erosion of masculinized privileging. Recalling the role of PMSCs as both appendage and enhancer, the repeated assertion from commentators that U.S. Marines should be guarding U.S. embassies further buttresses the assertion that the Kabul incident induces penile unease because it exposes PMSCs as a source of erectile deflation and the subsequent problems this causes for Anglo-American expressions of spectacular tumescence. Translated through discourses of penile unease, the concerns of POGO, the USDoS, media, and netizens would be written as follows: The distraction and stress generated by the alcohol-fueled parties made the ArmorGroup contractors flaccid in their duties to secure the U.S. embassy thereby jeopardizing "the diplomatic mission in Afghanistan" (Brian 2009, 2) along with NATO efforts to remain resilient in the face of continued threats from the Taliban and al-Qaeda.

Writing "flaccid in their duties" succinctly captures the second form of penile unease generated by the Kabul incident. Where discomfort with ArmorGroup's inability to aid Anglo-American tumescence in Afghanistan can be linked to broader concerns of the roles that PMSCs do and should have as erectile aids/force-multipliers, the cornucopia of problems with ArmorGroup's securing of the U.S. embassy demonstrate the emasculating/deflating effects on male bodies in (post)conflict spaces. As the Kabul incident demonstrates, corporeal emasculation/deflation need not be limited to injuries sustained to fleshy penises. In a letter obtained by POGO, Werner Illic (2009), guard force commander of the U.S. embassy, described how understaffing, work shifts, and the hostile environment of Kabul pushed the ArmorGroup contractors to the "threshold" of sleep deprivation: "When we have to work guys overtime or ramp up extra manpower (during scheduled off days) due to increased threat conditions etc . . . etc . . . we further compound the issue of sleep deprivation. This ultimately diminishes the [contractors'] ability to provide security." The lack of sleep combined with the stresses of working in a hostile space/place literally exhausted the bodies of the ArmorGroup contractors. Exhausted bodies are not hard bodies, not strong bodies. They are frail and weak bodies, prone to failure, prone to exposing the (onto-political) unease of actualizing the phallus and/or phallic security through the contingencies of flesh. With stress, lack of sleep, and exhaustion also noted to be contributing factors of ED, the working conditions of the ArmorGroup guards are further arranged as sources of penile unease with the inabilities of masculinized male bodies to perform the phallus and/or phallic security in (post)conflict spaces. Likewise, the desire to perform properly as expressed by those contractors who exposed the "unprofessional" activities (Attachment 2 2009; Attachment 3 2009) of their colleagues and superiors signals a further strain on achieving phallic security. The expressed discomfort with the "deviance," "intimidation," and unaccountability of their colleagues and superiors and its subsequent effects on the securing performances of the ArmorGroup contractors forms a circular chain of stress: desire-to-perform/inability to perform/stress of unfulfilled desire/furthers inability to perform. Or in short, the interpersonal working conditions experienced by the ArmorGroup contractors readily produced performance anxiety, thereby further dampening the vigorousness of the contractors.

The particular physical and interpersonal inabilities of the ArmorGroup contractors to uphold the phallic-securing standards expected of them demonstrates the irony of assembling masculinized male bodies/fleshy penises through spaces, places, and processes that will also dissemble or resemble the corporeal and symbolic meanings of those bodies. In the Kabul incident, this irony is articulated through discourses of penile unease. Admittedly, this discourse of penile unease must be read through metaphor, innuendo, and double entendre. That concerns with the dysfunction of the ArmorGroup contract are spectacularly visualized through performances of nonprocreative and nonpenetrative male intimacies make it methodologically appropriate to read unease with the Kabul incident as penile unease. Reading dysfunction as an analog for ED also exposes the unease with how (post)conflict spaces distort masculinized male bodies and subsequently masculinized privilege. Rather than being spaces where men can go to be(come) men or where nation-states can operationalize masculinized proxies in order to demonstrate spectacular tumescence, the Kabul incident demonstrates that the "mundane" material and symbolic practices of male bodies laboring in hostile, threatening, and warlike spaces actually expose the onto-political shakiness of locating and actualizing phallic authority in and through men's proximity to fleshy penises.

While PMSCs continue to be contracted by Anglo-American embassies for security services, the overtly sexualized character of the Kabul incident exposes the heteronormal and penile standards and practices that PMSCs and the men they employ are expected to uphold and perform. Whether reacting viscerally, reservedly, or in a deflective manner, or variously expressing concerns with the dysfunctions of ArmorGroup's contract, the unease of policymakers, media, and netizens exposes the import of the governance of sexualized practices and precepts in and through (post)conflict spaces. In transgressing and reevaluating the heteronormal ordering of space and male bodies, as well as demonstrating the ironies and conundrums of requiring contingent matter to substantiate universalized ideologies, the Kabul incident becomes strategically, tactically, and sociopolitically relevant. The Kabul incident demonstrates that the tactical, strategic, and sociopolitical processes that make (post)conflict spaces real and meaningful are affected by gendered and sexualized expectations of how men and their bodies are to perform. Such effects are not uniform as heteronormative and penile processes are not ahistorical—contrary to the demands of phallo-centrism. Hence, as argued in this chapter, heteronormative and penile unease is a constant feature of the privatizing, militarizing, securing, and commercializing practices that use and produce masculinized male bodies. What the Kabul incident does is spectacularly expose the ever-present unease and a subsequent tactical, strategic, and sociopolitical need to assuage concerns with the inabilities of masculinized male bodies to consistently perform heteronomally and phallically. Moreover, the Kabul incident demonstrates that heteronormative and penile unease is constituted through the mundane laboring of masculinized male bodies in (post)conflict spaces. Literal castration as a result of a battlefield injury is only just receiving public, popular attention, and primary attention is paid to personnel enlisted in Anglo-American militaries. The Kabul incident, however, serves as a reminder and example of the daily challenges of sustaining heteronormativity and phallo-centrism through male bodies especially when privatizing, militarizing, securing, and commercializing processes create spaces that simultaneously assemble and distort how male bodies can perform heteronormally and phallically.

NOTES

1. According to another Gawker article, publishers at Gawker became aware of the ArmorGroup photos through a story published on *Mother Jones* at 10:19 a.m. on September 1 (Cook 2009b).
2. Aegis was awarded the contract to guard the embassy in 2011. In January 2013, POGO released another report detailing continuing issues with the guard force (ABC News 2013).
3. Phallo-centric carnality can be understood as the hierarchical ordering of pleasure wherein pleasure is properly derived from the touch, sight, and expenditure of the erect penis and the penetrative fulfillment of the erect penis' metonymic counterpart the phallus. In practice phallo-centric carnalities need not be specifically erotic, and consequently pleasure can be derived from all that can be/is framed as long, hard, potentially penetrative, and ejaculatory.
4. It would not be surprising if a survey of the people who expressed disgust did not also harbor some serious homophobic conceptions. However, it should be

noted that at least one commentator wrote, "Some of that was disturbing and I'm gay" (JordanGold 2009), which suggests that the source of visceral unease is not wholly motivated by bigotry, hate, or moral disapproval.

5. To be sure, self-expression and exploration are highly affected by gendered, raced, and classed expectations that permit certain embodied expressions and explorations over others.

6. The aesthetics of celebration and enjoyment imaged in the documentation can also buttress assertions that visceral and staid expressions of unease are actualizations of unease with the violation of heteronormal intimacies and spaces.

7. Halberstam (2011, 57) makes a more convincing case that "Male stupidity masks the will to power that lies just behind the goofy grin, and it masquerades as some kind of internalization of feminist critiques . . . and this masks the gender inequality."

8. Spongberg (1997) contends that although the hegemonic penis has been publically invisible, the subaltern penis has played a crucially visible role in European colonial practices. In particular the invisibility or visibility of penises and genitalia was used to differentiate between civilized and uncivilized people: "Size was not, however, the only consideration. Length of prepuce, number of testicles and methods of circumcision were all seen as markers of difference" (23).

9. For the purposes of this chapter, I understand the phallus to be the symbolic manifestation of masculine privilege whereby masculine privilege is manifested through performances and reifications of strength, rigidity, visibility, virility, vigorousness, and penetration. Understood as such, the phallus can be easily recognized as the symbolic stand-in for fleshy penises, however, the phallus is more importantly the sign of masculine superiority over femininity and thus phallic performances are entangled in the often contradictory sorting, ordering, and privileging of culture over nature, ideology over matter, reason over emotion, male over female, universal over particular, and hetero over homo (Bordo 1999; Potts 2000; Brubaker and Johnson 2008). It should be acknowledged that masculinized male bodies are not the only bodies capable of wielding phallic power. According to Bordo (1999): "The phallus, remember, is not a real body part. Having one or not requires permission of culture and/or the exercise of attitude more than the possession of a particular kind of body . . . not having a penis—although it has historically been a monumental impediment—is not an insuperable obstacle to projecting phallic authority" (101).

10. International phallic performativity is also fraught with vulnerabilities, failings, and dysfunctions. For hegemonic or superpower states, economic and financial turmoil, military blunders, defeats, and diplomatic strife signal waning strength, shrinking influence, reduced virility, and subsequent dephallusization. Conversely, nation-states that "can't" achieve global military reach, greater export-to-import ratios, or are wholly dependent on foreign direct investment are consistently confronted with the inability to measure up.

11. The queering and transitioning necessary to claim phallic authority may readily disqualify the ability of "other" bodies to become phallusized, but if the lack of a penis can be properly sheathed or privatized, it is possible for "others" to accrue the privileges of phallic performativity.

12. "A lot of these companies fulfill an important need that does contribute to the good guys cause" by acting as force-multipliers for overstretched NATO forces (Blanchette, quoted in Montpetit 2010).
13. It is worth noting that PMSCs play an important role in the decision-making process for when and how the Anglo-American security, defense, and intelligence apparatus gets hard (Leander 2005a).

PART IV

Private In/Security

Gendered Problems of Accountability, Regulation, and Ethics

CHAPTER 9

Engendering Accountability in Private Security and Public Peacekeeping

VALERIE SPERLING

Peacekeeping missions—typically including some portion of private military contractors—often take up residence in postconflict zones, where state capacity is weak. These missions therefore provide fertile ground for exploring the nexus between transnational military forces and accountability (Mendelson 2005, 2).[1] As the growing field of feminist security studies has shown (e.g., Tickner 1992a; Blanchard 2003; Jacoby 2005; Sjoberg 2009; Kaufman and Williams 2010; Enloe 2013; Sylvester 2013a), the struggle to provide military security in fragile conflict zones can have unintended consequences for women's human security in those areas.

One means to explore accountability and private military contractors in peacekeeping missions is to examine the accountability relationships between peacekeepers, contractors, and women living in areas where the missions are located. These relationships are inescapably gendered, as they are intimately tied to the gendered politics of protection discussed in other chapters in this volume. Accountability problems have surfaced particularly in regard to the trafficking, prostitution, and exploitation of women and girls—by UN military peacekeepers, civilian UN personnel, and civilian contractors (including those hired as military support and those accompanying the mission as civilian police). In this chapter, I describe how employing private military and security companies (PMSCs) on peacekeeping missions contributed to the negative implications for accountability to local populations. The use of U.S.-based PMSCs as part of the peacekeeping mission in Bosnia, for instance, allowed contractors to violate human rights with impunity, even as it spurred changes to U.S. legislation in an effort to increase contractor accountability to local citizens.

Because regular (noncontractor) peacekeepers have also engaged in sexual exploitation and abuse, this chapter includes analysis of the United Nations' efforts to address accountability issues in peacekeeping operations, briefly surveying UN responses to allegations of sexual exploitation and abuse of women by peacekeepers from Cambodia to the Congo. The cases examined here illustrate the problematic relationship between transnational military forces and accountability. Although the use of transnational military force—including private contractors—can stabilize frail states, PMSCs are more likely to undercut than to strengthen the ties of political accountability between citizens and their governments, and transnational military forces in general—including peacekeepers—often lack accountability to the populations with whom they interact.

PEACEKEEPERS AND PMSCs IN BOSNIA: TRAFFICKING IN THE BALKANS

Transnational military/peacekeeping forces' engagement with sex trafficking during the UN Mission in Bosnia-Herzegovina (UNMIBH) between 1995 and 2002 sheds light on the accountability issues raised by private contractors on peacekeeping missions. Sex trafficking networks had grown dense in Bosnia and Herzegovina by 1999, several years after UNMIBH began its work as mandated by the 1995 Dayton Accords (Vandenberg 2002, 2005a). As of autumn 2002, UNMIBH believed 227 of Bosnia's nightclubs and bars were engaged in trafficking-related activity. A UN source in 2001 substantiated the widespread nature of sex trafficking in Bosnia, noting that roughly a quarter of the women and girls employed in these establishments had been trafficked (Vandenberg 2002, 4). Despite the fact that "purchasing sex is illegal in Bosnia"—to say nothing of trafficking—brothels featuring trafficked women proliferated in part to "service" the influx of peacekeepers and contractors affiliated with the mission (Mendelson 2005, 9; Vandenberg 2002, 11).

Among the personnel accompanying UNMIBH was an International Police Task Force (IPTF) composed of IPTF "monitors" (civilian police), intended to support the development of rule of law in postwar Bosnia by supervising local police forces. This civilian police force was staffed in part by private military contractors. IPTF monitors are typically mobilized from national police forces to serve on such missions. Given the fact that the United States has no national police force, IPTF monitors from the United States are recruited by private military contractors from among local and state police forces. Because of this decentralized recruiting practice, "information on disciplinary actions against particular officers rarely makes it back to a U.S. police officer's home force" and accountability suffers (Vandenberg 2002, 48). For the Bosnian mission, the U.S. IPTF personnel were hired by the U.S.-based PMSC, DynCorp.

Ironically, some IPTF personnel engaged in the trafficking-related activities that they should have been working to eradicate—such as purchasing sex in brothels enslaving trafficked women, and even purchasing the women themselves. Promoting democracy—one aspect of the UN's mission—was thus accompanied by violations of human rights and a striking absence of accountability for such violations, since IPTF monitors enjoyed immunity from criminal prosecution while serving on UN missions (Vandenberg 2002, 5, 14, 47).

The UNMIBH chose not to request that the UN secretary-general waive IPTF employees' immunity in cases where IPTF monitors were allegedly involved in activities related to trafficking. Instead, 18 monitors were merely repatriated for "incidents of sexual misconduct" over the course of the mission and (as of several years later) none were prosecuted upon return to their home countries (Vandenberg 2002, 5, 51). In one case from November 2000, IPTF monitors ostensibly from Spain, France, the United States, and elsewhere raided three brothels in Prijedor, and then transported some of the trafficked women to Sarajevo for assistance under an International Organization for Migration program. There, the women's testimony revealed that at least nine IPTF monitors, including those who had conducted the raids, were among their clients. In at least one case, a U.S. IPTF monitor purchased a trafficked woman from a brothel in Sarajevo, ostensibly in order to pay off her "contract." He was repatriated but not prosecuted (Vandenberg 2002, 49–50, 53). At that time, U.S. courts lacked jurisdiction in the event that civilian police monitors from the United States were to commit such crimes while on foreign missions, and none were prosecuted (Vandenberg, 2005a, 159).

The repatriation of IPTF monitors to their home states made it impossible for them to appear as witnesses to convict the brothel owners and traffickers; they were not even interrogated before repatriation, rendering accountability impossible. The UN addressed the investigation of the IPTF monitors only cursorily; one investigating officer was told by his supervisor that he should "only scratch the surface" (Vandenberg 2002, 59). Local officials in Bosnia were dismayed by the immunity enjoyed by IPTF officers. One state prosecutor interviewed for a Human Rights Watch report stated: "The allegations are not in the competence of the national prosecutor's office—they have immunity. It cannot be a case in this office. But I would welcome it if some kind of procedure would be brought against those people in their home countries. . . . I don't know of a single case where someone was charged at home. I am not entitled to bring charges" (Vandenberg 2002, 61).

Also participating in the Bosnian mission was a NATO-led stabilization force (SFOR), along with its own contractors—civilians providing logistical support to the troops in the area. Along with IPTF monitors, SFOR contractors also reportedly participated in sex trafficking during the Bosnian mission. Such contractors had immunity only for actions taken in relation to their official duties, but, like IPTF monitors, were not prosecuted locally for their alleged trafficking-related crimes, in part because they were repatriated before investigations could get off the ground (Vandenberg 2002, 5–6). Like their IPTF counterparts, U.S. SFOR contractors in Bosnia were hired through DynCorp under a Department of Defense contract. Although there was no evidence that SFOR soldiers participated in trafficking-related activities in Bosnia, U.S. civilian contractors faced fewer restrictions on their freedom of movement and were able to visit brothel-nightclubs as a result. The SFOR contractors in question "faced allegations of buying women, transporting trafficked women, and violence against trafficked women" (Vandenberg 2002, 62).

U.S. contractor involvement in sex trafficking-related activities in Bosnia has been closely scrutinized. A report based on an investigation by the U.S. Army's Criminal Investigation Division stated that approximately five DynCorp staff (contracted to SFOR) had been "involved in white slavery," purchasing women from brothels and selling them back "when tired of the women" (Vandenberg 2002, 62). One such contractor "purchased a trafficked Moldovan woman and an automatic weapon in a package deal from a brothel owner" for the price of 740 USD, according to his confession to U.S. Army investigators, but was not prosecuted upon return to the United States.

Other cases of contractors purchasing trafficked women have been reported, as have been instances of trafficking facilitated by contractors in Bosnia (Bolkovac and Lynn 2011). Between 1999 and 2002, Human Rights Watch documented "at least eight cases of U.S. contractors who allegedly purchased trafficked women and girls as chattel"—half of them were private contractors with the Department of Defense, and half were on contract to the State Department as police officers in the UN Mission in Bosnia and Herzegovina (Vandenberg 2005b). Yet none of the U.S. contractors involved "faced criminal prosecution in U.S. courts or abroad for trafficking or for purchase of a human being as chattel. In most instances, once the purchase was discovered overseas, the contractor simply fled back to the United States on the next flight out," making prosecution impossible (Vandenberg 2005b). When an American SFOR contractor was caught during a March 2001 raid of a local nightclub-brothel, a local judge sought to interview him the following day as a potential witness against the owner of the club, but the American had already left the country (Vandenberg 2002, 67). In one case from the Balkans, "a U.S. contractor country manager made ad hoc arrangements with local police to ensure that any of his personnel caught conducting illegal activities in the host nation would be immediately placed in his custody" from whence they would be swiftly repatriated to the United States (Vandenberg and Mendelson, 2005).

A former DynCorp employee, Ben Johnston, similarly testified (to the U.S. Congress) to contractors' engagement with the sex-trafficking system, explaining that DynCorp employees could bring trafficked women into "locked-down military installations because the [UN] vans will not get searched if you drive them on post." His testimony also described a pornographic videotape made in Bosnia in which his boss, the DynCorp contract manager "appeared to rape a female." Johnston testified: "There is my supervisor, the biggest guy there [in Bosnia] with DynCorp, videotaping having sex with these girls, girls saying no, but that guy now, to my knowledge, he is in America doing fine. There was no repercussion for raping the girl" (quoted in Mendelson 2005, 36).

Contractors in such a system face no accountability for their actions, although they are part of a U.S. mission. Despite the passage of MEJA (the Military Extraterritorial Jurisdiction Act) in 2000, which made Department of Defense contractors subject to U.S. felony law while working abroad, "right up until the U.S. pull-out from Bosnia and Herzegovina in November 2004, the purchases of women by U.S. contractors continued" (Vandenberg 2005b). As of April 2006, there had been no prosecutions of any peacekeepers from the United States for trafficking offenses (Vandenberg 2006).

Although MEJA could have been used to prosecute U.S. contractors hired through the Department of Defense (such as those working for SFOR in Bosnia), MEJA would not have allowed for the prosecution of U.S. contractors working as IPTF monitors, since they had no connection to the Department of Defense but rather were hired on a DynCorp contract to the State Department. In 2005, this loophole for contractors was closed by the Trafficking Victims Protection Reauthorization Act (TVPRA). Section 103 of the TVPRA in essence amended MEJA, making prosecutable in the United States any trafficking-related felony offense committed by anyone employed by or contracted to the agencies of the U.S. government not covered under MEJA (the contractors' dependents are also covered under the TVPRA). Under the TVPRA, any U.S. police officers hired by DynCorp to serve in a U.S. IPTF contingent would be, in effect, under contract to the State Department and could be prosecuted if they were to commit a trafficking-related offense (USDoS 2006; U.S. Code 2006, chs. 212 and 212A).[2]

Rapid repatriation, however, has served as a significant obstacle to prosecuting U.S. contractors under either MEJA or the TVPRA. Prosecution in the United States is plausible only if significant evidence in the case has been collected. Gathering such evidence after repatriation is impractical. When trafficking cases occur involving peacekeepers, the UN typically collects little data. Once a U.S.-contracted peacekeeper is repatriated, it would take enormous effort and expense for a U.S. prosecutor in the Criminal Division of the Department of Justice to investigate the case abroad, to find the woman (or women) in question, and to convince her to testify in order to build a prosecutable case (Vandenberg 2006).

Compared to U.S. military personnel, contractors have enjoyed relative impunity in cases of sex trafficking. A Department of Defense report from December 2003 concluded that there was "negligible evidence" of U.S. armed forces in the Balkans having engaged in prostitution or supporting sex trafficking, particularly because U.S. military personnel could leave their bases only under limited conditions. By contrast, Department of Defense contractors working for SFOR were not "subject to the same restrictions that are placed on U.S. Service members" and were allowed to "circulate in host country communities" in some cases; military personnel from other countries were also found to be more likely to be involved in such activities (USDoD Inspector General's Office, 2003). In contradiction to the Department of Defense report's findings, however, a special forces officer who served in Bosnia and a lieutenant colonel billeted to NATO in Kosovo both confirmed that U.S. military forces frequented prostitutes and trafficked women there. The finding of only "negligible evidence" of U.S. military involvement with trafficking and prostitution was perhaps not surprising, given the fact that the inspectors failed to "interview local police near the base in Bosnia, brothel owners near the bases in Bosnia or Kosovo, shelter directors, or victims" who would have been most likely to provide relevant evidence, relying almost entirely on witnesses from the U.S. military instead (Mendelson 2005, 34, 44).

Transnational support for building accountability and rule of law locally is grossly undermined when peacekeeping forces violate local and international laws, such as those on trafficking. In a detailed report on peacekeeping and trafficking in the Balkans, political scientist Sarah Mendelson (2005) notes that when uniformed peacekeepers or civilian contractors "get away with purchasing women or girls as chattel, that sends a strong message that criminality is condoned" (17). Just as problematic is the material support that men provide to traffickers when they purchase sex—money that traffickers then use to bribe local police, allowing the lucrative flow of trafficked women to continue and undermining attempts to establish an accountable legal system (17). The Norwegian NATO ambassador summarized the problem of peacekeepers' (even unwitting) support for trafficking:

> [N]ot only do we destroy the reputation of our country and our organization and the operation, we violate fundamentally [the] human rights of women and children. And we do harm to the objectives of our mission, which is to establish rule of law, establish the foundation for democracy and for a decent economy.

Not to tear down rule of law, not to create gray economies [and] stimulate corruption. (Quoted in Mendelson 2005, 18)

The UN's lack of response to peacekeepers' involvement in sexual abuse and trafficking reflects the fact that the UN had two conflicting agendas: one to support, at least rhetorically, human rights (including women's human rights), and the other, to avoid taking steps that could limit troop contributions, such as punishing peacekeepers who engaged in trafficking or sexual abuse. As a result, the UN's ability to support the construction of local accountability structures and rule of law suffered—not to mention the human cost when the UN turned a blind eye to the sexual slavery of women (Mendelson 2005, 51).

UN complicity in protecting peacekeepers who engage in prostitution and trafficking has gone beyond the failure to waive immunity in individual cases. When UNMIBH closed up shop at the end of 2002, it was replaced by the European Union Police Mission (EUPM), which discovered that UN personnel had taken with them "hundreds of files" on trafficking incidents during the mission. EUPM officials were told that "the files had either been archived in New York or burned"—quite possibly because "the information contained in the files implicated IPTF officers" and the UN did not want that information released (Mendelson 2005, 63–64). According to the International Organization on Migration's May 2004 report on Balkan trafficking, the UN's action meant that

no intelligence information collected by the UN/IPTF [on trafficking] was transferred to the national police. Databases containing thousands of details acquired in several years of work and related to criminals and victims of trafficking were never handed to the national police or to the monitoring EUPM mission . . . [including] details [for] approximately 1,500 potential victims and hundreds of potential traffickers, locations, etc. (Quoted in Mendelson 2005, 64)

Rapid repatriation from Bosnia, in combination with other choices—such as the failure to transfer the UN's collected data on trafficking incidents— meant that the Bosnian peacekeeping mission's accountability to the local population could not be enforced. The intentional "loss" of information also undermined the goal of rebuilding a local judicial system. The Bosnian government was thus left less accountable to the population because it was deprived of a means to punish the alleged violators.

Two years after the UN peacekeeping mission in Bosnia withdrew, an internal UN report referring to sexual abuse by peacekeepers in the Congo criticized the UN's culture of impunity, summarizing the situation as "zero compliance with [the UN policy of] zero tolerance" (quoted in Mendelson

2005, 68). The accumulated experience with these issues in Bosnia, as well as in other peacekeeping missions that preceded and followed it, led the UN to take additional steps to address the accountability issues that arise at the intersection of peacekeeping and sexual exploitation.

BEYOND BOSNIA: PEACEKEEPERS AND ACCOUNTABILITY

While private contractors were the focus of much attention in connection with trafficking in Bosnia, it is not only contractors accompanying peacekeeping missions, but also peacekeepers more generally who may engage in sexual exploitation, defined by the UN as "any actual or attempted abuse of a position of vulnerability, differential power, or trust, for sexual purposes" (Khaleeli and Martin 2004; Martin 2005).[3] UN peacekeeping missions, however well-intentioned, can be undermined because of peacekeepers' lack of accountability to the local population, made visible when exploitation of local women occurs. Examples of such violations have included the rampant use of prostitutes by UN peacekeepers in Cambodia; peacekeepers in the Democratic Republic of Congo, Liberia, and Sierra Leone demanding sex from children and women in exchange for food; and European peacekeepers in Eritrea having sex with local minors and making pornographic films (Martin 2005, 4–5; Lyall 2006; Lynch 2005; Gardiner 2007; UNHCR and Save the Children-UK 2002). A brief treatment of sexual exploitation and peacekeeping in the UN's Cambodian and Liberian missions provides some illustration of the issue.

Cambodia and Liberia

Although the United Nations Transitional Authority in Cambodia (UNTAC) supported accountability to women in the electoral process that the mission oversaw from 1991–1993, UNTAC personnel engaged in some of the abuse of women that would later be echoed in peacekeeping missions in West Africa and elsewhere (Whitworth 2004, 66).[4] Under UNTAC, prostitution, including child prostitution, flourished. A local women's NGO "estimated that the number of prostitutes in Cambodia grew from about 6,000 prostitutes in 1992 to more than 25,000 at the height of the mission" (Whitworth 2004, 67). The expansion of this industry was so dramatic that it appeared to become permanently fused with the UNTAC mission in popular memory. A wax museum exhibiting "scenes from Cambodia's history and culture" captured the UNTAC period with two life-size figurines—a UN peacekeeper, complete with beret, holding a female prostitute in his arms. The UNTAC mission brought not only an expansion of commercial sex but also complaints of sexual abuse at the hands of peacekeepers, ranging from street harassment by UNTAC personnel, to rape, and to "fake marriages" that terminated upon a peacekeeper's departure to his home country (Whitworth 2004, 69–70).

Yasushi Akashi, the head of UNTAC, when confronted by NGOs on the subject of such "sexual misconduct" shocked his audience by stating, "boys will be boys" and noting that he thought it "natural for [the soldiers]—to chase 'young beautiful beings of the opposite sex'" (quoted in Whitworth 2004, 13, 71). His comments were met with a letter of protest from 165 Cambodian citizens and expatriates objecting to violent behavior on the part of some of UNTAC's employees, whom they also held "responsible for the dramatic rise of prostitution and HIV/AIDS. The letter described how women felt restricted in their movements and powerless as a result of UNTAC's presence in Cambodia" (Whitworth 2004, 71). Although Akashi responded more appropriately to the letter, putting an officer in place to hear community complaints, the complaints suggest that as UNTAC was trying to create conditions for the establishment of an accountable Cambodian government, UNTAC itself had behaved unaccountably and left parts of the population feeling powerless and without a means to hold peacekeepers accountable for their actions (including rape, the impregnation of local women, and so forth).

A decade later, in 2002, UN operations in West Africa were wracked by scandal when peacekeepers, other UN staff, and NGO workers were allegedly found exchanging "scarce relief supplies for sex" (Refugees International 2004). Sexual exploitation continued within the UN's Liberian mission (UNMIL), established in 2003, where peacekeepers reportedly "routinely engage[d] in sex" with young girls, according to an "internal U.N. letter" penned by a UNICEF employee. The letter accused peacekeepers of visiting a club where "girls as young as 12 years of age are engaged in prostitution, forced into sex acts and sometimes photographed by U.N. peacekeepers in exchange for $10 or food or other commodities" (Lynch 2005). In the wake of these revelations, the UN mission in Liberia placed several known brothels off-limits to UN personnel, but civilians working for the UN could still purchase women and set them up in houses to evade the sanctions on nightclubs: "What I'd heard from different staff people I interviewed was men just buy a house or rent a house and put women in there," explained Sarah Martin, a senior advocate at the NGO Refugees International (quoted in Wadhams 2005).

In May 2006, a report by Save the Children (UK) found that sexual abuse of girls (aged 8 to 18) by aid workers and peacekeepers had continued in Liberia, particularly in displaced persons' camps and in communities where displaced people were now returning. A UN statement revealed that its workers had been involved in eight cases of sexual abuse and exploitation in the first four months of the year, and that one staff person had been suspended as a result. The Save the Children report called on the UN to prosecute the

abusers, and if they were found guilty, to prevent them from being rede-
ployed as peacekeepers elsewhere. At the time, no system to prevent such
redeployment existed (Lyall 2006).

Immunity, Impunity, and Accountability

Although the UN Department of Peacekeeping Operations (UNDPKO)
expressed a "zero tolerance" policy on the issues of sexual exploitation and
abuse, it was not observed uniformly in the field. Acknowledging its failure
to address the problem of accountability to local populations in the wake of
repeated violations, the UN's zero tolerance policy was supplemented in 2002
by a peacekeeper Code of Conduct, printed on cards handed out to peacekeepers in the field, titled *We Are United Nations Peacekeepers* and *Ten Rules—Code
of Personal Conduct for Blue Helmets* (Holt and Hughes 2004). The fourth of
the *Ten Rules* states, "Do not indulge in immoral acts of sexual, physical or
psychological abuse or exploitation of the local population or United Nations
staff; especially women and children." Similarly, *We Are United Nations
Peacekeepers* states, "We will never—commit any act that could result in
physical, sexual or psychological harm or suffering to members of the local
population, especially women and children; become involved in sexual liai-
sons which could affect our impartiality, or the well being of others" (quoted
in Khaleeli and Martin 2004).[5] According to UNDPKO, "Eradicating sexual
exploitation and abuse became a major priority for UNDPKO in 2005," when
the department implemented a "comprehensive strategy to eliminate sexual
exploitation and abuse in its peacekeeping missions, including the establishment of Peacekeeping Conduct and Discipline Units at UN Headquarters and
in the field" (UNDPKO Fact Sheet). These efforts were spurred by an investigation within the UN in late 2004, exposing the fact that "dozens of peacekeepers serving on a mission to the Congo had committed sex abuse crimes
against refugees, including many minors." In an attempt to stop the continuing abuses, the UN's Code of Conduct incorporated a ban on purchasing sex
from prostitutes and instituted a curfew for UNDPKO personnel (USDoS
2005).[6]

In October 2005, when asked about the UN's response to ongoing reports
of sexual abuse by peacekeepers, a UNDPKO official asserted that "tremen-
dous progress has been made over the past year to drive home the U.N.'s message of zero tolerance and zero impunity," represented by a dramatic increase
in the number of repatriations in the previous 20 months (88 troops had
been repatriated and 10 civilian employees fired as the result of investigations into the conduct of 221 peacekeepers). The official admitted, however,
that despite such progress, the "message had still not taken hold" (Hoge
2005). Over the course of 2005, according to UNDPKO statistics, there were

340 allegations of sexual exploitation and abuse (SEA) against peacekeepers worldwide, 193 of which involved military personnel, 24 involved civilian police, and 123 involved civilian staff on the peacekeeping mission (UN General Assembly 2006, 10).[7] From January 2004 through November 2006, investigations into 319 SEA cases involving peacekeeping personnel worldwide generated 18 dismissals (of UN civilian staff) and the repatriation of 144 troops and 17 civilian police; 56 percent of the cases deemed worthy of investigation resulted in termination of the person's participation in the mission (Dollarhide 2007). By the end of 2006, 357 allegations had been reported; in 2007 there were 127, and in 2008 there were only 83. Most of these were leveled against military personnel (61); the rest concerned civilian personnel and police (UN General Assembly 2009, 5). In 2009, the number rose to 112 (UN General Assembly 2010, 5).

The number of allegations declined from 2006 to 2008, although the UN report in which these numbers were presented noted that their method of counting allegations of sexual abuse had changed over the past few years. The report's authors, however, did not explain *how* their method had changed—which suggests that these data may not be comparable across multiple years at all. Also, the allegations of abuse in 2008 included a sharp increase in substantiated allegations of the rape of minors; these increased in 2009 as well (UN General Assembly 2009, 7; UN General Assembly 2010, 5). The UN report for 2008 also acknowledged the vast underreporting of such crimes (UN General Assembly 2009).

Under pressure—especially from NGOs like Refugees International—the UN took steps to address these human rights violations. One measure sought to make it clearer to the local community to whom to complain in the event of abuse and to develop campaigns to promote awareness of the sexual exploitation and abuse issue among the mission staff and the population. To that end, materials were made available on a UN training website (UN 2013a). Among these, for example, were an educational poster and photos of a T-shirt, both from the Liberian mission's awareness campaign in 2007, the theme of which was opposition to transactional sex. The slogan presented on the T-shirt (and illustrated in a cartoon that portrayed a conversation between a young woman, her mother, and a man offering to "help" the family in exchange for time spent with the young woman) was "No sex for help, no help for sex" (UN 2013a).

There exists a range of obstacles to peacekeeper accountability in the area of sexual exploitation and abuse. These include the immunity agreements between troop-donating countries and host countries (the Status of Mission or Forces Agreements—SOMA/SOFA), the weakness of the legal systems in most states where UN peacekeepers operate, and the "cumbersome bureaucratic procedures" in place for pursuing allegations against peacekeepers. The SOMA/SOFA agreements "reserve full jurisdiction over misconduct by military troops serving as peacekeepers to the country of origin of the peacekeeper," leaving the UN mission leaders with the sole option of sending offenders home if their "misconduct" is discovered (Khaleeli and Martin 2004). In the end, punishment upon repatriation varies according to the practices of the peacekeepers' states of origin; the UN has limited ability to follow up to see what (if anything) happens to repatriated troops. Jacques Paul Klein, the special representative to the UN secretary-general for Liberia, complained: "I don't have direct chain of command to contingents [of peacekeepers]. I send recommendations to DPKO [Department of Peacekeeping Operations] but I don't know what happens when soldiers are sent home. It's very frustrating" (Refugees International 2004). The chain of accountability between the UN mission and the local population thus broke down almost as soon as the abuse had occurred (Bedont 2005).[8]

In an attempt to address the accountability loopholes occurring in cases of SEA, in 2006 the UN Secretariat issued a new "draft model memorandum of understanding" (MOU)—an agreement signed between the UN and countries contributing troops to peacekeeping operations. It was debated during the 61st session of the UN General Assembly, which opened in September 2006. In July 2007, the revised MOU was endorsed by the UN General Assembly (2009, 7). The MOU brought troop-contributing countries under a new obligation (starting in 2008) to train their peacekeepers better on preventing sexual exploitation and abuse. Specifically, it included a section explicitly stating that all troop contingents and commanders would be obligated to abide by the UN's Codes of Conduct, including the prohibitions on SEA, and that troop-contributing countries would not only familiarize their troops with those standards and prohibitions, but that those states would "issue or promulgate the United Nations standards of conduct in a form or manner that makes them binding under their laws or relevant disciplinary code upon all members of its national contingent" (UN Secretary-General, 2006).[9] The UNDPKO also began to keep better track of allegations of abuse by using an online Misconduct Tracking System that was reportedly improved in 2008. Ostensibly, when allegations were substantiated, peacekeepers could more easily be repatriated and barred from serving on future missions.

Another approach to countering sexual exploitation and abuse on UN peacekeeping missions was to increase the presence of female peacekeepers. One effort in this regard was the Indian government's creation of an all-women peacekeeping police force that was deployed to Liberia in October 2006. Joanna Foster, the gender advisor to the mission noted that peacekeeping groups dominated by women resulted in "very little reporting of sexual exploitation" (quoted in Ross 2007). Yet women only made up 8 percent of the UN's police force and 2 percent of its military forces as of March 2010, limiting this approach as an option (Basu 2010).

In addition to troops, peacekeeping missions also involve military observers, civilian UN staff, and CIVPOL or civilian police (including private contractors). Unlike soldiers, they hold the status of "experts performing missions," and enjoy "functional immunity applicable under official functions." If they break local laws while doing something that is not regarded as part of their official mission, then they can be tried under local civil and criminal law. Local law enforcement bodies, however, are unlikely to serve as a reliable accountability mechanism since peacekeeping missions are typically found in states that lack functional judicial systems. As a result, "very few military observers or civilian police/staff have been tried by a host country" (Khaleeli and Martin 2004).

Less attention has been paid to abuses by civilian personnel on UN peacekeeping missions, though civilians may be responsible for a greater share of the problem of sexual exploitation in the field. Sarah Martin (2005) of Refugees International argues: "In reality, it is easier to discipline military personnel in peacekeeping missions than civilians. While there are command structures in place in the military, the multiplicity of civilian agencies and personnel in these missions makes investigating and punishing their abusive behavior more difficult" (ii). Civilian personnel working for UN missions are technically employed not by the UN but by a private contractor, which makes follow-up in the event of violations difficult. According to a peacekeeping expert interviewed by Refugees International, "Not only are we unsure if they are punished, we suspect that they are sometimes just rotated to another mission" and the appropriate follow-up with victims is nearly impossible (quoted in Martin 2005, 22).

A first step toward improving the external accountability of UN peacekeeping missions might lie in providing a procedure for complaints that would be transparent to the local community (Martin 2005, iii). Confusion over the proper route for complaints was a significant issue in the UN's Liberian mission (UNMIL). In December 2003, UNDPKO asked the Liberian mission to select a "community focal point"—a person to whom community complaints about sexual exploitation could be reported (Refugees International 2004). An investigation by Refugees International in 2004 revealed that the management of UNMIL could not identify an appropriate person to receive complaints about such violations—and found that local women who had been abused would have neither the means of reporting such a problem nor a person to whom to report (Martin 2006). Two years later, the UNMIL Conduct and Discipline Unit website listed a hotline number that could presumably be used to report cases of sexual abuse and exploitation, but this would be of little use if community members were not aware of it or lacked telephone access, as is the case in rural areas (UNMIL 2007[10]). According to a researcher who visited Liberia in March 2007, UNMIL's hotline was "up and running," and a handful of people affiliated with the UN and Liberia's national police made mention of it. "However, no one seemed to know whether and to what extent it was actually being used."[11]

The accountability principle would be further improved by a process informing victims of the outcome of any investigation or legal proceeding that takes place as a result of the complaint:

> Currently peacekeeping troops report to their home country commanders. If a soldier is found guilty, that person is sent back to his country for discipline. It is very difficult, if not impossible, for victims and their families to determine what, if any, actions have been taken. In order for local communities and victims to trust the UN enough to begin reporting violations, victims must know they will be protected and treated with respect when they report and that there will be action taken against the perpetrator. (Martin 2005, iii)

In July 2004, at the behest of UN Secretary-General Kofi Annan, former civilian peacekeeper and Jordanian ambassador to the UN Prince Zeid Ra'ad Zeid al-Hussein produced a report on eradicating sexual abuse and exploitation in peacekeeping missions.[12] Among other things, the Zeid report called for troop-contributing countries to create "on-site courts martial for guilty parties and [to] adopt formal memoranda of understanding in advance of deployment so that the cases of sexual exploitation and abuse [would be] forwarded to their competent national or military authorities" (Martin 2005, iii–iv). The Zeid report further recommended that victims of sexual exploitation by peacekeepers be compensated monetarily (from those peacekeepers' wages) and that in cases where paternity was established, peacekeepers should be held financially responsible. Individual UN peacekeepers could thus more easily and transparently be held accountable for their actions in the local community (Martin 2005, 1, 23).

Following the Zeid report, Refugees International's own report on this issue suggested that the UN raise the importance of eliminating peacekeepers' sexual abuse and exploitation of women by making compliance with UN policy on the issue an explicit criterion of job performance for UN managers and to fire senior UN officials who do not carry out the policies to eliminate such abuses. This would help hold mission commanders and managers accountable for any failures to disrupt a mission culture that tolerates sexual exploitation (Martin 2005, 1, 16).[13] Finally, to cut down on abuses, Refugees International recommended advanced training for peacekeeping troops, as well as careful "follow-up" and that "troop-contributing countries work more closely with local women's groups to incorporate culturally appropriate curriculum into their military training" and hence improve accountability (Martin 2005, iii).

According to the Conduct and Discipline Unit (CDU) of UNMIL, the concerns expressed in the Zeid and Refugees International reports were addressed, at least on paper. As of March 2007, the CDU's website alerted UNMIL personnel to the fact that sex with people under 18 violated the Code of Conduct and was "strictly prohibited," as was the "exchange of money, employment, goods, assistance or services for sex." Peacekeepers were warned that such violations would "result in administrative and/or disciplinary action and ineligibility to participate in future peacekeeping operations or access to any employment within the UN system once listed in the UNDPKO database for serious misconduct" in addition to possible punishment upon repatriation (UNMIL 2007). Sarah Martin, senior advocate for Refugees International, expressed skepticism about the utility of the database: "They've been saying that there was a database all along, but the database has never functioned."[14] Instead, the UN relied on troop-contributing countries to screen peacekeepers, but they failed to do so since it would further draw out the process of providing troops to missions.[15] Regarding accountability for paternity, the CDU also alerted "military contingent members" to the possibility of "paternity payments if pregnancy is confirmed to have occurred as a result of sexual exploitation or abuse" (UNMIL 2007). It is not clear how such a claim could be proven, however.[16]

The frequency and scale of sexual exploitation and abuse by transnational military or civilian peacekeeping forces, whether private contractors or otherwise, pales by comparison to that perpetrated by government soldiers and rebel forces in many of the states to which UN peacekeeping missions deploy. The probable percentage of Liberian women raped during the 14-year-long civil war approached 40 percent, for instance, compared to a total of 75 complaints of reported rape lodged against UN personnel in Liberia in 2005 and 2006 combined (according to UNMIL) (McConnell 2007). Similarly, the practice of girls and women exchanging sex for food, money, or protection from government soldiers in displaced persons camps is common (as is sexual violence more generally). A September 2005 Human Rights Watch report documented the widespread sex-for-protection racket (as well as flat-out rape) in such camps in northern Uganda. Government soldiers ostensibly guarding against rebel attacks are often the perpetrators; a Ugandan expatriate working for the UN commented on the frequency of rape by government soldiers, saying: "There is a complete culture of impunity—The soldiers feel that they own the women in the camps; that they can do anything with them" (quoted in Scheier 2006). Like the UN's failure to appropriately sanction peacekeepers who sexually abuse and exploit the women and girls under their care, government soldiers enjoy a lack of accountability and are rarely disciplined by the military. According to the report, "Even when a victim identifies her violator—in many cases, nothing happens to him or he is transferred elsewhere" (Scheier 2006).

Bearing in mind the backdrop of women's sexual exploitation that has pervaded conflict and postconflict situations, for peacekeepers to contribute to the exploitation of the local population—even in a small way—contravenes the purpose of peacekeeping as a means of building accountability. As one expert in the field of peacekeeping summed it up: "[T]he United Nations' mission is not to undermine rule of law but rather to strengthen it. When they blatantly disregard local laws about prostitution and encourage the cover-up of violations within the mission, they are poisoning the mission and corrupting the mandate" (quoted in Martin 2005, 4). Likewise, as the 2009 report from the UN secretary-general noted, "the fact remains that even one case of sexual abuse or sexual exploitation is one too many and that zero tolerance must remain the goal" (UN General Assembly 2009, 7). Integrating accountability to women across peacekeeping missions would not only improve the effectiveness of UN missions but could also set an example for postconflict governments, encouraging them to take seriously issues of accountability within their own military and security forces.

CONCLUSIONS: PRIVATE MILITARY CONTRACTORS, GENDER, AND ACCOUNTABILITY

Accountability issues are highlighted when we examine questions of state security and human security from a feminist perspective, and ask how state or military security can clash with women's security. In weak states, where peacekeeping interventions occur, the unintended consequences of those interventions have included the sexual exploitation of women by the very people who are supposed to be guaranteeing the population's physical security. While peacekeeping missions can play a critical role in moving conflict zones toward peace, it is the UN's obligation to simultaneously ensure that women's rights are not sacrificed on the altar of state and military security. Yet it has been difficult to accomplish compliance with "zero tolerance" policies both in the field (by mission participants) and by troop-contributing countries that serve as the responsible parties when violations occur.

There is no simple and straightforward way to hold transnational peacekeeping forces accountable to local populations for human rights abuses. This is true of both national-military peacekeeping troops and of contractors hired by PMSCs for international missions. Holding contractors accountable has presented a particular challenge. Private military and security companies may have an incentive to maintain a clean record and avoid human rights violations, so as to preserve a good reputation and future contracts (Singer 2003, 217). But the desire for future profits also creates incentives for PMSCs to cover up crimes committed by their employees at home or abroad (222). The case of DynCorp, the US PMSC that hired U.S. personnel for the Bosnian mission, is instructive. After several of its employees were caught violating women's rights in Bosnia through sex trafficking and other types of sexual exploitation, the company fired the "whistleblowers" who reported these abuses to their management (Robberson 2007). Having covered it up, DynCorp was then rewarded with the contract to train the Iraqi police force a few years later.[17]

The privatization of military force used internationally is a slippery slope for many reasons, among which is the relative absence of accountability for human rights violations committed by private contractors in the field. The violations of women's rights by private contractors on UN and other international peace-oriented missions could constitute a starting point for international collaboration to combat this problem. Such explorations could also lead to recognition of the fact that when private entities (like military contractors) undertake the provision of public goods (such as military and police security), they must be held publicly accountable to the populations whose lives they affect.

NOTES

1. An earlier version of this chapter was published in Valerie Sperling, *Altered States: The Globalization of Accountability* (Cambridge University Press, 2009), pp. 198–215. The author thanks Maya Eichler and Kristen Williams for their helpful feedback on this chapter.
2. MEJA is Chapter 212 of the U.S. Code of Laws; the TVPRA adds Chapter 212A.
3. Sexual abuse is defined as "actual or threatened physical intrusion of a sexual nature, whether by force or under unequal or coercive conditions" (see Khaleeli and Martin 2004; Martin 2005).
4. As part of the UNTAC effort, the UN Development Fund for Women (UNIFEM) encouraged women to vote and organized a four-day summit meeting at which women from across the country gathered to discuss their priorities and prepared themselves to lobby for women's issues within the new system to be ushered in by the 1993 election (Whitworth 2004, 66).
5. On the history of UNDPKO's policy regarding sexual exploitation and abuse (SEA), see Shotton 2006.
6. Chapter 11 of this volume similarly addresses issues regarding the intersection of morality and military protection.
7. There were 357 allegations against UNDPKO personnel in 2006, although the frequency of reported SEA declined over the course of the year. See UN General Assembly 2007.
8. One proposal for ameliorating the existing accountability gap is to change the SOFA agreements such that a contributor state would retain "primary jurisdiction" over its peacekeeping troops in the event of crimes committed, but the host state would have jurisdiction in the event that the contributor state chose not to prosecute. This is similar to the SOFA agreements under which NATO troops operate within NATO member states (see Bedont 2005).
9. I thank Yewande Odia, chief of the Conduct and Discipline Team (UNDPKO) for pointing me to this information.

10. Sarah Martin, senior advocate for Refugees International. Phone interview by author, March 29, 2007.
11. Esfahani, Asal, e-mail communication with author, April 4, 2007.
12. Jordan is a major contributor of troops to peacekeeping operations.
13. The leadership of the UN mission in Haiti was more devoted to expressing a clear policy on prostitution than was the one in Liberia; peacekeepers in Haiti (MINUSTAH) understood that sex with prostitutes was forbidden (Martin 2005, 16). Even so, 108 peacekeepers were expelled from Haiti in November 2007 after accusations of sexual exploitation surfaced ("U.N. Ousts Peacekeepers in Sex Case" 2007).
14. Sarah Martin, senior advocate for Refugees International. Phone interview by author, March 29, 2007.
15. Sarah Martin, senior advocate for Refugees International. Phone interview by author, March 29, 2007. The UNDPKO planned to establish a "global database on misconduct allegations and cases covering all missions" in 2007 (UNDPKO 2007).
16. Sarah Martin, senior advocate for Refugees International. Phone interview by author, March 29, 2007.
17. "Dyncorp should never have been awarded the Iraqi police contract" according to the chief UN human rights officer in Sarajevo, Madeleine Rees (Traynor 2003). Also see the 2011 movie *The Whistleblower* directed by Larysa Kondracki, and "The Whistleblower: An Interview with Kathryn Bolkovac and Madeleine Rees" by Prügl and Thompson (2013).

CHAPTER 10

Women, PMSCs, and International Law

ANA FILIPA VRDOLJAK

Public consciousness of private military and security companies (PMSCs) was raised when investigations and lawsuits concerning violence perpetrated against women as civilians and employees arose (De La Vega and Beck 2006; Krahmann 2007, 105; U.S. Department of Defense 2010). These events and their aftermath exposed inadequacies in existing international and national laws to hold PMSCs accountable and to ensure effective remedies for victims. Despite concerted efforts to address these deficiencies in the law and regulation in the intervening years, progress in respect of accountability and reparations for human rights violations committed by these companies and their personnel remains limited. This chapter considers present-day initiatives to regulate PMSCs through international law, particularly as they relate to women and gender issues more broadly.

It is deeply ironic that as the implementation and enforcement of international humanitarian law and human rights law has been strengthened in the last decades, through the establishment of individual complaint procedures, specialist tribunal and courts covering breaches of human rights law, international humanitarian law, and international criminal law, there has been an erosion of these principles and protections through the privatization of governmental and intergovernmental functions. Despite an exponential increase in contracting out these activities to PMSCs since 2001, the legal regulation of these companies and their personnel has been slow and fragmented (Mancini, Ntoubandi, and Marauhn 2011; Østensen 2011).

When assessing the regulation of PMSCs, legal experts have referred to the urgent need to address the "glaring gap" at the international level where they are "rarely held accountable" for violations of international humanitarian law and human rights law (UNWGM 2010a, 10). Feminist legal scholars have long highlighted the divide in law between the private sphere, which is left largely unregulated, and the public sphere, which is regulated (Charlesworth, Chinkin, and Wright 1991, 615). While this analysis was developed to expose the gendered nature of law and its adverse impact upon women, it is a useful tool for examining regulatory gaps concerning the activities of PMSCs.

The failure of the law and regulators to adequately keep up with the rapid expansion and diversification in the use of PMSCs has had a significant impact for victims of human rights violations perpetrated by PMSCs and their employees generally, and for women and girls in particular (Schulz and Yeung 2008). To explore these developments, this chapter is divided into two parts. Part one focuses on current initiatives at the international level to provide a regulatory framework for PMSCs and which encompass the obligations of states (and international organizations) in respect to international humanitarian law, human rights law, and use of force. Part two outlines the influence of civil society participation (including feminist academics, women's NGOs, and so forth) in breaking the "silence" within international organizations and international law concerning violence against women (VAW) and girls and its potential influence upon the regulation of PMSCs. Both parts serve to highlight evolving notions of force and violence, accountability and enforcement, and access to justice and reparations within international law today.

PMSCs AND THEIR LEGAL REGULATION

PMSCs do not operate in a legal lacuna. Indeed, there are various efforts at the international and national levels, state- and industry-based, to restate the existing laws and formulate good practice guidelines. The problem arises with the multiplicity of initiatives which are not harmonized, and because regulatory gaps remain. The need to address regulatory gaps is amplified because the rise of PMSCs is eroding the effectiveness of existing international humanitarian law and human rights law norms (UNOIGWG 2011, 1).

Accordingly, this part of the chapter provides a brief overview of current major regulatory initiatives in this field:

- *Multilateral, state-based, legally binding regulation:* The UN's draft Convention on Private Military and Security Companies (draft UN Convention) (UNWGM 2010b).
- *Multilateral, multistakeholder, self-regulatory initiatives:* The Montreux Document on pertinent international legal obligations and good practices for states related to operations of private military and security companies during armed conflict (Montreux Document) (ICRC 2008),

the related International Code of Conduct for Private Security Service Providers (ICoC) (Swiss Confederation 2010), and the International Code of Conduct for Private Security Service Providers' Association Articles of Association (ICoCA Articles) (Swiss Confederation 2013a).
- *National laws.*

These legal developments are examined specifically in respect to the international responsibility for violations of international law by PMSCs and their personnel and access to justice and remedies for victims of such violations. Victims may include civilians who come into contact with PMSCs, PMSC personnel, or members of armed forces. The discussion in this part focuses on international humanitarian law and human rights law more generally, while specific protections concerning women are covered in part two below.

Draft UN Convention on PMSCs

Within the United Nations, the regulation of PMSCs has primarily been driven by the Working Group on the Use of Mercenaries. By 2008, the Working Group proposed a definition of PMSCs that recognized the extensive range of activities these companies undertake during armed conflict and postconflict situations (UNWGM 2008, 1). While acknowledging the significance of the Montreux Document, discussed below, they affirmed their intention to pursue a legally binding instrument for states rather than companies (Nikitin 2009, 4).

Following consultations with states, NGOs, and academics, a draft Convention was released by the Working Group in 2010 (UNWGM 2010b). The draft reaffirms states' obligations concerning international human rights law and requires that they establish measures ensuring transparency, accountability, and responsibility of PMSCs and their personnel, and provide mechanisms for redress for victims (UNWGM 2010a, paras.39–41). The UN Human Rights Council established an Open-ended Intergovernmental Committee to consider the possibility of a binding instrument along the lines proposed by the Working Group (UN 2010e, para.5).

The draft Convention reaffirms the obligation of states to prevent, investigate, prosecute, and punish violations of international humanitarian and human rights law and that violations of these norms can be imputed to states, intergovernmental organizations, and nonstate actors including PMSCs.[1] However, only the legal responsibility of states parties, and intergovernmental organizations "within the limits of their competence" is extrapolated (UNWGM 2010a, paras.43–45). There is silence concerning the direct responsibility of PMSCs (UNWGM 2010a, 16; also see Clapham 1993). It emphasizes that states have a responsibility to protect those affected by human rights violations perpetrated by PMSCs whether they be civilians, military personnel, or PMSC employees. Like the Montreux Document before it, the draft enunciates differing obligations for contracting states (who directly contract the services of PMSCs), states of operation (on whose territory PMSCs operate), and home states (where the PMSC is incorporated, registered, or has its principal place of management) (UNWGM 2010b, Art.2). The draft Convention outlines the basic international law obligations owed by *states* in respect to international humanitarian law, human rights law, and use of force (Part II).

The draft UN Convention seeks to fill the current regulatory gap by affirming the application of international human rights and humanitarian law to PMSCs, that is, that they and their personnel must be held responsible for violations, and proposes a clear mode of implementation and enforcement missing from the current international and national initiatives. Under the proposed instrument, this gap will primarily be closed through the establishment of effective national legal frameworks by states parties which would cover regulation and oversight through licensing, registration, training, and vetting regarding human rights and humanitarian law norms, and regulation of the use of force (Part III).

A divergence of opinion has arisen with respect to the draft UN Convention's engagement with the regulation of use of force in international law. Understanding of force in international law remains very limited when compared with the manifold modes of violence experienced by women and the diverse consequences of armed violence on them (Milliken, Gilgen, and Lazarevic 2009, 11–13; UN 2011b, 6–25; UN 2012a; Geneva Declaration 2012, 113–138). Reflective of its preparation by the Working Group on Mercenaries, it seeks to define the legal use of force and "inherently" state functions which cannot be contracted out to third parties, including PMSCs (UNWGM 2010b, Arts.2 and 9). Divisions have arisen between states which regarded the proposed distinction acceptable and those that favored a restrictive approach (UNWGM 2010a, 17). While the European Union argued that parts of the draft convention were outside the competence of the Human Rights Council (UNOIGWG 2011a, 15), the proposed instrument makes clear that the regulation of the use of force must be understood within a human rights framework (UNWGM 2010b, Art.1). This way of interpreting the regulation of the use of force has the potential to move it beyond a purely statist rubric (Charlesworth, Chinkin, and Wright 1991, 22). For example, civilians, including women, have disproportionately higher mortality and injury rates arising from small arms (Farr, Myrttinen, and Schnabel 2009; UN 2012a, 13–14). The draft Convention seeks to regulate the outsourcing of the use of certain weapons, including firearms, by PMSCs (UNWGM 2010b, Arts.10 and 11).

Nonetheless, the draft Convention does endeavor to stem the erosion of controls on the use of force, through their contracting out to nonstate entities (CE 2009a). It does this in two ways: the reaffirmation of the "legitimate" use of force in its many guises as an inherently state (or intergovernmental) function, and that states parties will be held responsible for the international wrongful acts of PMSCs and personnel in certain circumstances. The draft Convention seeks to impose responsibility on states parties to ensure criminal, civil and/or administrative penalties for violators of international humanitarian and human rights law and those engaged in inherently state functions (UNWGM 2010b, Art.19). Furthermore, states parties must provide victims with effective remedies under national law (UNWGM 2010a, 10).

The chief criticisms of the current self-regulatory scheme are its nonbinding nature and lack of effective oversight mechanisms. The proposed UN Convention would require the establishment of an international committee made up of "experts of high moral standing, impartiality and recognised competence in the field" elected and nominated by the states parties, who will oversee and monitor its implementation (UNWGM 2010a, Art.29). Three modes of triggering investigations of violations of the convention are envisaged. All are dependent on the cooperation of the relevant state or states. First, the committee would receive, investigate, and issue findings and recommendations concerning grave or systematic violations of the convention. These proceedings would remain confidential (UNWGM 2010b, Art.33). If the matter is not resolved, the committee can with the consent of the states parties appoint an ad hoc Conciliation Commission to hear the matter and make recommendations (Arts.35 and 36).

Further, the committee could hear complaints against a state party brought by another, when it believes the other is not fulfilling its obligations under the proposed Convention (UNWGM 2010b, Art.34). A similar procedure is attached to existing human rights treaties, but it has not been utilized to date. Indeed, it is relatively weak compared to the UN Convention on the Elimination of All Forms of Discrimination against Women and the UN Convention on the Elimination of All Forms of Racial Discrimination which enables states parties to refer disputes to the International Court of Justice for resolution.[2]

Finally, the committee can also receive petitions from or on behalf of individuals or groups who are victims of violations by a state party. As with other human rights instruments, this only occurs if the relevant state has made a declaration recognizing its competence to receive such communications (UNWGM 2010b, Art.37). While such an international mechanism does have the potential to "give women's voices a direct audience in the international community" (Charlesworth, Chinkin, and Wright 1991, 645), it is significantly restricted. It is the state party that decides whether it will grant competence to the committee to receive such communications, the matter is heard in closed session, and there is no explicit requirement on the committee to refer potential grave breaches of international humanitarian law or serious violations of human rights law to a competent multilateral body for further investigation.[3]

It is important to note that the Working Group on Mercenaries itself can receive individual communications from "a state, state organ, intergovernmental and non-governmental organization, or the individuals concerned, their families or their representatives, or any other relevant source" (HRC Res.2005/2). The UNWGM will forward the complaint to the relevant state for reply. Its Opinion shall be forwarded to the state, the Human Rights Council, the relevant PMSC involved, and the complainant. The UNWGM shall follow up with the country to ensure that it is implementing its recommendations or explains its failure to do so.

The preamble and substantive provisions of the draft Convention reflect developments in international human rights law concerning the fight against impunity, that is, to ensure that perpetrators of serious violations are held to account legally and that their victims receive reparations (UNOIGWG 2011a, 14).[4] Like the Montreux Document before it, Part IV of the Convention concerns state responsibility to impose sanctions for violations and remedies for victims.[5] Complementary to these obligations is the proposed establishment of an international fund to provide reparations for victims and assist in their rehabilitation (UNWGM 2010b, Art.28). The creation of the fund would not absolve PMSCs and individuals who are criminally liable, from also compensating victims (Art.28(b)). The inclusion of this international fund in the draft text was "welcomed by many" (UNWGM 2010a, 16). The application of these principles pertaining to reparations as they related to women is examined in part two below.

The very need for a *binding* international agreement remains highly contested. There is division between states (and the African Union) that stressed the need for a new specialist treaty covering PMSCs because existing self-regulatory frameworks do not provide effective and enforceable accountability mechanisms or avenues for redress; and those countries (and the European Union) that maintain that existing regulatory initiatives like guiding principles and model legislation should be implemented and properly assessed (UNOIGWG 2011a, 12–16).

Critical legal scholars, including feminists, have long challenged states' monopoly in international law-making and argued for the need to acknowledge and embrace civil society in these processes (Chinkin 1992, 292). The proposed UN Convention was prepared with feedback from nonstate actors and draws heavily from self-regulatory regimes like the Montreux Document, a soft-law instrument propelled by multiple stakeholders including the International Committee of the Red Cross (ICRC). While there are a number of women on the UNWGM, the involvement of UN bodies or NGOs advocating on behalf of women has not been overt in this process to date.[6] Given the finite resources of such bodies and the persistent underrepresentation of women in the decision-making roles in the United Nations and within states, this is not unsurprising (Charlesworth, Chinkin, and Wright 1991, 23; UN 2010a). Importantly, the proposed convention would convert existing soft-law, good practice principles into binding obligations on matters that disproportionately impact "vulnerable" groups including women (cf. Chinkin 1989). The current draft's limited explicit engagement of issues pertaining directly to women (even compared to the Montreux Document) and ongoing resistance to a binding instrument hinders efforts to fight impunity and provide all victims with effective redress.

Montreux Document and International Code of Conduct (ICoC)

Co-sponsored by Switzerland and the ICRC, the Montreux Document focuses on the obligation of states, and with the ICoC and ICoCA Articles, which center on companies, it is intended to be read as a complementary regulatory framework. It is a multistakeholder initiative that has received broad support from the United Nations, states, and the industry (UN 2008c, 3). Part I summarizes existing obligations of states, PMSCs, and their personnel under international law; while Part II outlines "good practices" to facilitate states' adherence to these obligations. The subsequent draft UN Convention borrows heavily from the Montreux Document.

The Montreux Document and Good Practices, ICoC for PMSCs, and the ICoCA Articles must be viewed against the backdrop of diverse, multilateral initiatives to formulate a normative framework covering human rights and businesses, the foremost being the UN Guiding Principles (UN 2011c, Annex).[7] Prepared in response to failed efforts to impose responsibility on companies in international law, the UN Guiding Principles, endorsed by the Human Rights Council in 2011, work on the premise that there has been a fundamental shift from the public to the private spheres and this is having adverse implications for human rights and vulnerable groups including women. Like the Montreux Document, it does not create new international law obligations but seeks to provide a coherent framework of existing standards and practices, expose gaps, and facilitate future developments (UN 2011c, 5). The Montreux Document broadly follows the three pillars of the UN "Protect, Respect and Remedy" framework on Human Rights and Business. The duty of states to protect against the human rights violations of third parties, including PMSCs is covered by the Montreux Document and Good Practices. Corporate responsibility to respect human rights, including through international humanitarian law, is reflected in the ICoC. The requirement to provide access to effective remedies to victims of violations is intended to be realized through the ICoCA Articles and mechanisms to be developed by its Steering Committee (Swiss Confederation 2013b).

While it addresses the obligations of states and PMSCs in international law, the Montreux Document (ICRC 2008) makes clear its good practice recommendations would benefit international organizations, NGOs, and companies, including PMSCs (Preface, para.8). It covers the activities of PMSCs during armed conflict. However, the principles and good practice guidelines were prepared on the understanding that they may also be useful in nonconflict situations (Preface, para.5).

Like the UN Guiding Principles, the Montreux Document affirms that states are the primary duty bearers regarding human rights and international humanitarian law. And like the subsequent draft UN Convention, it places the primary obligation for monitoring and enforcement of these international norms on the state. It reaffirms that under international humanitarian law and human rights law certain activities cannot be contracted out by a state and that it retains its obligations under international law even if it contracts activities to third parties (ICRC 2008, Part I.A, para.2; UN Guiding Principle 5). Furthermore, states must prevent, investigate, and punish violators of international human rights law and provide effective remedies to victims of PMSCs and their personnel (ICRC 2008, Part I, paras.4–8, 10, 15, 20). It confirms that PMSCs and their personnel are bound by applicable national laws including those imposing international humanitarian law and human rights law standards upon them (Part I, para.22). The importance of domestic law in holding PMSCs and their personnel to account is discussed further below.

Part II of the Montreux Document covering "good practices" mimics the operationalization of legal obligations of states contained in the UN Guiding Principles but is tailored for states interacting with PMSCs and their personnel.[8] Like the Guiding Principles they are dominated by contractual-based devices. They are neither legally binding nor exhaustive, and are inappropriate when they clash with a state's international legal obligations. They are primarily directed to the contracting state, which is encouraged to select PMSCs with no record of serious crimes including violations of international humanitarian law, sexual offences, and violent crime (ICRC 2008, Part II, para.6). Enforcement procedures are contractually based and include termination of license for the PMSC and employment contract for its personnel, financial sanctions, and remedies for its victims. When negotiating agreements with territorial states, the contracting state must cover jurisdiction and immunity to ensure that there are adequate and appropriate civil and criminal jurisdiction and remedies concerning violations (Part II, paras.22 and 23). With respect to monitoring and compliance, it should provide for criminal jurisdiction under its national law including establishing corporate criminal responsibility and extraterritorial application covering acts committed abroad (Part II, para.19).[9]

Where the Montreux Document and related good practices are designed to reaffirm and elaborate upon the international humanitarian law and human rights law obligations of states with respect to their dealings with PMSCs and their personnel, the ICoC is the industry equivalent concerning the UN Guiding Principles (Swiss Confederation 2010, 3). Signatory companies are required to endorse the Montreux Document, the UN Principles, and to affirm that they will "respect the human rights of, and fulfil humanitarian responsibilities towards, all those affected by their business activities" (3). The ICoC also seeks to establish "common and internationally-recognized operational and *business* practices" (4), and an independent, external oversight and governance mechanism is being developed pursuant to the ICoC Code (Part C) and ICoCA Articles. Signatory companies must have an internal oversight mechanism and submit to auditing and verification by the tripartite Steering Committee (made up of representatives from governments, industry, and civil society). They must establish grievance procedures that are "fair, accessible, and offer effective remedies, including recommendations for the prevention of recurrence," and maintain sufficient funds to meet "reasonably anticipated commercial liabilities" arising from damages and claims for death, injury, or property damages (15). The ICoCA Articles provide for the establishment of a board with equal representation of member companies, affiliated civil society organizations, and affiliated governments; and a secretariat, which shall administer the ICoC and implement the board's decisions. In response to violations of the ICoC, the board is empowered to suspend or terminate the membership of a member company (Swiss Confederation 2013a, Art.13.2.7).

John Ruggie observed that effective access to remedies for victims of human rights violations by corporations is "underdeveloped" and "flawed" (UN 2010b, 7, 18). The UN Guiding Principles affirm states have a duty to not only protect against human rights abuses by companies within their jurisdiction but also to ensure that victims of violations have access to an effective remedy (UN 2011c, 25). It envisages that state-based grievance procedures can be "supplemented or enhanced" by "collaborative initiatives" (24). Unlike earlier drafts, the ICoCA Articles adopted in 2013 do not allow for third-party complaints (UNWGM 2013, 15). A complaint may be made by an individual or their representative specifying violations of the ICoC and alleged harm to one or more of the individuals arising from the violation (Swiss Confederation 2013a, Art.13.2.1). In order to ensure that nonjudicial grievance mechanisms, whether state or nonstate based, are effective, the UN Principles stipulate that they must be legitimate, accessible, predictable, equitable, transparent, rights-compatible, that is, that the results and remedies comply with international human rights norms (UN 2011c, 28–29).

While the ICoCA Articles do provide for monitoring, including a "human rights risk assessment" (Swiss Confederation 2013a, Art.12), the Working Group on Mercenaries and others charge that its grievance mechanism does not comply with the UN Guiding Principles (UNWGM 2012a, 6–7), even though participants are required to adhere to them. For example, the complainant may be provided with information concerning other possible avenues to resolve the grievance including the relevant company's own internal grievance procedures, other existing independent dispute resolution bodies, private counsel, or law enforcement authorities. This falls short of the UN Guiding Principles requirements of actively assisting potential complainants who are seeking access to redress (UN 2011c, 31).

However, many commentators argue that the greatest deficiency of the proposed grievance mechanism lies in that it only covers procedural aspects of a company's grievance process and not substantive elements concerning remedies for violations (UNWGM 2012a, 6; Cockayne 2012a; ICJ 2012). While the benefits of nonjudicial modes of redress are acknowledged, perhaps the primary drawback of the self-regulatory, multistakeholder codes of conduct, like the ICoC and its proposed grievance mechanism, is that they are voluntary in their membership and their modes of enforcement are not binding (UN 2011b). These significant limitations are exemplified by "so-called rogue business actors" who actively and deliberately avoid any form of regulation (MacLeod 2011, 360).

Much of the language around these self-regulatory, multistakeholder initiatives is driven by managerial concepts of due diligence and risk management, rather than legal concepts of obligations and rights (Richemond-Barak 2011; UNWGM 2012b, 13). While the UN Guiding Principles are a positive step (Cockayne 2012b), the ongoing impasse at the international level on extending legal responsibility to nonstate actors like corporations regarding human rights abuses means that an "implementation gap" remains for the effective enforcement of international law norms (CE 2012). And while the Montreux Document and ICoC's tailoring of these principles to PMSCs is also a welcome development, the limitations of the UN Guiding Principles is exacerbated with respect to such companies. PMSCs are increasingly undertaking activities previously the exclusive preserve of states and intergovernmental organizations. Drafted prior to this shift to privatization, existing human rights and international humanitarian instruments have been found wanting. The self-regulatory initiatives concerning PMSCs cover not only human rights norms but also international humanitarian law and use of force—they address the most volatile of circumstances and impact upon the most vulnerable groups. For this reason, any regulatory regime must not only be binding, but it must also ensure that contemporary developments in these fields are not wound back. Good practices and codes of conduct can only complement binding legal norms and not substitute them.

National Legal Regime

As noted above, the draft UN Convention on PMSCs and the Montreux Document place primary regulatory and remedial responsibility on states. Until a binding international agreement is adopted that extends responsibility for human rights violations to nonstate actors, enforcement of international humanitarian law and human rights law norms through domestic law remains imperative. There are a number of branches of national law that are potentially relevant, like criminal law, contract law, and torts, and that have been explicitly or implicitly referenced in the draft UN Convention and Montreux Document as possible avenues for accountability and access to justice for victims of human rights abuses by nonstate actors (Dickinson 2002, 2006; Ryngaert 2008; Richemond-Barak 2011).

However, the significant limitations of these areas of law and domestic avenues of oversight, accountability, and enforcement have also been increasingly exposed (ICJ 2012a). These difficulties range from the limited number of criminal prosecutions of PMSC personnel to the lack of jurisdiction regarding corporate criminal responsibility (U.S. 2010), and to civil actions stymied by protections normally afforded governments being extended to PMSCs and their activities (Ryngaert 2008). Added to these legal barriers to effective access to justice are those exacerbated by the transnational nature of PMSCs, and the volatile environments in which they operate, which hinder reporting, collection of evidence, and cooperation with relevant legal systems.

One NGO has succinctly noted, the right to effective redress is intimately related to the duty of states to investigate, prosecute, and punish human rights violations—"[t]hese tasks cannot be left solely to private mechanisms," particularly where "the public interest and the interests of justice are at stake" (ICJ 2012b, 8, 13). Consequently, the Human Rights Council has observed, national laws can only be a part of the "proper regulation" of the impact of businesses on human rights (HRC Res.17/4(2011)). The UNWGM has pointed to the work of the Inter-American Commission on violence against women to make a similar point in regard to states' international law obligations concerning human rights violations by nonstate actors (UNWGM 2013, 16).

VIOLENCE AGAINST WOMEN AND ACCESS TO JUSTICE

Lack of clarity about the application of international law norms and inadequacies of existing regulatory regimes covering PMSCs have reinforced concerns about transparency and accountability with respect to gender-related violence, harassment, and discrimination. While international humanitarian law and human rights law have dedicated, or "special," provisions for women, feminist legal scholars have done much to expose the gendered nature of these branches of international law (Gardam and Jarvis 2001). In recent decades, the jurisprudence of international criminal courts has addressed large-scale and systematic sexual violence in a number of conflicts, the United Nations' campaign of mainstreaming women's issues has impacted significantly on relevant human rights law (SC Res.1325(2000)), and the ICRC has sought to investigate and address women's concerns (ICRC 1995; Lindsey 2001). This part of the chapter focuses on efforts to address violence against women to illustrate the reinterpretation of existing international human rights and humanitarian law norms through the involvement of civil society at international forums and its potential impact on the regulation of PMSCs.

Jurisprudence of International Criminal Tribunals and VAW

These processes are exemplified through the recent shift in the manner in which sexual violence, including rape, is perceived in international law. The ad hoc International Criminal Tribunals for the former Yugoslavia (ICTY) and Rwanda (ICTR) from the 1990s to date through their interpretation and enforcement of international humanitarian law and international criminal law have been instrumental in the recognition of rape as a grave breach of international humanitarian law. When adopting the ICTY statute, the Security Council flagged "its grave alarm at continuing reports of widespread and flagrant violations of international humanitarian law occurring within the territory of the former Yugoslavia . . . including reports of . . . organised and systematic detention and rape of women" (SC Res.827 (1994); Gardam and Javis 2005, 148–160). Both ICTY and ICTR governing statutes list rape as a crime against humanity.[10] These tribunals have elaborated on rape,[11] and other sexual violence (including enslavement and sexual slavery),[12] as a war crime and a crime against humanity. Significantly, they have also extended these acts to come within the definition of persecution (on the grounds of gender even though not explicitly contained in their respective governing statutes),[13] torture,[14] and genocide.[15]

United Nations

Until recently, the United Nations' response to women's issues, particularly violence against women, was "silence" (Charlesworth, Chinkin, and Wright 1991). Today, its activities in this field fall into the areas of human rights, international criminal law, and UN reform. The Declaration on the Protection of Women and Children in Emergency and Armed Conflict adopted in 1974 and the Convention on the Elimination of all Forms of Discrimination against Women (CEDAW) in 1979 do not explicitly refer to sexual violence during armed conflict.[16] An understanding of violence against women as a violation of human rights is contained in the 1992 general recommendation on "Violence against Women" adopted by the Committee on the Elimination of Discrimination against Women. The UN Declaration on the Elimination of Violence against Women of 1993 requires states to "exercise due diligence to prevent, investigate and, in accordance with national legislation, punish acts of violence against women" whether perpetrated by the state or private persons.[17] It acknowledges that women are especially vulnerable to violence during armed conflict. In the same year, the Vienna Declaration and Programme of Action stated that violations of the human rights of women, "including in particular murder, systematic rape, sexual slavery, and forced pregnancy, require a particularly effective response."[18] During this period, the UN human rights bodies appointed a Special Rapporteur on Violence against Women, Its Causes, and Consequences and a Special Rapporteur on the Situation of Systematic Rape, Sexual Slavery, and Slavery-like Practices. Their periodic reports are central to documenting the nature, extent, and prevalence of these and related issues, and fostering law reform. Feminist legal scholars and the UN Special Rapporteur on VAW have challenged interpretations of international humanitarian law that fail to acknowledge the violence occasioned by rape and other forms of sexual violence (UN 1998; UN 2008a).

The 1995 Beijing Platform of Action reiterated that states had an obligation to exercise due diligence in preventing, investigating, and prosecuting sexual violence against women by nonstate actors (UN 1995, 27). From this initiative arose Security Council Resolution 1325 adopted in October 2000, which guides the work of the UN and its member states in this area. It "emphasizes the responsibility of all States to put an end to impunity and to prosecute those responsible for genocide, crimes against humanity, and war crimes including those relating to sexual and other violence against women and girls" (Art.11). It was augmented by the Secretary-General's In-Depth Study on all Forms of Violence against Women of 2006, which enumerated several areas in need of reform including data collection, more effective preventative and remedial services, comprehensive victim services, and bridging the gap between international and national laws for those seeking redress (UN 2006b, 67, 95,106; UN 2011e).

These changes have had a transformative impact not only on the substantive law but also on the manner of its implementation and enforcement. This has extended to the procedures and practices of international courts through to the appointment and training of investigative and prosecutorial staff,[19] and judicial officers;[20] the tailoring of remedies to the requirements of women and girls (discussed further below); and the engagement of women in postconflict reconciliation and reconstruction efforts (SC Res.1325, para.8; UN 2008b; SC Res.1888(2009); SC Res.1889(2009); SC Res.1960(2010); Schnabel and Tabyshalieva 2012).

Within the United Nations, these developments have led to a broader move to mainstream issues related to women, including peacekeeping and peace-building operations (UN 2000; UN 2006a). Its organs, agencies, and member states must report on their implementation of Resolution 1325. As explained below, the United Nations is addressing some of these issues as it reviews its relations with armed private security contractors retained to undertake work on its behalf. While not specific to the organization's retention of PMSCs, it is bound by international human rights and human-itarian law as confirmed in the 1999 Bulletin of the Secretary-General (UN 1999) and its own 2011 Human Rights Due Diligence Policy concerning UN support to non-UN security forces (UN 2013b). The UN Policy on Armed Private Security Companies and Guidelines on the Use of Armed Security Services from Private Security Companies was adopted by its Department of Safety and Security (DSS) in 2012 and requires companies to train their personnel in human rights law and its application and in preventing sex-ual harassment, prior to the commencement of contractual services (UN 2012b, 10).

International Committee of the Red Cross and Red Crescent

The protection of women has always been part of the remit of the ICRC. During World War II, it raised awareness of the plight of female prisoners of war, and this was later incorporated into the Geneva III Convention (ICRC 1995). Its work during the Yugoslav conflicts led to the recognition of rape as "wilfully causing great suffering or serious injury to body and health" and therefore was a grave breach under the Geneva Conventions (ICRC 1992; ICRC 1993, 337). The ICRC stressed the need to enforce existing interna-tional humanitarian law norms, to recognize that rape conducted in armed conflict was a war crime, and that investigators and prosecutors be trained appropriately.

The ICRC's contribution to the 1995 Beijing Conference led to interna-tional recognition of the impact on women and girls of the "us[e] [of] sys-tematic rape as a tactic of war and terrorism" (UN 1995, 57). Its 2001 *Women Facing War* report, a global survey of the impact of armed conflict on women, highlighted specific areas of concerns for female civilians, namely, safety (e.g., personal safety, sexual violence, freedom from arbitrary displacement, and freedom of movement) and legal issues (e.g., access to effective remedy) (Lindsey-Curtet, Holst-Roness, and Anderson 2004, Part1.2). It argued for a stronger role for women in peacekeeping and stability operations, and the need to tailor military manuals and training (ICRC 2007). These moves formed the backdrop to the specific recommendations concerning women in the Montreux Document, an ICRC initiative.

Regulation and Redress

In 2001, UN Special Rapporteur on VAW, Radhika Coomaraswamy, referred to the "particular difficulties in enforcing international standards with regard to non-State actors" and called on the international community to ensure that they complied with international humanitarian law and human rights law (UN 2001, 15). Recent international regulatory initiatives, like the draft UN Convention, UN Guiding Principles, Montreux Document, UN-INSTRAW Tool Kit on Gender and PMSCs, and the UN Guidelines on its use of armed private security companies, have emphasized four areas of action: vetting personnel, education and ongoing training of personnel, reporting, and investigation and accountability. They explicitly cover dealings between states and/or intergovernmental organizations and PMSCs.

First, the Montreux Document recommends that vetting the past conduct of the PMSCs or their personnel, including verified records of sexual offenses, be a prerequisite for awarding contracts (ICRC 2008, 14, 20, 25; UN 2001, 8–10).[21] The ICoC requires signatory companies to establish selection and vetting procedures for its personnel and subcontractors that include disqualification from carrying a weapon if past conduct has included rape, sexual abuse, or trafficking in persons (Swiss Confederation 2010, 11). This is important because regulation of PMSCs remains primarily confined to self-regulation and contractual obligations (Schulz and Yeung 2008, 9). The UN-INSTRAW Report requires that PMSCs improve "vetting standards . . . to ensure those who have committed human rights violations or gender-based violent crimes be excluded" (17). The draft UN Convention does not refer to gender-based violence or women specifically, but it does require states parties to establish criteria for granting licenses and authorizations to PMSCs that take into account records or reports of human rights violations (UNWGM 2010b, Art.14(3)). The UN Guidelines require any contractor to have signed onto ICoC to verify that there is "no evidence or suspicion of previous criminal offences or human rights violations" by its personnel (UN 2012b, para.24).

Second, these recent initiatives emphasize the need for gender awareness training.[22] The Montreux Document requires contracting, host, and territorial states when selecting and authorizing PMSCs to take into account that their personnel are "sufficiently trained" prior to deployment and on a continuing basis regarding international humanitarian law, human rights law, and specific topics like gender (ICRC 2008, paras.128 and 130). The ICoC likewise requires companies to maintain records of training (Swiss Confederation 2010, 12). The draft UN Convention does not have a specific provision concerning gender awareness training but does cover the obligation of states parties to ensure that the PMSCs that they contract are trained in international humanitarian law and human rights law generally (UNWGM 2010b, Arts.4(2) and 14(3)). The UN-INSTRAW Review made a similar recommendation. UN Guiding Principle 7 emphasizes that states provide assistance to companies working in conflict zones to assess and address risks of abuses, particularly gender-based and sexual violence. To this end, the framework established under Res.1325 that covers training of peacekeepers is implicitly extended to PMSCs working alongside them on UN missions by the 2012 UN Guidelines (UN 2012b, para.23).

Third, the ICoC stipulates that signatory companies and their personnel must report sexual or gender-based violence and human trafficking to competent military and civilian authorities (Swiss Confederation 2010, 9). The Code prohibits signatory companies, and their personnel, supporting or benefiting from national or international crimes, including "sexual or gender-based violence, [or] human trafficking," and that they report "known or responsible suspicion[s]" of such acts to competent authorities in the country where the acts took place, country of nationality of victim, and/or country of nationality of the perpetrator. The UN-INSTRAW Review recommends that states and PMSCs develop national and international standards for monitoring and reporting sexual and physical violence perpetrated by PMSCs, particularly in the post-conflict situations discussed in Valerie Sperling's chapter in this volume (Schulz and Yeung 2008, 17). Likewise, the UN Guidelines have reporting requirements for PMSCs retained by the United Nations (UN 2012b, paras.25 and 27).

Fourth, as noted in part one, recent efforts to regulate PMSCs have emphasized the need for PMSCs' accountability. The 2001 UN Special Rapporteur on VAW's report called on states to prosecute perpetrators of war crimes and human rights abuses and ensure victims are eligible for compensation (UN 2001, 42). The Montreux Document states that the obligation to prosecute covers contracting, home, and territorial states (ICRC 2008, paras.6, 12, 17, and 21). Under the related ICoC, signatory companies and their personnel will not invoke contractual obligations, superior order, or exceptional circumstances (like armed conflict, public emergency, etc.) as justification for national or international crimes including sexual or gender-based violence or human trafficking. The Code also requires these companies to facilitate these processes by reporting to competent authorities, making records of allegations and findings available on request, cooperating with official investigations, and protecting whistleblowers (Swiss Confederation 2010, 7, 15).

In his report concerning the protection of civilians during armed conflict in 2006, the UN Secretary-General noted in regard to SC Res.1325 (2000) and SC Res.1674 (2006) that "more decisive and rigorous action is needed to bridge the gap between the rhetoric of those resolutions and the reality on the ground and to treat acts of sexual violence for what they are—despicable war crimes and crimes against humanity that must be punished" (UN 2007, 13). Ruggie has also called on states to provide more comprehensive guidance to corporations operating in conflict zones (UN 2011d). The United Nations has sought to coordinate and strengthen its advocacy, accountability, and support of national efforts to prevent sexual violence and respond to victims' needs through the UN Action against Sexual Violence in Conflict initiative. Also, under its amended memorandum of understanding with countries contributing to peacekeeping missions, the sending states have exclusive jurisdiction to investigate and prosecute offenses concerning sexual violence perpetrated by their contingent (UN 2007, 14; GA Res.61/291(2007)).

The question of accountability is closely aligned with access to justice and redress for victims. As the UN Guiding Principles indicate, the requirements of accountability enunciated under the twin pillars of states' obligation to protect and the corporations' obligation to respect reinforce the third pillar of states' obligation to provide effective remedies for victims. As examined above, this is reflected to varying degrees in the draft UN Convention, the Montreux Document, the ICoC, and the 2012 UN Guidelines covering UN contracts with PMSCs. When establishing the Working Group on Human Rights and Transnational Corporations in July 2011, the Human Rights Committee mandated that it make recommendations at the national, regional, and international levels "for enhancing access to remedies available to those whose human rights are affected by corporate activities, including those in conflict areas" (HRC Res.17/4(2011)). Also, it is required to take into account "a gender perspective" and "give special attention to persons living in vulnerable situations" (CE 2012, 21). Likewise, the draft UN Convention on PMSCs stipulates that when imposing sanctions for violations, states parties should have "due consideration . . . to offences committed against vulnerable groups" (UNWGM 2010b, Art.19(5)). Yet, it fails to list rape and sexual or gender-based violence in the draft's preamble of a nonexhaustive catalogue of international crimes that attract "the right to a comprehensive and effective remedy in accordance with international law."

The Updated Principles to Combat Impunity adopted by the UN Commission on Human Rights in 2006 provide that women should participate in public consultations for the development, implementation, and assessment of reparation programs (UN 2005b). As noted earlier, much has been made of the "implementation gap" and deficiencies of the current regulatory regimes covering PMSCs. There is an emerging body of work undertaken by academics, NGOs, and the Special Rapporteur on VAW concerning reparations and women, which is starting to have an impact on the jurisprudence of international human rights courts (Rubio-Marin 2009; UN 2010d).[23] Like the transformative work on violence against women before it, feminist scholars and women's advocacy groups are promoting women- and girl-centered processes that challenge and redefine procedural and substantive reparation mechanisms. Recognizing that violence and denial of access to redress is fueled by existing, systemic inequality, reparations cannot feasibly seek to return individuals to their circumstances prior to these crimes. Instead, the aim is transformative and seeks to "subvert, instead of reinforce . . . the root causes" (UN 2010d, 11). It is imperative that when designing remedial processes in the context of the regulation of PMSCs, drafters and negotiators engage fully with these developments and seek the active participation of representatives of vulnerable groups, including women.

CONCLUSION

Sadly, it is not surprising that the circumstances which brought the activities of PMSCs to the consciousness of the general public were acts of violence against women. By breaking the "silences" within international organizations and states and in international and domestic law, feminist scholars and women's NGOs have raised awareness of violence and inequalities suffered by women from the familial through to the transnational spheres, which are further exacerbated when the rule of law and state authority are compromised. The regulatory or implementation gaps surrounding PMSCs have a disproportionately negative impact upon women and other vulnerable groups. As noted above, current efforts to formulate regulatory frameworks offer glimpses of awareness in this regard. However, when women-centered issues are explicitly raised by these initiatives they remain confined to the realm of nonbinding good practice guidelines. A binding, specialist, international instrument regulating PMSCs is necessary to fight against impunity—to hold perpetrators accountable and to ensure effective reparations for their victims. As the international community works its way toward this goal, drafters and negotiators must harness developments in international law concerning women from the redefinition of key concepts in international criminal law to the reconceptualization of reparations. Additionally, it is crucial that civil society, particularly in the form of women's NGOs, UN bodies like UN Women (the umbrella body concerning women's issues at the United Nations), and relevant special rapporteurs be engaged in the process.

NOTES

1. PMSCs are defined as "corporate entit[ies] which provide on a compensatory basis military and/or security services by physical persons and/or legal entities" (UNWGM 2010b, Art.2(a)).

2. Art.29 (an opt out provision), Convention on the Elimination of All Forms of Discrimination again Women, December 18, 1979, in force September 3, 1981, GA Res. 34/180, UN Doc. A/34/46, 1249 UNTS 13; and Art.22, International Covenant on the Elimination of All Forms of Racial Discrimination, December 21, 1965, in force January 4, 1969, GA Res. 2106 (XX), Annex, 20. UN Doc.A/6014 (1966), 660 UNTS 195.

3. Its preamble refers to the International Criminal Court, and Art.38(c) draft UN Convention would enable the committee to refer urgent matters to the General Assembly, Security Council, specialized committees, or request that the General Assembly or Security Council pursuant to Art.96 of the UN Charter seeks an advisory opinion from the International Court of Justice.

4. Referencing Reparations Principles (UN 2005a). See also the related Impunity Principles (UN 2005b).

5. For customary international law and state practice concerning reparations including to individuals see Shelton (2005); and Rule 150 Reparation, ICRC Customary International Humanitarian Law Database, http://www.icrc.org/customary-ihl/eng/print/v1_cha_chapter42_rule150 (accessed November 25, 2012).

6. Three, Faiza Patel (chair/rapporteur), Patricia Arias, and Elżbieta Karska, of the five members of the UN Working Group on Mercenaries who prepared the draft Convention are women.

7. See UN 2003a (endeavoring to establish binding international legal obligations on business for human rights violations); UN Global Compact (UNGC) 2012; EU 2006, 2 (which emphasizes corporate social responsibility (CSR)); and the OECD 2011, a hybrid model, incorporating the legal obligations of states and domestic implementation and amended in May 2011 to align itself with the UN Guiding Principles.

8. The operationalization of the UN "Protect, Respect and Remedy" Framework was intended to provide "concrete and practical recommendations for its implementation" which have become the UN Guiding Principles (UN 2011c, 4).

9. With respect to corporate criminal liability see, for example, Art.12 Convention on Cybercrime ETS No.185, 23 November 2001, entered into force, 1 July 2004; and Art.18 Criminal Law Convention on Corruption, ETS No.173, 27 January 1999, entered into force, 1 July 2002. Certain human rights treaties require extension of jurisdiction to acts of natural or legal persons outside the territory of the state party: see Art.44, Convention on Preventing and Combating Violence against Women and Domestic Violence, CETS No.210, 11 May 2011, not entered into force.

10. Art.5(g) Statute of the International Criminal Tribunal for the Former Yugoslavia, GA Res.827 of 25 May 1993; Arts 3(h) and 4(g), Statute of the International Criminal Tribunal for Rwanda, SC Res.955 of 8 November 1994. The ICTR statute enumerates it and other forms of sexual violence as a violation of Common Article 3 of the 1949 Geneva Conventions. The Tokyo International Military Tribunal referred to sexual crimes in its indictment, and both the Nuremberg and Tokyo Tribunals heard evidence in respect of them, but neither mentioned rape in their judgments.

11. Prosecutor v. Akayesu, Trial Judgment, Case No.ICTR-96-4-T, 2 September 1998, para.688; Prosecutor v. Delalić et al. Trial Judgment, Case No.IT-96-21-T, 16 November 1998 (Čelibići), para.495; Prosecutor v. Furundžija, Trial Judgment, Case No.IT-95-17/1-T, 10 December 1998, para.271; Prosecutor

v. Kunarac et al., Trial Judgment, Case No.IT-96-23-T and IT-96-23/1-T, 22 February 2001, paras.460 and 495; and Prosecutor v. Kvočka et al., Trial Judgment, Case No.IT-98-30-T, 2 November 2001.

12. Kunarac et al., Trial Judgment, paras.540 and 542. See UN 2006.

13. Prosecutor v. Gacumbtsi, Trial Judgment, Case No.ICTR-2001-64-T, 17 June 2004, paras.321-333, and Prosecutor v. Gacumbtsi, Appeals Judgment, Case No.ICTR-2001-64-T, 7 July 2006, paras.102–3, 147–57; Prosecutor v. Musema, Trial Judgment, Case No.ICTR-96-13, 27 January 2000, paras.962–6; Prosecutor v. Semanza, Trial Judgment, Case No.ICTR-97-20-I, 15 May 2003, para.477–9; Prosecutor v. Tadić, Trial Judgment, Case No.IT-94-1-T, 7 May 1997, para.715; Prosecutor v. Kupreskić, Trial Judgment, Case No.IT-95-16-T, 14 January 2000, para.627; Kvočka Trial Judgment, paras.196–7, 233–4; Prosecutor v. Krstić, Trial Judgment, Case No.IT-98-33-T, 2 August 2001, paras.617–8; Furundžija, Trial Judgment, para.172; and Prosecutor v. Delalić et al,. Appeals Judgment, Case No.IT-96-21-A, 20 February 2001 (Čelibići Appeals Judgment).

14. Akayesu, Trial Judgment, para.594; Semanza, Trial Judgment, paras.482–5; and Prosecutor v. Furundžija, Appeals Judgment, Case No.IT-95-17/1-A, 21 July 2000, para.111. Cf. Kunarac, Trial Judgment, *supra* note 79, at paras.473, 482 and 497, and Kvočka Trial Judgment, para.139. See also UN Doc.A/HRC/7/3.

15. Gacumbtsi, Trial Judgment, paras.259–92; Akayesu, Trial Judgment; and Musema, Trial Judgment, para.933.

16. GA Res.34/180 of 18 December 1979, in force 3 September 198, 1249 UNTS 13, in particular Art.2.

17. GA Res.48/104, 20 December 1993, Art.4(c).

18. Art.38, Vienna Declaration and Programme of Action, adopted by World Conference on Human Rights, 25 June 1993, UN Doc.A/CONF.157/23.

19. Art.42(9), Rome Statute; for ICTY and ICTR see UN Division for the Advancement of Women, "Sexual Violence and Armed Conflict: United Nations Response," at http://www.un.org/womenwatch/daw/public/w2apr98.htm (accessed December 12, 2012); and Art.15(4) Statute of the Special Court for Sierra Leone requires the office of the prosecutor to give due consideration to the appointment of staff including prosecutors and investigators experienced in gender-related crimes (see also UN 2010c; UN 2011e, 21).

20. Art.36(8)(a)(iii) and (b), Rome Statute. The requirement that the Assembly of States Parties ensure fair representation of men and women and judges with legal expertise on specific issues, including but not limited to violence against women and children, has entailed the election of at least six female and six males judges, see ICC, *Procedure for the nomination and election of judges, the prosecutor and the deputy prosecutor of the International Criminal Court, Consolidated version* ICC-ASP/3/Res.6, para.19.

21. UN Guiding Principle 7 stipulates that with respect to companies operating in conflict zones, states should withdraw support for those involved in gross human rights violations (UN 2011c).

22. Gender has been defined by the ICRC as "culturally expected behaviour of men and women based on roles, attitudes and values ascribed to them on the basis of their 'sex'" (Lindsey-Curtet, Holst-Roness, and Anderson 2004, 7).

23. See Nairobi Declaration on Women's and Girls' Right to a Remedy and Reparations, March 2007; Declaration of the Goma Forum on the Rights of Victims of Sexual Violence, December 2009; and González et al. ("Cotton Field") v. Mexico, Judgment of 16 November 2009, I-ACtHR. Cf. Opuz v. Turkey, No.33401/02, Judgment of 9 June 2009, ECHR.

CHAPTER 11

Empathy, Responsibility, and the Morality of Mercenaries

A Feminist Ethical Appraisal of PMSCs

JILLIAN TERRY

While engagement by feminist IR scholars with private military and security companies (PMSCs) and their impact on processes of international political violence continues to grow, existing feminist scholarship has yet to address the complex moral and ethical implications of employing private force. This chapter examines the use of private military contracting in the post-9/11 period through a lens of feminist ethics. My argument is twofold: First, that a critical feminist ethical framework is a useful way to assess the ethics of contemporary warfare practices such as the hiring of PMSCs. Second, that prioritizing ethics in the development of feminist security studies offers a fruitful way forward for the field. Unlike other moral and ethical investigations of the hiring of PMSCs to date, an analysis that privileges a feminist ethical understanding of global politics asks us to think more deeply and critically about *relations* when examining the use of private force in the contemporary age and allows us to question if and how concepts such as *empathy* and *responsibility* play a part in shaping the day-to-day experiences of PMSC employees. The second part of my argument is based on an acknowledgement that in order for feminist security studies to deepen its contribution to security studies more broadly, it must engage and analyze a wide variety of phenomena in modern conflict and war—and do so in a way that opens up such analyses for dialogue with other perspectives in the field. For example, by engaging with ethical concepts and principles on the question of modern warfare and the changing nature of combatants, feminist security studies may delve deeper into conversations and debates surrounding the preeminence of just war theorizing in mainstream discussions of the ethics of war. This, I suggest, is essential in demonstrating the usefulness of a feminist framework as an integral part of, rather than a supplement to, dominant security discourses in the discipline. Furthermore, as feminist security studies continues to grow as a subfield of feminist IR, it would be useful to make connections with the as yet largely untapped resource of feminist ethical scholarship that lies outside the boundaries of the discipline. Feminist philosophers and social theorists in recent decades have, in their role as ethicists, questioned how gendered understandings of the world have shaped mainstream ethical conversations and led us to prioritize particular sets of moral and ethical principles regarding everyday life. Using these theoretical contributions and applying them to situations of international security, political conflict, and war enriches how feminists within IR talk about ethics and provides us with a new, alternative vocabulary to use when asking difficult moral and ethical questions about practices of war that move beyond the dominant just war framework.

Unlike the traditional soldiers of public military forces, private military contractors operate within a realm of morality guided not by military ethics training but instead by the actions of private economic actors and the shifting market related to the changing nature of contemporary war. Questions about private force that have been especially significant for feminists—including those surrounding accountability and the treatment of civilians in war—suggest that responsibility and empathy can be important conceptual tools for unpacking the ethical complexities of PMSCs. This chapter argues that it is imperative for feminist security scholarship to engage with questions of ethics in order to better understand the privatization of military force and to uncover the moral dilemmas of the practice that are often obscured by mainstream analyses in IR. Applying a feminist framework demonstrates that employing PMSCs actually results in a more complex and varied set of moral uncertainties than existing analyses have suggested. Rather than the ethical difficulties surrounding PMSCs being located primarily within the realm of financial motivation and "rogue" immoral behaviors owing to the lack of national sentiment connected to their work in war zones—as has been suggested in many IR discussions to date—examining private force through a feminist ethical lens uncovers moral dilemmas that center on the relationships between PMSC employees, official military personnel, combatants, and civilians and are closely connected to how we can understand questions of responsibility and empathy within the realm of these relational experiences. Moving away from an individualistic, self-motivated approach when considering ethics in private force is essential to building a more accurate understanding of the moral and ethical complexities inherent within the practice, and I argue here that a feminist ethical approach allows us to make this move in a valuable and reflective manner.

In order to support this argument, the chapter first builds a two-part feminist ethical framework to examine morality in private force, which is premised on empathy and responsibility. Foregrounding empathy as an ethical consideration in private security asks us to reflect on the unique relationship between paid security professionals and those impacted by living in war zones. Furthermore, a feminist ethical concept of responsibility and obligation to others that exists in contrast to a masculine ethics of justice based on the impersonal—and arguably inhuman—conceptions of rationality and objectivity can help us understand the ethical and moral decisions taken during the day-to-day operations of private military security contractors. The second section of the chapter applies a feminist ethical framework to an analysis of the existing literature within IR and security studies on PMSCs in order to interrogate its ethical and moral commitments to date. Despite the proliferation of work in the discipline dedicated to the exploration of how PMSCs impact contemporary conflict, the ethical dimension of private security has rightly been described as undertheorized in existing scholarship (Pattison 2008, 143). The final section of the chapter articulates some of the ways in which thinking about feminist ethics may provide new and fruitful avenues for feminist security scholarship to grapple with the difficult moral complexities of war more broadly and suggests some next steps for examining empathy and responsibility in the realm of PMSCs.

While this chapter demonstrates the difficulties in identifying a clear path forward for answering questions about the morality of PMSCs in the contemporary age, it also works to broaden and deepen the examination of this multifaceted element of warfare that is being developed by feminist scholarship in IR—in this volume and elsewhere—and challenges mainstream ethical analyses of PMSCs by highlighting the value of a feminist approach to the moral dilemmas inherent in private force.

FEMINIST ETHICS AND PRIVATE FORCE: ON EMPATHY AND RESPONSIBILITY

In an attempt to move beyond existing ethical analyses seen in IR as well as strands of political philosophy, applying a feminist ethical framework to the private military and security industry provides new lenses through which to see the complex behaviors and practices of PMSCs in the contemporary era. In particular, the feminist framework that I propose contains elements to examine both the *behavioral* side of PMSC operations—that is, what do private military contractors do, how do they do it, and who is impacted by their actions and in what ways—as well as the broader, *organizational* discussion surrounding the morality of private force as an industry and the ways in which it interacts with formal militaries and states themselves. To this end, I argue that it is necessary to rethink the ethics of PMSCs by foregrounding feminist ethical conceptual tools of empathy and responsibility. In so doing, it is possible to uncover a new and important set of understandings about the moral and ethical judgments to be made about PMSCs and how we might increase their moral and ethical standing as significant actors in contemporary warfare—particularly, we see that the ethical questions raised by private force as a practice of war are intrinsically tied to contractors' relationships with each other, as well as with public military forces, combatants, and civilians. This relational perspective exists as an alternative to the individual, self-motivated moral analyses that have been made about private force to date, centering largely on financial motivations and the lack of ties to a nationalist sentiment or patriotic identity leading to immoral or ethically questionable actions and behaviors.

The concept of empathy has been explored most commonly by feminist care ethicists such as Virginia Held (2006) in recent years but has thus far received almost no attention from mainstream scholarship examining the ethics of war. I suggest that it is an essential aspect of a feminist ethical framework as it acknowledges the importance of emotion and feeling, taking another step in moving beyond the abstraction and oversimplification of war seen in the contemporary just war tradition. Further, foregrounding empathy serves to bolster the ethical considerations brought to bear by thinking about war relationally and experientially. Christine Sylvester's (2013a) assertion that war as both physical and emotional experience has been largely ignored in IR has important implications here—as she remarks, thinking about experience in war "is a realm full of disorienting and generative bodily feelings and political possibilities" (86). When we suggest that it is ethically important not only to think about the relationships and experiences we have with others but also to have *empathy* for them, the moral questions surrounding war—and in particular, wars fought in highly technologized and privatized ways—become more complex and difficult to answer using a strictly delineated set of abstract principles or criteria.

A focus on empathy also serves to highlight the important distinction between sympathy and empathy, articulating a need to move beyond a simple recognition of or appreciation for the situations of others and instead feel as they do. As Laura Sjoberg (2006) suggests: "Empathy is not sharing others' experience, nor is it pitying others' plights. Instead it is, in some non-trivial way, feeling their pain" (48). This understanding of the pain and suffering caused by political violence is radically different than one where such emotions are considered morally acceptable because a war is just and suggests a need for thinking more critically about the ethics of war based on the importance of empathy as a central concern. Similarly, Fiona Robinson

(1999) suggests that using empathy as an ethical guideline allows us to consider context, relationality, and particularity in care in order to mitigate the effects of difference. Daryl Koehn's (1998) discussion of empathy provides a useful example of the potential benefits of such a concept in an ethical framework for war—as she suggests, "empathy allows someone else's experience and perspective to become a part of our moral baseline and therefore can function to help us overcome prejudices and misconceptions" (57). She goes on to highlight empathy's ability to assess our own efficacy as moral agents, rightly claiming that "if an empathetic conversation with another shows us that what we thought was a benefit is in fact a harm, then we had better rethink our claim to be just" (57).

The focus on relational thinking and practices of care is at the heart of a feminist conception of empathy—one whose primary aim is to shift our moral understandings away from the self and toward others. A feminist ethical approach is therefore distinguishable from other, more individualistic and justice-centered ethical approaches that maintain a prominent foothold in discussions of ethics in international political life. Thinking about empathy in this way allows us to build an alternative ethical lens for looking at private force: if we foreground the feeling of others' pain, the particularity and uniqueness of the experience of war, and the inclusion of a perspective other than our own, we are left asking a very different set of moral questions about the actions of PMSCs—namely, do those engaged in contracted private force operations think empathetically while doing their (paid) job, and if so, how? The experiences—and resultant empathetic interactions—of a private military contractor, working in Kandahar as an employee of a company operating with a specific contract, goals, and deadlines, will undoubtedly be different from that of a member of the official state military and graduate of a military academy who has already completed several tours of duty in Afghanistan. These differences impact the ethical and moral decision-making of each actor in war. Given the training and institutional supports provided to soldiers within the sprawling organization of contemporary militaries, we might expect to see an increased attention to the tenets of empathy described above—particularly as counterinsurgency operations and "winning hearts and minds" of civilians have played an increasingly important role in post-9/11 warfare. Conversely, an individual without the same relational experiences as a member of an official military—instead employed on an ad-hoc basis for short-term contracts—may well find it more difficult to think empathetically when faced with moral and ethical quandaries in the workplace (i.e., in a warzone).

Empathy, as feminist scholars have conceived it, therefore plays an important role as an ethical guideline for thinking about war generally and about the practices of PMSCs specifically. There is often a disconnect between the employees of PMSCs and the individuals around them, including official state military personnel, civilians, and combatants. For many private military contractors, there is little link between their job, which provides them with a salary, and the lives of those impacted by war on the ground. This economic motivation and detachment from the political and emotional realities of conflict has the possibility to lead to highly destructive and unethical consequences whereby PMSC employees find themselves wrongly identifying civilians as enemy combatants or not providing adequate support to official military personnel due to a lack of empathetic connection as colleagues. By thinking seriously about the importance of empathy as an ethical principle, we can begin to formulate ways to encourage moral and ethical behavioral standards among those working in private force—whether it is through an inclusion of a discussion on empathy into the codes of conduct and ethics written by PMSCs themselves; increased attention to empathetic interaction between private military contractors and civilian populations; or attempts to educate PMSC employees about the importance of empathy, relationships, and shared experience.

Just as foregrounding a feminist ethical understanding of empathy may allow us to make new moral judgments about the behaviors and practices of PMSCs and their employees, so too can placing an additional focus on the concept of responsibility. Thinking about responsibility as an ethical guideline means acknowledging the importance of ascribing moral responsibility for actions, as well as an understanding of the responsibilities that we have to each other. Specifically with respect to the ethics of war, I suggest that thinking about responsibility is critical as there is a need for the recognition of concrete realities and atrocities of war as well as the assigning of responsibility for them, regardless of whether a war is deemed morally justifiable. The contemporary just war tradition's failure to adequately assess questions of responsibility in its ethical appraisal of war serves as a fundamental shortcoming in the literature. A feminist ethical framework that acknowledges the need for responsibility and its ethical importance in thinking about contemporary practices of political violence allows us to think more substantively about *what* international actors are responsible for and *when* to ascribe responsibility to one party rather than another. Importantly, a feminist understanding of responsibility also asserts the importance of the existence of shared responsibilities that we have for each other. As Heidi Grasswick (2003) suggests, there have been many significant developments in thinking about responsibility within feminist ethics, chief among them the need to move beyond a strictly delineated praise/blame version of moral responsibility and acknowledge the *impurities* of moral agency in a careful and contextual way when assigning responsibility for particular moral actions or decisions (99). Thinking about responsibility through a feminist lens requires a nuance not present in other conceptions of responsibility, which concentrate largely on the ascription of blame on particular actors in a given moral situation. Robinson (2011) articulates the importance of this specific form of responsibility when she theorizes that feminist care ethics have "a focus on attention, responsiveness, and responsibility to the needs of particular others as the substance of morality" (29). In this sense, responsibility is explicitly feminist, as it calls our attention to how moral decision-making is constantly entwined with the complex relationships we have with others and the ways in which care features in those relationships. Therefore, responsibility is not simply a means of labeling the actions of individuals (as moral/ ethical or otherwise) but instead highlights the importance of our shared collective responsibilities to and for the lives of others as a pillar of a feminist ethical framework.

Scholars investigating the ethics of the private military and security industry have long grappled with the question of responsibility. Peter Singer (2008) suggests that the exact lines of responsibility between PMSCs and state governments are quite difficult to assess in cases where private military firms (PMFs, as he calls them) are seen to have done something wrong. He rightfully asks: "Who can and should be punished for these crimes? The soldiers who did the actual deeds? Their government? The individual employees of PMFs? The overall military companies? Their clients? The clients' owners (stockholders)?" (221). Such questions are highly contentious and demonstrate the complicating effect that privatizing security has on what is already a complex issue of responsibility in war. Foregrounding a feminist ethical conception of responsibility as a contextual and relational tool with which we can untangle the intricate web of accountability helps us navigate a world in which PMSCs are subject only to the laws of the market rather than to the wide range of checks and balances that oversee traditional state militaries. Specifically, utilizing a feminist understanding of responsibility—that both moves beyond an oversimplified praise/blame system and thinks about the moral and ethical responsibilities we have to each other as a collectivity— asks us to question existing paradigms of responsibility in discussions surrounding the ethics of private force. Instead of thinking about responsibility in terms of ascription, for example as a particular company's code of ethics assigning responsibility for the ethical and moral decisions made by its employees to those individuals themselves, using a feminist ethic of responsibility means foregrounding the feelings of interconnectedness individuals have toward others, the contexts they find themselves in, and their experiences. This understanding of responsibility, stemming from the early work on the ethics of care by Carol Gilligan (1982) and Nel Noddings (1984), may be characterized by nurturing and places particular focus on responsibilities to others. It exists in contrast to more mainstream ethical arguments premised on justice, expressions of autonomy, and the formation of abstract and universal principles characterized by rationality and an emphasis on the rights of individuals.

Because the daily experiences of private contractors are necessarily filled with interactions with a variety of others—colleagues, official military personnel, insurgents, and civilians—a feminist understanding of responsibility is essential for revealing the moral characteristics of those relationships. Therefore, a feminist ethical framework that includes responsibility as a central component is able to make more accurate ethical judgments about the actions of private forces in contemporary war zones than ethical approaches focused on the individual. This is not to say that there remains no space in this framework for particular forms of individual responsibility. Certainly, the intent of an ethical argument rooted in feminist notions of responsibility is not to exclude the possibility of individual blame or punishment when contextually appropriate—for example, in the torture and abuse cases reported at the Abu Ghraib prison in Iraq. Rather, such an expression of responsibility is meant to highlight the necessarily relational experiences of PMSC employees and the resulting need for an ethical framework that acknowledges this relationality rather than assumes the existence of an isolated and individual moral actor in battle.

Rather than seeing the use of PMSCs as a force "that pushes responsibility and liability outwards through contracting and privatization" (Taussig-Rubbo 2009b, 144), using a feminist lens of responsibility asks us to take seriously the need for a comprehensive approach to ascribing responsibility for atrocities in war—an approach that acknowledges the state's role as client and customer of PMSCs, the companies themselves, and the individual employees of the firms in question. In particular, it questions the holding of responsibility as an individual act, suggesting instead that it is in the relationships with others that it is possible to think more carefully about responsibility as an ethical guideline. It is not sufficient to simply label the realm of private force as too difficult or diffuse to accurately identify responsible parties—rather, a feminist ethical approach to responsibility would suggest that in order to make judgments about the moral and ethical status of private force, it is absolutely vital that responsibility be of primary concern to those both inside the theoretical/academic community and those practitioners in governments and conflict zones around the world.

The concepts of empathy and responsibility as put forward by the work of feminist ethicists both inside and outside the contours of IR serve as two small, but important, first steps toward a more fruitful feminist dialogue and debate surrounding the ethics of PMSCs, as they highlight the need for a more experiential and collective understanding of how PMSCs operate day-to-day and how these conditions affect their abilities to act in morally or ethically nebulous circumstances. A feminist ethical framework premised on empathy and responsibility offers an alternative to mainstream theoretical discussions surrounding the regulation and motivations of PMSCs—by moving away from an autonomous, justice-based ethical approach to understanding

PMSCs and toward a collective, relational, and contextual one, it becomes evident that PMSC operations are morally and ethically problematic in ways that existing scholarship in IR has not been aware of.

ETHICS AND MORALITY IN PRIVATE FORCE: FROM CONVENTIONAL TO FEMINIST CONVERSATIONS

Having identified a feminist ethical framework with which we can study the ethics of private force, it is necessary to assess the usefulness of such a framework, built on the concepts of empathy and responsibility, against existing debates and analyses in IR about the morality of PMSCs. When surveying the field, it is quickly evident that there has been a marked proliferation of both academic scholarship and media coverage examining the rise of PMSCs, particularly in the years following the American-led invasion of Iraq in March of 2003. However, as Singer (2008) points out, the concept of private force itself is not a new one, and there is a significant historical legacy of states hiring outsiders to assist in the fighting of their battles (19). Increases have been seen in military operations undertaken by the United States (and its allies) in Afghanistan and Iraq as part of the "war on terror," and it is now unlikely for any major deployment of U.S. military forces overseas to succeed without the employment of private companies (Franke and Boemcken 2009, 11). Despite this, startlingly few analyses have focused on the ethical and moral dimensions of private force. In this section, I demonstrate the effectiveness of a feminist ethical framework by assessing what the limited existing analyses of ethics in private force have missed out on: namely, to provide an alternative vision to the justice-based, individual, and autonomous understanding of ethics that is offered by mainstream approaches to ethics in war, and to consider contextual, relational, and experiential factors that serve to shape the ethical and moral decisions made by PMSC employees.

Much of the existing ethical and moral analysis of PMSCs has tended to focus on their capacity as providers of direct military force and engagement in combat, despite the empirical evidence suggesting that this represents only a small fraction of the work PMSCs are contracted to complete. It is therefore important for future debates around the ethical and moral complexities of PMSCs—including this discussion—to recognize the diversity of functions and roles played by private actors in military contexts and to acknowledge that the ethical judgments we make about private force cannot always be generalized across the spectrum of private military and security employment. Rather, a feminist ethical framework premised on concepts of empathy and responsibility allows for a deeper and more contextually aware discussion of how the ethics of private force is far more particularized than existing scholarship would suggest.

As one might expect, much of the literature on PMSCs that does take up a discussion of ethics and/or morality introduces its analysis by pointing toward the impact of economics as a motivation for success and the different ethical implications brought forth by the market as a driving force for PMSC activities in conflict zones. Sarah Percy (2007), in her analysis of mercenaries and the history of the norm against their use in international relations, uses the *Oxford English Dictionary* definition of "mercenary" to demonstrate the industry's pervasive links to financial motivation: " 'mercenary' is used as adjective meaning 'a person whose actions are motivated primarily by personal gain, often at the expense of ethics' " (241). As she points out, the norm against mercenary use in international relations has a significant ethical component and the moral definitiveness with which society sees killing in the abstract sense has influenced the specific political norm that has developed, suggesting that only the citizens of a state should be used as its military personnel. Percy's suggestion, however, is that it is the ways in which private force have traditionally been seen— that is, as reckless mercenaries with a psychopathic desire to kill—which have contributed to its institutionalization as a morally problematic practice in warfare. If examined from a different perspective, she argues, the norm against the use of private military fighters becomes more complex, and we may well see situations where the use of private force may be the most moral option in a particular conflict (240). Percy's assertion echoes that of other scholars (e.g., Mandel 2002; Singer 2008; Carmola 2010) in the discipline who have argued that the moral realities of private military contracting are significantly more complex than they have been portrayed and that more attention is needed in order to make more accurate ethical and moral judgments about the use of private force in contemporary conflicts.

While this type of argument is useful in acknowledging the complexity of the moral and ethical questions surrounding PMSCs, Percy does not go far enough in unpacking the term "mercenary" and its economic roots. While her analysis stops at the point of economic motivations, a feminist ethical framework of empathy and responsibility asks us to step outside the boundaries of the market and examine the particular contexts and experiences of contractors, both as individuals and in their relationships with others. In so doing, an image appears not simply of a lone warrior intent on bringing home the largest salary but instead of a complex web of relations that impact the ethical and moral decision-making practices of PMSC employees and demand a new attention on empathetic interactions and questions of responsibility and care for others. This move away from the individualistic, self-interested financial factor as the *only* concern for PMSC ethics allows us to understand that while the behavior of individual contractors may well be largely related to the promise of a paycheck, it is through their relationships and experiences with a variety of others that the true complexities of their ethical and moral decision-making is revealed.

Another relevant area of discussion surrounding ethics and PMSCs is in the realm of regulation. For many, it is the lack of regulation, professional standards, and behavior-monitoring principles that are primary sources for moral and ethical quandaries about the use of private force by states. Some PMSCs have begun to focus on these ethical questions by participating in discussions about and subsequent implementation of corporate responsibility policies, including creating standards for professional behavior and signing agreements for regulation and monitoring by objective groups (Avant 2007, 192). Many of these standards are enshrined in codes of conduct that PMSCs use for both recruitment and marketing purposes, often to distance themselves from the negative connotations given to private force discussed earlier in this chapter. For example, Vesper Group, a Swedish-based private security firm founded in 2004 with subsidiaries in Afghanistan, Pakistan, Uganda, and Iraq, expresses its values in the "guiding principles" of the company's code of ethics: "[B]eing a Swedish based company we understand development work and human rights issues. We get the job done efficiently, but we also consider the ethical implications of how our services are being implemented" (quoted in Berndtsson 2012, 312). Similarly, ArmorGroup—a large British private security firm acquired by G4S in 2008—emphasizes on its "Regulation and Ethical Standards" web page its strong commitment to monitoring by external groups including the International Red Cross (Krahmann 2010, 7). Other firms such as DynCorp and Bechtel have written extensive codes of ethics and business conduct that deal mainly with "harassment of co-workers, organizational conflicts of interests and the production of company assets, while leaving out more sensitive issues such as the use of armed force" (151). The connotations of morality and professionalism in these companies' codes of ethics are familiar themes throughout the private force sector, demonstrating a desire among PMSCs to set the ethical rules and benchmarks by which their own conduct is measured.

In assessing the area of regulation, a feminist ethical framework highlights some of the main issues we encounter when PMSCs attempt to self-regulate, the most important of which is related to the notion of responsibility. By creating these codes of conduct and ethical guidelines for their employees, PMSCs inscribe an individualistic, autonomous, rights-based identity onto those working in the field, and subscribe primarily to a praise/blame system of responsibility that does not take into account the subjectivities and impurities of moral agency inherent in discussions of responsibility itself. These codes of conduct do not question the broader legitimacy and morality of the work being done, instead choosing to focus on individual ethical transgressions in the realm of coworker harassment. In addition, these ethical guidelines do not ascribe responsibility to the company itself or suggest that it is at all capable of morally or ethically questionable behavior. As PMSCs describe themselves as ethical, these codes of conduct often serve as a form of advertising, raising questions about the maintenance of a particular corporate reputation and questions of accountability and control (Avant 2007, 194). Empirically, the ethical codes that have been voluntarily created by PMSCs, either as individual companies or as a collectivity, appear not to have had much impact on the conduct of PMSC employees. As James Cockayne (2007) points out, the interrogators implicated in the Abu Ghraib Iraqi prison abuse scandal were supplied by the large PMSC CACI, and their behavior was not shaped or affected by the company's own Standards of Ethics and Business Conduct, which explicitly forbids sexual harassment (207). Cases such as this one highlight the problem of accountability in self-regulation—even if an increasing number of PMSCs claim to adhere to codes of conduct and ethics, they do so when and if it is suitable for them (Leander 2007b, 62; also see Vrdoljak's chapter in this volume on more recent developments, such as the International Code of Conduct for Private Security Service Providers).

While the concerns regarding this lack of regulation in existing analyses generally center on the emergence of private security actors and its effects on the state's monopoly over the use of force, a feminist ethical framework points to an additional significant quandary—the lack of desire by governments to regulate the actions of PMSCs and their reliance on self-regulatory schemes devised by the companies is yet another byproduct of a practice whereby responsibility is theorized and practiced at an individual, rather than collective, level. The PMSCs are left to create rules and standards that punish individuals for ethical and moral transgressions, such as coworker harassment, without pointing to the larger questions surrounding the moral status of the companies' actions and the legitimacy of their contracts. Thinking about responsibility in this caring, collective manner could lead to increased attention toward the behaviors of PMSCs on the part of governments and organizations, while ideally maintaining an awareness of the contextual and varied nature of PMSC activities. I acknowledge that a one-size-fits-all regulation scheme for private force is unlikely, given the wide swath of activity encompassed under its banner. Rather, an understanding of responsibility that shifts the focus from individual punishments to a more collective conception of morality and ethics could bring about positive change within the ongoing developments of regulation in the private military and security industry. This drive for broader regulation has been discussed in the literature, though there has not been a direct link made to questions of responsibility. Several policy reports and recommendations about the future of private force in global politics have also suggested that existing schemes of self-regulation are ineffective—as Caroline Holmqvist (2005) argues, the codes of conduct and ethics that PMSCs have written "are often unhelpfully vague and suffer from being directed at the individual company rather than the industry level" (47). She suggests that a broader approach to regulation is needed whereby states become important actors in enforcing legislation or regulation to hold PMSCs accountable to the ethical standards they set out for themselves in codes of conduct. To date, few steps have been taken in this direction by state governments, and many questions remain surrounding how PMSCs articulate their own moral and ethical commitments as actors in conflict zones. As these questions evolve, a feminist understanding of responsibility—moving away from individualistic, praise/blame approaches—would serve governments and organizations to move forward with increased regulatory schemes that can have a positive impact on the moral status of PMSCs and act independently of the companies' wish to maintain their corporate reputation as ethical. More specifically, feminist conceptions of responsibility through care prioritize our responsibilities to the needs of others and bring into focus the significant problems inherent in the existing self-regulation schemes by PMSCs. These codes of conduct and behavior, directed at employee transgressions and workplace harassment, miss an important element of ethical judgment about private force over-all—namely, when and where it is appropriate to deploy PMSCs and for what purpose. Practically speaking, existing forms of regulation do little to help navigate the murky waters of morality in the contracting of private force and to what extent their services may be used as a means to an unethical end. An understanding of responsibility that sees the importance of collective well-being is better tailored to make judgments about these broader implications on the legitimacy and morality of PMSC action.

Another area in which there has been some explicit analysis of moral and ethical judgment in the existing literature is through examinations of private force employees themselves. Elke Krahmann's (2010) investigation of private contractors provides a helpful distinction between what she calls the two preferred models of the soldier in liberalism—the politically neutral, professional soldier or the private military contractor (18). For her, the distinction between these two models is quite clear in terms of the ways in which democratic control over their actions is enforced. While the professional soldier is controlled through a combination of obligation and duty, patriotic sentiment, a collective professional ethos among official state military soldiers, and a clear distinction between the political and military roles of citizens, the "private military contractor has no general obligations other than to the employer or contract, is motivated by private gain, is alienated from society and is held accountable through market rather than institutional relations" (18). In recent years, this type of description has been substantiated with firsthand field and interview-based research in Afghanistan and Iraq, suggesting that the rogue, cowboy identity ascribed to many working in the private military and security industry is a product of reality.[1] From these differences, we can begin to imagine the variation in ethical training and consideration between state-sanctioned members of the military and private company employees. However, to date, this professional divide has been at least partially bridged by the heavy recruitment of private military contractors from among the ranks of former soldiers and defense department employees, particularly in the case of the United States. For those who have already been subject to state military training practices, it can be argued that the personal morals and high ethical behavioral standards of "serving your country" are transferred to those individuals' work in private force (Krahmann 2010, 151). Of course, the ethical standards to which state military employees are actually held have been subject to much debate in the fields of war and conflict studies in recent years. However, given the current military climate that is becoming more reliant on PMSCs for a variety of support roles in contemporary conflicts, those with official military training currently working in private force will increasingly be replaced by employees who have little to no experience of military professionalism. This is due largely to the changing nature of war, whereby states enter into contracts with PMSCs to fill supporting and specialist roles in military missions, many of which rely on the skills of highly trained civilians with particular areas of expertise, such as communications technology or geographic mapping, rather than on ex-military personnel. The resulting labor pool, drained of those former military officials who will have undergone at least some official military ethics training, will in the future increasingly consist of individuals with varied ethical backgrounds, raising concerns about the possibility for sound moral and ethical judgments to be made in the context of war.

Indeed, even the ex-military members who join the ranks of private force are likely to see some shift in the ethical norms they would have previously absorbed in training. This is due largely to the fundamental change in the work environment whereby economic factors now impact the actions of PMSC employees in a way not previously seen in their careers as soldiers. As Steve Fainru suggests in 2008's *Big Boy Rules*, "because the mercs weren't soldiers anymore . . . they could walk away at any time and often did, contract-hopping their way through a war and another people's nation with a gun. The money, it was always there and that was the ultimate goal: not peace, not victory, not a better Iraq" (215). While many private military contractors who were once members of official militaries undoubtedly are aware of the norms and obligations of war ascribed in international law, the allure of financial gain significantly obfuscates the application of this awareness to their work outside state military life. This distinct character of private force employment may well account for the fact that even ex-military personnel seem to portray a lack of concern for the ethical and moral obligations they would have likely been taught in military academy ethics-training classes and serves as a lens through which their relationships and daily experiences in war are shaded. A feminist ethical framework premised on empathy and responsibility can move past a vision of economic gain as the exclusive factor motivating contractor behavior, while still acknowledging its undeniable impact on the ethics of private contractors.

As Paul Higate (2012a) discovered through his engagement with British contractors' memoirs of their experiences in Iraq, there is evidence to suggest that the sense of professionalism that was so important for the contractors to convey stemmed at least in part from a strategic way to legitimize their involvement in military operations (340). While this professional identity may well have historical and cultural ties to a sense of national pride, as Higate (2012a) suggests, there is more emphasis on highly skilled and expert aspects of contractor identity than to their "service to country." This distinctly professional identity, when analyzed through a feminist ethical framework, takes on another role—that of the autonomous individual, abstracted from particular contexts and experiences, only there "to get the job done." Without an understanding of the relational and experiential aspects of war, the ability to engage in empathetic interactions or think ethically about the nature of responsibility is obscured, instead leaving the market or the firm to decide the best course of action rather than a judgment made in acknowledgment of the variety of relationships and unique experiences undertaken as a PMSC employee. In this sense, a feminist ethical framework can serve to call into question the existing identity of the private soldier as "professional" and ask how a more complex vision of how PMSC employees see themselves may lead us to ask very different questions about the ethics and morality of their day-to-day operations in the context of war.

Interestingly, the UK government has suggested that the outsourcing of military work to the private sector has actually served to "enhance morale, cohesion, combat effectiveness and ethos of the armed services" (Uttley 2005, 16) as soldiers are relieved from routine support roles and focus on more stimulating and rewarding tasks (Krahmann 2010, 106). It is important to recognize the many impacts this has on the environment of war—for example, as Isabelle Barker points out in this volume, it is often low-wage migrant men from South Asia who perform the reproductive labor tasks previously performed in families (by women), such as doing laundry and cooking, that maintain the military apparatus and allow soldiers to continue living with the conveniences of a middle-class lifestyle, even in a war zone. Looking at the inclusion of private contractors in conflict zones from a critical ethical perspective, however, leads us to question how particular situations and actions may be interpreted differently through a lens of market (rather than moral) accountability. In other words, what are the impacts on moral and ethical judgments in war when states are increasingly reliant on private force for the successful accomplishment of missions? Deborah Avant (2005) suggests that answering this question necessitates thinking about an important link to international law. Western military personnel (for the most part) understand the importance of abiding by the obligations of international law in terms of conduct in war. Such obligations are an integral element of professional military education both as moral imperatives and as a necessary element of effective military operations. Therefore, respecting the rights of noncombatants and abiding by domestic law with respect to civilian authorities are seen as essential ingredients in a successful military mission (51–52). Conversely, private military contractors are less concerned with the moral obligations ascribed in international law as their training is much less likely to include substantive discussions about the importance of the norms of proper behavior in war that have been enshrined in international legal doctrine in recent decades. Given that the primary motivator for PMSCs is profit, there are clear reasons to be concerned about the operations of such firms in practice, as well as the problems they pose for the credibility and viability of these norms and well-known principles of war, such as the combatant/civilian distinction (Alexandra 2012).

As the preceding discussion has demonstrated, there is no consensus within existing scholarship on the ethics of PMSCs. The limited work to date has focused largely on questions of regulation, accountability, education, and behavioral standards to make a variety of claims about if and when private military contractors can be seen as ethical or moral actors in contemporary conflict. A feminist ethical framework that foregrounds concepts of empathy and responsibility makes important claims about the tenuous ethical standing upon which the foundations of the private military and security industry are built. Feminist ethics, I suggest, is a useful way to think about questions of justice and morality in private force as it privileges an understanding of PMSCs that focuses on the contextual and relational elements of private force—as well as an awareness of the lived experiences of individuals working in and impacted by the industry—rather than discussing PMSCs solely in terms of markets, firms, and the states that hire them.

NAVIGATING THE GRAYNESS: THE FUTURE OF ETHICAL JUDGMENTS ON PRIVATE FORCE

Former UN adviser David Shearer (1998) states: "Private military forces cannot be defined in absolute terms: they occupy a gray area that challenges the liberal conscience. Moral judgments on the use of mercenaries are usually passed at a distance from the situations in which these forces are involved. Those facing conflict and defeat have fewer moral compunctions" (13). Given the nebulous nature of the morality and ethics of private force, particularly as it has been discussed in existing IR scholarship, it is an area in serious need of new approaches and critical perspectives. Echoing the thoughts of Shearer, Singer (2008) suggests that private military firms possess an ambiguous status when it comes to morals and ethics, and to make a blanket normative statement about whether the private military and security industry is moral would be both analytically incorrect and ethically unfair (228). Similarly, Avant (2005) warns against rushing to normative judgment about whether the privatization of security is "good" or "bad," suggesting that this impedes analysis of the wide range of effects of privatization and prevents us from fully understanding the dilemmas associated with private security (254). Such caveats are important reminders of the dynamic and complex nature of private force and suggest that we need an ethical outlook that is both reflexive and flexible, able to process the many contours of the industry without describing the ethics of PMSCs in stark, either/or terms. In my view, a feminist ethical framework premised on empathy and responsibility as important elements for understanding the debate surrounding PMSCs is able to achieve this in ways that existing scholarship on the ethics of private force has not been able to—namely, by pointing to the need for an increasingly collective and relational understanding.

As Kimberly Hutchings (2000) rightly points out, "a feminist ethics of care is most powerful when voiced as a claim about the nature of the world we inhabit rather than a claim about what ought to be the case" (123). Indeed, using a feminist ethics of care approach—grounded in understandings of empathy and responsibility—allows us to more accurately examine the workings of the contemporary private military and security industry, exposing its relational and experiential elements in a way not possible in mainstream ethical approaches. The resulting benefit is significant for the academic community, as it allows for a shift away from prescriptive, abstract, and universal solutions to the complex moral quandaries of private force. Instead, we are asked to think contextually and reflexively about the actions of PMSC employees in war. This shift is also likely to result in positive influences on the industry itself, particularly in the realms of regulation and ethics training where policymakers may look to existing studies on the morality of private force in developing future guidelines about their use and actions.

Moving forward, it is necessary to expand this framework into other areas of research about PMSCs. Feminist ethicists may want to think about how best to use our conceptual tools to make further practical recommendations in order to improve the ethical and moral standing of PMSCs, particularly as they gain importance and prevalence in conflict zones in virtually all corners of the world. As this chapter has suggested, it is unhelpful to rely on abstract moral principles in order to make judgments about the ethical status of PMSCs and their employees. Rather, a feminist framework constructed around empathy and responsibility asks us to push our assessments of PMSCs further and take seriously their varied experiences and relationships. This awareness allows us to make more careful, contextual claims about the morality of PMSCs and foreground the importance of care as an ordering ethical concept in international politics. For feminist IR scholars, care ethics provides an important addition to the meaningful contributions that have already been made about the gendered and masculinized nature of private force (see the chapters by Stachowitsch and Eichler in this volume) and asks us to think carefully about the moral basis on which the industry is built. Using empathy and responsibility as first steps will serve to help feminists navigate the grayness of the private military and security industry and engage in substantive analyses of the many moral and ethical complexities surrounding PMSCs in global politics.

NOTE

1. There have been a number of monographs in the past decade dedicated to profiling the lives and activities of PMSC employees (see, for example, Pelton 2006; Scahill 2007; Fainaru 2008; Isenberg 2009).

Conclusion

MAYA EICHLER

What is the role of gender in the privatization of military security? How does gender intersect with other categories of difference in shaping the practices of PMSCs? How is the privatization of military security connected to changes in national and global gender orders? What type of gendered organizations are PMSCs and what notions of masculinity and femininity do they rely on and reinforce, in intersection with race, class, citizenship, national identity, and sexuality? What gendered conceptions of protection, sacrifice, and security are (re)produced or disrupted by the privatization of security? And, how does the private security industry affect women's and men's security, both as employees and locals in the field? What gendered problems of accountability exist in relation to private security, and what is the potential for regulating and reforming private security from a feminist perspective?

This volume has offered answers to these and other questions but, of course, not exhausted the potential avenues for studying gender and private security in global politics. This volume has covered a wide array of themes in private security including the gendered causes and effects of security privatization; the interactions between gendered states and gendered global markets; gendered and racialized employment practices in the private security industry; the remaking of gendered protection, sacrifice, and violence through privatization; the negative effects of PMSCs on women's security; the gender-specific blind spots and limitations of existing accountability, regulatory, and ethical frameworks pertaining to PMSCs; and the place of PMSCs in sustaining a gendered global order.

The book has illustrated the potential breadth of scope for "critical gender studies in private security." Most importantly, the volume has aimed to enliven current scholarly debates on private security in contemporary global politics by foregrounding gender. As such, it has established gender as a key analytical category for the study of private security in global politics and put forward a framework for critical gender studies in private security. Moreover it has advanced the field of feminist security studies by contributing new empirical and theoretical insights into the gendering of security today. In this concluding chapter, I first highlight the book's contributions to private security scholarship by briefly reviewing the book's chapters. I then outline how the book's chapters contribute to a critical gender framework for the study of private security. Third, I identify the volume's contributions to feminist security studies. Finally, I conclude by considering the implications of the volume for a feminist politics of security and for future critical gender scholarship on private security.

GENDER AND PRIVATE SECURITY IN GLOBAL POLITICS

The chapters contained in this book make the case that gender analysis is crucial to improved and more nuanced theoretical, empirical, and normative understandings of security privatization, PMSCs, and private contractors in global politics. The book illustrates the varied and complex ways in which gender is significant to the body, local, national, regional, and global politics of private security. The chapters in part I, "Beyond the Public/Private Divide: Feminist Analyses of Military Privatization and the Gendered State," took as their starting point the gendering of states and recent transformations in this gendering to trace the gendered processes and effects of security privatization. Rejecting dichotomous categories, these contributors investigated how the relations between public and private spheres, state and market, and national and international realms are being reconstituted under neoliberalism. The analyses of private security here focused on the interactions between gendered states and global markets undergoing neoliberal restructuring (Stachowitsch), the gendered politics of sacrifice in states engaged in postmodern warfare (Baggiarini), and the global rescaling of the gendered politics of protection historically tied to the nation-state (Eichler). Together these chapters underscored the importance of taking seriously the role of the state in facilitating gendered security privatization, while also being attentive to the ways in which the market is shifting gender norms and remasculinizing security.

Part II, "Rethinking the Military Contractor I: Third-Country Nationals and the Making of Empire," challenged dominant stereotypes of the employees of PMSCs as Western, white, and trigger-happy "tough guys." The chapters by Barker, Chisholm, and Joachim and Schneiker investigated through a variety of methodologies (including ethnography and discourse analysis) the significant role of "third-country nationals"—primarily men from the global South—in the globally operating private security industry, whether as logistics workers or armed and unarmed security guards. Scholars have generally overlooked the role of men from the global South—much like the role of female camp followers during an earlier era—which has led to a privileging of Western (public and private) militarized masculinities. These chapters highlighted the racialized and gendered hierarchy of masculinities in the industry and how it is implicated in the making of empire and neocolonial global relations. By focusing on the exploitation as well as agency of the racialized men who work, often under poor conditions, in the industry the chapters show the intimate connections between security and political economy in local, national, regional, and global contexts.

Part III, "Rethinking the Military Contractor II: Masculinities and Violence," further reexamined norms of masculinity in the private security sector. The chapters by Higate and Hendershot investigated how the violent and transgressive behavior of some white Western contractors is interpreted within and beyond the industry, in ways that help legitimate (and informally regulate) the industry and uphold (post)conflict zones as heteronormal, masculinized spaces. Drawing on participant-observation during close-protection training, Higate argued that, contrary to expectations of the remasculinization thesis, trainers emphasized the importance of restraint, juxtaposing the hypermasculinity and hyperaggressiveness of U.S. contractors to the professional and disciplined masculinity of UK contractors. Hendershot's analysis of the Kabul hazing scandal showed that in addition to the hypermasculine other, the ideal contractor is constructed in opposition to the deviant homosexual or the potentially impotent other. As he argued, male contractors are expected to uphold heteronormativity— "including the proper functioning of both symbolic and fleshy penises." Together, parts II and III demonstrate the importance of subordinate masculinities for the industry's day-to-day functioning and of norms of hegemonic masculinity for its legitimacy.

Part IV shed light on a major theme in private security scholarship, that of accountability, regulation, and ethics, from a variety of feminist perspectives. Sperling showed that transnational forces, including PMSCs, used for peacekeeping purposes create particular problems of accountability when it comes to women's security. Vrdoljak's chapter detailed the limitations and gaps in the international legal framework that exists in relation to PMSCs and women. As these two chapters together show, women's security is negatively impacted in the context of the privatization and transnationalization of force, in particular when national regulation is weakened and international law is lagging behind. Terry's chapter added a feminist ethical perspective that foregrounded empathy and responsibility in place of individualism and profit, as is usually the case in analyses of the ethical dilemmas faced by private contractors. Her analysis suggested that debate on ethics and PMSCs move beyond a focus on the market to additionally explore "the particular contexts and experiences of contractors, both as individuals and in their relationships with others."

CRITICAL GENDER STUDIES IN PRIVATE SECURITY

Collectively, the volume's contributors have put forward a framework for studying and understanding security privatization as gendered and intersectional but also as a multiscalar and profoundly gendered political process. Gender, as discussed in the introduction to the volume, refers to socially constructed notions of masculinity and femininity that have historically helped maintain unequal gendered relations of power. A critical gender perspective, informed by feminism, investigates how masculinities and femininities are being contested, reproduced, and reconstituted by contemporary security practices, and how these practices are affecting gender hierarchies and women's security. Unlike "problem-solving" approaches that integrate a gender perspective in order to arrive at solutions to the industry's problems of legitimacy or open up new fields of employment for women, the critical gender perspective adopted in this volume has treated gender not as a variable but as constitutive of private security in global politics.

Significantly, the volume has gone beyond a narrow focus on gender to include intersectionality. The bulk of the volume's chapters highlighted the intersections of gender with other categories of difference and the relevance of these intersections for understanding private security. Stachowitsch argued that the inequalities of ethnicity, nationality, race, class, and gender found in the private security sector are not simply an outcome of marketization or, more specifically, the globalization and deregulation of labor but are as much shaped by race, class, national, and gender differences within the state that have become internationalized through privatization. In my chapter I put forth the argument that privatization enables a global rescaling of protection which relies on gendered, racialized, and classed discourses and practices (such as global narratives of protection, divisions of labor, and understandings of who is worth protecting) that intersect but are also distinct from other shifts in the national gendered politics of protection. The intersectional analysis of global privatized labor markets was further developed in the chapters by Barker, Chisholm, and Joachim and Schneiker. Here the privatization of security was studied through the intersections of masculinities with race, class, and citizenship, and the construction of subordinate masculinities. Higate's chapter highlighted the importance of the intersection of gender with nationality in discourses within the industry (specifically among trainers), while Hendershot shed light on the intersection of gender and sexuality in public discourse surrounding the Kabul hazing scandal.

The gender analyses developed throughout this volume have also revealed that security privatization and the practices of PMSCs shape and are shaped by multiple scales and scalar processes. Feminist attention to bodies, citizenship, and national gender orders allowed for new questions about and insights into private security. Security privatization produces new vulnerabilities for women's bodies (Sperling, Vrdoljak) while facilitating the pursuit of bloodless "bodyless" war (Baggiarini). Private *body*guarding was considered as a site for the construction of masculine and national identities (Higate), while the private market for force has made some gendered, racialized, and classed bodies more exploitable than others (Barker, Chisholm, Joachim and Schneiker). The body of the private contractor and its gendered and sexualized depictions were also shown to be central to the legitimacy of military outsourcing (Hendershot). Terry's chapter suggested that ethical debates could benefit from a focus on the individual contractors and their relationships, stressing experience and context rather than market logics. Other chapters foregrounded the national scale in their analyses of security privatization. The importance of gendered citizenship and the remaking of the gendered citizen-soldier to understanding security privatization were underscored in analyses of gendered states (Stachowitsch), gendered sacrifice (Baggiarini), and gendered protection (Eichler). The global scale (in interaction with local and national scales) was highlighted through analyses of the gendered and racialized global division of labor in the private security sector (chapters in part II), the significance of gendered global markets (Stachowitsch), the emerging global gendered politics of protection (Eichler), international peace operations and local accountability (Sperling), and the gendered limitations of international law in regard to PMSCs (Vrdoljak).

Furthermore, the critical gender analyses presented in this book revealed new ways in which we can recognize security privatization as political. Security privatization affects gendered relations of power not just between masculinities and femininities and between hegemonic and subordinate masculinities, but between states and markets, the global North and global South, government and citizens, "protectors" and "protected," "sacrificing" and "unsacrificable," and others. Baggiarini, for example, argued that privatization "depoliticizes war by rendering violence beyond the scope of the social contract," which itself is gendered. Stachowitsch highlighted the gendered aspects of the loss of transparency and democratic control that accompany privatization (including security privatization), such as the weakening of gender equality policies. Eichler showed that PMSCs do not simply fill a void in the market for security but (re)shape the gendered politics of protection. Joachim and Schneiker in a similar vein argued that PMSCs, while often depicted as neutral and apolitical actors, are implicated in the construction of societal and global gender norms, including hegemonic and subordinate masculinities. Higate and Hendershot illustrated that the gendered politics of security privatization can be located in unexpected sites such as the classroom or the comment sections of websites. The political impact of PMSCs also came to the fore in the chapters on gendered accountability, regulation, and feminist ethics in part IV of the volume. As these chapters argued, attempts to regulate or reform PMSCs need to be attentive to feminist concerns regarding violence against women, and can be enhanced with the conceptual tools of feminist ethics such as empathy and responsibility.

ADVANCING FEMINIST SECURITY STUDIES

Despite the varied disciplines of the group of scholars represented in this volume, all chapters draw on and are to a certain extent informed by key insights from feminist IR and security studies. These insights include the mutually constitutive relationship between gender, war, and militarism; the gendered organization of militarized institutions and labor markets; and the often negative effects of security policies on women's security. In applying feminist IR and security studies insights to an examination of private security, the chapters in this volume develop new understandings of the gendering of security today and suggest potential avenues for future research. In particular, the volume can be seen to advance the field of feminist security studies in three key ways: (1) it firmly establishes private security as a field of feminist investigations, (2) it furthers the study of masculinities and intersectional feminist analysis in security studies, and (3) it contributes to the development of a feminist political economy of security.

Feminist security studies scholars have thus far primarily focused on the realm of public militaries when examining militarization and war. While more recent feminist security scholars have investigated paramilitary groups and other nonstate armed actors (Sjoberg and Gentry 2007; MacKenzie 2010; McEvoy 2010), the private military sector has been neglected as a site for feminist investigations of security. Recent overviews of the field of feminist security studies do not mention private security as an area of research (Shepherd 2010b; Sjoberg and Martin 2010). Most of the contributors to this volume had previously published articles on gender and private security, but this book, for the first time, has brought together this scholarship to establish private security as a key area of study for feminist security studies. Indeed, the importance of private security to the waging of war in the twenty-first century underlines the need for feminists to pay attention to the myriad ways in which militarized gender identities are being reconstituted in intersection with race, class, sexuality, citizenship, and nationality and in which masculinization and feminization are being reinforced.

Crucially, security privatization is occurring alongside and in conjunction with changes in the gendered order of public militaries, which requires us to examine the interactions and interrelationships between public and private security sectors. As I have argued elsewhere (Eichler 2013), conceptualizing security as organized along a public–private continuum is not only analytically productive but also a necessary corrective to understanding military force and its gendering in contemporary global politics.

Second, this volume furthers the study of masculinities and of intersectional analysis in feminist security studies. Masculinity, in particular militarized masculinity, has been a key concept in feminist explorations of war, militarization, and security (Enloe 2000b; Tickner 2001). Feminist IR and security studies scholars have argued that the valorization of masculinity in and through militarism is a key factor in the legitimation of state leadership, the waging of war, and women's gender subordination. Militarized masculinity informs the gendered basis on which states organize for violence and on which international conflict occurs (Sjoberg 2013). But the relationship between masculinity, militarization, and states is in flux globally. Over the past few decades, an increasing number of countries have abolished male conscription and moved to all-volunteer forces, and states such as the United States and United Kingdom are heavily relying on PMSCs to wage war. These developments indicate a remaking of militarized masculinity rather than its demise. While we tend to assume that private contractors represent a "tough" version of militarized masculinity vis-à-vis more feminized public soldiers, the chapters in parts II and III of this volume compellingly show that there is a more complicated story to be told about masculinities in private security. While security privatization reinforces masculinization in some ways (see Stachowitsch, Eichler), there is no necessary or straightforward relationship between hypermasculinity and private security. As the chapters in part II demonstrate, gender subordination in the private security sector includes the feminization of racialized men from the global South whose exploitation plays a key part in making military outsourcing "cost-efficient." At the same time, the chapter by Higate in part III illustrates an example of the rejection of hypermasculinity and the celebration of restraint as a "truly" masculine trait among private contractors. Hendershot's chapter makes evident the ever-present unease with the inabilities of masculinized male bodies to consistently perform heteronomally and phallically, and the perceived need to reaffirm war zones as heteronormal, masculinized spaces. In addition to and in conjunction with furthering the study of masculinities, this volume demonstrates the importance of intersectional analysis to feminist security studies (Peterson 2009), already summarized above in the previous section.

Finally, one of the key contributions of this volume is to bring "the market" into feminist security studies and to contribute to the development of a feminist political economy of security. Several authors have identified the division and lack of conversation between feminist security studies and feminist GPE as one lacuna in the contemporary feminist study of war and militarization (Tickner and Sjoberg 2011, 234–235; True 2012, 194–195). While this volume does not directly speak to the economic root causes of gendered violence, it does much to advance a feminist integration of political economy and security studies by analyzing the multiple ways in which security privatization, the market for force, and PMSCs as both security and economic actors are gendered. The neoliberal market logic that drives privatization has also led to various new forms of gender subordination and insecurity, as the chapters in this volume illustrate. A critical gender analysis of security privatization can be furthered by integrating feminist security studies with feminist GPE. Feminist GPE approaches, as Stachowitsch argues in this volume, "help us contextualize private security within the neoliberal transformation of capitalism, processes of marketization and commodification of public goods, shifting power relations between markets and states, and their combined effects on gender relations." At the same time, a feminist political economy of security goes beyond a focus on the market. As several chapters in this volume argue (e.g. Chisholm, Higate, Terry), the market for force relies on and is sustained by personal, private, everyday relations as much as it is by state policies and company strategies. Moreover, a feminist political economy of security is relevant not only to the study of the private sector. As market logics and commercialization have begun to pervade the public sector, a feminist political economy of security will need to go beyond the market for force to also investigate the gendered effects of commercialization in public military and security spheres.

FEMINIST POLITICS AND THE POLITICS OF SECURITY:
FINAL THOUGHTS AND FUTURE RESEARCH

Security privatization not only changes some of the questions we need to ask in feminist security studies, but it also poses a challenge for feminist politics and activism on war and peace. Cynthia Enloe (2010) reminds us that "any war takes place in a particular moment in the history of gender," including in the "history of women's relationship to the state" (4). The same observation can be made about security privatization which has emerged at a time in the history of military gender relations, when militaries are being forced to increasingly open up to women and to expand women's military roles (Baggiarini in this volume; Eichler 2013). While privatization does not simply indicate a remasculinization of security, as the chapters in this volume have shown, it does reinforce notions of security tied to masculinity while at the same time reducing transparency about gender relations and depoliticizing the issue of gender equality (Stachowitsch). Privatization also has emerged at a time when international humanitarian law that addresses violence against women has been strengthened, but we see a parallel erosion of these principles and protections through the privatization of governmental and intergovernmental functions, thus impeding regulation in regard to PMSCs (Vrdoljak). Privatization depoliticizes security questions and makes it that much harder for feminists and other activists to shape security policies, while untangling the complex set of ethical and moral dilemmas entailed in the use of private force (Terry).

Feminist scholars have argued that we need to move beyond militarized security and understand security in its multiple and interrelated dimensions including human, economic, and environmental. This task has become more challenging today. While recognizing the multidimensionality of security, the urgency of security privatization, not to mention the global war on terror that has dominated the past decade and a half, has led many of us to renew our focus on military-related security questions. However, while focusing on militarized private security, the contributors to this volume explicitly and implicitly recognize security in its multidimensionality. As we have shown, for example, economic insecurity can push men on the margins of the global political economy into private security work (chapters in part II), while unaccountable transnational forces that include PMSCs threaten women's human security (Sperling). While the contributors to this volume are critical about the increased use of PMSCs in global politics, they also recognize that there are no simple answers to the question, "What should be done about PMSCs?" Instead, what emerges from the analyses presented is the need for a multi-pronged strategy that critiques privatization without romanticizing statist alternatives, questions the global expansion of security markets, calls for nondiscriminatory employment practices within the industry, keeps an eye on regulatory gaps and the statist bias of international law, questions media portrayals of private contractors that reinforce hypermasculinity and heterornormativity, aims to bring more nuance to our ethical perspectives, and recognizes and resists the depoliticization of security inherent in privatization.[1] More robust national and international regulation that is informed by feminist concerns and ethical considerations will have to be accompanied by a sustained critique of the gendered power relations and insecurities wrought by both private and public force.

This volume has only begun the tasks of unpacking the complex gendered politics of private security and of questioning the gendered normalization of militarized security through privatization. Future research will need to probe more deeply into the multidimensional aspects of security and into alternative models of security in the context of privatization. It will also need to explore the gendered privatization of security in multiple local and historical contexts—beyond the U.S.-led wars in Iraq and Afghanistan—which will bring new insights into private security and open new avenues for feminist reconceptualizations of security. The contributors to this volume come from multiple disciplines and have employed a wide range of feminist and feminist-informed approaches and methodologies. What unites this group of scholars is a common interest in the critical gender analysis of private security. In staking out the emerging field of critical gender studies in private security, it is our hope that the volume will animate critique and debate, and further feminist research into this important and complex phenomenon and its implications for contemporary global politics.

NOTE

1. I thank one of the anonymous reviewers for highlighting these contributions of the book for me.

Afterword

Engendering Knowledge and Shifting the Spaces of "Private Security" and "Global Politics"

ANNA LEANDER

The title of this book *Gender and Private Security in Global Politics* may come across as reassuringly conventional. It could easily be (mis)read as promising its reader a neat ordering, a locating of gender and private security in the space of global politics. This misreading will no doubt be useful for the career of this volume. It assigns the book to a neatly delimited place in the professional academic landscape; it fills the relatively empty spot where gender studies, global politics/IR, and private security studies meet. This misreading would be doubly welcome as it would allow the specialists of each field to confirm their own openness, to congratulate themselves on it, and possibly even to extend this celebration to each other's (but that is less likely). If this reading of the title was correct, it would make the book profoundly conservative. The book would conserve existing spaces of academic specialization. Each discipline could go on with a slightly enriched version of business as usual; specialists in each field could continue to operate "within narrow, 'safe' spaces in which accredited members toe the line" (A. Tickner 2013, 218).

Fortunately for the readers, *Gender and Private Security in Global Politics* is doing something rather different. By putting feminist approaches to work, it is engendering knowledge that shifts the spaces of the established disciplines rather than just "locating gender" within them. This afterword is about how and why. More specifically, it points to four themes that the feminist perspectives in the volume bring to the fore—(in)visibility, materiality, affect, and expertise. It suggests that each of these themes generates research agendas that not only span the boundaries of disciplinary space (and hence undermine their secluded safety) but also raise fundamental questions about how these spaces are constituted, operating, and evolving. As this afterword therefore concludes, rather than tucking gender and private security into a confined location of global politics, the chapters in this volume collectively destabilize the spatial separations that would make such a project feasible. In the process they open up fundamental questions about the politics of these spaces. The *Gender and Private Security in Global Politics* of the title must be read without comfy, conservative connotations.

(IN)VISIBILITIES

Making women, and gender more generally, visible has been at the core of feminist approaches. It should hence come as no surprise that the theme of (in)visibilities runs through many if not all the contributions to this volume. By way of exemplifying, Ana Vrdoljak's chapter analyzing accountability under international law shows how women remain largely (in)visible in international law. Regulation pertaining to their concerns and rights related to private security markets tend to be voluntary in form with far-reaching consequences for women's abilities to hold companies and those employing them legally accountable. Isabelle V. Barker shows that rendering the menial, lowly, and feminine support side of soldiering (in)visible through outsourcing is core to reproducing American soldiers. Maya Eichler argues in her chapter that the selling of protection by companies competing in markets reinforces and reproduces the (in)visibility of the violence that the conventional male protection role entails for women. This violence is "symbolic." It places women in the inferior position as those in need of protection. The symbolic turns disturbingly physical as gendered violence becomes a privileged way for one side to demonstrate its superiority by proving the incapacity of the other side to protect its women. Futhermore, as Saskia Stachowitsch explains in her chapter, the "hybrid," "neoliberal" forms of security governance to which private security is linked also reproduce the gender orders to which security governance is linked both at the level of the state and at the level of international relations. At the heart of her argument is the claim that the (in)visibility of these transformations makes "a strong case" for a feminist approach.

This insistence on (in)visibility and its significance is characteristic of feminist work in IR and beyond. Cynthia Enloe's (1994, 2000, 2007) work is emblematic in this respect. She has demonstrated the ways in which the (in)visibility of women in conventional IR is a political choice with the consequence of eliminating politics linked to women from the discussion. Even when the focus on (in)visibility is thus situated in a well-established tradition, it profoundly challenges attempts to "locate" gender and private security in global politics. The aim of this tradition is to change what private security studies and global politics are. The very idea that (in)visibility plays a core role in producing politics questions the idea of safe disciplinary spaces that would be desirable to reproduce. Focusing on (in)visibilities requires a constant questioning of the ways in which the disciplines reproduce invisibilities. For gender studies scholars, precisely this questioning is the precondition for politically relevant research. To engage in relevant research means to "refuse to start off thought and research from the conceptual frameworks of the disciplines or of the public institutions served by [them]" as Sandra Harding (2004, 29) puts it. This is unsettling for any discipline, including the three at play in this volume.

MATERIALITY

A second recurring theme through which this book shifts rather than consolidates existing academic spaces is its insistence on the central role of materiality in politics. This insistence takes a range of very different forms across the chapters. Bodies abound. Bodies of different colors, including the white and the Gurkha in Amanda Chisholm's chapter; bodies with different parts, including penises and butts in Chris Hendershot's chapter on hazing rituals; and body parts of different sizes such as the big and small bollocks in Paul Higate's chapter on a security training course. The material is extended to include the technological. The (nonfunctional) hotline meant to link the voices of Bosnian women and their concerns with sexual violence to accountability in the postconflict environment for example plays a core role in Valerie Sperling's chapter. Finally, Internet technologies in the form of the web pages through which companies represent themselves are at the heart of Joachim's and Schneiker's analysis of the gendered hierarchies that companies create to grant themselves a license to exploit.

By insisting on bodies and more broadly on technologies "that matter," the authors of this volume speak to a major and well-established research program in gender studies, including in IR, that is nonetheless prone to shift the terrain of established disciplines. They are engaged in asking questions about how the material is integral to politics; to the politics of global, gendered, and private security. These are precisely the kinds of questions that led Donna Haraway (1991) to formulate her "Cyborg Manifesto." It is also a research program that is rapidly growing in IR more generally, often under the banner of actor-network-approaches (see e.g., Connolly 2013; Walters and Best 2013). The gendered approach to these issues, including the one adopted in this volume, has the virtue of placing the politics of materiality at the center—a politics of oppression but also of possibilities. In Haraway's (1991) words, "The main trouble with cyborgs of course, is that they are the illegitimate offspring of militarism and patriarchal capitalism, not to mention state socialism. But illegitimate offspring are often exceedingly unfaithful to their origins. Their fathers after all are inessential" (151). Thus opening up questions about the politics of materiality is not innocent. It plows the ground of disciplinary spaces, unsettling not only their contours and boundaries but also their topography. The disciplinary space is no longer inhabited and labored only (or even mainly) by the familiar cast of characters including individuals, institutions, states companies, discourses, and people but also by all kinds of other things including Internet and telephone cables, and bodies with colors, sizes, and shapes. Worse still, these familiar characters lose their purity as the take hybrid (or cyborg) shapes. No wonder the disciplinary terrain becomes unsettled and seems to be shifting under our feet.

AFFECT

As this book opens up the themes of (in)visibility and materiality just outlined, it also opens up affect—a third, well-established gender studies theme that tends to shift the spaces of established disciplines. As Margaret Wetherell (2012) puts it, "affect is principally topic based. It is about infusing social analysis with what could be called psychosocial texture [marking a] shift away from research based on discourse and disembodied talk and texts, towards more vitalist, post-human and process based perspectives" (2–3). Interest in both the psychological and vitalist sides of affect are at the core of some of the volume's chapters. Hendershot's chapter is one of these. It focuses on the ways in which "penile anxieties" were at the heart of the scandal involving ArmorGroup, which he argues only makes sense because it was disrupting how contractors and military personnel reinforce "heteronormativity." Bianca Baggiarini's chapter on the transformation of the "affective economies" that sacrifice sustains and the "mimetic processes" that uphold it is another. However, the theme of affect runs through many of the chapters in the volume. Emotional labor and care are core concerns in Barker's discussion of the reproduction of American soldiers. The way "Rich" (the instructor) engages the affective and embodied dimensions of his students with his references to Billy Big Bollocks and his old mother figure prominently in Higate's account of how contractor training works. And, finally, intergenerational affect is core to Chisholm's account of how the Gurkhas are reimagining themselves as contractors.

While the focus on affect in this volume is no doubt part of the wider "affective turn" (Clough 2008) that is mirrored in the growing interest in affect and emotions also in IR (Bleiker and Hutchison 2008; Bially-Mattern 2011; Sylvester 2011), it is important to underscore the extent to which taking this "turn" also means shifting disciplinary spaces. Following the affective road leads to terrains where questions of emotions and affect—where they come from, what they do, how they spread, and how they change action and rationality—have a long pedigree. Acknowledging the extent to which this terrain overlaps with or, more strongly, is fully part of the disciplinary spaces of private security and global politics must also alter mappings of these spaces. The disciplinary maps need to be redrawn. They should depict also the space of the research agendas opened up in this book regarding the role of affect in practices of private security so as to indicate the links between these affective practices and global politics. The maps will also need to show that these research agendas can be taken further. Research might strive, for example, to become better at understanding the affective dimensions by drawing links to work on the affective dimensions of security advertising and consumption, on regulatory arrangements for private security, or on the digitalization of much security politics (see e.g., Goold and Loader 2010; Amoore 2011; Leander 2013). As this indicates, taking the affective turn would pose serious questions about how the maps should be drawn. For anyone who thought that this book was plotting gender and private security into the space of global politics, it must feel unsettling to say the least. The space is shifting to an extent where there is no longer a map to plot on.

EXPERTISE

This leads straight to a final theme that runs through this book, namely, the theme of who should be involved in drawing the maps in the first place; that is, what authoritative knowledge or "expertise" about gender and private security in global politics is and how it can best be gathered. Arguably the book is a collective statement that feminist approaches can engender (authoritative) knowledge in which others should take an interest. Some chapters make this claim by mainly focusing on academic knowledge. Stachowitsch makes a case for integrating feminist approaches. Jillian Terry argues that responsibility and ethics in contracting are particularly "suited" to a feminist ethical analysis and in turn demonstrate the usefulness of an ethical focus for feminist approaches generally. These claims are of a familiar kind. IR theories are often presented as evolving through "debates" about which kind of academic knowledge is most authoritative. Even if the scope of these debates may be decreasing as each camp gathers around its own fire (Sylvester 2013), disagreement over which academic expertise is most authoritative is familiar. However, the book also opens up a second discussion about expertise; namely, a discussion about the role of nonacademics in defining authoritative knowledge, including in academia, and hence the ties between "theory" and "practice." This theme stands out most clearly in the ethnographically grounded chapters, which may not be particularly surprising as the "symmetry of knowledge" (of observer and observed) and "reflexivity" (about the relation between observer and observed) are central to the ethnographic repertoire. Hence, Chisholm reflects on how her status as an "expert" fashioned the kind of access she had to the knowledge of the Gurkhas to whom she spoke. Similarly, Higate notes the importance of being enrolled on par with the other students and of having a background in the military for his access to the version of authoritative knowledge about private security that was produced in the course, which he then uses to question the authoritative knowledge about gender and private security in global politics in academia.

Opening up the question of who the expert is makes moot the prospect of easily plotting gender and private security onto a map of global politics to the point of appearing impossible. It draws attention to the disagreement that would immediately arise about who should be allowed to do the plotting. In addition to contending academic expertise, nonacademic experts would throw themselves into the fray over who should be allowed access to the drawing board. In the contention over how gender and private security are to be fitted into global politics, this would include companies, NGOs, regulators, and governments that would not only be present indirectly through their influence on individual academics and their research projects (as in Chisholm's and Higate's discussions) but most certainly also directly with their own views and hence their influence over what research should be carried out in the first place. Opening up the question of expertise as this book does, in other words, also opens up the fundamental question of who defines the disciplinary space in the first place.

PATHWAYS THROUGH SHIFTING SPACES

This book is about engendering knowledge and shifting the spaces of private security and global politics. Even more strongly, this book unsettles the established spaces, making them seem more like wandering dunes that change shape depending on when and from where they are approached. I have insisted that the themes of expertise, affect, materiality, and (in)visibility that play a core role in this book conspire to produce this unsettling effect. If anyone had misread the title (and skipped all the chapters), I hope that this afterword leaves them with little doubt that this is what the book does, at least this is my reading. What are the implications for further research? Moving dunes may be beautiful, but they may also be unsettling and worrisome. As Terry points out, her analysis "demonstrates the difficulties in identifying a clear path forward." As I see it, the core difficulty it and the other chapters in the volume point to is that there is no ready path in the singular to be identified. That, however, is only a difficulty if one thinks that walking the trodden path is what is called for. I tend to side with those who don't necessarily think so (including e.g., Spelman 1988 and Stengers 1995, who both forcefully make this point). Rather, I think walking new paths may often be more interesting and fruitful. Continuing along the paths this book has begun in rethinking private security, global politics, and gender is one example. It is not difficult to see that this could help deepen and widen the very significant contributions made in this book. However, I am wrong to present this as a matter of personal preferences! There are no established paths on wandering dunes. If, indeed, engendering knowledge means shifting spaces, as this book clearly shows it does, there is little choice but to invent new paths through the moving terrain. This book provides some very helpful ideas about how this might be done.

BIBLIOGRAPHY

ABC News. 2013. "US Embassy in Kabul 'Dangerously Vulnerable' to
    Attack: Report." Accessed December 15. http://bit.ly/18UDaNm.
Abrahamsen, Rita and Michael C. Williams. 2008. "Selling Security: Assessing the
    Impact of Military Privatization." *Review of International Political Economy* 15
    (1): 131–46.
———. 2011. *Security Beyond the State: Private Security in International Politics.*
    Cambridge: Cambridge University Press.
Adair-Toteff, Christopher. 2005. "Max Weber's Charisma." *Journal of Classical
    Sociology* 5 (2): 189–204.
Adamsky, Dima. 2010. *The Culture of Military Innovation: The Impact of Cultural Factors
    on the Revolution in Military Affairs in Russia, the US, and Israel.* Stanford: Stanford
    University Press.
Agamben, Giorgio. 1998. *Homo Sacer: Sovereign Power and Bare Life.*
    Stanford: Stanford University Press.
Agathangelou, Anna M. 2002. "'Sexing Globalization' in International
    Relations: Migrant Sex and Domestic Workers in Cyprus, Greece and Turkey."
    In *Power, Postcolonialism and International Relations: Reading Race, Gender
    and Class,* edited by Geeta Chowdhry and Sheila Nair, 142–69. London and
    New York: Routledge.
Agathangelou, Anna and Lily Ling. 2003. "Desire Industries: Sex Trafficking, UN
    Peacekeeping, and the Neo-Liberal World Order." *Brown Journal of World
    Affairs* 10 (1): 133–48.
———. 2009. *Transforming World Politics: From Empire to Multiple Worlds.*
    Oxon: Routledge.
Agathangelou, Anna and Heather M. Turcotte. 2010. "Postcolonial Theories
    and Challenges to 'First World-ism.'" In *Gender Matters in Global Politics.
    A Feminist Introduction to International Relations,* edited by Laura J. Shepherd,
    44–58. New York: Routledge.
AKE. 2010a. "About." Accessed May 4. http://www.akegroup.com/about-ake/.
———. 2010b. "Benefits of AKE Support." Accessed April 10. http://www.akegroup.
    com/about-ake/benefits-of-ake-support.php.
Alexandra, Andrew. 2012. "Private Military and Security Companies and
    the 'Civilianization of War.'" In *Protecting Civilians During Violent
    Conflict: Theoretical and Practical Issues for the 21st Century,* edited by David
    W. Lovell and Igor Primoratz, 183–97. Farnham, UK: Ashgate.
Alison, Miranda H. 2009. *Women and Political Violence: Female Combatants in
    Ethno-National Conflict.* London: Routledge.

Altvater, Elmar and Birgit Mahnkopf. 1996. *Grenzen der Globalisierung: Ökonomie, Ökologie und Politik in der Weltgesellschaft.* Münster: Westfälisches Dampfboot.

Amoore, Louise. 2011. "Data Derivatives: On the Emergence of a Security Risk Calculus for Our Times." *Theory, Culture & Society* 28 (6): 24–43.

Anders, Birthe. 2013. "Tree-Huggers and Baby-Killers: The Relationship between NGOs and PMSCs and Its Impact on Coordinating Actors in Complex Operations." *Small Wars & Insurgencies* 24 (2): 278–94.

Anderson, Benedict. 1991. *Imagined Communities: Reflections on the Origin and Spread of Nationalism.* London: Verso.

Apelt, Maja and Cordula Dittmer. 2007. "'Under Pressure'—Militärische Männlichkeiten im Zeichen neuer Kriege und veränderter Geschlechterverhältnisse." In *Dimensionen der Kategorie Geschlecht: Der Fall Männlichkeit,* edited by Mechthild Bereswill, Michael Meuser, and Sylka Scholz, 68–83. Münster: Westfälisches Dampfboot.

Associated Press. 2007. "5 More Sri Lankan Workers Rescued from Iraq, Agency Says." *International Herald Tribune, Europe,* March 23.

Assured Risks. 2010a. "Careers." Accessed May 4. http://www.assuredrisks.com/careers.html.

———. 2010b. "Main." Accessed May 4. http://www.assuredrisks.com/.

———. 2011. "About Assured Risks." Accessed March 30. http://www.assuredrisks.com/about_assured_risks.html.

Attachment 2. 2009. "Email Attached to POGO Letter to Secretary of State Hillary Clinton Regarding U.S. Embassy in Kabul." Project on Government Oversight. Accessed December 15, 2013. http://bit.ly/1mgQX9G.

Attachement 3. 2009. "Email Attached to POGO Letter to Secretary of State Hillary Clinton Regarding U.S. Embassy in Kabul." Project on Government Oversight. Accessed December 15, 2013. http://bit.ly/1mgQX9G.

Avant, Deborah. 2005. *The Market for Force: The Consequences of Privatizing Security.* Cambridge: Cambridge University Press.

———. 2006. "The Implications of Marketized Security for IR Theory: The Democratic Peace, Late State Building, and the Nature and Frequency of Conflict." *Perspectives on Politics* 4 (3): 507–28.

———. 2007. "The Emerging Market for Private Military Services and the Problems of Regulation." In *From Mercenaries to Market: The Rise and Regulation of Private Military Companies,* edited by Simon Chesterman and Chia Lehnardt, 181–95. Oxford: Oxford University Press.

———. 2011. "Military Contractors and the American Way of War." *Daedalus* 140 (3): 88–99.

Avant, Deborah and Lee Sigelman. 2009. "What Does Private Security in Iraq Mean for US Democracy?" Paper presented at the International Studies Association Annual Convention, New York, February 15–18.

———. 2010. "Private Security and Democracy: Lessons From the US in Iraq." *Security Studies* 19 (2): 230–65.

Aylwin-Foster, Nigel. 2005. "Changing the Army for Counterinsurgency Operations." *Military Review* (November–December): 1–15.

Bacevich, Andrew J. 2010. *Washington Rules: America's Path to Permanent War.* New York: Metropolitan Books.

Baggiarini, Bianca. 2013. "Private War, Private Suffering, and the Normalizing Power of Law." In *Gendered Perspectives on Conflict and Violence,* edited by Marcia Texler Segal and Vasilikie P. Demos, 165–88. Bingley: Emerald.

———. 2014. "Re-Making Soldier-Citizens: Military Privatization and the Biopolitics of Sacrifice." *St. Anthony's International Review* 9 (2): 9-23.

Bakker, Isabella. 2003. "Neo-Liberal Governance and the Reprivatization of Social Reproduction: Social Provisioning and Shifting Gender Orders." In *Power, Production and Social Reproduction*, edited by Isabella Bakker and Stephen Gill, 66–82. London-New York: Macmillan-Palgrave.

———. 2007. "Social Reproduction and the Constitution of a Gendered Political Economy." *New Political Economy* 12 (4): 541–56.

baracine. 2009. "Kabul Embassy Orgies—The Investigation." YouTube. Accessed December 15, 2013. http://bit.ly/18MFKCF.

Barker, Isabelle V. 2009. "(Re)producing American Soldiers in an Age of Empire." *Politics and Gender* 5 (2): 211–35.

Barrett, Frank J. 1996. "The Organizational Construction of Hegemonic Masculinity: The Case of the US Navy." *Gender, Work and Organization* 3 (3): 129–42.

———. 2001. "The Organizational Construction of Hegemonic Masculinity: The Case of the US Navy." In *The Masculinities Reader*, edited by Stephen M. Whitehead and Frank J. Barrett, 77–99. Cambridge: Polity Press.

Basu, Moni. 2010. "Indian Women Peacekeepers Hailed in Liberia." CNN.com, March 5. Accessed May 15, 2012. http://www.cnn.com/2010/WORLD/africa/03/02/liberia.women/index.html.

Bedont, Barbara. 2005. "The Renewed Popularity of Rule of Law: Implications for Women, Impunity, and Peacekeeping." In *Gender, Conflict and Peacekeeping*, edited by Dyan Mazurana, Angela Raven-Roberts, and Jane Parpart, 89–92. Lanham, MD: Rowman and Littlefield.

Belkin, Aaron. 2012. *Bring Me Men: Military Masculinity and the Benign Facade of American Empire 1898–2001*. London: Hurst/Columbia.

Benhabib, Seyla. 1992. "Models of Public Space: Hannah Arendt, the Liberal Tradition, and Jürgen Habermas." In *Habermas and the Public Sphere*, edited by Craig Calhoun, 73–98. Cambridge, MA: MIT Press.

———. 2004. *The Rights of Others*. Cambridge: Cambridge University Press.

Berlant, Lauren and Michael Warner. 1998. "Sex in Public." *Critical Inquiry* 24 (2): 547–66.

Berndtsson, Joakim. 2012. "Security Professionals for Hire: Exploring the Many Faces of Private Security Expertise." *Millennium: Journal of International Studies* 40 (2): 303–20.

———. 2013. "Exploring PSC-Military Relations: Swedish Officers and the Private Security Sector in Peace Operations." *Cooperation and Conflict* 48 (4): 484–501.

Bezanson, Kate and Meg Luxton, eds. 2006. *Social Reproduction: Feminist Political Economy Challenges Neo-Liberalism*. Montreal/Kingston: McGill-Queens University Press.

Bhabha, Homi K. 2004. *The Location of Culture*. London: Routledge.

Bhattacharyya, Gargi. 2008. *Dangerous Brown Men: Exploiting Sex, Violence and Feminism in the War on Terror*. London: Zed Books.

Bially-Mattern, Janice. 2011. "A Practice Theory of Emotion for International Relations." In *International Practices*, edited by Emanuel Adler and Vincent Pouliot, 63–86. Cambridge: Cambridge University Press.

Bigo, Didier. 2006. "Protection: Security, Territory and Population." In *The Politics of Protection: Sites of Insecurity and Political Agency*, edited by Jef Huysmans, Andrew Dobson, and Raia Prokhovnik, 84–100. London: Routledge.

Blanchard, Eric M. 2003. "Gender, International Relations, and the Development of Feminist Security Theory." *Signs: Journal of Women in Culture and Society* 28 (4): 1289–312.

———. 2011. "The Technoscience Question in Feminist International Relations: Unmanning the US War on Terror." In *Feminism and International Relations: Conversations About the Past, Present, and Future,* edited by J. Ann Tickner and Laura Sjoberg, 146–63. London and New York: Routledge.

Bleiker, Roland and Emma Hutchison. 2008. "Fear No More: Emotions and World Politics." *Review of International Studies* 34 (S1): 115–35.

Blom, Ida. 2000. "Gender and Nation in International Comparison." In *Gendered Nations: Nationalism and Gender Order in the Long Nineteenth Century*, edited by Ida Blom, Karen Hagemann, and Karen Hall, 3–26. Oxford and New York: Berg Publishers.

Blue Hackle. 2011. "Operating in Remote, Hostile and Austere Environments." Accessed April 1. http://www.bluehackle.com/en-GB/Environments/.

———. 2013a. "History & Philosophy." Accessed December 19. http://www.bluehackle.com/?page_id=119.

———. 2013b. "Our People." Accessed December 19. http://www.bluehackle.com/?page_id=80.

Bolkovac, Kathryn and Cari Lynn. 2011. *The Whistleblower: Sex Trafficking, Military Contractors, and One Woman's Fight for Justice*. Basingstoke: Palgrave Macmillan.

Bordo, Susan. 1994. "Reading the Male Body." In *The Male Body: Features, Destinies, Exposures*, edited by Laurence Goldstein, 265–306. Ann Arbor: University of Michigan Press.

———. 1999. *The Male Body: A New Look at Men in Public and Private*. New York: Farrar, Straus and Giroux.

Boyd, Susan B. 1997. *Challenging the Public/Private Divide: Feminism, Law, and Public Policy*. Toronto: University of Toronto Press.

Brand, Ulrich. 2010. "Der Staat als soziales Verhältnis." In *Kritische politische Bildung,* edited by Bettina Lösch and Andreas Thimmel, 145–56. Schwalbach: Wochenschau Verlag.

———. 2013. "Internationalisierung des Staates." In *Theorien der Internationalen Politischen Ökonomie*, edited by Josha Wullweber, Antonia Graf, and Maria Behrens, 299–313. Wiesbaden: Springer Fachmedien.

Brian, Danielle. 2009. "POGO Letter to Secretary of State Hillary Clinton Regarding U.S. Embassy in Kabul." Project on Government Oversight. September 1. Accessed December 15, 2013. http://bit.ly/1mgQX9G.

Briody, Dan. 2004. *The Halliburton Agenda: The Politics of Oil and Money*. Hoboken: John Wiley.

Broder, John. 2007. "Filling Gaps in Iraq, Then Finding a Void at Home." *New York Times*, July 17.

Broder, John and James Risen. 2007. "Death Toll for Contractors Reaches New High in Iraq." *New York Times,* May 19.

Brodsky, Robert. 2009. "Embassy Fires Security Guards over Appearance in Vulgar Photos." *Government Executive*. Accessed December 15, 2013. http://bit.ly/1acOGGi.

Brooks, Doug. 2000. "Messiahs or Mercenaries? The Future of International Private Military Services." *International Peacekeeping* 7 (4): 129–44.

———. 2002. "Protecting People: The PMC Potential. Comments and Suggestions for the UK Green Paper on Regulating Private Military Services." July 25. Accessed September 15, 2013. http://bit.ly/1C7lkUy.

———. 2010. "A Local Issue: The Trade-Offs Involved in Using Local Nationals." *Journal of International Peace Operations* 6 (1): 4, 42.

———. 2011. "Stopping 'Traffick': TCNs and the Challenges of Human Resources in Stability Operations." *International Journal of Peace Operations* 7 (1): 6, 39.

———. 2012. "Attention: Trafficking. Translating Policy Initiatives in to Successful Compliance." *International Journal of Peace Operations* 7 (6): 5, 20.

Brooks, Doug and Matan Chorev. 2008. "Ruthless Humanitarianism: Why Marginalizing Private Peacekeeping Kills People." In *Private Military and Security Companies: Ethics, Policies and Civil-Military Relations*, edited by Andrew Alexandra, Deane-Peter Baker, and Marina Caparini, 116–30. London: Routledge.

Brotz, Howard and Everett Wilson. 1946. "Characteristics of Military Society." *The American Journal of Sociology* 51 (5): 371–5.

Brown, Wendy. 1988. *Manhood and Politics: A Feminist Reading of Political Theory*. Totowa, NJ: Rowman and Littlefield.

———. 1992. "Finding the Man in the State." *Feminist Studies* 18 (1): 7–34.

———. 1995. *States of Injury: Power and Freedom in Late Modernity*. Princeton, NJ: Princeton University Press.

Brubaker, Rogers. 1992. *Citizenship and Nationhood in France and Germany*. Cambridge, MA: Harvard University Press.

Brubaker, Sarah Jane and Jennifer A. Johnson. 2008. "'Pack a More Powerful Punch' and 'Lay the Pipe': Erectile Enhancement Discourse as a Body Project of Masculinity." *Journal of Gender Studies* 17 (2): 131–46.

Bullock, Christopher. 2009. *Britain's Gurkhas*. London: Third Millennium.

Burchell, David. 2002. "Ancient Citizenship and Its Inheritors." In *Handbook of Citizenship Studies*, edited by Engin Isin and Bryan Turner, 89–105. London: Sage.

Butler, Judith. 1990. *Gender Trouble: Feminism and the Subversion of Identity*. New York: Routledge.

———. 2006. *Precarious Life: The Powers of Mourning and Violence*. London: Verso.

Caplan, Lionel. 1995. *Warrior Gentlemen: "Gurkhas" in the Western Imagination*. Oxford: Berghahn Books.

Carmola, Kateri. 2010. *Private Security Contractors and New Wars: Risk, Law, and Ethics*. New York: Routledge.

Castles, Stephen and Mark J. Miller. [1993] 2003. *The Age of Migration: International Population Movements in the Modern World*. New York: Guilford Press.

CBS News. 2009a. "Embassy Guards Fired for Lewd Behavior." September 3. http://cbsn.ws/14sh5pt.

———. 2009b. "U.S. Kabul Security Gone Wild." September 1. Accessed December 15, 2013. http://bit.ly/18MFKCF.

Cerjan, Paul. 2005. "Interview." Boston: *Frontline* WGBH. June 21. Accessed April 15, 2008. http://to.pbs.org/1njPimR.

Chambers, Samuel A. 2007. "'An Incalculable Effect': Subversions of Heteronormativity." *Political Studies* 55 (3): 656–79.

Chang, Kimberly A. and L. H. M. Ling. 2000. "Globalization and Its Intimate Other: Filipina Domestic Workers in Hong Kong." In *Gender and Global Restructuring:*

Sighting, Sites and Resistances, edited by Marianne H. Marchand and Anne Sisson Runyan, 27–43. London and New York: Routledge.

Charlesworth, Hilary, Christine Chinkin, and Shelley Wright. 1991. "Feminist Approaches to International Law." *American Journal of International Law* 85 (4): 613–45.

Chesterman, Simon and Chia Lehnardt, eds. 2007. *From Mercenaries to Market: The Rise and Regulation of Private Military Companies.* Oxford: Oxford University Press.

Chinkin, Christine. 1989. "The Challenge of Soft Law: Development and Change in International Law." *International and Comparative Law Quarterly* 38: 850–66.

———. 1992. "A Gendered Perspective to the International Use of Force." *Australian Yearbook of International Law* 12: 279–93.

Chatterjee, Pratap. 2006. "Doing the Dirty Work." *Colorlines: The National Newsmagazine on Race and Politics* 33 (July–August). Accessed August 15, 2012. http://bit.ly/1voDZfS.

———. 2009. "Not Necessarily a Glamorous Existence: A Tough Choice Faces Many Third Country Nationals." *Journal of International Peace Operations* 4 (6): 19–20.

Chisholm, Amanda. 2010. "Racialized Representations of Masculinities in Private Security: An Ethnographic Exploration of Gurkhas in Afghanistan." Paper presented at the International Studies Association Annual Convention, New Orleans, February 17–20.

———. 2014a. "The Silenced and Indispensable: Gurkhas in Private Military Security Companies." *International Feminist Journal of Politics* 16 (1): 26–47.

———. 2014b. "Marketing the Gurkha Security Package: Colonial Histories and Neoliberal Economies of Private Security." *Security Dialogue* 45 (4): 349-72.

Clapham, Andrew. 1993. *Human Rights in the Private Sphere.* Oxford: Oxford University Press.

Clough, Patricia T. 2008. "The Affective Turn: Political Economy, Biomedia and Bodies." *Theory, Culture and Society* 25 (1): 1–22.

CNN.com/asia. 2009. "14 from U.S. Embassy Security Staff in Afghanistan Fired." Accessed December 15, 2013. http://bit.ly/JJVq.

Cockayne, James. 2007. "Make or Buy? Principal-Agent Theory and the Regulation of Private Military Companies." In *From Mercenaries to Market: The Rise and Regulation of Private Military Companies,* edited by Simon Chesterman and Chia Lehnardt, 196–216. Oxford: Oxford University Press.

———. 2008. "Regulating Private Military and Security Companies: The Content, Negotiation, Weaknesses and Promise of the Montreux Document." *Journal of Conflict Security Law* 13 (3): 401–28.

———. 2012a. "Comments: Draft Charter of the ICoC Mechanism." Accessed November 21. http://bit.ly/1o8iJc9.

———. 2012b. "Submission for the Second Session of the UN Human Rights Council's Open-ended Intergovernmental Working Group." Accessed December 1. http://bit.ly/1saYx7D.

Cohn, Carol. 1987. "Sex and Death in the Rational World of Defense Intellectuals." *Signs: Journal of Women in Culture and Society* 12 (4): 687–718.

———. 2007. "Motives and Methods: Using Multi-Sited Ethnography to Study US National Security Discourses." In *Feminist Methodologies for International*

Relations, edited by Brooke A. Ackerly, Maria Stern, and Jacqui True, 91–107. Cambridge: Cambridge University Press.

———, ed. 2013. *Women and Wars.* Cambridge, UK: Polity.

Coleman, Arthur P. 1999. *A Special Corps: The Beginnings of Gorkha Service with the British.* Edinburgh: Pentland Press.

Colás, Alejandro and Richard Saull, eds. 2006. *The War on Terrorism and the American "Empire" after the Cold War.* London: Routledge.

Cook, John. 2009a. "Our Embassy in Afghanistan Is Guarded by Sexually Confused Frat Boys." Gawker. Accessed December 15, 2013. http://bit.ly/3fHSd6

——— 2009b. "How Gawker Launched a State Department Investigation." Gawker. Accessed December 15, 2013. http://bit.ly/FgWUJ

Connell, Raewyn. 1987. *Gender and Power: Society, the Person and Sexual Politics.* Stanford: Stanford University Press.

———. 1998. "Masculinities and Globalization." *Men and Masculinities* 1 (1): 3–23.

———. 2000a. "Arms and the Man: Using the New Research on Masculinity to Understand Violence and Promote Peace in the Contemporary World." In *Male Roles, Masculinities and Violence,* edited by Ingeborg Breines, Raewyn Connell, and Ingrid Eide, 21–33. Paris: UNESCO.

———. 2000b. *The Men and the Boys.* Berkeley and Los Angeles: University of California Press.

———. 2005. "Globalization, Imperialism and Masculinities." In *Handbook of Studies on Men and Masculinities,* edited by Raewyn Connell, Jeff Hearn, and Michael Kimmel, 71–89. ThousandOaks: Sage.

———. 2012. "Masculinity Research and Global Change." *Masculinidades y cambio social* 1 (1): 4–18.

Connolly, William E. 2013."The 'New Materialism' and the Fragility of Things." *Millennium: Journal of International Studies* 41 (3): 399–412.

Cornwall, Andrea and Nancy Lindisfarne. 1994. "Dislocating Masculinity: Gender, Power and Anthropology." In *Dislocating Masculinity: Comparative Ethnographies,* edited by Andrea Cornwall and Nancy Lindisfarne, 11–47. London and New York: Routledge.

Cooper, Helen. 2007. "Foreign Service Officers Resist Mandatory Iraq Postings." *New York Times,* November 1.

CorpWatch. 2004. *Houston, We Have a Problem: An Alternative Annual Report on Halliburton.* April.

———. 2005. *Houston, We Still Have a Problem: An Alternative Report on Halliburton.* May.

———. 2006. *Hurricane Halliburton. Conflict, Climate Change & Catastrophe: An Alternative Annual Report on Halliburton.* May.

Cossman, Brenda and Judy Fudge. 2002. *Privatization, Law, and the Challenge to Feminism.* Toronto: University of Toronto Press.

Council of Europe (CE). 2009a. *Recommendation 1858 (2009) Private Military and Security Firms and Erosion of the State Monopoly on the Use of Force.* Council of Europe Parliamentary Assembly. Adopted January 29.

———. 2009b. *Report on Private Military and Security Firms and Erosion of the State Monopoly on the Use of Force.* Adopted by the Venice Commission at the 79th Plenary Session, Study no. 531. CDL-AD(2009)038.

———. 2010a. *Resolution 1757 (2010) Human rights and Business.* Council of Europe Parliamentary Assembly. October 6.

———. 2010b. *Resolution 1722 (2010) Piracy—A Crime and a Challenge for Democracies.* Council of Europe Parliamentary Assembly. Adopted April 28.

Council of Europe (CE). 2012. *Draft Feasibility Study on Corporate Social Responsibility in the Field of Human Rights*. Steering Committee for Human Rights. November 16. CDDH(2012) 017.

Cowen, Deborah. 2006. "Fighting for 'Freedom': The End of Conscription in the United States and the Neoliberal Project of Citizenship." *Citizenship Studies* 10 (2): 167–83.

——. 2008. *Military Workfare: The Soldier and Social Citizenship in Canada*. Toronto: University of Toronto Press.

Cowen, Deborah and Emily Gilbert, eds. 2008. *War, Citizenship, Territory*. New York: Routledge.

Cowen, Deborah and Neil Smith. 2009. "After Geopolitics? From the Geopolitical Social to Geoeconomics." *Antipode* 41 (1): 22–48.

Cox, Michael. 2007. "Is the United States in Decline—Again? An Essay." *International Affairs* 83 (4): 643–53.

Cox, Robert. 1981. "Social Forces, States and World Orders: Beyond International Relations Theory." *Millennium: Journal of International Studies* 10 (2): 126–55.

Cross, Gary. 2008. *Men to Boys: The Making of Modern Immaturity*. New York: Columbia University Press.

Cross J. P. and Buddhiman Gurung. 2007. *Gurkhas at War: Eyewitness Accounts from World War II to Iraq*. Greenhill Books: London.

Crouse, Janice Shaw. 2011. "The Crisis of Modern Male Immaturity." *American Thinker* 25 (March). Accessed December 15, 2013. http://bit.ly/e6reIV.

Dalby, Simon. 2008. "Geopolitics, the Revolution in Military Affairs, and the Bush Doctrine." *YCISS Working Paper* 49. Toronto: York Centre for International Security Studies.

Dahmer, F. C. et al. 2009. "Roadblocks to Healthcare: What Contractors Need to Know About Medical Services in Conflict and Post-Conflict Environments." *Journal of International Peace Operations* 5 (3): 25–6, 34.

Darby, Phillip. 2009. "Rolling Back the Frontiers of Empire: Practising the Postcolonial." *International Peacekeeping* 16 (5): 699–716.

Das, Veena. 2007. *Life and Words: Violence and the Descent into the Ordinary*. Berkeley: University of California Press.

Dauphinée, Elizabeth and Cristina Masters, eds. 2007. *The Logics of Biopower and the War on Terror: Living, Dying, Surviving*. New York: Palgrave Macmillan.

Dawson, Ashley and Malini Johar Schueller, eds. 2007. *Exceptional State: Contemporary U.S. Culture and the New Imperialism*. Durham, NC: Duke University Press.

Dawson, Graham. 1994. *Soldier Heroes: British Adventure, Empire and the Imagining of Masculinities*. London: Routledge.

Dean, Mitchell. 1999. *Governmentality: Power and Rule in Modern Society*. Thousand Oaks, CA: Sage.

De La Vega, Connie and Alyson Beck. 2006. "The Role of Military Demand in Trafficking and Sexual Exploitation." Human Rights Advocates, UN Commission on the Status of Women, 50th Session. Berkeley: Human Rights Advocates.

Del Rosso, Jared. 2011. "The Penis as Public Part: Embodiment and the Performance of Masculinity in Public Settings." *Sexualities* 14 (6): 704–24.

De Nevers, Renée. 2009. "(Self) Regulating War?: Voluntary Regulation and the Private Security Industry." *Security Studies* 18 (3): 480–516.

Des Chene, Mary K. 1991. *Relics of Empire: A Cultural History of Gurkhas, 1815–1987.* Standford: Standford University Press.

Dickinson, Laura A. 2002. "Contract as a Tool for Regulating PMCs." In *From Mercenaries to Market: The Rise and Regulation of Private Military Companies,* edited by Simon Chesterman and Chia Lehnardt, 217–38. Oxford: Oxford University Press.

———. 2006. "Public Law Values in a Privatized World." *Yale Journal of International Law* 31 (Summer): 383–426.

———. 2011. *Outsourcing War and Peace: Preserving Public Values in a World of Privatized Foreign Affairs.* New Haven, CT: Yale University Press.

DiMaggio, Paul J. and Walter W. Powell. 1983. "The Iron Cage Revisited: Institutional Isomorphism and Collective Rationality in Organizational Fields." *American Sociological Review* 48 (2): 147–60.

Dodge, Toby. 2005. "Iraqi Transitions: From Regime Change to State Collapse." *Third World Quarterly* 26 (4): 705–21.

dogeater99. 2010. Comments Section—"Kabul U.S. Embassy Guard: Sexual Deviancy Required for Promotion." ABC News. Accessed December 15, 2013. http://abcn.ws/15YoKrv.

Dollarhide, Maya. 2007. "Sexual Abuse: The UN Under Fire." *Voices-Unabridged: The E-Magazine on Women and Human Rights Worldwide* 11. Accessed April 25. http://www.voices-unabridged.org/article.php?id_article=169&numero=11.

Doty, Roxanne L. 1996. *Imperial Encounters: The Politics of Representation in North-South Relations.* Minneapolis: University of Minnesota Press.

dsnj1-2009. 2009. Comments Section—"Embassy Guards Fired for Lewd Behavior." CBS News. Accessed December 15, 2013. http://cbsn.ws/14sh5pt.

Duffield, Mark. 2001. *Global Governance and the New Wars: The Merging of Development and Security.* London: Zed Books.

Duncanson, Claire. 2009. "Forces for Good? Narratives of Military Masculinity in Peacekeeping Operations." *International Feminist Journal of Politics* 11 (1): 63–80.

Dunigan, Molly. 2011. *Victory for Hire: Private Security Companies' Impact on Military Effectiveness.* Stanford: Stanford University Press.

DynCorp International. 2012. "DynCorp International Core Values." Accessed September 7. http://www.dyn-intl.com/about-us/values-code-of-conduct.aspx.

———. 2013. "Security Services." Accessed December 19. http://www.dyn-intl.com/what-we-do/security-services.aspx.

Edelman, Lee. 2004. *No Future: Queer Theory and the Death Drive.* Durham, NC: Duke University Press.

Edkins, Jenny. 2003. *Trauma and the Memory of Politics.* Cambridge: Cambridge University Press.

Ehrenreich, Barbara and Arlie Russell Hochschild, eds. 2002. *Global Woman: Nannies, Maids, and Sex Workers in the New Economy.* New York: Henry Holt.

Eichler, Maya. 2012a. *Militarizing Men: Gender, Conscription, and War in Post-Soviet Russia.* Stanford: Stanford University Press.

———. 2012b. "Gender and the Global Market for Force: A Feminist Analysis." Paper presented at the International Studies Association Annual Convention, San Diego, CA, April 1–4.

———. 2013. "Gender and the Privatization of Security: Neoliberal Transformation of the Militarized Gender Order." *Critical Studies on Security* 1 (3): 311–25.

Eichler, Maya. 2014. "Contracting Out Military Work: From National Conscription to Globalized Recruitment." *Citizenship Studies* 18 (6-7): 600-14.

Eisenstein, Zillah. 1978. *Capitalist Patriarchy and the Case for Socialist Feminism.* New York: Monthly Review Press.

———. 2007. *Sexual Decoys: Gender, Race and War in Imperial Democracy.* London: Zed Books.

Elsea, Jennifer and Nina M. Serafino. 2007. "Private Security Contractors in Iraq: Background, Legal Status, and Other Issues." CRS Report for Congress. Accessed September 7. http://www.hsdl.org/?view&did=477868.

Elshtain, Jean Bethke. 1993. "Sacrifice and Sovereignty." In *Remaking the Nation,* edited by Marjorie Ringrose and Adam J. Lerner, 159-75. Buckingham: Open University Press.

———. 1995. *Women and War.* Chicago: University of Chicago Press.

Elson, Diane and Ruth Pearson. 1981. "'Nimble Fingers Make Cheap Workers': An Analysis of Women's Employment in Third World Export Manufacturing." *Feminist Review* 7 (Spring): 87–107.

Enloe, Cynthia. 1981. *Ethnic Soldiers: State Security in a Divided Society.* Middlesex: Penguin Books.

———. 1988. *Does Khaki Become You? The Militarization of Women's Lives.* London: Pandora.

———. 1989. *Bananas, Beaches, and Bases: Making Feminist Sense of International Politics.* Berkeley: University of California Press.

———. 1994. *The Morning After: Sexual Politics at the End of the Cold War.* Berkeley: University of California Press.

———. 2000a. "Masculinity as Foreign Policy Issue." *Foreign Policy in Focus* 5 (36), October 1. Accessed January 20, 2004. http://fpif.org/masculinity_as_foreign_policy_issue/.

———. 2000b. *Maneuvers: The International Politics of Militarizing Women's Lives.* Berkeley: University of California Press.

———. 2004. *The Curious Feminist: Searching for Women in a New Age of Empire.* Berkeley: University of California Press.

———. 2007. *Globalization and Militarism: Feminists Make the Link.* Lanham: Rowman and Littlefield.

———. 2010. *Nimo's War, Emma's War: Making Feminist Sense of the Iraq War.* Berkeley: University of California Press.

———. 2013. *Seriously! Investigating Crashes and Crises as If Women Mattered.* Berkeley: University of California Press.

Erickson, Bonnie H., Patricia Albanese, and Slobodan Drakulic. 2000. "Gender on a Jagged Edge: The Security Industry, Its Clients and the Reproduction and Revision of Gender." *Work and Occupations* 27 (3): 294–318.

European Union. 2006. "Implementing the Partnership for Growth and Jobs: Marking Europe a Pole of Excellence on Corporate Responsibility." Communication from the Commission to the European Parliament, the Council and the European Economic and Social Committee, March 22. COM(2006) 136 Final.

Fainaru, Steve. 2008. *Big Boy Rules: America's Mercenaries Fighting in Iraq.* Cambridge, MA: Da Capo Press.

Faludi, Susan. 1994. "The Naked Citadel." *The New Yorker,* September 5, 62–81.

Fanon, Frantz. 1967. *Black Skin, White Masks.* New York: Grove Press.

Farr, Vanessa, Henri Myrttinen, and Albrecht Schnabel, eds. 2009. *Sexed Pistols: Gender Perspectives on Small Arms and Light Weapons*. Tokyo: UN University Press.

Feil, Moira, Susanne Fischer, Andreas Haidvogl, and Melanie Zimmerman. 2008. *Bad Guys, Good Guys and Something Inbetween: Corporate Governance Contributions in Zones of Violent Conflict*. Frankfurt am Main: Peace Research Institute.

Feinman, Rose Ilene. 2000. *Citizenship Rites: Feminist Soldiers and Feminist Antimilitarists*. New York: New York University Press.

Ferguson, Niall. 2004. *Colossus: The Price of America's Empire*. New York: Penguin.

Fitzsimmons, Scott. 2012. "The Market for Force in the United States." Paper presented at the International Studies Association Annual Convention, San Diego, CA, April 1–4.

Forster, Tristan. 2012. In-person interview with Amanda Chisholm, August 28.

Forster Tristan and James Sinclair. 2009. "Ethical Recruitment Practices: The Importance of Operating Above-Board with TCNs." *Journal of International Peace Operations* 4 (6): 15–6.

Foucault, Michel. 1978. *The History of Sexuality, Vol.1: An Introduction*, translated by Robert Hurley. New York: Random House.

———. 2003. *Society Must Be Defended: Lectures at the Collège de France, 1975–76*, edited by Mauro Bertani and Alessandro Fontana, translated by David Macey. New York: Picado.

———. 2010. "Nietzsche, Genealogy, History." *The Foucault Reader*, edited by Paul Rabinow, 76–100. New York: Vintage Books.

Fox News. 2009. "U.S. Embassy in Afghanistan Fires Lewd Guards." Accessed December 15, 2013. http://fxn.ws/nAIeO.

Francesco, Francioni and Natalino Ronzitti, eds. 2011. *War by Contract: Human Rights, Humanitarian Law and Private Contractors*. Oxford: Oxford University Press.

Franke, Volker and Marc von Boemcken. 2009. "Attitudes, Values and Professional Self-Conceptions of Private Military Security Contractors in Iraq: An Exploratory Study." DSF Forschung 24. Bruck, Germany: Deutsche Stiftung Friedensforschung (DSF).

Franzway, Suzanne, Diane Court, and Raewyn Connell. 1989. *Staking a Claim: Feminism, Bureaucracy, and the State*. Cambridge: Polity Press.

Frevert, Ute. 1996. "Soldaten, Staatsbürger: Überlegungen zur historischen Konstruktion von Männlichkeit." In *Männergeschichte—Geschlechtergeschichte: Männlichkeit im Wandel der Moderne*, edited by Thomas Kühne, 69–87. Frankfurt: Campus.

Friedman, Thomas L. 2009. "The Best Allies Money Can Buy." *New York Times*, November 4.

Gardam, Judith. 2005. "Women and Armed Conflict: The Response of International Humanitarian Law." In *Listening to the Silences: Women and War*, edited by Helen Durham and Tracey Gurd, 109–24. The Hague: Martinus Nijhoff.

Gardam, Judith G. and Michelle J. Jarvis. 2001. *Women, Armed Conflict and International Law*. The Hague: Kluwer.

Gardiner, Nile. 2005. "The UN Peacekeeping Scandal in the Congo: How Congress Should Respond." The Heritage Foundation, March 22. Accessed February 22, 2007. http://www.heritage.org/Research/InternationalOrganizations/hl868.cfm.

Gates, Robert. 2007. "News Transcript." Washington DC: Department of Defense. Accessed December 11, 2007. http://www.defenselink.mil/transcripts/transcript.aspx?transcriptid=4050.

Gaviria, Marcella and Martin Smith. 2005. *Private Warriors* [video]. Boston: *Frontline* WGBH.

Geneva Declaration on Armed Violence and Development. 2012. *Global Burden of Armed Violence 2011*. Geneva: Geneva Declaration on Armed Violence and Development.

Gibson-Graham, J. K. 2006. *The End of Capitalism (As We Knew It): A Feminist Critique of Political Economy*. Minneapolis: University of Minnesota Press.

Gill, Stephen. 2005. "The Contradictions of U.S. Supremacy." In *Empire Reloaded: Socialist Register*, edited by Leo Panitch and Colin Leys, 23–45. Halifax: Fernwood.

Gilligan, Carol. 1982. *In a Different Voice: Psychological Theory and Women's Development*. Cambridge, MA: Harvard University Press.

Girard, René. 1979. *Violence and the Sacred,* translated by Patrick Gregory. Baltimore: Johns Hopkins University Press.

Glanz, James. 2009. "Contractors Outnumber US Troops in Afghanistan." *New York Times,* September 2.

Glanz, James and Andrew W. Lehren. 2010. "Use of Contractors Added to War's Chaos in Iraq." *New York Times*, October 23.

Gobo, Giampetro. 2008. *Doing Ethnography,* translated by Adrian Belton. Los Angeles: Sage.

Goldstein, Joshua S. 2001. *War and Gender: How Gender Shapes the War System and Vice-Versa*. Cambridge: Cambridge University Press.

Goold, Benjamin and Ian Loader. 2010. "Consuming Security? Tools for a Sociology of Security Consumption." *Theoretical Criminology* 14 (3): 3–30.

Gould, Tony. 1999. *Imperial Warriors: Britain and the Gurkhas*. London: Granta Books.

Gowan, Peter. 2006. "The Bush Turn and the Drive for Primacy." In *The War on Terrorism and the American "Empire" after the Cold War*, edited by Alejandro Colás and Richard Saull, 131–54. London: Routledge.

Graham, Stephen. 2008. "Imagining Urban Warfare." In *War, Citizenship, Territory,* edited by Deborah Cowen and Emily Gilbert, 33–56. New York: Routledge.

Grasswick, Heidi. 2003. "The Impurities of Epistemic Responsibility: Developing a Practice Oriented Epistemology." In *Recognition, Responsibility, and Rights: Feminist Ethics and Social Theory*, edited by Robin N. Fiore and Hilde Lindemann Nelson, 89–104. Lanham, MD: Rowman and Littlefield.

Gray, Chris. 2003. "Posthuman Soldiers in Postmodern War." *Body and Society* 9 (4): 215–26.

Gregory, Derek. 2011. "Everywhere War." *The Geographical Journal* 177 (3): 238–50.

Grespin, Whitney. 2012. "Anatomy of a Kidnapping: Helping Companies and Individuals Understand the Process and Aftermath of an Incident." *Journal of International Peace Operations* 7 (6): 17–9.

Guerrero, Hugo. 2008. "Perspective of a Third Country National: A Response from a Colombian Private Security Contractor." *Journal of International Peace Operations* 4 (1): 21–2.

Gumedze, Sabelo. 2007. "Sexual Exploitation and Sexual Abuse: The Need for Special Measures within the Private Security/Military Industry." *Institute*

for Security Studies Today, January 16. Accessed June 2, 2011. http://bit.
ly/1jvbNUf.

Gunaratnam, Yasmin. 2003. *Researching "Race" and Ethnicity: Methods, Knowledge and Power.* London: Sage.

Hagemann, Karen and Ralf Pröve, eds. 1998. *Landsknechte, Soldatenfrauen und Nationalkrieger: Militär, Krieg und Geschlechterordnung im historischen Wandel.* Frankfurt am Main: Suhrkamp.

Hansen, Karen V. and Ilene J. Philipson, eds. 1990. *Women, Class, and the Feminist Imagination: A Socialist-Feminist Reader.* Philadelphia: Temple University Press.

Halberstam, Judith. 2011. *The Queer Art of Failure.* Durham, NC: Duke University Press.

Hall, Lucy and Laura J. Shepherd. 2013. "WPS and R2P: Theorising Responsibility and Protection." In *Responsibility to Protect and Women, Peace and Security: Aligning the Protection Agendas*, edited by Sara E. Davies et al., 53–80. Leiden: Martinus Nijhoff.

Haraway, Donna J. 1988. "Situated Knowledges: The Science Question in Feminism and the Privilege of Partial Perspective." *Feminist Studies* 14 (3): 575-99.

———. 1991. *Simians, Cyborgs and Women: The Reinvention of Nature.* New York: Routledge.

Harding, Sandra. 2004. "A Socially Relevant Philosophy of Science? Resources from Standpoint Theory's Controversiality." *Hypathia* 19 (1): 25–47.

Hardt, Michael and Antonio Negri. 2000. *Empire.* Cambridge, MA: Harvard University Press.

Harper, Karen. 2009. "US Embassy in Kabul Sex Photos—State Dept. Responds." YouTube. September 2. Accessed December 15, 2013. http://bit.ly/14sidt9.

Harrington, Carol. 2005. "The Politics of Rescue: Peacekeeping and Anti-trafficking Programmes in Bosnia-Herzegovina and Kosovo." *International Feminist Journal of Politics* 7 (2): 175–206.

Harvey, David. 2006. *Spaces of Global Capitalism: Towards a Theory of Uneven Geographic Development.* London: Verso.

Hearn, Jeff and Wendy Parkin. 2002. *Gender, Sexuality and Violence in Organizations: The Unspoken Forces of Organization Violations.* London: Sage.

Held, Virginia. 2006. *The Ethics of Care: Personal, Political, and Global.* Oxford: Oxford University Press.

Hemmings, Clare. 2012. "Affective Solidarity: Feminist Reflexivity and Political Transformation." *Feminist Theory* 13 (2): 147–61.

Herbert, Melissa S. 1998. *Camouflage Isn't Only for Combat: Gender, Sexuality, and Women in the Military.* New York: New York University Press.

Hibou, Béatrice. 2004. *Privatizing the State.* New York: Columbia University Press.

Higate, Paul, ed. 2003a. *Military Masculinities: Identity and the State.* Greenwood: Praeger.

———. 2003b. "'Soft Clerks' and 'Hard Civvies': Pluralizing Military Masculinities." In *Military Masculinities: Identity and the State*, edited by Paul Higate, 27–42. Westport: Praeger.

———. 2009. "Putting Mercenary Masculinities on the Research Agenda." Working Paper 03-09. School of Sociology, Politcs and International Studies, University of Bristol.

———. 2011. "'Cat Food and Clients': Gendering the Politics of Protection in the Private Militarised Security Company." Working Paper 08-11. School of Sociology, Politics and International Studies, University of Bristol.

Higate, Paul. 2012a. "'Cowboys and Professionals': The Politics of Identity Work in the Private and Military Security Company." *Millennium: Journal of International Studies* 40 (2): 321–41.

———. 2012b. "The Private Militarized Security Contractor as Geocorporeal Actor." *International Political Sociology* 6 (4): 355–72.

———. 2012c. "Drinking Vodka from the 'Butt-Crack': Men, Masculinities and Fratriarchy in the Private Militarized Security Company." *International Feminist Journal of Politics* 14 (4): 50–69.

———. 2012d. "In the Business of (In)Security: Mavericks, Mercenaries and Masculinities in the Private Security Company." In *Making Gender, Making War: Violence, Military and Peacekeeping Practices*, edited by Annica Kronsell and Erica Svedberg, 182–96. London and New York: Routledge.

———. 2012e. "Martial Races and Enforcement Masculinities of the Global South: Weaponising Fijian, Chilean, and Salvadoran Postcoloniality in the Mercenary Sector." *Globalizations* 9 (1): 35–52.

Higate, Paul and Alisa Cameron. 2006. "Reflexivity and Researching the Military." *Armed Forces & Society* 32 (2): 219–33.

Higate, Paul and Marsha Henry. 2004. "Engendering (In)security in Peace Support Operations." *Security Dialogue* 35 (4): 481–98.

Higate, Paul and Saskia Stachowitsch. 2013a. "The Problems of PMSCs or PMSCs as a Problem? Reflections on Gender Scholarship and the Legitimization of Violence in Private Security." Paper presented at the International Studies Association Annual Convention, San Francisco, April 3–6.

———. 2013b. "(De)Constructing the 'Hypermasculine' Private Military Contractor: Critiques of Masculinity and the Legitimization of the Private Security Industry." Paper presented at the Political Masculinities: Structures, Discourses and Spaces in Historical Perspective Conference, Vienna, November 15–17.

Hobsbawm, Eric. 1989. *The Age of Empire 1875–1914*. New York: Vintage.

Hockey, John. 2003. "No More Heroes: Masculinity in the Infantry." In *Military Masculinities: Identity and the State*, edited by Paul Higate, 15–25. Westport: Praeger.

Hoge, Warren. 2005. "Report Finds U.N. Isn't Moving to End Sex Abuse by Peacekeepers." *New York Times*, October 19, A5.

Holmqvist, Caroline. 2005. "Private Security Companies: The Case for Regulation." SIPRI Policy Paper 9 (January). Stockholm: Stockholm International Peace Research Institute.

Holt, Kate and Sarah Hughes. 2004. "Sex and Death in the Heart of Africa." Refugees International, May 25. Accessed February 22, 2007. http://www.refugeesinternational.org/content/article/detail/1093.

Hooper, Charlotte. 1998. "Masculinist Practices and Gender Politics: The Operation of Multiple Masculinities in International Relations." In *The "Man" Question in International Relations*, edited by Marysia Zalewski and Jane Parpart, 28–53. Boulder, CO: Westview Press.

———. 1999. "Masculinities, IR and the 'Gender Variable': A Cost-Benefit Analysis for (Sympathetic) Gender Sceptics." *Review of International Studies* 25 (3): 475–91.

———. 2001. *Manly States: Masculinities, International Relations, and Gender Politics*. New York: Columbia University Press.

Howe, Herbert M. 1998. "Private Security Forces and African Stability: The Case of Executive Outcomes." *The Journal of Modern African Studies* 36 (2): 307–31.

Hubbard, Philip. 2000. "Desire/Disgust: Mapping the Moral Contours of Heterosexuality." *Progress in Human Geography* 24 (2): 191–217.

———. 2008. "Here, There, Everywhere: The Ubiquitous Geographies of Heteronormativity." *Geography Compass* 2 (3): 640–58.

Hubert, Henri and Marcel Mauss. 1964. *Sacrifice.* Chicago: University of Chicago Press.

Hunt, Krista and Kim Rygiel, eds. 2006. *(En)Gendering the War on Terror: War Stories and Camouflaged Politics.* Hampshire, UK: Ashgate.

Huskey, Kristine A. 2012. "Accountability for Private Military and Security Contractors in the International Legal Regime." *Criminal Justice Ethics* 31 (3): 193–212.

Hutchings, Kimberly. 2000. "Towards a Feminist International Ethics." *Review of International Studies* 26 (5): 111–30.

———. 2008a. "1988 and 1998: Contrast and Continuity in Feminist International Relations." *Millennium: Journal of International Studies* 37 (1): 97–105.

———. 2008b. "Making Sense of Masculinity and War." *Men and Masculinities* 10 (4): 389–404.

Huysmans, Jef. 2006. "Agency and the Politics of Protection: Implications for Security Studies. In *The Politics of Protection: Sites of Insecurity and Political Agency*, edited by Jef Huysmans, Andrew Dobson, and Raia Prokhovnik, 1–18. London: Routledge.

Hyndman, Jennifer. 2008. "Whose Bodies Count? Feminist Geopolitics and Lessons." In *Feminism and War: Confronting U.S. Imperialism,* edited by Robin L. Riley, Chandra Talpade Mohanty, and Minnie Bruce Pratt, 194–206. London: Zed Books.

Ikenberry, G. John. 2004. "Illusions of Empire: Defining the New American Order." *Foreign Affairs* 83 (2): 144-54.

Illic, Werner. 2009. "Email Attached to POGO Letter to Secretary of State Hillary Clinton Regarding U.S. Embassy in Kabul." Project on Government Oversight. Accessed December 15, 2013. http://bit.ly/1mgQX9G.

Imam, Ayesha M. 1997. "The Dynamics of WINning: An Analysis of Women in Nigeria (WIN)." In *Feminist Genealogies, Colonial Legacies and Democratic Futures,* edited by M. Jacqui Alexander and Chandra Talpade Mohanty, 280–307. London and New York: Routledge.

International Committee of Jurists (ICJ). 2012a. "Corporations and Human Rights: Comments by the International Commission of Jurists on the Draft Feasibility Study on Corporate Social Responsibility in the Field of Human Rights." November.

———. 2012b. "Submission of the International Commission of Jurists to the Second Session of the Open-ended Intergovernmental Working Group (IGWG) to Consider the Possibility of an International Regulatory Framework on the Regulation of PMSCs." August.

International Committee of the Red Cross (ICRC). 1992. "Update on Aide-Memoire." December 3.

———. 1993. "Final Declaration of the International Conference for the Protection of War Victims." *International Review of the Red Cross* 33 (296): 337.

———. 1995. Statement of Renée Guisan, ICRC delegate to the Fourth World Conference on Women, Beijing, September 4, 1995. Accessed April 10, 2009. http://www.un.org/esa/gopher-data/conf/fwcw/conf/una/950912110707.txt.

International Committee of the Red Cross (ICRC). 2007. *International Humanitarian Law and Gender, Report Summary, International Expert Meeting "Gender Perspectives of International Humanitarian Law,"* October 4–5. Stockholm and Geneva: ICRC.

———. 2008. Montreux Document on Pertinent International Legal Obligations and Good Practices for States Related to Operations of Private Military and Security Companies During Armed Conflict, Attached to letter dated 2 October 2008 from the Permanent Representative of Switzerland to the UN Secretary-General." UN Doc.A/63/467-S/2008/636, Annex.

International Stability Operations Association. 2012. "Media Advisory 2012—07 05: ISOA Releases new Stability Operations Magazine." Accessed September 7. http://www.stability-operations.org/index.php.

Isenberg, David. 2009. *Shadow Force: Private Security Contractors in Iraq.* Westport, CT: Praeger Security International.

Isin, Engin and Kim Rygiel. 2007. "Abject Spaces: Frontiers, Zones, Camps." In *The Logics of Biopower and the War on Terror: Living, Dying, Surviving,* edited by Elizabeth Dauphinée and Cristina Masters, 181–203. New York: Palgrave Macmillan.

Jackson, David and Jason Grotto. 2008. "US: Inside the World of War Profiteers." *Chicago Tribune,* February 21.

Jackson, Stevi. 2006. "Gender, Sexuality and Heterosexuality: The Complexity (and Limits) of Heteronormativity." *Feminist Theory* 7 (1): 105–21.

Jacoby, Tami Amanda. 2005. *Women in Zones of Conflict: Power and Resistance in Israel.* Quebec: McGill-Queen's University Press.

Jay, Nancy. 1992. *Throughout Your Generations Forever: Sacrifice, Religion and Paternity.* Chicago: University of Chicago Press.

Jeffords, Susan. 1989. *The Remasculinization of America: Gender and the Vietnam War.* Bloomington: Indiana University Press.

Jeffreys, Sheila. 2007. "Double Jeopardy: Women, the US Military and the War in Iraq." *Women's Studies International Forum* 30 (1): 16–25.

Jessop, Bob. 2001. "Bringing the State Back In (Yet Again): Reviews, Revisions, Rejections, and Redirections." *International Review of Sociology* 11 (2): 149–73.

Joachim, Jutta and Andrea Schneiker. 2012a. "Of 'True Professionals' and 'Ethical Hero Warriors': A Gender Discourse Analysis of Private Military and Security Companies." *Security Dialogue* 43 (6): 495–512.

———. 2012b. "New Humanitarians? Frame Appropriation through Private Military and Security Companies." *Millennium: Journal of International Studies* 40 (2): 365–88.

———. 2012c. "(Re)Masculinizing Security? Gender and Private Military and Security Companies." In *Gender, Agency and Political Violence,* edited by Linda Åhäll and Laura J. Shepherd, 70–92. Basingstoke: Palgrave Macmillan.

Johnson, Carol. 2002. "Heteronormative Citizenship and the Politics of Passing." *Sexualities* 5 (3): 317–36.

Johnson, Chalmers. 2004. *The Sorrows of Empire: Militarism, Secrecy, and the End of the Republic.* New York: Metropolitan Books.

Johnstone, Rachael Lorna. 2009. "Unlikely Bedfellows: Feminist Theory and the War on Terror." *Chicago-Kent Journal of International and Comparative Law* 9 (1): 1–45.

JordanGold. 2009. Comments Section—"Our Embassy in Afghanistan Is Guarded by Sexually Confused Frat Boys." Gawker. Accessed December 15, 2013. http://bit.ly/3fHSd6.

Kagan, Robert and William Kristol. 2000. "Introduction: National Interest and Global Responsibility." In *Present Dangers: Crisis and Opportunity in American Foreign and Defense Policy,* edited by Robert Kagan and William Kristol, 17–22. San Francisco: Encounter Books.

Kahn, Paul. 2008. *Sacred Violence: Torture, Terror and Sovereignty.* Ann Arbor: University of Michigan Press.

Kantola, Johanna. 2007. "The Gendered Reproduction of the State in International Relations." *British Journal of Politics and International Relations* 9 (2): 270–83.

Kaplan, Robert D. 2005. *Imperial Grunts: The American Military on the Ground.* New York: Random House.

Kaufman, Joyce P. and Kristen Williams. 2010. *Women and War: Gender Identity and Activism in Times of Conflict.* Boulder, CO: Kumarian Press.

Kaufman, Michael. 1994. "Men, Feminism, and Men's Contradictory Experiences of Power." In *Theorizing Masculinities,* edited by Harry Brod and Michael Kaufman, 142–63. Thousand Oaks, CA: Sage.

Kaufman-Osborn, Timothy. 2005. "Gender Trouble at Abu Ghraib?" *Politics and Gender* 1 (4): 597–619.

Keene, Jennifer D. 2001. *Doughboys, the Great War, and the Remaking of America.* Baltimore: Johns Hopkins University Press.

Kempadoo, Kamala. 1999. "Continuities and Change: Five Centuries of Prostitution in the Caribbean." In *Tourism and Sex Work in the Caribbean,* edited by Kamala Kempadoo, 3–34. Lanham, MD: Rowman and Littlefield.

Kennedy, Paul. 1988. *The Rise and Fall of the Great Powers: Economic Change and Military Conflict from 1500 to 2000.* London: Unwin Hyman.

Kerber, Linda K. 1980. *Women of the Republic: Intellect and Ideology in Revolutionary America.* Chapel Hill: University of North Carolina.

Khaleeli, Jehan and Sarah Martin. 2004. "Addressing the Sexual Misconduct of Peacekeepers." Refugees International, September 23. Accessed February 2, 2006. http://www.refugeesinternational.org/content/article/detail/4047/.

Khalidi, Omar. 2001/02. "Ethnic Group Recruitment in the Indian Army: The Constrasting Cases of Sikhs, Muslims, Gurkhas and Others." *Pacific Affairs* 74 (4): 529–52.

Killingray, David. 1999. "Guardians of Empire." In *Guardians of Empire: The Armed Forces of the Colonial Powers c. 1700–1964,* edited by David Killingray and David Omissi, 1–24. Manchester, UK: Manchester University Press.

Kimmel, Michael. 1994. "Masculinity as Homophobia: Fear, Shame, and Silence in the Construction of Gender Identity." In *Theorizing Masculinities,* edited Harry Brod and Michael Kaufman, 119–41. Thousand Oaks, CA: Sage.

———. 1997. *Manhood in America: A Cultural History.* Oxford: Oxford University Press.

Kinsey, Christopher. 2006. *Corporate Soldiers and International Security: The Rise of Private Military Companies.* New York: Routledge.

Kochhar-George, Che Singh. 2010. "Nepalese Gurkhas and Their Battle for Equal Rights." *Race and Class* 52 (2): 43–61.

Koehn, Daryl. 1998. *Rethinking Feminist Ethics: Care, Trust, and Empathy.* London: Routledge.

Kovitz, Marcia. 2003. "The Roots of Military Masculinity." In *Military Masculinities: Identity and the State,* edited by Paul Higate, 1–14. Westport: Praeger.

Krahmann, Elke. 2007. "Transitional States in Search of Support: Private Military Companies and Security Sector Reform." In *From Mercenaries to Market: The Rise and Regulation of Private Military Companies,* edited by Simon Chesterman and Chia Lehnardt, 94–112. New York: Oxford University Press.

Krahmann, Elke. 2008. "Security: Collective Good or Commodity?" *European Journal of International Relations* 14 (3): 379–404.

———. 2010. *States, Citizens and the Privatisation of Security.* Cambridge: Cambridge University Press.

Kreisky, Eva. 1994. "Das ewig Männerbündische? Zur Standardform von Staat und Politik." In *Wozu Politikwissenschaft? Über das Neue in der Politik,* edited by Claus Leggewie, 191–208. Darmstadt: Wissenschaftliche Buchgesellschaft.

Kronsell, Annica. 2012. *Gender, Sex, and the Postnational Defense: Militarism and Peacekeeping.* Oxford: Oxford University Press.

Kruck, Andreas and Alexander Spencer. 2013. "Contested Stories of Commercial Security: Self- and Media Narratives of Private Military and Security Companies." *Critical Studies on Security* 1 (3): 326–46.

Kuehnast, Kathleen, Chantal de Jone Oudrast, and Helga Hernes, eds. 2011. *Women and War: Power and Protection in the 21st Century.* Washington, DC: US Institute for Peace.

Leander, Anna. 2004. "Drafting Community: Understanding the Fate of Conscription." *Armed Forces & Society* 30 (4): 571–99.

———. 2005. "The Power to Construct International Security: On the Significance of Private Military Companies." *Millennium: Journal of International Studies* 33 (3): 803–26.

———. 2006. "Privatizing the Politics of Protection: The Authority of Military Companies." In *The Politics of Protection: Sites of Insecurity and Political Agency,* edited by Jef Huysmans, Andrew Dobson, and Raia Prohkovnik, 19–33. London and New York: Routledge.

———. 2007a. "Portraits in Practice: The Private Security Business and the Reconfiguration of International Politics." Paper presented at the 6th Pan-European Conference of the Standing Group on International Relations (SGIR) of the European Consortium for Political Research, Torino, September 12–15.

———. 2007b. "Regulating the Role of Private Military Companies in Shaping Security and Politics." In *From Mercenaries to Market: The Rise and Regulation of Private Military Companies,* edited by Simon Chesterman and Chia Lehnardt, 49–64. Oxford: Oxford University Press.

———. 2009a. "The Privatization of International Security." Working Paper 10. Department of Intercultural Communication and Management, Copenhagen Business School.

———. 2009b. "Contractualized Citizenship, Nationalized Contracting, Militarized Soldiering: The Market for Force and the Right to Have Protection Rights." Working Paper presented at the ECPR workshop Practices of Citizenship and the Politics of Insecurity, Lisbon, April 14–19.

———. 2010. "Commercial Security Practices." In *The Routledge Handbook of New Security Studies,* edited by Peter J. Burgess, 208–16. London: Routledge.

———. 2012. "What Do Codes of Conduct Do? Hybrid Constitutionalization and Militarization in Military Markets." *Global Constitutionalism* 1 (1): 91–119.

———. 2013. "The Politics of Whitelisting in Commercial Security." In *The Politics of the List: Law, Security, Technology.* University of Canterbury: Kent Law School.

Leander, Anna and Rens Van Munster. 2007. "Private Security Contractors in the Debate about Darfur: Reflecting and Reinforcing Neoliberal Governmentality." *International Relations* 21 (2): 201–16.

Levy, Yagil. 2007. "Soldiers as Laborers: A Theoretical Model." *Theory and Society* 36 (March): 187–208.

Lieber, Keir. 2005. *War and the Engineers: The Primacy of Politics over Technology.* Ithaca: Cornell University Press.

Lindsey, Charlotte. 2001. *Women Facing War: ICRC Study of the Impact of Armed Conflict on Women.* Geneva: ICRC.

———. 2005. "The Impact of Armed Conflict on Women." In *Listening to the Silences: Women and War,* edited by Helen Durham and Tracey Gurd, 21–35. The Hague: Martinus Nijhoff.

Lindsey-Curtet, Charlotte, Florence Tercier Holst-Roness, and Letitia Anderson. 2004. *Addressing the Needs of Women Affected by Armed Conflict: An ICRC Guidance Document.* Geneva: ICRC.

Lister, Ruth. 2002. "Sexual Citizenship." In *Handbook of Citizenship Studies,* edited by Engin F. Isin and Bryan S. Turner, 191-207. London: Sage.

Löffler, Marion. 2011. *Feministische Staatstheorie: Eine Einführung.* Frankfurt am Main: Campus.

———. 2012. *Geschlechterpolitische Strategien: Transformationen von Staatlichkeit als politisch gestaltbarer Prozess.* Frankfurt am Main: Campus.

Ludwig, Gundula. 2011. *Geschlecht regieren: Staat, Subjekt und heteronormative Hegemonie.* Frankfurt am Main: Campus.

Ludwig, Gundula, Birgit Sauer, and Stefanie Wöhl, eds. 2009. *Staat und Geschlecht: Grundlagen und aktuelle Herausforderungen feministischer Staatstheorie.* Baden-Baden: Nomos.

Lunn, Joe. 1999. "Les Races Guerrieres: Racial Preconceptions in the French Military about West African Soldiers During the First World War." *Journal of Contemporary History* 34 (4): 517–36.

Lutz, Catherine. 2002. "Making War at Home in the United States: Militarization and the Current Crisis." *American Anthropologist* 104 (3): 723–73.

Lyall, Sarah. 2006. "Aid Workers Are Said to Abuse Girls." *New York Times,* May 9, A8.

Lynch, Colum. 2005. "U.N. Faces More Accusations of Sexual Misconduct." *Washington Post,* March 13.

Lynch, Tony and A. J. Walsh. 2000. "The Good Mercenary." *Journal of Political Philosophy* 8 (2): 133–53.

MacKenzie, Megan. 2010. "Securitization and De-securitization: Female Soldiers and the Reconstruction of Women in Post-Conflict Sierra Leone." In *Gender and International Security: Feminist Perspectives,* edited by Laura Sjoberg, 151–66. New York: Routledge.

———. 2012. "Let Women Fight: Ending the U.S. Military's Female Combat Ban." *Foreign Affairs* 91 (6): 32-42.

MacKinnon, Catherine. 1989. *Toward a Feminist Theory of the State.* Cambridge, MA: Harvard University Press.

MacLellan, Nic. 2007. "Fiji, Iraq and Pacific Island Security." *Race and Class* 48 (3): 47–62.

MacLeod, Sorcha. 2011. "The Role of International Regulatory Initiatives on Business and Human Rights for Holding Private Military and Security Contractors to Account." In *War by Contract: Human Rights, Humanitarian Law and Private Contractors,* edited by Francesco Francioni and Natalino Ronzitti, 343–61. Oxford: Oxford University Press.

MacNicol, Glynnis. 2009. "Does the Long Arm of Gawker Reach the State Department?" Mediaite. Accessed December 15, 2013. http://bit.ly/Pn3y2.

Mahmood, Saba. 2005. *Politics of Piety. The Islamic Revival and the Feminist Subject.* Princeton, NJ: Princeton University Press.

Mamdani, Mahmood. 2009. *Saviors and Survivors: Darfur, Politics, and the War on Terror.* New York: Pantheon Books.

Mancini, Marina, Faustin Z. Ntoubandi, and Thilo Marauhn. 2011. "Old Concepts and New Challenges: Are Private Contractors the Mercenaries of the Twenty-First Century?" In *War by Contract: Human Rights, Humanitarian Law and Private Contractors,* edited by Francesco Francioni and Natalino Ronzitti, 321–40. Oxford: Oxford University Press.

Mandel, Robert. 2002. *Armies without States: The Privatization of Security.* London: Lynne Rienner.

———. 2004. *Security, Strategy, and the Quest for Bloodless War.* Boulder, CO: Lynne Rienner.

Manigart, Philippe. 2003. "Restructuring the Armed Forces." In *Handbook of the Sociology of the Military,* edited by Giuseppe Caforio, 323–43. New York: Springer.

Mannitz, Sabine. 2011. "Redefining Soldierly Role Models in Germany." *Armed Forces & Society* 37 (4): 680–700.

Marchand, Marianne H. 1996. "Reconceptualising 'Gender and Development' in an Era of Globalization." *Millennium: Journal of International Studies* 25 (3): 577–603.

Marchand, Marianne H. and Anne Sisson Runyan. 2000. *Gender and Global Restructuring: Sightings, Sites and Resistances.* London and New York: Routledge.

Martin, Sarah. 2005. "Must Boys Be Boys? Ending Sexual Exploitation and Abuse in UN Peacekeeping Missions." Refugees International, October. Accessed February 22, 2007. http://www.refugeesinternational.org/content/publication/detail/6976/.

———. 2006. "'Must Boys Be Boys? Confronting Sexual Exploitation and Abuse in UN Peacekeeping Operations." Lecture at Fletcher School, Tufts University, February 1.

Maruska, Jennifer Heeg. 2010. "When Are States Hypermasculine?" In *Gender and International Security: Feminist Perspectives,* edited by Laura Sjoberg, 235–55. New York: Routledge.

Masters, Cristina. 2005. "Body Counts: the Biopolitics of Death." In *The Logics of Biopower and the War on Terror: Living, Dying, Surviving,* edited by Elizabeth Dauphinée and Cristina Masters, 43–57. New York: Palgrave Macmillan.

———. 2008. "Bodies of Technology and the Politics of the Flesh." In *Rethinking the Man Question: Sex, Gender and Violence in International Relations,* edited by Jane Parpart and Marysia Zalewski, 87–107. New York: Zed Books.

Mathers, Jennifer G. 2013. "Women and State Military Forces." In *Women and Wars,* edited by Carol Cohn, 124–145. Cambridge: Polity.

McConnell, Tristan. 2007. "All-Female Unit Keeps Peace in Liberia." *Christian Science Monitor,* March 21.

McClintock, Anne. 1993. "Family Feuds: Gender, Nationalism and the Family." *Feminist Review* 44 (Summer): 61–80.

McEvoy, Sandra. 2010. "Loyalist Women Paramilitaries in Northern Ireland: Beginning a Feminist Conversation about Conflict Resolution." In *Gender and International Security: Feminist Perspectives,* edited by Laura Sjoberg, 129–50. New York: Routledge.

McIntosh, Mary. 1978. "The State and the Oppression of Women." In *Feminism and Materialism: Women and Modes of Production*, edited by Annette Kuhn and Annmarie Wolpe, 245–89. London: Routledge and Kegan Paul.

McVeigh, Karen. 2013. "Sexual Assault Crisis Tempers Euphoria Over End of Combat Ban." *Guardian*, January 25.

Melloy, Kilian. 2009. "Homoerotic 'Hazing' Turns U.S. Kabul Embassy into 'Animal House.'" *Edge Boston*, September 3. Accessed December 15, 2013. http://bit.ly/1xP4oSl/.

Memmi, Dominique. 2002. "Public-Private Opposition and Biopolitics: A Response to Judit Sandor." *Social Research* 69 (1): 143–47.

Mendelson, Sarah E. 2005. *Barracks and Brothels: Peacekeepers and Human Trafficking in the Balkans*. Washington, DC: CSIS Press.

Messner, J. J. 2007. "What's It Worth to You? Expatriates, Third Country Nationals, Local Nationals and Pay Disparity." *Journal of International Peace Operations* 3 (2): 32.

Mies, Maria. 1986. *Patriarchy and Accumulation on a World Scale: Women in the International Division of Labor*. London: Zed Books.

Milliken, Jennifer, with Elisabeth Gilgen and Jasba Lazarevic. 2009. *Tackling Violence against Women: From Knowledge to Practice Initiatives*. Geneva: Geneva Declaration.

Mohanty, Chandra Talpade. 1997. "Women Workers and Capitalist Scripts: Ideologies of Domination, Common Interests, and the Politics of Solidarity." In *Feminist Genealogies, Colonial Legacies and Democratic Futures*, edited by M. Jacqui Alexander and Chandra Talpade Mohanty, 3–29. London and New York: Routledge.

———. 2003. *Feminism without Borders: Decolonizing Theory, Practicing Solidarity*. Durham, NC: Duke University Press.

Monaghan, Lee F. 2004. "Doorwork and Legal Risk: Observations from an Embodied Ethnography." *Social Legal Studies* 13 (4): 453–80.

Montpetit, Jonathan. 2010. "Canadian Military Using Private Afghan Security Despite Pending Ban." *Toronto Star*, October 25.

Morgan, David H. J. 1994. "Theater of Combat: The Military and Masculinities." In *Theorizing Masculinities*, edited by Harry Brod and Michael Kaufmann, 165–82 London: Sage.

Morgan, Matthew. 2006. "American Empire and the American Military." *Armed Forces & Society* 32 (2): 202–18.

Morrell, Robert and Sandra Swart. 2005. "Men in the Third World: Postcolonial Perspectives on Masculinities." In *Handbook of Studies of Men and Masculinities*, edited by Michael S. Kimmel, Jeff Hearn, and Raewyn Connell, 90–113. Thousand Oaks, CA: Sage.

Moskos, Charles. 2000. "Toward a Postmodern Military: The United States as a Paradigm." In *The Postmodern Military*, edited by Charles Moskos, John Allen Williams, and David R. Segal, 14-31. Oxford: Oxford University Press.

Moskos, Charles, John Allen Williams, and David R. Segal, ed. 2000. *The Postmodern Military*. Oxford: Oxford University Press.

MoxNewsDotCom. 2009. "Wild Parties and Deviant Hazing By ArmorGroup Guards at US Embassy in Afghanistan." YouTube, video no longer available.

Mutimer, David. 2007. "Sovereign Contradictions: Maher Arar and the Indefinite Future." In *The Logics of Biopower and the War on Terror: Living, Dying,*

Surviving, edited by Elizabeth Dauphinée and Cristina Masters, 159–79. New York: Palgrave Macmillan.

Nagl, John A. 2002. *Learning to Eat Soup with a Knife: Counterinsurgency Lessons from Malaya and Vietnam*. Chicago and London: University of Chicago Press.

Nancy, Jean-Luc. 1991. "The Unsacrificeable." *Yale French Studies* 79: 20–38.

Nandy, Ashis. [1983] 1988. *The Intimate Enemy: Loss and Recovery of Self under Colonialism*. New York: Oxford University Press.

Narayan, Uma. 1997. *Dislocating Cultures: Identities, Traditions, and Third World Feminism*. New York: Routledge.

National Priorities Project. 2006. "Military Recruiting 2006." Accessed December 11, 2007. http://www.nationalpriorities.org/Publications/Military-Recruiting-2006.html.

Netter, Sarah. 2010. "Blast Boxers Hit Military Market to Protect Soldiers' Most Sensitive Areas." ABC News, 29 October. Accessed December 15, 2013. http://abcn.ws/b6aW6R.

Nikitin, Alexander I. 2009. "Oral Statement of President." UN Working Group on the Use of Mercenaries, Human Rights Council, 10th session, March 6.

Niva, Steve. 1998. "Tough and Tender: New World Order Masculinity and the Gulf War." In *The "Man" Question in International Relations*, edited by Marysia Zalewski and Jane Parpart, 109–28. Boulder, CO: Westview Press.

Noddings, Nel. 1984. *Caring: A Feminine Approach to Ethics and Moral Education*. Berkeley: University of California Press.

Nordland, Rod. 2009. "Ex-Blackwater Workers May Return to Iraq Jobs." *New York Times*, April 4.

Norton, Anne. 2004. *Leo Strauss and the Politics of American Empire*. New Haven. CT: Yale University Press.

Nuciari, Marina. 2006. "Models and Explanations for Military Organization: An Updated Reconsideration." In *Handbook of the Sociology of the Military*, edited by Giuseppe Caforio, 61–85. New York: Springer.

O'Reilly, Maria. 2012. "Muscular Interventionism: Gender, Power and Liberal Peacebuilding in Post-Conflict Bosnia-Herzegovina." *International Feminist Journal of Politics* 14 (4): 529–48.

Orford, Anne. 1999. "Muscular Humanitarianism: Reading the Narratives of the New Interventionism." *European Journal of International Law* 10 (4): 679–711.

———. 2011. "Passions of Protection: Sovereign Authority and Humanitarian War." In *Experiencing War*, edited by Christine Sylvester, 8–27. New York: Routledge.

Organisation for Economic Co-operation and Development (OECD). 2011. *Guidelines on Multilateral Enterprises*. Rev. ed. Paris: OECD.

Østensen, Åse Gilje. 2011. *UN Use of Private Military and Security Companies: Practices and Policies*. Geneva: DCAF.

Ouzgane, Lahoucine and Robert Morrell. 2005. *African Masculinities: Men in Africa from the Late Nineteenth Century to the Present*. New York: Palgrave MacMilian.

Owens, Patricia. 2008. "Distinctions, Distinctions: 'Public' and 'Private' Force?" *International Affairs* 84 (5): 977–90.

Pan, Esther. 2004. "Iraq-Military Outsourcing." Council on Foreign Relations, May 20. Accessed December 11, 2007. http://www.cfr.org/publication/7667/#6.

Parsons, Timothy H. 1999. "Wakamba Warriors Are Soliders of the Queen: The Evolution of the Kamba as a Martial Race, 1890–1970." *Ethnohistory* 46 (4): 671–701.

Pemble, John. 1971. *Britain's Gurkha War: The Invasion of Nepal, 1814–16*. Barnsley: Frontline Books.

Parashar, Swati. 2010. "Women, Military, and Security: The South Asian Conundrum." In *Gender and International Security: Feminist Perspectives*, edited by Laura Sjoberg, 168–87. New York: Routledge.

Parenti, Christian. 2007. "Planet America: The Revolution in Military Affairs as Fantasy and Fetish." In *Exceptional State: Contemporary U.S. Culture and the New Imperialism*, edited by Ashley Dawson and Malini Johar Schueller, 88–104. Durham, NC: Duke University Press.

Paris, Michael. 2000. *Warrior Nation: Images of War in British Popular Culture, 1850-2000*. London: Reaktion Books.

Parker John. 1999. *The Gurkhas: The Inside Story of the World's Most Feared Soldiers*. London: Headline Book.

Patterson, Malcom Hugh. 2009. *Privatising Peace: A Corporate Adjunct to United Nations Peacekeeping and Humanitarian Operations*. Basingstoke: Palgrave Macmillan.

Pattison, James. 2008. "Just War Theory and the Privatization of Military Force." *Ethics & International Affairs* 22 (2): 143–62.

———. 2010. "Deeper Objections to the Privatization of Military Force." *Journal of Political Philosophy* 18 (4): 425–47.

Peers, Douglas M. 1991. "'The Habitual Nobility of Being': British Officers and the Social Construction of the Bengal Army in the Early Nineteenth Century." *Modern Asian Studies* 25 (3): 545–69.

Pelton, Robert Young. 2006. *Licensed to Kill: Hired Guns in the War on Terror*. New York: Crown.

Percy, Sarah. 2007. *Mercenaries: The History of a Norm in International Relations*. Oxford: Oxford University Press.

Petersen, Alan. 2003. "Research on Men and Masculinities: Some Implications of Recent Theory for Future Work." *Men and Masculinities* 6 (1): 54–69.

Peterson, V. Spike, ed. 1992a. *Gendered States: Feminist (Re)Visions of International Relations Theory*. Boulder, CO: Rienner.

Peterson, V. Spike. 1992b. "Security and Sovereign States: What Is at Stake in Taking Feminism Seriously?" In *Gendered States: Feminist (Re)Visions of International Relations Theory*, edited by Spike V. Peterson, 31–64. Boulder, CO: Lynne Rienner Publishers.

———. 2003. *A Critical Rewriting of Global Political Economy: Integrating Reproductive, Productive, and Virtual Economies*. New York: Routledge.

———. 2005. "How (the Meaning of) Gender Matters in Political Economy." *New Political Economy* 10 (4): 499–521.

———. 2007. "Rewriting (Global) Political Economy as Reproductive, Productive, and Virtual (Foucauldian) Economies." *International Feminist Journal of Politics* 4 (1): 1–30.

———. 2008. "'New Wars' and Gendered Economies." *Feminist Review* 88 (1): 7–20.

———. 2009. "Gendered Identities, Ideologies, and Practices in the Context of War and Militarism." In *Gender, War, and Militarism*, edited by Laura Sjoberg and Sandra Via, 17–29. Santa Barbara, CA: Praeger.

———. 2010. "International/Global Economy." In *Gender Matters in Global Politics: A Feminist Introduction to International Relations*, edited by Laura J. Shepherd, 204–17. New York: Routledge.

Pictet, Jean et al. 1958. *Geneva Convention Relative to the Protection of Civilian Persons in Time of War.* Geneva: ICRC.

Pieterse, Jan Nederveen. 2004. *Globalization or Empire?* New York: Routledge.

Pin Fat, Véronique and Maria Stern. 2005. "The Scripting of Private Jessica Lynch: Biopolitics, Gender, and the 'Feminization' of the US Military." *Alternatives: Global, Local, Political* 30 (1): 25–53.

Pingeot, Lou. 2012. *Dangerous Partnership: Private Military and Security Companies and the UN.* New York: Global Policy Forum.

Pintchman, Tracy. 2009. "Reflections on Power and the Postcolonial Context: Tales from the Field." *Method and Theory in the Study of Religion* 21 (1): 66–72.

Plain, Jill. 2006. *John Mills and British Cinema.* Edinburgh: Edinburgh University Press.

Potts, Annie. 2000. "'The Essence of the Hard On': Hegemonic Masculinity and the Cultural Construction of 'Erectile Dysfunction.'" *Men and Masculinities* 3 (1): 85–103.

———. 2001. "The Man with Two Brains: Hegemonic Masculine Subjectivity and the Discursive Construction of the Unreasonable Penis-Self." *Journal of Gender Studies* 10 (2): 145–56.

Poulantzas, Nicos. 1978. *Staatstheorie: Politischer Überbau, Ideologie, Autoritärer Etatismus.* Hamburg: VSA.

Pratt, Nicola. 2013. "Reconceptualizing Gender, Reinscribing Racial-Sexual Boundaries in International Security: The Case of UN Security Council Resolution 1325 on Women, Peace and Security." *International Studies Quarterly* 57 (4): 772–83.

Pringle, Rosemary and Sophie Watson. 1992. "'Women's Interest' and the Post-structuralist State." In *Destabilizing Theory: Contemporary Feminist Debates*, edited by Michèle Barrett and Anne Philipps, 53–73. Cambridge: Polity Press.

Project for the New American Century. 1997. "Statement of Principles." Accessed April 14, 2009. http://www.newamericancentury.org/statementofprinciples.htm.

Prügl, Elisabeth and Haley Thompson. 2013. "The Whistleblower: An Interview with Kathryn Bolkovac and Madeleine Rees." *International Feminist Journal of Politics* 15 (1): 102–9.

Puar, Jasbir K. 2006. "Mapping US Homonormativities." *Gender, Place and Culture* 13 (1): 67–88.

Rai, Shirin. 2004. "Gendering Global Governance." *International Feminist Journal of Politics* 6 (4): 579–601.

Ramazanoglu, Caroline and Janet Holland. 2002. *Feminist Methodology: Challenges and Choices.* London: Sage.

Ratti, Oscar and Adele Westbrook. 1991. *Secrets of the Samurai: A Survey of the Martial Arts of Feudal Japan.* North Clarendon, VT: Tuttle.

Raz, Guy. 2007. "U.S. Contractors in Iraq Rely on Third-World Labor." National Public Radio, October 16.

Reid, Julian. 2006. *The Biopolitics of the War on Terror: Life Struggles, Liberal Modernity, and the Defence of Logistical Societies.* Manchester: Manchester University Press.

Refugees International. 2004. "Sexual Exploitation in Liberia: Are the Conditions Ripe for Another Scandal?" April 20. Accessed February 22, 2007. http://www.refugeesinternational.org/content/article/detail/957.

Richemond-Barak, Daphné. 2011. "Regulating War: A Taxonomy in Global Administrative Law." *European Journal of International Law* 22 (4): 1027–69.

Riley, Robin L., Chandra Talpade Mohanty, and Minnie Bruce Pratt, eds. 2008. *Feminism and War: Confronting U.S. Imperialism.* London: Zed Books.

Robberson, Tod. 2007. "Employees Not Convinced Whistle-Blowers Are Safe." *Dallas Morning News*, February 9. Accessed August 13, 2008. http://bit.ly/1ywx8SV.

Robinson, Fiona. 1999. *Globalizing Care: Ethics, Feminist Theory, and International Relations.* Boulder, CO: Westview Press.

———. 2011. *The Ethics of Care: A Feminist Approach to Human Security.* Philadelphia: Temple University Press.

Robtice. 2009. Comments Section. "Lord of the Flies at U.S. Embassy in Kabul?" NBC News. Accessed December 15, 2013. http://bit.ly/1eFwmsS.

Rose, Nikolas. 1999. *Powers of Freedom.* New York: Cambridge University Press.

Ross, Brian, Rhonda Schwartz, and Kirit Radia. 2009. "Kabul U.S. Embassy Guard: Sexual Deviancy Required for Promotion." ABC News, September 2. http://abcn.ws/15YoKrv.

Ross, Will. 2007. "Liberia Gets All-Female Peacekeeping Force." BBC News, Liberia, January 31. Accessed March 1. http://news.bbc.co.uk/2/hi/africa/6316387.

Roy, Kaushik. 2001. "The Construction of Regiments in the Indian Army: 1859–1913." *War and History* 8 (2): 127–48.

Rubio-Marin, Ruth, ed. 2009. *The Gender of Reparations: Unsettling Sexual Hierarchies While Redressing Human Rights Violations.* Cambridge: Cambridge University Press.

Runyan, Anne Sisson. 1990. "Gender Relations and the Politics of Protection." *Peace Review: A Journal of Social Justice* 2 (4): 28–31.

Runyan, Anne Sisson and V. Spike Peterson. 2013. *Global Gender Issues in the New Millennium.* 4th ed. Boulder, CO: Westview Press.

Rygiel, Kim. 2006. "Protecting and Providing Identity: The Biopolitics of Waging War through Citizenship in the Post-9/11 Era." In *(En)Gendering the War on Terror: War Stories and Camouflaged Politics*, edited by Krista Hunt and Kim Rygiel, 145–67. Aldershot, UK: Ashgate.

———. 2008. "The Securitized Citizen." In *Recasting the Social in Citizenship*, edited by Engin Isin, 268–300. Toronto: University of Toronto Press.

Ryngaert, Cedric. 2008. "Litigating Abuses Committed by Private Military Companies." *European Journal of International Law* 19 (5): 1035–53.

Said, Edward W. 1978. *Orientalism: Western Conceptions of the Orient.* New York: Random House.

Samanta, Amiya K. 1996. *Gorkhaland: A Study in Ethnic Separatism.* New Delhi: Khama.

Sauer, Birgit. 2001. *Die Asche des Souveräns: Staat und Demokratie in der Geschlechterdebatte.* Frankfurt am Main: Campus.

———. 2008. "Neuliberale Verhältnisse: Staatlichkeit und Geschlecht." In *Neoliberalismus—Analysen und Alternativen*, edited by Christoph Butterwegge, Bettina Lösch, and Ralph Ptak, 34–49. Wiesbaden: Verlag für Sozialwissenschaften.

Sauer, Birgit and Stefanie Wöhl. 2011. "Feminist Perspectives on the Internationalization of the State." *Antipode* 43 (1): 108–28.

Scahill, Jeremy. 2007. *Blackwater: The Rise of the World's Most Powerful Mercenary Army.* New York: Nation Books.

Scheier, Rachel. 2006. "Soldier Verdict Spotlights Rape in Ugandan Camps." *Women's E-news*, May 29. Accessed June 2. http://www.womensenews.org/article.cfm?aid=2756.

Schnabel, Albrecht and Anara Tabyshalieva. 2012. *Defying Victimhood: Women and Post-Conflict Peacebuilding.* Tokyo: UN University Press.

Schott, Robin. 2010. *Birth, Death, and Femininity: Philosophies of Embodiment.* Bloomington and Indianapolis: Indiana University Press.

SCG International. 2013a. "Tier One: High Risk Projects." Accessed December 19. http://198.65.2.10/DO/consultantTIER1.htm.

———. 2013b. "Tier Four: Host Country Nationals (HCN)." Accessed December 19. http://198.65.2.10/DO/consultantTIER4.htm.

Schulman, Daniel. 2009. "Animal House in Afghanistan." *Mother Jones*, September 1. Accessed December 15, 2013. http://bit.ly/cwvUlz.

———. 2011. "Vodka Butt-Shot Contractor STILL Guarding the Kabul Embassy." *Mother Jones*, February 17. Accessed December 15, 2013. http://bit.ly/fBv4mW.

Schulz, Sabrina and Christina Yeung. 2008. "Private Military and Security Companies and Gender." In *Gender and Security Sector Reform Toolkit*, edited by Megan Bastick and Kristin Valasek. Geneva: DCAF, OSCE/ODIHR, UN-INSTRAW.

Schumacher, Gerald. 2006. *A Bloody Business: America's War Zone Contractors and the Occupation of Iraq.* New York: Zenith Press.

Scott, Joan W. 1986. "Gender: A Useful Category of Historical Analysis." *American Historical Review* 91 (5): 1053–75.

Scranton, Deborah. 2008. *Bad Voodoo's War* [video]. Boston: *Frontline* WGBH.

Seccombe, Ian. 1985. "International Labor Migration in the Middle East: A Review of Literature and Research, 1974–84." *International Migration Review* 19 (2): 335–52.

Segal, Mady Wechsler. 1995. "Women's Military Roles Cross-Nationally: Past, Present, and Future." *Gender and Society* 9 (6): 757–75.

———. 1999. "Gender and the Military." In *Handbook of the Sociology of Gender,* edited by Janet Saltzman Chafetz, 563–81. New York: Kluwer Academic/Plenum.

Seidman, Steven. 2005. "From Polluted Homosexual to Normal Gay: Changing Patterns of Sexual Regulation in America." In *Thinking Straight: The Power, Promise and Paradox of Heterosexuality,* edited by Chrys Ingraham, 39–62. Routledge: New York.

Sharoni, Simona. 2008. "De-Militarizing Masculinities in the Age of Empire." *Österreichische Zeitschrift für Politikwissenschaft* 37 (2): 147–64.

Shearer, David. 1998. "Private Armies and Military Intervention." *Alelphi Paper* 316 (February). London: International Institute for Strategic Studies.

Shelton, Dinah. 2005. *Remedies in International Human Rights Law.* Oxford: Oxford University Press.

Shepherd, Laura J., ed. 2010a. *Gender Matters in Global Politics: A Feminist Introduction to International Relations.* London: Routledge.

Shepherd, Laura J. 2010b. "Feminist Security Studies." In *The International Studies Encyclopedia,* edited by Robert A. Denemark. doi 10.1111/b.9781444336597.2010.x.

Sheppard, Eric and Robert B. McMaster, eds., 2004. *Scale and Geographic Inquiry: Nature, Society, and Method.* Malden, MA: Blackwell.

Sherman, Jake and Victoria DiDomenico. 2009. *The Public Cost of Private Security in Afghanistan*. New York: Centre on International Cooperation.

Shimko, Kenneth. 2010. *The Iraq Wars and America's Military Revolution*. Cambridge: Cambridge University Press.

Shotton, Anna. 2006. "A Strategy to Address Sexual Exploitation and Abuse by United Nations Peacekeeping Personnel." *Cornell International Law Journal* 39 (1): 97–107.

Shrestha, Slesh A. 2011. "Effect of Education Returns Abroad on Domestic Schooling: A British Gurkha Army Experience." Unpublished Paper. Department of Economics. Ann Arbor: University of Michigan.

Sigal, Clancy. 2011. "The US Isn't Facing Up to the Literal Emasculation of Its Soldiers." *Guardian*, April 19. Accessed December 15, 2013. http://bit.ly/16s6UVx.

Simpson, Cam. 2005. "Into a War Zone, On a Deadly Road." *Chicago Tribune*, October 10.

———. 2006a. "U.S. to Probe Claims of Human Trafficking: Tribune Series on Iraq Abuses Sparked Action." *Chicago Tribune*, January 19.

———. 2006b. "Iraq War Contractors Ordered to End Abuses." *Chicago Tribune*, April 23.

Simpson, Cam and Aamer Madhani. 2005. "U.S. Cash Fuels Human Trade." *Chicago Tribune*, October 9.

Singer, Peter W. 2001/02. "Corporate Warriors: The Rise of the Privatized Military Industry and Its Ramifications for International Security." *International Security* 26 (3): 186–220.

———. 2003. *Corporate Warriors: The Rise of the Privatized Military Industry*. Ithaca: Cornell University Press.

———. 2004. "The Private Military Industry and Iraq: What Have We Learned and Where to Next?" Geneva Centre for the Democratic Control of Armed Forces (DCAF) Policy Paper. Proceedings of the International Security Forum (ISF), Montreux, Switzerland, October 4–6.

———. 2005. "Outsourcing War." *Foreign Affairs* 84 (2): 119–133.

———. 2008. *Corporate Warriors: The Rise of the Privatized Military Industry*. Updated ed. Ithaca: Cornell University Press.

Sinha, Mrinalini. 1995. *Colonial Masculinity: The "Manly Englishman" and The "Effeminate Bengali" in the Late Nineteenth Century*. Manchester: Manchester University Press.

Sjoberg, Laura. 2006. *Gender, Justice, and the Wars in Iraq: Feminist Reformulation of Just War Theory*. Lanham, MD: Rowman and Littlefield.

———. 2007. "Gendering the Empire's Soldiers: Gender Ideologies, The United States Military, and the 'War on Terror.'" Paper presented at the Gender, Militarism, and War Conference, University of Pennsylvania, October 25.

———. 2008. "Scaling IR Theory: Geography's Contribution to Where IR Takes Place." *International Studies Review* 10 (3): 471–99.

———, ed. 2010. *Gender and International Security: Feminist Perspectives*. London and New York: Routledge.

———. 2011. "Gender, the State, and War Redux: Feminist International Relations across the 'Levels of Analysis.'" *International Relations* 25 (1): 108–34.

———. 2013. *Gendering Global Conflict: Towards a Feminist Theory of War*. New York: Columbia Press.

Sjoberg, Laura and Caron E. Gentry. 2007. *Mothers, Monsters, Whores: Women's Violence in Global Politics*. London: Zed Books.

Sjoberg, Laura and Jillian Martin. 2010. "Feminist Security Theorizing." In *The International Studies Encyclopedia*, edited by Robert A. Denemark. doi 10.1111/b.9781444336597.2010.x.

Sjoberg, Laura and Jessica Peet. 2011. "A(nother) Dark Side of the Protection Racket: Targeting Women in Wars." *International Feminist Journal of Politics* 13 (2): 163–82.

Sky News. 2009. "US Guards 'Drunk at Obscene Kabul Parties." September 3. Accessed December 15, 2013. http://bit.ly/1aSOIlS.

Skeggs, Beverley. 2009. "Feminist Ethnography." In *Handbook of Ethnography*, edited by Paul Atkinson et al., 426–42. Los Angeles: Sage.

Snyder, R. Claire. 1999. *Citizen-Soldiers and Manly Warriors: Military Service and Gender in the Civic Republican Tradition*. Lanham, MD: Rowman and Littlefield.

———. 2003. "The Citizen-Soldier Tradition and Gender Integration of the U.S. Military." *Armed Forces & Society* 29 (2): 185–204.

Spearin, Christopher. 2008. "Private, Armed and Humanitarian? States, NGOs, International Private Security Companies and Shifting Humanitarianism." *Security Dialogue* 39 (4): 363–82.

Specops Company. 2012. "Our Services Your Success." Accessed August 29. http://www.specops-company.com/service.

Spelman, Elizabeth V. 1988. *Inessential Woman: Problems of Exclusion in Feminist Thought*. Boston: Beacon Press.

Sperling, Valerie. 2009. *Altered States: The Globalization of Accountability*. New York: Cambridge University Press.

Spivak, Gayatri. 1988. "Can the Subaltern Speak?" In *Marxism and the Interpretation of Culture*, edited by Cary Nelson and Lawrence Grossberg, 271–316. London: Macmillan.

Spongberg, Mary. 1997. "Are Small Penises Necessary for Civilisation? The Male Body and the Body Politic." *Australian Feminist Studies* 12 (25): 19–28.

Stachowitsch, Saskia. 2012a. "Military Gender Integration and Foreign Policy in the United States: A Feminist International Relations Perspective." *Security Dialogue* 43 (4): 305–21.

———. 2012b. "Professional Soldier, Weak Victim, Patriotic Heroine: Gender Ideologies in Debates on Women's Military Integration in the US." *International Feminist Journal of Politics* 15 (2): 157–76.

———. 2012c. *Gender Ideologies and Military Labor Markets in the U.S.* London: Routledge.

———. 2013. "Military Privatization and the Remasculinization of the State: Making the Link between the Outsourcing of Military Security and Gendered State Transformations." *International Relations* 27 (1): 74–94.

———. 2014. "The Reconstruction of Masculinities in Global Politics: Gendering Strategies in the Field of Private Security." *Men and Masculinities*. doi: 10.1177/1097184X14551205.

Stanovsky, Derek. 2007. "Postcolonial Masculinities." In *International Encyclopedia of Men and Masculinities*, edited by Michael Flood, Judith Kegan Gardiner, Bob Pease, and Keith Pringle, 493–96. London: Routledge.

Steinhauer, Jennifer. 2013. "Veterans Testify on Rapes and Scant Hope of Justice." *New York Times*, March 13.

Steinhoff, Uwe. 2011. "Ethics and Mercenaries." In *New Wars and New Soldiers: Military Ethics in the Contemporary World*, edited by Paolo Tripodi and Jessica Wolfendale, 137-52. Farnham, UK: Ashgate.

Stengers, Isabelle. 1995. *L'invention Des Sciences Modernes*. Paris: Flammarion.

Stiehm, Judith Hicks. 1982. "The Protected, the Protector, the Defender." *Women's Studies International Forum* 5 (3): 367–76.

Stiglitz, Joseph and Linda Blimes. 2008. "Hidden Wounds and Accounting Tricks: Disguising the True Costs." In *Lessons from Iraq: Avoiding the Next War*, edited by Miriam Pemberton and William D. Hartung, 48–64. Boulder, CO: Paradigm.

Stoler, Ann Laura. 2002. *Carnal Knowledge and Imperial Power: Race and the Intimate in Colonial Rule*. Berkeley: University of California Press.

Strange, Susan. 1996. *The Retreat of the State: Diffusion of Power in the World Economy*. Cambridge: Cambridge University Press.

Streets, Heather. 2004. *Martial Races: The Military, Race and Masculinity in British Imperial Culture, 1857–1914*. Manchester: Manchester University Press.

Swiss Confederation. 2010. "International Code of Conduct for Private Security Service Providers." November 9. Accessed November 22, 2012. http://bit.ly/1sEnQOT.

———. 2013a. "International Code of Conduct for Private Security Service Providers' Association: Articles of Association." February. Accessed June 22, 2014. http://bit.ly/1sEo20G.

———. 2013b. "The International Code of Conduct for Private Security Service Providers (ICoC): Framework for the Steering Committee." K.221.244-PMSC-RON. Accessed June 22, 2014. http://bit.ly/1oLnJjr.

Sylvester, Christine. 1994. *Feminist Theory and International Relations in a Postmodern Era*. Cambridge: Cambridge University Press.

———. 2002. *Feminist International Relations: An Unfinished Journey*. Cambridge: Cambridge University Press.

———. 2010. "Tensions in Feminist Security Studies." *Security Dialogue* 41 (6): 607–14.

———. 2011. "Emotion and the Feminist IR Researcher (Forum)." *International Studies Review* 13 (4): 687–708.

———. 2012. "War Experiences/War Practices/War Theory." *Millennium: Journal of International Studies* 40 (3): 483–503.

———. 2013a. *War as Experience: Contributions from International Relations and Feminist Analysis*. London and New York: Routledge.

———. 2013b. "Experiencing the End of International Relations." *European Journal of International Relations* 19 (3): 609–26.

Taussig-Rubbo, Mateo. 2009a. "Sacrifice and Sovereignty." In *States of Violence: War, Capital Punishment, and Letting Die*, edited by Jennifer L. Culbert and Austin Sarat, 83–126. Cambridge, MA: Cambridge University Press.

———. 2009b. "Outsourcing Sacrifice: The Labor of Private Military Contractors." *Yale Journal of Law & the Humanities* 21 (1): 101–64.

———. 2011. "The Unsacrificeable Subject." In *Who Deserves to Die?*, edited by Austin Sarat and Karl Shoemaker, 131–50. Amherst and Boston: University of Massachusetts Press.

Tétreault, Mary Ann. 2006. "The Sexual Politics of Abu Ghraib: Hegemony, Spectacle, and the Global War on Terror." *National Women's Studies Association Journal* 18 (3): 33–50.

TheFlex21. 2009. Comments Section—"US Embassy in Kabul Sex Photos—State Department Responds." YouTube. Accessed December 15, 2013. http://bit.ly/14sidt9.

Thomas, Claire. 2010. "Why Don't We Talk about 'Violence' in International Relations?" *Review of International Studies* 37 (4): 1815–36.

Tickner, Arlene B. 2013. "By Way of Conclusion: Forget IR?" In *Claiming the International*, edited by Arlene B. Tickner and David L. Blaney. 214–32. New York: Routledge.

Tickner, J. Ann. 1992a. *Gender in International Relations: Feminist Perspectives on Achieving Global Security*. New York: Columbia University Press.

———. 1992b. "Foreword." In *Gendered States: Feminist (Re)Visions of International Relations Theory*, edited by V. Spike Peterson, ix–xi. Boulder, CO: Lynne Rienner.

———. 1996. "Identity in International Relations Theory: Feminist Perspectives." In *The Return of Culture and Identity in IR Theory*, edited by Yosef Lapid and Friedrich Kratochwil, 147–62. Boulder, CO: Lynne Rienner.

———. 2001. *Gendering World Politics: Issues and Approaches in the Post–Cold War Era*. New York: Columbia University Press.

———. 2006. "Feminism Meets International Relations: Some Methodological Issues." In *Feminist Methodologies in International Relations*, edited by Brooke A. Ackerly, Maria Stern, and Jacqui True, 19–41. Cambridge: Cambridge University Press.

———. 2013. "Ann Tickner on Feminist Philosophy of Science, Engaging the Mainstream and Still Remaining Critical in/of IR." Theory Talks no. 54: Ann Tickner. April 22. Accessed January 15, 2014. http://www.theory-talks.org/2013/04/theory-talk-54.html.

Tickner, J. Ann and Laura Sjoberg. 2011. "Conclusion: Looking Forward for Feminist International Relations." In *Feminism and International Relations: Conversations about the Past, Present, and Future*, edited by J. Ann Tickner and Laura Sjoberg, 221–36. New York: Routledge.

Tonkin, Hannah. 2011. *State Control over Private Military and Security Companies in Armed Conflict*. Cambridge: Cambridge University Press.

Traynor, Ian. 2003. "The Privatisation of War." *Guardian*, December 10. Accessed October 9, 2013. http://bit.ly/ZBIdDg.

True, Jacqui. 2012. "Securitizing Feminism or Feminist Security Studies? Review of *Gender and International Security: Feminist Perspectives*, edited by Laura Sjoberg. New York: Routledge, 2010." *International Studies Review* 14 (1): 193–95.

Tucker, F. 1957. *Gorkha: The Story of the Gurkhas of Nepal*. London: Constable.

Uesseler, Rolf. 2008. *Servants of War: Private Military Corporations and the Profit of Conflict*, translated by Jefferson Chase. New York: Soft Skull Press.

"U.N. Ousts Peacekeepers in Sex Case." 2007. *New York Times*, November 3, A10.

United Nations (UN). 1994. "Reports and Recommendations Made by the Panel of Commissioners Concerning Part One of the Second Instalment of Claims for Serious Personal Injury or Death (Category 'B' Claims)." December 15, UN Doc.S/AC.26/1994/4.

———. 1995. "Fourth World Conference on Women, Action for Equality, Development and Peace, Beijing Declaration and Platform for Action." UN Doc.A/Conf.177/20.

———. 1998. "Report Submitted by the Special Rapporteur on Violence against Women, Its Causes and Consequences, M. R. Coomaraswamy." January 26, UN Doc.E/CN.4.1998/54.

———. 1999. "Secretary-General's Bulletin: Observance by United Nations Forces of International Humanitarian Law." August 6, UN Doc.ST/SGB/1999/13.

———. 2000. "The Windhoek Declaration and the Namibia Plan of Action on Mainstreaming Gender Perspective in Multidimensional Peace Support Operations." Windhoek, Namibia, May 31, UN Doc.A/55/138, Annex I.

———. 2001. "Violence against Women Perpetrated and/or Condoned by the State During Times of Armed Conflict (1997–2000)." Report of the Special Rapporteur on Violence against Women, Its Causes and Consequences, M. R. Coomaraswamy. January 23, UN Doc.E/CN.4/2001/73.

———. 2003a. "UN Norms on the Responsibilities of Transnational Corporations and Other Business Enterprises with Regard to Human Rights, UN Sub-commission on the Promotion and Protection of Human Rights." August 26, UN Doc.E/CN.4/Sub.2/2003/12/rev.2.

———. 2005a. "Basic Principles and Guidelines on the Right to a Remedy and Reparation for Victims of Gross Violations of International Human Rights Law and Serious Violations of International Humanitarian Law (Reparations Principles), GA Res.60/147 of 16." December, UN Doc.A/Res/60/147.

———. 2005b. "Updated Set of Principles for the Protection and Promotion of Human Rights through Action to Combat Impunity (Impunity Principles)." February 8, UN Doc.E/CN.4/2005/102/Add.1.

———. 2006a. *Securing Equality: Engendering Peace. A Guide to Policy and Planning on Women, Peace and Security* (UN SCR 1325). New York: UN-INSTRAW.

———. 2006b. "In-Depth Study on All Forms of Violence Against Women, Report of the Secretary-General." July 6, UN Doc.A/61/122/Add.1.

———. 2007. "Report of the Secretary-General on the Protection of Civilians in Armed Conflict." October 28, UN Doc.S/2007/643.

———. 2008a. "Report of UN Special Rapporteur on Violence against Women, Y. Ertürk, Mission to the Democratic Republic of the Congo." February 28, UN Doc.A/HRC/7/6/Add.4.

———. 2008b. "Women and Peace and Security, Report of the Secretary-General." September 25, UN Doc.S/2008/622.

———. 2008c. "Informal Summary of the Montreux Document by Switzerland." October 6, UN Doc.A/63/467.

———. 2010a. "The Status of Women in the United Nations System and in the Secretariat, as at 31 December 2010, Focal Point for Women in the UN System." August 23, 2011. Accessed December 3, 2012. http://www.un.org/womenwatch/osagi/fg.htm

———. 2010b. "Report of the Special Representative of the Secretary-General on the Issues of Human Rights and Transnational Corporations and other Business Enterprises." April 9, UN Doc.A/HRC/14/27.

———. 2010c. "Turning the Lens: Victims and Affected Communities on the Court and the Rome Statute System, Review Conference of the Rome Statute." May 30, Doc.RC/ST/V/INF.2.

———. 2010d. "Report of the Special Rapporteur on Violence against Women, Its Causes and Consequences: Reparations to Women Who Have Been Subjected to Violence in the Context of Both Peace and Post-conflict. R. Manjoo." April 23, UN Doc.A/HRC/14/22.

———. 2010e. "HRC Res.15/26(2010) Open-Ended Intergovernmental Working Group to Consider the Possibility of Elaborating an International Regulatory Framework on the Regulation, Monitoring and Oversight of the Activities of Private Military and Security Companies." October 7, Doc.A/HRC/RES/15/26.

———. 2011a. "Report of Working Group on Use of Mercenaries as a Means of Violating Human Rights and Impeding the Exercise of the Rights of Peoples to Self-Determination, Note of Secretary-General." August 22, UN Doc.A/66/317.

———. 2011b. "Advancement of Women, Note by the Secretary-General." August 1, UN Doc.A/66/215.

———. 2011c. "Guiding Principles on Business and Human Rights: Implementing the United Nations 'Protect, Respect and Remedy' Framework, Report of the Special Representative of the Secretary-General on Issues of Human Rights and Transnational Corporations and Other Business Enterprises, J. Ruggie." March 21, UN Doc.A/HRC/17/31. Endorsed by Human Rights Council Res.17/4 June 16.

———. 2011d. "Business and Human Rights in Conflict-Affected Regions: Challenges and Options for State Responses, Report of SPSG J. Ruggie." May 27, UN Doc.A/HRC/17/32.

———. 2011e. "Advancement of Women: Note by the Secretary General. Report of the Special Rapporteur on Violence against Women, R. Manjoo." August 1, UN Doc.A/66/215.

———. 2012a. "Report of the Special Rapporteur on Violence against Women, Its Causes and Consequences: Gender-Related Killings of Women, R. Manjoo." May 22, UN Doc.A/HRC/20/16.

———. 2012b. "United National Security Management System, Manual, *Guidelines on the Use of Armed Security Services from Private Security Companies*, Annex A—Statement of Works, UNDSS." November 8.

———. 2013a. "Protection from Sexual Exploitation and Abuse by UN and Related Personnel. Tools Repository: Prevention." Accessed June 4. https://www.un.org/en/pseataskforce/tools_prevent.shtml.

———. 2013b. "Human Rights Due Diligence Policy on United Nations Support to Non-United Nations Security Forces." March 5, UN Doc.A/67/775–S/2013/110.

UN Department of Peacekeeping Operations. N.D. "Fact Sheet." Accessed April 19, 2007. http://www.un.org/Depts/dpko/factsheet.pdf.

———. 2007. "DPKO's Comprehensive Strategy on Sexual Exploitation and Abuse." Accessed April 19. http://www.un.org/Depts/dpko/CDT/strategy.html.

UN General Assembly. 2006. "Special Measures for Protection from Sexual Exploitation and Sexual Abuse. Report of the Secretary General." May 24.

———. 2007. "Special Measures for Protection from Sexual Exploitation and Sexual Abuse. Report of the Secretary-General." June 15.

———. 2009. "Special Measures for Protection from Sexual Exploitation and Sexual Abuse. Report of the Secretary-General." February 17.

———. 2010. "Special Measures for Protection from Sexual Exploitation and Sexual Abuse. Report of the Secretary-General." February 18.

UN Global Compact. 2012. Accessed December 3. http://bit.ly/1fOaAPt.

UNHCR and Save the Children-UK. 2002. "Sexual Violence & Exploitation: The Experience of Refugee Children in Guinea, Liberia and Sierra Leone." February. Accessed June 30, 2014. http://bit.ly/1mUxqHY.

UN Mission in Liberia. 2007. "Conduct and Discipline Unit." Accessed November 23. http://unmil.org/content.asp?ccat=cdu.

UN Open-ended Intergovernmental Working Group to Consider the Possibility
of Elaborating an International Regulatory Framework on the Regulation,
Monitoring and Oversight of the Activities of Private Military and
Security Companies (UNOIGWG). 2011. "Summary of the First Session,
Chairperson-Rapporteur, L. L. Ndimeni." UN Doc.A/HRC/WG.10/1/
CRP.2.

UN Secretary-General. 2002. *Women, Peace and Security.* New York: United Nations.
Accessed October 15, 2010. http://bit.ly/1rf1LDm.

———. 2006. "Revised Draft Model Memorandum of Understanding between the
United Nations and [participating State] Contributing Resources to [the
United Nations Peacekeeping Operation]." October 3. Accessed April 19,
2007. http://bit.ly/1jw1Ohu.

UN Working Group on the Use of Mercenaries as a Means of Violating
Human Rights and Impeding the Exercise of the Rights of Peoples to
Self-Determination (UNWGM). 2004. "Report." UN Doc.E/CN.4/2005/14.

———. 2008. "Report." UN Doc.A/HRC/7/7.

———. 2010a. "Report." UN Doc.A/HRC/15/25.

———. 2010b. "Draft of a Possible Convention on Private Military and Security
Companies (PMSCs) for Consideration and Action by the Human Rights
Council." July 5, UN Doc.A/HRC/15/25, Annex.

———. 2010c. "Note by the Secretary-General." UN Doc.A/65/325.

———. 2012a. "Report." UN Doc.A/HRC/21/43.

———. 2012b. "Note by the Secretary-General." UN Doc.A/67/340.

———. 2013. "Report." UN Doc.A/68/339.

U.S. Army. 1983. *Dictionary of United States Army Terms.* AR 310–25, October 15.

U.S. Code. 2006. Title 18 Crimes and Criminal Procedure, Chapter 212: Military
Extraterritorial Jurisdiction (MEJA) of 2000. Accessed June 30, 2014.
http://1.usa.gov/1n31QN7.

U.S. Department of Defense, Inspector General's Office. 2003. "Assessment of DOD
Efforts to Combat Trafficking in Persons. Phase II: Bosnia-Herzegovina and
Kosovo." December 8. On file with Valerie Sperling.

———. 2010. "Efforts to Prevent Sexual Assault/Harassment Involving
DOD Contractors During Contingency Operations." April 10, Report
No.D.-2010-052.

U.S. Department of Defense, Office of the Deputy Assistant Secretary of Defense,
2011. "Contractor Support of U.S. Operations in the USCENTCOM Area of
Responsibility, Iraq, and Afghanistan." October. Accessed January 10, 2013.
http://www.acq.osd.mil/log/PS/CENTCOM_reports.html.

U.S. Department of State. 2005. "Trafficking in Persons Report." Government Office
to Monitor and Combat Trafficking in Persons. June 3. Accessed February 22,
2007. http://www.state.gov/g/tip/rls/tiprpt/2005/46606.htm.

———. 2006. "Trafficking Victims Protection Reauthorization Act of 2005 (TVPRA)."
Accessed June 20, 2014. http://www.state.gov/j/tip/laws/61106.htm.

U.S. Government Accountability Office. 2005. "Reporting Additional Service Member
Demographics Could Enhance Congressional Oversight." GAO-05-952.

U.S. Senate. 2009. "New Information about the Guard Force Contract at the
U.S. Embassy in Kabul." Senate Committee on Homeland Security and
Governmental Affairs, Subcommittee on Contracting Oversight. Accessed
December 15, 2013. http://1.usa.gov/Tp0d8O.

U.S. White House. 2002. "National Security Strategy of the United States." September. Washington DC.

Uttley, Matthew 2005. "Contractors on Deployed Military Operations: United Kingdom Policy and Doctrine." Carlisle, PA: Strategic Studies Institute.

Vandenberg, Martina. 2002. "Hopes Betrayed: Trafficking of Women and Girls to Bosnia and Herzegovina for Forced Prostitution." Human Rights Watch, November. Accessed November 23, 2007. http://www.hrw.org/reports/2002/bosnia/Bosnia1102.pdf.

———. 2005a. "Peacekeeping, Alphabet Soup, and Violence against Women in the Balkans." In *Gender, Conflict and Peacekeeping*, edited by Dyan Mazurana, Angela Raven-Roberts, and Jane Parpart, 150-67. Lanham, MD: Rowman and Littlefield.

———. 2005b. "Out of Bondage." *Legal Times*, February 14.

———. 2006. Presentation at Harvard University Following the film *The Peacekeepers and the Women*. April 18.

Vandenberg, Martina and Sarah Mendelson. 2005. "Comments on DFARS Case 2004-D017, Defense Federal Acquisition Regulation Supplement: Combating Trafficking in Persons." August 22. On file with Valerie Sperling.

Väyrynen, Tarja and Berit von der Lippe. 2011. "Co-opting Feminist Voices for the War on Terror: Laura Bush Meets Nordic Feminism." *European Journal of Women's Studies* 18 (1): 19–33.

Via, Sandra. 2010. "Gender, Militarism, and Globalization: Soldiers for Hire and Hegemonic Masculinity." In *Gender, War, and Militarism*, edited by Laura Sjoberg and Sandra Via, 42–53. Santa Barbara, CA: Praeger.

Virchow, Fabian. 2008. "Der neoliberale Staat, die private Produktion von 'Sicherheit' und die Transformation der Bürgerrechte." In *Neoliberalismus—Analysen und Alternativen,* edited by Christoph Butterwegge, Bettina Lösch, and Ralph Ptak, 224–42. Wiesbaden: Verlag für Sozialwissenschaften.

Vrasti, Wanda. 2008. "The Strange Case of Ethnography and International Relations." *Millennium: Journal of International Studies* 37 (2): 279–301.

Vrdoljak, Ana Filipa. 2011. "Women and Private Military and Security Companies." In *War by Contract: Human Rights, Humanitarian Law and Private Contractors,* edited by Francesco Francioni and Natalino Ronzitti, 151–70. Oxford: Oxford University Press.

Wadhams, Nick. 2005. "Civilian Employees, Not Soldiers, Will Be Big Problem as United Nations Tackles Sex Abuse, Official Says." Associated Press, March 15. Accessed February 22, 2007. http://www.refugeesinternational.org/content/article/detail/6356.

Wadley, Jonathan D. 2010. "Gendering the State: Performativity and Protection in International Security." In *Gender and International Security: Feminist Perspectives*, edited by Laura Sjoberg, 38–58. New York: Routledge.

Walters, William, and Jacqueline Best. 2013. "'Actor-Network Theory' and International Relationality: Lost (and Found) in Translation (Forum Introduction)." *International Political Sociolgy* 7 (3): 332–34.

Warner, Michael. 2005. *Publics and Counterpublics.* Zone Books: New York.

Weber, Cynthia. 1999. *Faking It: U.S. Hegemony in a "Post-Phallic" Era.* Minneapolis: Minnesota University Press.

Weber, Max. 1994. *Weber: Political Writings.* Cambridge: Cambridge University Press.

Wedel, Janine R. 2008. "The Shadow Army: Privatization." In *Lessons from Iraq: Avoiding the Next War*, edited by Miriam Pemberton and William D. Hartung, 116–23. Boulder, CO: Paradigm.

Westcott Kathryn. 2010. "'Pirate' Death Puts Spotlight on 'Guns for Hire.'" BBC News, March 24. Accessed June 8. http://news.bbc.co.uk/2/hi/africa/8585967.stm.

Wetherell, Margaret. 2012. *Affect and Emotion: A New Social Science Understanding.* London: Sage.

The Whistleblower. 2011. DVD. Directed by Larysa Kondracki. Iver Heath, Bucks, UK: High Fliers Films.

Whittell, Giles. 2009. "Embassy at Risk as 'Deviant' Guards Let Their Hair Down: Private Contractors in Kabul under Investigation." *The Times*, September 3, 35.

Whitworth, Sandra. 2004. *Men, Militarism, and UN Peacekeeping: A Gendered Analysis.* Boulder, CO: Lynne Rienner.

Wibben, Annick T. R. 2011. *Feminist Security Studies: A Narrative Approach.* London: Routledge.

Wilcox, Lauren. 2010. "Gendering the Cult of the Offensive." In *Gender and International Security: Feminist Perspectives*, edited by Laura Sjoberg, 61–82. New York: Routledge.

Wing, Adrien Katherine, ed. 1997. *Critical Race Feminism: A Reader.* New York: New York University Press.

Wolcott, James. 2012. "The Hung and the Restless." *Vanity Fair*. March. http://vnty.fr/1dKBOHN

The Women's Research and Education Institute. 2013. *Women in the Military: Where They Stand*, 8th ed. Arlington: The Women's Research and Education Institute.

Woods, Steven G. 2004. "The Logistics Civil Augmentation Program: What is the Status Today?" Strategic Research Report. Carlisle: U.S. Army War College.

Woodward, Rachel and K. Neil Jenkings. 2011. "Military Identities in the Situated Accounts of British Military Personnel." *Sociology* 45 (2): 252–268.

Young, Iris Marion. 2003. "The Logic of Masculinist Protection: Reflections on the Current Security State." *Signs: Journal of Women in Culture and Society* 29 (1): 1–25.

Young Pelton, R. 2006. *Licensed to Kill: Hired Guns in the War on Terror.* London: Crown.

Youngs, Gillian. 2000. "Breaking Patriarchal Bonds: Demythologising the Public/Private." In *Gender and Global Restructuring: Sightings, Sites and Resistances*, edited by Marianne A. Marchand and Anne Sisson Runyan, 44–58. London: Routledge.

Yuval-Davis, Nira. 1997. *Gender and Nation.* London: Sage.

Zalewski, Marysia. 2010. "Feminist International Relations, Making Sense . . . " In *Gender Matters in Global Politics: A Feminist Introduction to International Relations*, edited by Laura J. Shepherd, 28–43. New York: Routledge.

———. 2013. *Feminist International Relations: Exquisit Corpes.* London: Routledge.

Zarate, Juan Carlos. 1998. "The Emergence of a New Dog of War: Private International Security Companies, International Law, and the New World Disorder." *Stanford Journal of International Law* 34 (Winter): 75–162.

INDEX

private security, 4, 9, 230
  critical gender studies in, 2, 229–31
  in global politics, 3–5, 227–29
  Gurkhas in, 95–113
  as political, 230, 233–35
Private Warriors (documentary), 75–76
privatization, 36n. 2
  of protection, 69–72
  of violence, 27, 44, 46–51
  See also military privatization
problem-solving approach, 8, 229
profane, 42
Project on Government Oversight (POGO),
  151, 161
prostitution, 176, 177
protection, 7, 33–35
  from feminist perspective,
    58–60, 69–72
  gendered, 58–60, 64–66
  global labor market, 67–72
  of Gurkhas, 109–10
  market-based, 61–67
  and masculinity, 59–60, 64–66, 133
  military, 55
  myths, 41
  and PMSCs, 56, 57, 62, 64–69, 115
  politics of, 55–57, 60–69
  privatization of, 69–72
  and violence, 56
  of women, 45, 58–59, 133, 200, 237

Quatta (Gurkha), 106

Rabindra (Gurkha), 108
racialized contractors, 104–6
racism, 90
Randhoj (Gurkha), 105, 110, 111
rape, 198, 199, 200, 201
Red Cross. *See* International Committee
  of the Red Cross
reflexivity, 98–99, 241
Refugees International, 179, 181, 182, 183
remasculinization, 131–32, 135, 141,
  142–44, 233
Remasculinization of America, The
  (Jeffords), 132
repatriation, 173
republican motherhood, 80–81
research, 98–99, 134–42, 144, 238
responsibility, 208–25

revolution in military affairs (RMA),
  46–47, 49, 50
Robinson, Fiona, 211, 214
Ruggie, John, 195, 203
Rumsfeld, Donald, 49, 83
Runyan, Anne Sisson, 71
Rwanda, 198, 205n.10

sacred, 42, 51
sacrifice
  in current war-making, 51
  and disciplining of citizenship, 39–46
  as gendered, 45
  legitimacy of, 44, 52
  macrohistorical dimension, 41
  masculine grammar of, 53
  military, 40
  military privatization and gendered
    politics of, 37–54
  of mothers of fallen soldiers, 44
  politics of, 37–54
  as religious act, 41
  of soldier-citizens, 43
  theories of, 41
  turn away from, 54
  women's, 40
Said, Edward, 88
Sante (Gurkha), 104
Schneiker, Andrea, 133, 141, 144
Schott, Robin, 38, 42
Schulman, Daniel, 147
Secret Service, 138
security
  definitions of, 33–34
  feminist studies of, 6–7,
    55–72, 231–33
  source of legitimacy, 48
  See also contractors; private military
    and security companies; protection
security privatization. *See* military
  privatization; private security
Service Employees International, 124
sex-role stereotypes, 41
sex tourism, 123
sex trafficking, 170–76, 185, 201, 202
sexual exploitation/abuse, 176–85, 201
sexualized coercion, 152–53
sexual practices, 149–50, 152, 162
sexual slavery, 198, 199
sexual violence, 51, 199, 202, 203, 205n.10